Library of
Davidson College

# TEMPERAMENT
# PERSONALITY
# ACTIVITY

# TEMPERAMENT PERSONALITY ACTIVITY

### Jan Strelau

*Institute of Psychology
University of Warsaw
Poland*

1983

ACADEMIC PRESS

*A Subsidiary of Harcourt Brace Jovanovich, Publishers*

London  New York
Paris  San Diego  San Francisco
São Paulo  Sydney  Tokyo  Toronto

ACADEMIC PRESS INC. (LONDON) LTD
24-28 Oval Road
London NW1 7DX

*U.S. edition published by*
ACADEMIC PRESS INC.
111 Fifth Avenue
New York, New York 10003

Copyright © 1983 by Academic Press Inc. (London) Ltd

*All Rights Reserved*
No part of this book may be reproduced in
any form by photostat, microfilm, or any other means,
without written permission from the publishers

*British Library Cataloguing in Publication Data*

Strelau, Jan
   Temperament—personality—activity.
   1. Personality
   I. Title
   155.2    BF698

ISBN 0-12-673280-9

LCCCN 83-70585

Photoset by Paston Press, Norwich
and printed in Great Britain by St Edmundsbury Press, Bury St Edmunds, Suffolk

# FOREWORD

East and West, as we all know, are separated by a political closed door, occasionally pierced by dissidents or fellow-travellers, but closed nonetheless. It is less generally known, however, that there is also a scientific counterpart to this political barrier; and in no field is the scientific barrier more prominent than in psychology. There are several reasons for this particular division. One, of course, is the closed door itself: science thrives on the free exchange of ideas, but this is severely hampered by the limits on travel and discussion set by the political differences between East and West. A second reason is linguistic: much of the impetus for the development of psychological theory in the East derived from a long succession of deservedly influential Russian scientists who, naturally enough, have chosen to write in their own language, both before and after the Soviet Revolution. This literature is therefore much more accessible to the other Slavic nations of the East than to the Latins and Anglo-Saxons of the West. A third reason stems from the very separation of the two halves of our psychological world. The political and linguistic isolation of the East (as seen from our side of the great divide) has had the consequence that the theories they use over there, the language (even after translation) they employ to decribe their experiments and observations, the assumptions taken so much for granted as not even to figure in such descriptions—all these are now so profoundly different from our own practices that it requires a great effort simply to find out what the Eastern Europeans are up to. And, no doubt, the same could be said of one from the East wishing to find out what *we* are up to.

Fortunately, the scientific barrier between East and West is less rigid than the political one—it is a semi-permeable membrane rather than a rigid barrier; and the permeability of the membrane increases steadily as one approaches Poland. As in political, so in scientific affairs; that country occupies a special place in Europe, attuned to developments in Washington, London, and Paris almost as much as to those in Moscow. It was, for example, from his strategic listening post in Warsaw that

Jerzy Konorski was able to offer both East and West the first real attempt to synthesize Pavlovian conditioned reflexes out of Sherringtonian unconditioned reflex arcs. In much the same spirit Jan Strelau offers us in this book an important synthesis of neo-Pavlovian concepts in personality theory and their Western equivalents (themselves often originally developed from the same Pavlovian starting-point, though by a circuitous route). Moreover, this is a synthesis which, again like Konorski's, is more than a synthesis, for it bears the stamp of originality that can come only from someone who has himself done significant pioneering research in the field. In consequence, there is matter here from which we can all learn: those who know the Western literature, but wish to find out what is going on in the Soviet Union (the "Pavlovian bloc", I had almost said); those who wish to look again at the Western literature but seen now from the special vantage point that is Warsaw; and those who, for the first time in English, have an opportunity to learn *in extenso* of the important research that has been taking place over the last 25 years in Professor Strelau's own laboratory. For all, indeed, who have a serious interest in the biological basis of personality, Professor Strelau's book will be required reading.

*Oxford, 1983* *J. A. Gray*

# PREFACE

Twenty-five years ago I started my research on Pavlovian typology, by paying particular attention to the contributions of the Moscow psychologists Boris M. Teplov and Vladimir D. Nebylitsyn and the Ural group working under Volf S. Merlin. The experience accumulated in the course of these studies has given birth to the development of a new concept of temperament which I have entitled the *regulative theory of temperament*. This theory could not have been founded without making use of other concepts in psychology too; the most important of which were the activation theories developed in Western psychology and the theory of action primarily formulated by Russian psychologists and originally developed in Poland by my teacher Tadeusz Tomaszewski. The 25 years we spent together could not be without influence on my thinking in psychology, but I have also learned much from Professor Tomaszewski about people and the world in which they act.

The main idea of the regulative theory of temperament is that temperament, being a product of biological evolution, plays an important role in regulating the interrelations between the humans and their environment. Two basic features comprising the energetic characteristic of behaviour, reactivity and activity, have been particularly acknowledged. Their significance consists mainly in regulating the stimulative value of the surroundings and the individual's own behaviour, as a safeguard on his need for stimulation. The role of temperament in human action has also been presented in this volume. Taking as a point of departure the understanding of temperament as a product of biological evolution, and personality as a result of socio-historical conditions, emphasis is placed on the interdependencies of both phenomena in question.

During my long period of research and after ten years of studies on my own, I was gradually joined by students whose numbers grew from year to year. There are now ten of us working at the Department of Psychophysiology and Psychology of Individual Differences, not to mention numerous Ph.D. and graduate students. Since so much of our exploration in the area of temperament was a joint effort it is rather difficult to separate my own contribution from that of my students. Thus it seems reasonable to speak of our research into temperament and, hence, one of the main aims of this volume is to summarize the results we have collected over the last fifteen years of joint studies. I am not mentioning the names of my collaborators here because there are too many of them, but they may frequently be found in the text of the last three chapters in which the research has been summarized.

A large portion of the book deals with Pavlovian typology, with special focus on current research in this area. As mentioned at the very beginning, our concept has much in common with this theory and I have never ceased to take an interest in the neo-Pavlovian approach, which should be included within the concept of temperament. My own research in this area (which started in 1957) along with a six-month fellowship used for intensive studies, in the Teplov–Nebylitsyn laboratory in 1966, and innumerable and permanent contacts with my Russian friends have given me the confidence to make a competent summary of work in this area, all the more so since many years have lapsed since Jeffrey A. Gray and Vladimir D. Nebylitsyn published their excellent monographs on Pavlov's typology. It should also be added that no book exists, even in Russian, summarizing the current status of this field of research.

Since a large portion of my own research concerns studies on nervous system properties (NSP) assessed by means of an inventory I decided to devote part of the book to the discussion of the Strelau Temperament Inventory (STI), which seems to be the only questionnaire aimed at diagnosing nervous system properties. This inventory has also been used in several countries in the West over recent years. The inventory approach to NSP enabled, more efficiently than any other method, the nervous system properties to be related to several popular personality dimensions measured on the same level of behaviour, such as extraversion–introversion, neuroticism, and anxiety. Thus the many results collected in our laboratory concerning these relationships may be considered to be new links between the psychology of individual differences in the West and in the East.

The list of people to whom I owe my thanks for help and contribution in writing this book is, as usual, very long. No doubt I owe my greatest dept to my associates and students who enriched the regulative theory of temperament with new facts and ideas, thus substantially influencing the final shape of this conception. Two of my students, Andrzej Eliasz and Tatiana Klonowicz, were with me from the very beginning of my new approach to temperament and today their own contribution to this field is of great importance.

I did not believe myself capable of writing this monograph in English. Alexander Thomas and Grace W. Shugar convinced me that it was not a lost cause to attempt to do so. But it was Helena Grzegołowska-Klarkowska, one of my former students, who decided to undertake the risk of bringing my English to a shape which could at least communicate with the reader. This was a difficult and time-consuming work for which I am deeply indebted to her. The responsibility for the final text is, however, mine and I ask the reader's forbearance.

The content of the book would be far from what it is if it were not for the kindness and help of the many of my psychologist friends and colleagues scattered around the world. This help consists mainly in continually sending the books and reprints that my students and I use in our everyday work. In our situation, where, primarily for economic reasons, it is rather difficult to buy books and to pay subscription fees for psychological journals from the West, this help is of especial importance to us and I would like to take this opportunity to express my deepest gratitude to all who contribute to this more or less unilateral exchange.

I owe a special debt of appreciation to Dr Era A. Golubeva and to Dr Inna V. Ravich-Shcherbo. Thanks go to Era Golubeva, who carefully revised the two first chapters I was able to put into the text dealing with the Pavlovian typology and made certain corrections and completions. Inna Ravich-Shcherbo expended a lot of effort to complete a number of Russian psychologists' references not available in Polish libraries.

Cordial thanks should be given to my daughter, Krysia, who produced all the figures; it was a pleasure to see how involved she became.

Acknowledgement is also due to the publisher who displayed much patience in waiting for the manuscript and who decided to co-operate with the author, though conscious that he would be deprived of easy and rapid contact with his partner.

Most of the research presented in this book was supported by the Polish Academy of Sciences (grants: P-70 and W-11.8). However, it is the University of Warsaw, where I have worked since 1957, that has primarily helped me in many respects to conduct the intensive studies of temperament presented in this book.

*Warsaw, 1983*                                                                                         *Jan Strelau*

# CONTENTS

| | |
|---|---|
| *Foreword* | v |
| *Preface* | vi |

**1. Pavlovian Typology: Traditional Research and Current Approach** — 1
  Pavlov's research on types of nervous system — 1
  Nervous system typology as developed by Pavlov's students — 13
  The Teplov–Nebylitsyn school: neo-Pavlovian typology — 25
  Main directions of research in Pavlov's typology presented by the Ural group — 62

**2. Laboratory Methods Used by Neo-Pavlovian Typologists to Diagnose the Nervous System Properties** — 73
  Introduction — 73
  Methods for diagnosing the strength of the nervous system with regard to excitation — 77
  Diagnostic methods for lability of the nervous system — 97
  Diagnosis of mobility of the nervous processes — 104
  Background alpha rhythm characteristics as indices of equilibrium of excitation and inhibition (activatability) — 108

**3. The Temperament Inventory as a Result of Studies in Methods for Diagnosing Nervous System Properties** — 111
  Discrepancies in the estimation of nervous system properties diagnosed in laboratory conditions — 111
  Interview and observation as diagnostic methods in Pavlov's typology — 115
  The Strelau temperament inventory (STI) — 118

**4. Pavlovian Typology and some Personality Dimensions Based on Biological Endowment** — 138
  Introduction — 138
  Extraversion–introversion and nervous system properties — 143
  Anxiety and neuroticism as related to the basic properties of the nervous system — 154
  General conclusions — 164

## 5. Regulative Theory of Temperament — 167
The Pavlovian concept of nervous system properties and its critical analysis as a starting-point for the regulative theory of temperament — 167
The understanding of temperament — 171
The energetic level of behaviour as one of the main components of temperament — 174
Temporal characteristics of behaviour — 193
Methods used for diagnosing temperament features — 197

## 6. Temperament and Activity — 207
Style of action related to temperament and as a regulator of stimulative value of situations — 207
The influence of temperament on the choice of activity and situation of a given stimulative value — 225
Efficiency of action and psychophysiological changes under situations imposed upon stimulative value and temperament traits — 240

## 7. Temperament and Personality — 255
Theoretical considerations — 255
Empirical evidence as regards the relation between temperament and personality — 263
Final remarks — 283

## References — 286

## Chapter Notes — 330

## Appendixes
1. Strelau temperament inventory (STI) — 337
2. Nursery school child's reactivity rating scale ($RRS_1$) — 342
3. Pupil's reactivity rating scale ($RRS_2$) — 345
4. Pupil's reactivity rating scale ($RRS_3$) — 349
5. Temporal traits inventory (TTI) — 353

## Author Index — 359

## Subject Index — 368

*To Krystyna, my wife*

# 1
# Pavlovian Typology:
# Traditional Research and Current Approach

## PAVLOV'S RESEARCH ON TYPES OF NERVOUS SYSTEM

Systematic observations of the behaviour of dogs, during experiments on classical conditioning, led Pavlov and his students to the conclusion that there exist strongly expressed individual differences in the speed and accuracy with which both positive and negative (inhibitory) conditioned reflexes are elaborated: in their efficiency, strength, and durability, in the ease with which they may be changed and, finally, in the manner in which animals behave in the experimental chamber.

Basing his approach on the concept of "nervism", according to which any behaviour is governed and regulated by the central nervous system (CNS), Pavlov hypothesized that certain properties of the nervous processes exist which are responsible for the observed individual differences in conditioning or, more generally, in the dogs' behaviour. In his first papers, when speaking about the basic properties of the nervous system (NS) he mentioned the strength of the nervous processes of excitation and inhibition and the equilibrium between the strength of both these processes. In the 1930s he added a third property, the mobility of nervous processes.

According to Pavlov (1951–52), the configuration of the basic properties of the nervous processes constitute the so-called type of nervous system (TNS). It was in one of his reports given in 1909–10 to the Association of Russian Physicians in Petersburg that he first used this concept; however, it was not explained at that time.

Contrary to popular belief, it was not Pavlov who first described the types of NS. In 1910, his student, Nikiforovsky, in his Ph.D. dissertation devoted to the pharmacology of conditioned reflexes, gave a description of three types of NS. The equilibrium of nervous processes (NPs) was the main criterion for separating these types. Referring primarily to the behaviour of dogs in the experimental chamber, Nikiforovsky (1910) characterized these as follows:

(1) the type with predominance of excitation over inhibition. These dogs are sensitive and mobile, they do not behave quietly during the experiment and the smallest changes in the experimental situation evoke strong expressed reactions;
(2) the type with predominance of inhibition over excitation. Dogs belonging to these type do not usually change their posture during the experimental procedure and their reaction to unexpected or unusual stimuli is slight. Evoked conditioned reflexes become very quickly inhibited;
(3) the balanced type, which Nikiforovsky characterizes as the usual, average type. This includes dogs in which the nervous processes of excitation and inhibition are well developed.

Pavlov referred in his publications to the classification of types introduced by Nikiforovsky. In his 1925 paper on the inhibitory type of nervous system, he suggested a strong analogy between his types of NS, where the balance of nervous processes still appears to be the main criterion for discriminating types, and the classical typology of temperaments proposed by Hippocrates. The type with predominance of excitation over inhibition has been compared by Pavlov with the sanguine, and the type with the predominance of inhibition over excitation has been identified with the melancholic. An intermediate place has been reserved for the balanced type where the strength of both processes, excitation and inhibition, is expressed at the same level. However, he abandoned this analogy in the face of evidence collected in his laboratory.

Over the 30 years devoted to studies in conditioned reflexes (CRs) in dogs, Pavlov somewhat modified his TNS classification.

The most comprehensive and consistent classification of TNS, along with a detailed description of the separate properties of the NS and methods used for diagnosing them, was introduced in the paper *General Types of Higher Nervous Activity in Animals and Man* published by Pavlov in 1935. This paper has been used by Pavlov's students and other investigators concentrating on TNS research as the main basis of information in this area. In describing Pavlov's typology, I will refer mainly to this fundamental publication in which Pavlov summarized his and his students' results and experience in research on the types of nervous system.

## 1. Traditional Research and Current Approach

As mentioned before, there are three fundamental properties of the nervous system, the combination of which constitutes the TNS: the strength, balance (equilibrium), and mobility of the nervous processes of excitation and inhibition.

Because there is still considerable misunderstanding as to what Pavlov's NS typology really is (e.g. Eysenck, in press) let me give a more detailed description of these properties as they were, in my opinion, understood by Pavlov, taking into account the specific diagnostic methods used in his laboratory.

### Strength of the Nervous System as Regards Excitation

Apparently, Pavlov considered the strength of the nervous system to be the most important property of the NS. He suggested (Pavlov, 1951–52) that the significance of the strength of nervous processes, particularly the excitatory process, follows clearly from the fact that the environment often conveys unusual, extraordinary events—stimuli of great intensity.

According to Pavlov, the strength of excitation means simply the ability of cortical cells to work; or, in other words, their working capacity. The strength of the NS refers to the functional capacity and it is manifested principally in the withstanding of either prolonged or short-lived, but exceedingly strong, excitation without slipping into protective inhibition. The strength of excitation can be estimated by recording the organism's responses to strong, prolonged, or recurrent stimulation.

Concerning the essence of the process of excitation, Pavlov's publications provide us with little information. He limited himself to stating that the fundamental significance for work is borne by a hypothetical "excitable substance" underlying the ability of the nerve cells to work, or that the excitatory process is connected with dissimilation.

Despite the fact that Nebylitsyn (1972a) has suggested that the neurophysiological and biochemical theories of the excitatory process were well known to Pavlov, one must state that Pavlov never referred to them when describing the essence of excitation as well as inhibition. He always concentrated on the functional, rather than the neurophysiological or biochemical aspects of excitation and inhibition.

Pavlov used the terms "strength of the nervous system" and "strength of excitation" interchangeably, treating them as a property of the nervous system. This has been a source of many misunderstandings in TNS investigation, as Nebylitsyn (1963a) points out. The strength of the nervous processes, though fundamentally conceptualized by Pavlov as a trait, may simultaneously be viewed as a state, i.e. the level of the excitatory process at a particular moment. The strength of the excitatory process understood as a current state may depend on at least three variables:

(1) intensity of the stimuli;
(2) the so-called tonus of the cortex, or in other words, the level of activation which may depend in turn on such variables as hunger, fatigue, motivation etc.;
(3) a given property of the NS underlying individual differences in the strength of excitatory process evoked by a stimulus of the same intensity and on the basis of the same tonus (activation) of the cortex.

This third variable, which influences the strength of the excitatory process (understood as a state), is precisely what is meant by strength of the NS as regards excitation, or, less exactly, "strength of the excitatory process".

The role of these three variables in determining the strength of the process of excitation has been discussed by Pavlov (1951–52) and by Gray (1964), the pioneer of Pavlovian typology in the Western countries.

As may be assumed, a reverse relation occurs between the strength of the nervous system as a property and the intensity of the excitatory process as a state, other variables being equal. The stronger the nervous system, i.e. the more resiliant it is to strong stimuli, the smaller the excitatory process, understood as an evoked state.

To avoid misunderstandings in TNS investigation it seems more reasonable to use the expression "strength of the nervous system as regards excitation". Using the term "strength of excitation" we should bear in mind that it is used as an abbreviation of the former expression and means, in Pavlov's typology, a trait rather than a state. When discussing excitation as a state later on I will use the term "intensity of excitation". This intensity is a function of the intensity of stimuli, assuming other variables are equal.

A turning-point in describing the methods used in Pavlov's laboratory to diagnose the strength of nervous system as regards excitation, was his statement that the ability of the nerve cells to work may be measured in different ways:

(a) by determining the intensity of stimuli to which the individual is able to react adaptively;
(b) by increasing the excitability of the nerve cells by means of, e.g. food deprivation or caffeine;
(c) by using prolonged stimulation.

# 1. Traditional Research and Current Approach

During the whole period of research on TNS Pavlov moved more and more from the observational data collected on the basis of animal behaviour (the so-called life indicators of the TNS) to laboratory techniques, which permitted more accurate and quantitative characterization of NS properties.

Four main laboratory methods used by Pavlov and his collaborators for diagnosing the strength of excitation may be mentioned.

(i) The application of strong conditioned stimuli of increasing intensity until the threshold of endurance is reached. The stronger the stimuli at which the CR can be evoked the stronger the excitation process of the individual. This method enables the limit of the capacity to work to be directly described.

(ii) The animal is food deprived, which causes increased excitability. During this state, conditioned stimuli of different intensity are applied. In individuals with a strong excitatory process, strong stimuli enhance the efficiency of CR as a result of the increased excitability of the nerve cells. In individuals with a weak excitatory process the application of stimuli of equal intensity leads to protective inhibition and, at the same time, to a decrement in efficiency of CRs.

(iii) Instead of using food deprivation, the excitability of the NS may be increased pharmacologically. For this reason caffeine, a stimulant drug, is used. After giving the animal a dose of caffeine, the CR activity to stimuli of different intensity is measured. In individuals with a strong excitatory process caffeine increases the effect of excitation; in individuals with a weak excitatory process a decrease occurs, resulting in the limits of working capacity being exceeded. Caffeine increases the excitability of the nerve cells thus causing stimuli of weak intensity to produce similar effects to stronger stimuli under normal conditions. The limit of working capacity may be measured by the amount of caffeine with which the animal is able to perform. The larger the amount of a stimulus of given intensity (doses of 0.05–3.00 g have been used) to which the dog continues to react adequately, the greater the strength of the NS as regards excitation.

(iv) A positive CR is developed. The speed of aquisition of a CR and its durability are used as the criteria of the strength of excitation. The speed with which the CR is evoked is determined by the magnitude of the unconditioned stimulus (UCS) needed to evoke the CR. The durability of CR is measured by the number of presentations of the conditioned stimulus (CS) without reinforcement needed to extinguish the CR to this stimulus. In dogs with a strong excitatory process the CR is quickly evoked and is stable. Dogs with a weak excitatory process do not readily develop CRs and if they are acquired they are rather unstable.

The methods established in Pavlov's laboratory for diagnosing the strength of excitation, as well as other properties of the NS, were used as a starting-point for TNS investigation in animals and, to some extent, in humans.

## Strength of the Nervous System as Regards Inhibition

Pavlov refers not only to the strength of excitation but also to the strength of inhibition; however, this feature of the nervous system plays rather a secondary role in his typology. In substance, there is no information in Pavlov's publications suggesting the meaning of the strength of the NS with regard to inhibition. All we find are statements indicating that inhibition is connected with the process of assimilation, or that excitation and inhibition are inseparable. In Pavlov's work the concept of "inhibition" is variously defined and the differences between so-called unconditioned inhibition and conditioned inhibition are conceived differently (e.g. Konorski, 1958; Anokhin, 1958; Mayorov, 1962).[1]

At the beginning Pavlov, in distinguishing the types of NS, mentioned the so-called "inhibitory type", identified with the melancholic, who was characterized as the type with predominance of inhibition over excitation.[2] In his paper *The Inhibitory Type of the Nervous System in Dogs* Pavlov characterized individuals representing this type as subjects with weak nerve cells (he therefore subsequently referred to the weak type rather than the inhibitory type) and whose inhibitory CRs are well developed and of high durability. The ease of evoking inhibitory CRs and their stability are, according to Pavlov, indicators of conditioned inhibition, especially its strength. Therefore, it could be assumed that the inhibitory type developed strong conditioned inhibition. But Pavlov radically altered this idea in his 1931 paper, *Experimental Neurosis*. He emphasized that, in the weak type, which he no longer called the "inhibitory type", both the nervous processes—excitation and inhibition—are weak, with reference to conditioned inhibition.

On the other hand, the weak type is characterized by strong external inhibition which is a variation of unconditioned inhibition. He wrote:

> In the weak type, with weak internal inhibition, conversely, the external inhibition (negative induction) dominates and this mainly influences the behaviour of the animal. Hence the name of this type—weak, restrained (Pavlov, 1952, p. 488).[3]

Finally, when Pavlov, like other investigators involved in TNS research, spoke about the strength or weakness of inhibition, he was referring to conditioned, acquired inhibition.

## 1. Traditional Research and Current Approach

When considering the strength of inhibition we have to remember that it was assumed by Pavlov to be a trait, as was the case with the strength of excitation (see p. 3). To be precise, we should use the term: strength of the nervous system as regards inhibition.

In general, it seems that Pavlov's views on the strength of inhibition were unclear and confused (see e.g. Teplov, 1956, 1964a; Strelau, 1969), causing considerable reluctance among Pavlov's students and followers to investigate this property of the NS (e.g. Rozhdestvenskaya, 1963a; Yermolayeva-Tomina, 1963). As a rule, the strength of inhibition was only diagnosed when the equilibrium of nervous processes—excitation and inhibition—had to be estimated.

As far as the diagnosis of strength of inhibition is concerned Pavlov described several methods used in his laboratory for quantifying strength of inhibition; of these, the following four methods seem to be the most important.

(1) The experimenter evokes an inhibitory CR, e.g. using differentiation. At the beginning the inhibitory stimulus is applied for about 15 s. Then the presentation of this stimulus is prolonged to 5–10 min. This is the method for investigating the "durability" of the inhibitory process. The purpose is to ascertain how long the nerve cell is able to maintain a state of internal inhibition. Animals with a weak inhibitory process are unable to sustain internal inhibition for long, the result being disturbance of CR activity or even neurosis. In individuals with a strong inhibitory process prolonged inhibition does not cause disturbances. According to Pavlov this method determines the absolute strength of the inhibitory process.

(2) The inhibitory CR is evoked by using different modes of non-reinforcement of the conditioned stimulus, depending on the kind of CR. The number of inhibitory stimulus presentations needed to decrease the reaction to this stimulus is used as the criterion of the speed of evoking the inhibitory CR. A high speed of evoking different kinds of inhibitory CRs indicates a strong inhibitory process in animals, whereas the slowness or inability to evoke this inhibitory reaction is used as an indicator of the weakness of the nervous process.

(3) Prior to testing, a dose of bromine is given to the animal. Next, CRs are evoked or tested. Bromine increments the effect of inhibitory stimuli. This pharmacological agent, a depressant, exacerbates the process of inhibition and an appropriate dose drives the nerve cell's capacity to its limits. The stronger the nervous system as regards inhibition the greater the dose of bromine needed to lower the nerve cells down to their capacity limit, i.e. to the state of protective inhibition.

(4) After evoking a positive CR to a given stimulus, we have to measure the magnitude of the CR. Next we begin the process of differentiation presenting several stimuli, similar to the CS but without reinforcement. This procedure is terminated as soon as the animal no longer reacts to these stimuli. Depending on the strength of inhibition two different effects are observed. The effect of the CS may be enhanced or diminished with reference to its magnitude before differentiation.

> In the first case the strong inhibitory process concentrates and evokes positive induction; in the second, being weak, the inhibitory process fades gradually, decreasing the effect of the positive stimulus (Pavlov, 1952, p. 554).

In conclusion, the entrancing effect of the positive stimulus, after differentiation, indicates a strong inhibitory process, whereas the diminishing effect, i.e. the diminishing of the positive CR, is assumed to be an indicator of the weakness of the inhibitory process.

## Equilibrium (Balance) of the Nervous Processes

Equilibrium or balance (the terms are interchangeable) of the nervous processes was the first NS property distinguished by Pavlov, and, as has been shown, it was used in the first NS typology described by Nikiforovsky (see p. 2), as the main criterion for distinguishing types.

Pavlov, analysing the essence of the equilibrium of the nervous system, regarded this feature from the functional point of view, as was the case with other properties of the NS.

During the life of humans and animals it is often necessary to inhibit certain excitations in order to evoke other reactions, which are adequate for new stimuli in the environment (Pavlov, 1952, p. 540).

When writing about the equilibrium or balance of nervous processes Pavlov was referring to the equilibrium between the strength of excitation and inhibition. This position remained unchanged from the 1920s up to the last period of his life, when he wrote that the equilibrium of nervous processes should be regarded as the ratio of the strength of excitatory process to the strength of inhibition (Pavlov, 1952, pp. 543, 602).

Curiously, Pavlov's major TNS paper on methods of diagnosing NS properties makes no reference to the measurement of NS balance. This is also the case in his other works. Probably he assessed the equilibrium of nervous processes by comparing the values of strength of excitation and strength of inhibition. So, for example, characterizing the strong, unbalanced type, with predominance of excitation over inhibition he wrote: "If the positive conditioned reflexes in this type are easily evoked, the negative reflexes, conversely, are very slowly moulded" (Pavlov, 1952, p. 543). He makes similar conclusions about the balance of nervous processes in other cases.

## Mobility of the Nervous Processes

Mobility was the third and last property of the nervous system to be discovered. According to Pavlov, the essence of mobility is "the ability to give way—according to external conditions—to give priority to one impulse before the other, excitation before inhibition and conversely" (1952, p. 540). It means that mobility manifests itself by the speed with which a reaction to a given stimulus, when required, is inhibited in order to yield to another reaction evoked by other stimuli, etc. The environment is continuously changing, therefore the individual, in order to adapt to these conditions, must modify his nervous processes in line with these changes.

Disturbances in the mobility of nervous processes may lead to pathological inertia or lability, both of these traits representing the extreme poles of mobility of the nervous system. In Pavlov's publications there is no information about the hypothetical neurophysiological mechanism of mobility of nervous processes.

The methods used to diagnose the mobility of the nervous system are all based on the idea that this feature refers to the speed of alteration of excitation into inhibition and vice versa. I will limit the description to the following four techniques used by Pavlov.

(1) The experimenter evokes in the animal a so-called trace conditioned reflex. To achieve this effect we apply the stimulus, which should be conditioned without reinforcement. After approximately 30 s to 3 min from the moment this CS terminates we begin to apply the UCS. The duration of the isolated action of the stimulus to which the trace CR should be developed may be modified (from 5–30 s), as can be the interval between the termination of the CS and the beginning of the UCS. The duration of both these variables has been used as an indicator of the inertia of the nervous system. The inertia, understood as opposite in character to mobility, will be larger the shorter the duration of the CS and the longer the interval between the termination of the CS and the UCS to which a CR may be formed. The formation of trace CR was considered by Pavlov to be the most precise method for diagnosing mobility of the nervous processes.

(2) A neutral stimulus is applied to the animal repeatedly, e.g. a bulb

of a given colour, which is reinforced every other trial. The applications follow consecutively (B+, B−, B+, B−, . . .). This task is known as rhythmic reinforcement and non-reinforcement of the same stimulus. The rhythmic intervals between stimuli are changed. The longer the interval required between the stimuli to keep up with these changes the smaller the mobility of the animal's nervous system. On the other hand, the shorter the interval the more rapidly the process of excitation passes into the process of inhibition and, conversely, the larger the mobility of nervous processes.

(3) A positive and negative CR is formed in the animal. A neutral stimulus (e.g. a tone of 500 Hz) is associated with the UCS, the other one (e.g. a tone of 800 Hz) is not. After the positive CR is formed to the reinforced sound and the inhibitory one (lack of reaction) to the non-reinforced sound the experimenter reverses the procedure. The hitherto inhibitory stimulus is now reinforced whereas the previously reinforced CS is now applied without the UCS. So, the signal value of both stimuli is changed, hence the method is appropriately known as alteration of the signal value of a pair of conditioned stimuli, or just "alteration". The fewer the applications of stimuli needed to change their signal value, the higher the mobility of the NS. As will be shown, this method has been used by many investigators as the main indicator of the mobility of nervous processes.

(4) Stimuli in a given, constant order are applied to the animal. With some of them a positive CR is evoked by systematic unconditioned reinforcement. Other stimuli in the configuration are not reinforced. This way a given set of CRs is formed—the so-called dynamic stereotype. Once the stereotypic reactions are consolidated the set of conditioned stimuli is changed, e.g. the stimuli might be applied in reverse order. This is the change of the dynamic stereotype. Mobile dogs react adequately to the sequence of stimuli in the new, changed set whereas in inert dogs, either the CRs do not conform to stimulus significance, or the CR activity disappears altogether.

## Types of Nervous System

Different configurations of the properties of nervous processes described above constitute the types of nervous system also referred to by Pavlov as types of higher nervous activity.

Referring to the strength of NS, he distinguished the strong and the weak TNS. The equilibrium between the strength of excitation and inhibition allowed him to make the next distinction, though within the strong type only, that of the balanced and unbalanced types. The

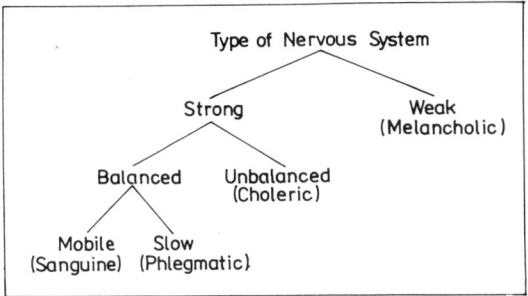

FIG. 1. Pavlov's nervous system typology and its relation to the Hippocrates–Galen typology of temperaments.

unbalanced type occurs in one form: with predominance of excitation over inhibition. Finally, taking mobility as the next criterion, the strong, balanced individuals may appear modified in two ways: into the mobile and the slow type. Pavlov argued consistently that the four types of NS corresponded to the classical types of temperament proposed by Hippocrates and Galen, as portrayed in Fig. 1.

As can be seen from this characterization, Pavlov did not construct his classification in a logical manner by simply combining the three basic properties of the NS. Had he done so, he would have had to distinguish more types; as he wrote, there would have been at least twenty-four types of NS in all.

Commenting on his limited choice of possible alternatives Pavlov argued that the existence of the four types had been vindicated by his many years of study of the behaviour of dogs, under both laboratory and natural conditions.

Pavlov conceptualized NS type as being innate and, hence, relatively immune to environmental influences, including rearing. He referred to it as the genotype, in contradiction to the traditional meaning of the term, thus giving rise to various misinterpretations of his position.[4]

He conceived nervous system type as a physiological basis of temperament, the latter being simply a psychological manifestation of the TNS. He sometimes even used both these terms interchangeably. According to Pavlov, the types of nervous system established in animal investigation could be justifiably extended to humans.

> . . . the mentioned types are what we call in man temperaments. The temperament constitutes the most general characteristic of every man, the most general and most essential characteristic of his nervous system (Pavlov, 1952, p. 389).

Much space has been dedicated in Pavlov's publications to the role of the TNS or its separate properties in the process of adjustment of the organism to the environment. The most convenient way to present his position is to give a short description of the four TNS.

(1) The strong, balanced, and mobile type (sanguine) is a healthy, resistant, and vitally efficient type of NS. He takes the Aristotelian golden mean, together with the slow (phlegmatic) type. This individual is lively and active when stimulated by the surroundings, in non-stimulating situations is prone to drowsiness and to sleep, and develops positive and inhibitory CRs easily. It is difficult to develop nervous diseases in representatives of this type, even in unfavourable conditions. Pavlov considered this type to be the most perfect, since it guarantees the maintenance of equilibrium between the organism and the surroundings more than the other types do.

(2) The strong, balanced, and slow type (phlegmatic). Alongside the sanguine, one of the types of NS which are well adjusted to life. Such properties as considerable strength and equilibrium of excitation and inhibition processes cause a healthy and resistant type of NS. Positive and negative CRs are developed with ease, and once they are formed they remain stable. It is difficult to develop nervous diseases in this individual, even in difficult situations. However, because of the high inertia of the nervous processes, individuals belonging to this type have difficulty in adapting to rapidly changing conditions.

(3) The strong, unbalanced type (choleric). Positive conditioned reflexes are formed quickly and with ease, whereas inhibitory CRs develop with difficulty. The predominance of excitation over inhibition predisposes the choleric to neurotic states. The type has difficulty interrupting activity when necessary. In difficult situations, requiring strong inhibition, individuals belonging to this type are inclined to be depressive and sleepy or, on the contrary, they may be aggressive and irrepressible.

(4) The weak type (melancholic). Characterized as the limited type with a narrow vital range, who needs special conditions to survive. CRs develop with difficulty and they may be disturbed or even extinguished under distracting stimuli. The nerve cells are weak in this type, and therefore stimuli of normal intensity may cause overstimulation leading to the development of protective inhibition. This type is most frequently to be found among neurotics. The weak type also has little capacity to respond adequately to the action of inhibitory stimuli. Their behaviour is easily disrupted by rapid and frequent changes in the environment. The small capacity of the NS causes its other properties to play a secondary role and for that reason weak types are more or less

vitally defective. They should be recognized as maladapted to life, quick to collapse, and often prone to sickness. Individuals representing this type may be recognized as valuable under special conditions only, i.e. if reared in "hot-house" conditions (Pavlov, 1952, p. 558).

As may be seen by the above brief descriptions, Pavlov strongly related NS typology to the individual's ability to adapt to the environment, giving highest credit to the two strong, well-balanced types, and the lowest to the weak TNS.

## NERVOUS SYSTEM TYPOLOGY AS DEVELOPED BY PAVLOV'S STUDENTS

The Pavlovian typology of the NS has been variously interpreted by investigators involved in this area, one source of differences in interpretation being the changes in Pavlov's own understanding of the concepts of nervous system types and the separate properties of nervous processes over more than 30 years of studies in the higher nervous activity in animals.

Withholding myself from any definitive judgements as to what is and what is not Pavlovian typology of the NS I would like to provide some information about the main contributions—in my opinion—which have been made in this area since the 1930s.

First of all it should be stated that research in Pavlovian typology has been conducted almost exclusively in the Soviet Union and, within a limited scope, in other socialist countries, like Hungary (e.g. Marton and Urban, 1966; Marton, 1972), Czechoslovakia (Halmiova, 1978, 1980), Rumania (Popescu-Neveanu, 1954; Voicu and Olteanu, 1972), and Poland (Strelau, 1965a, 1969, 1970a, 1972a, 1972b, 1975a). Recently, several people in the West, greatly influenced by Gray's fundamental monograph *Pavlov's Typology*, have been showing growing interest in TNS investigation (see e.g. Mangan, 1967a, 1967b, 1967c, 1978, 1982; Eysenck and Levey, 1972; Eysenck, in press; Orlebeke, 1972; Loo, 1978, 1979; Paisey and Mangan, 1982; Strelau, et al., in press).

Among the Soviet TNS researchers I have counted more than one hundred people currently publishing in this area. In my opinion the most important research contributed to Pavlov's idea of TNS has been conducted in three centres. The first is the Leningrad group working in Koltushe, near Leningrad, where Pavlov set up his laboratory. This group, the most influential members of which have been Kupalov, Krasusky, and Fedorov, has been continuing TNS investigation in animals, directly following Pavlov's tradition.

Teplov and his students, especially Nebylitsyn who was the most active, have made by far the greatest contribution to the investigation of the basic properties of NS in humans, and some publications of the Teplov group, working in Moscow, have been translated into English (e.g. Gray, 1964; Nebylitsyn, 1972a; Nebylitsyn and Gray, 1972).

The third centre, unknown in the psychological literature of the West, is the Ural group working since the middle of the 1950s under Merlin. The main interests of this group centre on the psychological interpretation of the TNS with special emphasis on the role of TNS and temperament in human activity.

It would be an oversimplification to assume that all psychologists and physiologists in the Soviet Union who contributed to this area may be categorized within these three groups. As an example Krasnogorsky, Ivanov-Smolensky and their students may be mentioned. They developed their own original ideas which were not without impact on further TNS research, especially in that germane to human behaviour.

Characterizing the contributions to the concept of the type of nervous system since Pavlov I will begin with research conducted in animals. Since, however, we are more interested in human beings, it will be a rather short review, only emphasizing the data which strongly influenced research on humans.

## Research on Type of Nervous System in Animals

After Pavlov, one of the main directions in TNS research was the development of methods for diagnosing the types of NS in animals, mainly in dogs. A special attempt has been made to objectify these methods and to establish standard TNS investigation procedures (see e.g. Kolesnikov and Troshikhin, 1951; Mayorov and Troshikhin, 1952; Krasusky, 1953).

Mayorov and Troshikhin published the *Standard for the investigation of nervous system type in dogs* accepted by the Academy of Medical Sciences in 1950. It includes most of the methods elaborated in Pavlov's laboratory. For example, to diagnose the strength of excitation, the following techniques are recommended: (a) the speed of positive CR formation;[5] (b) the elevating of excitability by food deprivation cure; (c) increasing the intensity of stimuli; (d) administering caffeine of different doses.

All these methods, notably, had been used by Pavlov. What seems to be interesting, however, is that the standard does not include special methods for diagnosing the equilibrium of nervous processes. A full diagnosis of the TNS in the dog using all the techniques included within the so-called large standard takes about a year and a half to two years. For this reason this standard is devoid of any practical meaning. The data collected did, however, show correlations between the alternative techniques for diagnosing the separate properties of NS (see Krasusky, 1953).

Almost at the same time the so-called small standard was developed (see Kolesnikov and Troshikhin, 1951). It permitted the formulation of a diagnosis within 6–7 months, still rather a long time compared with the time needed to diagnose human psychological traits. The small standard includes: (a) strength of excitation—the caffeine trial; (b) strength of inhibition—the speed of differentiation; (c) mobility of nervous processes—the alteration of the signal value of a pair of stimuli.

In most TNS investigations these techniques are still used. The caffeine method, used exclusively in animal research, has been improved by taking into account the weight of the animals (see Troshikhina, 1971; Krasuskaya, 1971) or by a more quantitative approach based on the curve of normal distribution (Lovchikov and Roshchina, 1971; Krasuskaya, 1971).

The two other methods mentioned in the small standard for diagnosing strength of inhibition and mobility are often used in TNS investigation in humans, as will be shown in Chapter 2.

Some of the scientists working with animals paid special attention to the essence of the separate properties of the NS. The problem of mobility was thoroughly investigated by Pavlov's student, Yakovleva. Based on her mentor's works she concluded that the

> mobility of nervous processes—excitation and inhibition—might be characterized by the speed of the course of these processes, by the speed with which they arise and disappear when the stimulus has ceased to act and the speed of concentration after the initial phase of irradiation. Another index of mobility is the speed with which one process is replaced by the opposing process (Yakovleva, 1938, p. 32).

This position, which suggests that mobility might be a temporal characteristic of the NS (see also Asratyan, 1939) was developed by Teplov (1964a).

A series of studies have been carried out to elucidate the nature of mobility of nervous processes. Most well known is the research on mice conducted by Fedorov, who, in my opinion, might be regarded as the first psychophysiologist in the Soviet Union to use genetic behaviour methods in TNS investigation. On the bases of data collected over many years, he and his students showed that the genetic factor contributed to a considerable extent to the variance of mobility in mice

(Fedorov, 1964, 1969). He also stated that the characteristic of mobility undergoes changes during maturation and ageing (Fedorov, 1951).

Pavlov's view, according to which the equilibrium of nervous processes relates only to the balance between the strength of excitation and inhibition, was not accepted by Kupalov. Discussing this problem Kupalov concluded that the only primary basic properties of the NS are the strength of excitation and inhibition and mobility of nervous processes. Equilibrium is a secondary feature, which appears as a result of a given combination of the strength of excitation and inhibition on the one hand, and as the ratio of mobility of excitation to mobility of inhibition on the other; meaning that the excitatory process may be more mobile than the inhibitory one and vice versa (Kupalov, 1952, p. 466). This idea of treating equilibrium as a secondary property has been further developed in Teplov's laboratory (see p. 136).

The most systematic study of changes in the NS properties during maturation has been conducted by a Kiev group under Troshikhin, who carried out a developmental study in rats and dogs, controlling all three properties of the NS (Troshikhin et al., 1971). For example, measuring the strength of excitation in dogs by the caffeine trial the authors concluded that the strength of excitation is maximal at the age of 2 months. Beginning from the fourth month of life it gradually drops, as implied by the fact that the older the dog the smaller the dose of caffeine needed to evoke protective inhibition (see Fig. 2). Similar regularities have been found in rats. The authors' study, supported also by other data collected in dogs, rabbits and goats (e.g. Obraztsova, 1971) demonstrates very clearly the dynamics of the development of NS properties a study yet to be carried out in TNS research in humans.

Since the classical experiment conducted by Pavlov's students, Vyrzhikovsky and Mayorov (1957), who showed that rearing dogs for 2 years in prison conditions (closed cages) does not change their NS properties, many animal studies have been reported which aimed at determining the limits to which the TNS could change under training and other environmental factors. The results are rather confusing and do not lead to any unequivocal conclusions. Fedorov (1953) for example, reported that, under training, the speed of alteration of the signal value of a pair of stimuli grows. Because this technique was used as the sole method to diagnose the mobility of nervous processes in mice he concluded that, under training, the mobility of nervous processes must improve. In another publication (Strelau, 1969) the groundlessness of this conclusion was shown. Krasusky, who repeated Vyrzhikovsky and Mayorov's experiment in 37 dogs (the former authors limited their sample to eight dogs) supported the latter's conclusion about the

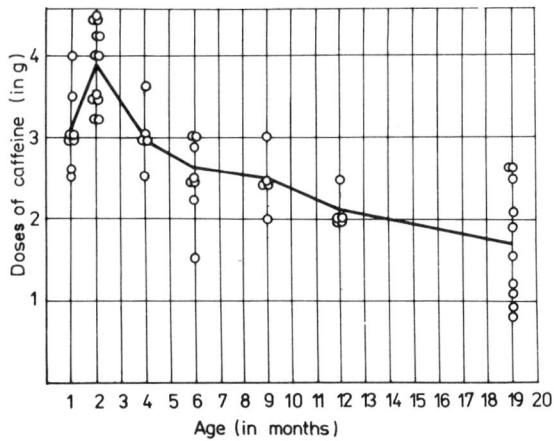

FIG. 2. Developmental characteristic of strength of excitation in dogs (adapted from Troshikhin et al., 1971).

unchangeability of NS properties, showing at the same time that advanced changes in the dogs' behaviour (especially as expressed in the so-called passive defensive reflex) was to some degree a behavioural expression of anxiety. This reflex is much greater in dogs reared in closed cages (Krasusky, 1959; Burdina et al., 1960).

In the study previously mentioned, Troshikhin referred to the possibility of training NS properties. Taking into account several categories of age at which the dogs were trained and different intervals between training sessions, the authors conclude that periods of development exist during which the dogs are more prone to changes in the properties of higher nervous activity. Early ontogenesis seems to be of special significance (Troshikhin et al., 1971).

These animal data, which show the possibilities and limits in changing NS properties as well as their developmental specificity, are highly relevant for the understanding of the type of NS in humans.

A special line of NS investigation has been developed by a Ukrainian group under Kavetsky, who showed the significance of the TNS in adaptation processes in dogs. Taking as a starting-point the hypothesis that a relationship exists between the physiological reactivity of the organism and the animal's TNS, the authors stated that individual differences in reactivity, revealed by sensitivity to pathogenic factors and medical drugs, by predispositions to diseases and their development, depended on the dog's NS properties (Kavetsky et al., 1961).

An experiment may serve as an example where the authors set out to test the hypothesis that, dependent on the TNS, differences exist in the process of regeneration of albumin and morphological components in the blood after losing a given amount of them. Twenty per cent of the general volume of blood was released (1% in relation to body weight) in a group of dogs, divided into strong, weak, and intermediate types. The number of erythrocytes and the levels of haemoglobin and albumin were determined 10 min before bleeding and then at given intervals until base level was reinstated.

In dogs with a strong NS the amount of erythrocytes and level of haemoglobin reverted to the norm within 2–3 days after bleeding; 19–23 days were required for weak TNS dogs; and in individuals characterized as intermediate, the initial level was restored after 9 days. The level of albumin reverted to the norm within 2–3 days in the strong type, whereas dogs with the weak type needed 22–23 days for regeneration.

Food deprivation, causing a state of constant hypoproteinaemia, yields similar effects. The regeneration of albumins and the process of erythrocyte and haemoglobin production following food deprivation occurs approximately twice as fast in the strong type of NS than in the weak type.

A similar experiment was conducted by Pshenichnyi (1960), in order to establish the relationship between the dynamics of leukocyte changes and the mobility of nervous processes. Tolerance to glucose as a function of the strength of NS in dogs was studied by Komarova (1971) who even recommended this trial as an indicator of the strength of the NS as regards excitation.

Unfortunately, research seeking relationships between NS properties and specific diseases in humans is sparse, although such investigation could be of great practical importance.

Since Pavlov established the four types of NS few investigators have objected to this magic number of four taken from Hippocrates typology. So the study conducted by Krasusky in dogs (1963) is all the more interesting. Using the small standard (see p. 15) to diagnose the type of NS in 116 dogs, the author names 48 different types of NS. Taking into account several degrees of strength, equilibrium, and mobility, and all possible combinations between them, Krasusky distinguished 120 variants (more than the number of dogs under investigation!) which might be characterized quantitatively.

This rather exaggerated tendency to differentiate types of nervous systems did, however, warn investigators against limiting the richness of the individuals' activity in which the temperament traits are revealed in only four patterns of behaviour.

## 1. Traditional Research and Current Approach

Finally, it must be stressed that the investigation of TNS, primarily conducted in dogs, gradually spread to many other animal species. Apart from mice and rats which first served as experimental subjects in Fedorov and Troshikhin's investigations, as has been partially illustrated above, other animals have also been used. For example, Vatsuro showed that in monkeys the mobility of nervous processes is higher in the kinesthetic sensory system than other modalities (Vatsuro, 1945; Vatsuro and Shtodin, 1947). Using animals from the same population Norkina (1961) argued that the TNS in monkeys did not change during a period of 6 years, starting with 3 to 4-year-old subjects. Kokorina (1971), investigating the type of nervous system in cows, presents data illustrating procedures for quantitative and qualitative TNS analysis in these animals.

A comparative study, using dogs, rabbits, and goats was conducted by Obraztsova (1964, 1971), who, among others, was interested in the developmental specificity of the NS properties across the species under investigation.

Two volumes written mainly by the Leningrad group: *Methods of Study of Typological Features of Higher Nervous Activity in Animals* (Chernigovsky, 1964) and *Methods for Studying the Typological Features of Higher Nervous Activity* (Krasusky and Fedorov, 1971) may serve as an example of the variety of methods used in TNS investigation and different kinds of experiments conducted in many species (besides the above-mentioned, horses, sheep, and guinea pigs have been studied).

The TNS in animals, outlined above, provides a comprehensive but by no means exhaustive account of the problems under discussion. However, more space will be devoted to TNS research in humans, since this is our main interest.

### Early Attempts to Apply Pavlov's Typology to Human Beings

The first attempts to apply Pavlov's theory of TNS to the study of humans were made by Krasnogorsky and by Ivanov-Smolensky, two students of the great physiologist.

It was in 1917 when Krasnogorsky, investigating the inhibitory reactions in children, distinguished two types of nervous system—the normal and the inert type of higher nervous activity. He published his conception of TNS several times (e.g. 1939, 1953, 1954); however, the most systematic and exhaustive description of his typology was presented in his monograph devoted to higher nervous activity in children (Krasnogorsky, 1958).

Krasnogorsky, like Pavlov, distinguished three basic properties of the NS—the strength, equilibrium, and mobility of nervous processes. However, he did not assign equilibrium to the relation between the strength of excitation and inhibition as was the case in Pavlov's typology, but he referred it to the relationship between the strength of excitation in the cortex and strength of excitation in the subcortex. The equilibrium of excitation between the cortex and subcortex areas eventually became the major criterion of his typology.

Using unconditioned and conditioned reactions (the salivary CR being the technique most extensively used), as well as taking into account verbal reactions and the global behaviour of the child, Krasnogorsky, like Pavlov, identified four types of nervous system, and linked them to the ancient typology of temperament. This is the first well-described and empirically supported characterization of temperament understood as the manifestation of the types of NS. The description of these four types is as follows (Krasnogorsky, 1958).

(1) The strong type with optimal excitation, balanced and quick, with harmonious co-operation of all segments of the brain is known as the sanguine. Both positive and inhibitory CRs are formed quickly and they are durable. The strength of reaction corresponds with the intensity of the stimuli. The strength of nerve cells in the cortex and a normal level of excitation in the subcortex guarantee good adaptation to the demands of the surroundings. The activity of the cortex is highly mobile. This type might be characterized as a vivid temperament, not causing problems in upbringing. Verbal reactions are formed quickly and they are in accordance with the age norms. The speech of the sanguine is, as a rule, loud, quick, clear, balanced, and fluent. It is accompanied by a lively gesticulation, well-expressed mimicry, and emotional arousal.

(2) The strong type, with optimal excitation, balanced, and slow is known as the phlegmatic. Both positive and inhibitory CRs are strong, durable, and formed with normal speed. Adequate co-operation between the cortex and subcortex insures the control of the cortex over the inborn reflexes. The phlegmatic adapts with ease to the social environment. Speech, reading, and writing are quickly acquired. The speech of this type is slower than in the sanguine. It is calm, uniform, and without emotional expression, vivid mimicry, or gesticulation.

(3) The strong type, excitable, immoderate, unbalanced, with domination of excitation in the subcortical centres is known as the choleric. This type can be characterized by the development of strong CRs, which are under considerable influence from the subcortex. Its increased activity is insufficiently regulated by the cortex. The elabora-

tion of CRs proceeds more slowly than in both the above-mentioned types due to the increased excitability of the subcortex, which has inhibitory effects on the cortex. The inhibitory conditioned reflexes of the choleric type are unstable. Children of this type usually have satisfactory school grades; however, they have difficulty adjusting their reactions and emotions to school requirements. Their speech is rather quick, but uneven, and develops with more difficulty than in both the former types.

(4) The weak type, with low excitation of both cortical and subcortical centres and lack of balance between excitation and inhibition corresponds to the melancholic. This is an energetic type. The decreased activity of the cortex is accompanied by low activity of the subcortex, which reveals itself in small emotional expression. Children of this type tire easily and fail to react to strong and long-lasting stimuli. The conditioned reflexes are weak and the formation of CRs proceeds slowly. The magnitude of CRs does not conform to the law of strength. This type is characterized by a predominance of external inhibition. The speech of the melancholic is slow and silent. Children with weak TNS are more prone to disorders in higher nervous activity.

Krasnogorsky states that the types of higher nervous activity (HNA) are not unchangeable. Since they are based on unconditioned and conditioned reactions, and especially on verbal behaviour, they may be modified under the influence of learning, nutrition, social events, education, and various diseases (Krasnogorsky, 1958, p. 226). This position, as will be seen later, is not accepted by most Soviet typologists, especially by the Teplov–Nebylitsyn school (see p. 42) which stressed the stability of the TNS in humans.

Teplov (1960) acknowledged the fact that Krasnogorsky's typology differs from Pavlov's first of all in the criteria used to identify the types of NS; however, like Pavlov, he did not avoid the magic number of four types.

Pavlov, characterizing separate properties of the nervous system, did not refer to their anatomical differentiation, assuming these to be properties of the "upper segment" of the NS, especially the cortex. The very clear differentiation between the NS properties of the cortex and subcortex seems to me to have been at the time one of the most important contributions in Krasnogorsky's typology. It is similarly stressed by Ilin (1978), who also mentions that, in Krasnogorsky's typology, excitation and inhibition tend to be treated as one indivisible process. This monistic concept is revealed by the fact this typology reflects the degree of excitability (intensity of excitation), but not the relation between excitation and inhibition.

In Krasnogorsky's typology the speed of CR formation and learning are strongly emphasized. The question arises as to whether the ability to form CRs and to learn may be assumed to be a temperamental trait, a contention not in sympathy with the usual interpretation of temperament and not in the main line of Pavlov's understanding of TNS as the physiological basis of temperament. The conditionability, measured by the speed of formation of CRs, and the problem of learning seem to be the domains of the psychology of abilities (see, e.g. Gagné, 1967). Moreover, the relation between the strength of NS and the speed of CR formation seems to be one of the most controversial problems in NS typology. In many publications, especially in the first period of investigation, it was assumed that the strength of nervous processes correlated positively with the speed of CR aquisition (see Pavlov, 1951–52; Mayorov and Troshikhin, 1952; Gurevich and Kolesnikov, 1955; Maizel, 1956; Biryukova, 1961; Elkin *et al.*, 1961; Kokorina, 1963, 1971). Since the 1950s, the opposite relation between the strength of nervous system and the speed of conditioning has been revealed, i.e. the CRs are formed more slowly the stronger the process of excitation. This has been stated, among others, by Krasusky (1953), Chebykin (1961), and Yermolayeva-Tomina (1963). Even Nebylitsyn, who denied that speed of conditioning is an indicator of strength of NS writes: "The high sensitivity of the sensory apparatus is a factor favouring the speed of CR formation" (1959b, p. 87). As will be shown, sensitivity is one of the poles of the strength dimension (see p. 29). I have argued in detail (see Strelau, 1969) that this regularity seems to be theoretically justified if one assumes that high sensitivity is, according to Teplov and Nebylitsyn (1963a), one of the characteristic traits of the weak type of NS. Semagin (1971), taking into account over 7000 results collected in white rats in which conditioned motor and alimentary reflexes were investigated, stated that the speed and durability of CRs does not depend on the strength of NS with regard to excitation and inhibition. The intensity of positive and negative (differentiation) CRs were used as indices of strength. It is also probable that an inverted U-curve relationship exists between the strength of excitation and the speed of CR formation which may lead to contradictory statements depending on the UCS–CS pair used. The degree to which the physical characteristics of the stimuli used and the temporal relationship in their exposition may influence speed of conditioning, depends on individual differences in temperament traits, as has been clearly shown by Eysenck and Levey (1972).

Returing to Krasnogorsky's typology one more remark should be made. It seems that the unequivocal subordination of the verbal characteristic of behaviour to the child's TNS is not supported by the author's own data, and thus forming direct conclusions about the individual's behaviour on the basis of his temperament traits is an oversimplification, as will be seen in Chapter 5.

Almost at the same time Ivanov-Smolensky, referring to Pavlov's idea of TNS, elaborated a typology which differs from both his mentor's and Krasnogorsky's conceptions (Ivanov-Smolensky, 1935, 1952, 1953). Investigations into NS properties were conducted on hundreds of kindergarten and school-age children, in Ivanov-Smolensky's laboratory. In all cases, a modified form of the motor-reaction method was used. Wherever possible this method was combined with the recording of heart rate and respiration. For younger children, special motor-reaction methods with alimentary and orienting reinforcements were used. On all developmental levels the so-called motor-verbal method, known also as the Ivanov-Smolensky method[6] was applied.

Taking into account the facility and speed of conditioned response formation Ivanov-Smolensky (1953) proposed the following four types:

(1) the mobile type—both positive and inhibitory temporal connections are formed easily and quickly;
(2) the slow type—both positive and inhibitory connections are formed slowly, with difficulty;
(3) the excitable type—positive temporal connections are formed easily and quickly, and inhibitory connections slowly and with difficulty;
(4) the inhibited type—positive temporal connections are formed slowly, inhibitory connections easily and quickly.

In contradistinction to Pavlov's view, Ivanov-Smolensky refers to "types of closing (reflex-forming) activity" by which he means to stress that his typology does not aspire to characterizing the so-called general types of NS and is only concerned with the process of CR formation. Many authors, however, disregarding Ivanov-Smolensky's own standpoint, erroneously take his typology to be a faithful transposition of Pavlov's typology from animals to human beings (e.g. Povorinsky, 1954; Ivanova, 1957; Sukhanova, 1959; Mateyev and Georgiyev, 1960; Umansky, 1960; Cytawa and Jakubowicz, 1961).

Two features of the NS constitute the basis of Ivanov-Smolensky's (1953) typology, namely mobility and equilibrium. He neglects such an important property of the NS as the strength of excitation and inhibition, assumed by Pavlov to be the most important feature. Though Ivanov-Smolensky himself did not permit the strength of NS to be measured, using his own criteria, one may find examples where Ivanov-

Smolensky's method has been used to diagnose NS strength (see Mateyev and Georgiyev, 1960; Cytawa and Jakubowicz, 1961).

Ivanov-Smolensky, like Krasnogorsky, shared the opinion that NS properties are closely related to the individuals' former experiences, to their ontogenesis and that the knowledge of NS properties is very important for education and medicine. These properties may be improved under social influences, especially in the case of extreme values of the separate features (Ivanov-Smolensky, 1953, p. 50). However, Teplov (1964a) argued very convincingly against this position. He also criticized the "closing temporal connection" typology for limiting the number to four types, although the criteria for its construction differed from Pavlov's. It is, he maintained, a kind of slavish and incomprehensible attachment to the ancient Hippocrates–Galen typology.

The idea of relating the properties of the NS to given diseases and to take them into account in programming treatment and therapy, never gained great popularity in TNS investigation; it has, however, been partially continued by others such as Birman (1951), Pervomaysky (1964), Simanovsky (1964), Kachura (1965), Rebrov (1965), Sklarova (1965), and Apter (1966).

The speed of conditioning used, especially in animal research (see p. 14), as an indicator of NS strength has been adapted by Ivanov-Smolensky as an index of mobility. This position, traceable to earlier publications (Asratyan, 1939; Davidenkov, 1947), has not been acknowledged in subsequent TNS research. In the light of contemporary research in this area, Ivanov-Smolensky's classification can be seen to rest squarely on the dynamism of nervous processes and on the balance between excitation and inhibition in dynamism (see p. 33), especially where speed of conditioning is the most crucial factor. As Nebylitsyn writes:

> In our opinion, therefore, the classifacatory system of Ivanov-Smolensky is one of the first attempts to generalize from experimental work on dynamism of nervous processes in man (1972a, p. 28).

For the same reason, which has also been mentioned on p. 22, it would be difficult to accept Ivanov-Smolensky's typology, where the speed of conditioning of positive and negative reactions seems to be the main criterion, as a physiological basis for temperament—an idea of Pavlov's.

One of the main contributions of Ivanov-Smolensky and his students to NS typology consists of drawing attention to the fact that the diagnosis of NS properties depends on the kind of stimuli used in the experiments. Findings of Korotkin, Sinkevich, and Khozak (see Ivanov-Smolensky, 1935) have shown that children may be ascribed different types of NS depending on the kind of reinforcement used in the CR experiment whether alimentary, defensive, or orienting. Interpreting this fact Ivanov-Smolensky concluded that, apart from the general, synthetic TNS, partial types also exist which refer to the separate functions of the organism—alimentary, defensive, sexual, orienting. They differ, among others, in strength, equilibrium, and mobility of nervous processes (Ivanov-Smolensky, 1935, p. 137). This means that NS properties may be differently characterized depending on the subcortical areas to which they are connected, or, in other words, depending on the kind of unconditioned stimuli used.

Thus the concept of the partial type was introduced to Pavlov's typology of the NS, although it had been known since the beginning of differential psychology (Stern, 1921).

The fact that TNS characteristic varies according to the kind of UCSs used has been supported by others such as Alekseyeva (1953), who used alimentary and acid-defence reinforcements in dogs, and by Fedorov. Fedorov showed that the diagnosis of mobility of nervous processes in mice measured by the alteration of the signal value of a pair of stimuli differs depending on whether food or electric shock are used as UCSs (Fedorov, 1962a, 1962b).

The only study conducted in adults with the aim of testing whether the diagnosis of NS type depends on the quality of the UCSs used has been conducted by the present author (see p. 112).

Systematic studies, the aim of which was to investigate the phenomenon of partiality in NS type investigations, have been conducted by the Teplov–Nebylitsyn school (e.g. Teplov, 1964a; Nebylitsyn, 1972a, 1972b; Rusalov, 1977), whose contribution to research into Pavlov's typology will be discussed in the next section, and by Strelau (1965a, 1969, 1972a).

## THE TEPLOV–NEBYLITSYN SCHOOL: NEO-PAVLOVIAN TYPOLOGY

Undoubtedly, the most significant contribution to Pavlov's typology adapted to humans, especially to adults, has been made by the Moscow group working since the middle 1950s under Teplov and, about ten years later, under Nebylitsyn, who was his first and most creative student. After Nebylitsyn's premature death in 1972, several smaller independent groups were organized which worked further in this area and developed Teplov and Nebylitsyn's ideas. Among these groups I would like to mention Gurevich and his students, whose studies concentrate on the significance of NS properties for the process of professional fitness. Ravich-Shcherbo and her group have been developing twin studies in this area to show the significance of the genetic factor in determining NS properties. Golubeva contributed first of all to the application of the electroencephalogram (EEG) technique for diagnosing NS properties which she and her collaborators have been linking with investigations in memory. Rozhdestvenskaya, the author of several methods elaborated for diagnosing NS properties has completed many systematic studies with the aim of showing the significance of the strength of NS in the effectiveness of behaviour in situations of different stimulation load. Rusalov and his co-workers, almost exclusively using the EEG method in NS properties research, have made interesting contributions to the further development of diagnostic methods and in seeking connections between NS properties and abilities. There are also other workers whose contribution to NS properties investigation seems very important (e.g. Leites, Borisova, Olshannikova). Since all of them were students of Teplov and/or Nebylitsyn, it seems justified to speak about the Teplov–Nebylitsyn school when broadly characterizing their contribution to Pavlov's typology.

As has been mentioned on p. 14 it is this development of Pavlov's typology which is best known in Western psychology. The contribution of the Moscow group is contained, among others, in nine more or less systematic published volumes. The first five were edited by Teplov under the title: *Typological Features of Higher Nervous Activity in Man* (Teplov, 1956, 1959, 1963, 1965, 1967). The next four volumes (VI–IX) changed their title into: *Problems of Differential Psychophysiology* and were edited by Nebylitsyn (1969, 1972c, 1974) and by Borisova *et al.* (1977). There are also some other volumes reporting results on research conducted by this group (see Smirnov, 1977; Lomov and Ravich-Shcherbo, 1978; Rusalov and Golubeva, 1980) as well as several monographs summarizing research in different areas of NS properties investigation (Teplov, 1961; Nebylitsyn, 1972a,[7] 1976; Gurevich, 1970; Rusalov, 1979; Golubeva, 1980a; Rozhdestvenskaya, 1980).

I have mentioned some of the people and their publications to illustrate the range and amount of research activity which has been invested in the area of NS properties by the group known under the label "Teplov–Nebylitsyn school". Now let me start with a more systematic characterization of their contribution without pretending to exhaust this area. I would, however, like to show that Powell's view, when he wrote—"Russian work as propounded by Pavlov, Teplov and Nebylitsyn begins with properties and types of nervous activity—and stops there" (1979, p. 25)—is not true.

## Methodological Bases of Nervous System Properties Investigation

Since the beginning of research into the area of Pavlov's typology Teplov formulated several methodological principles (1954, 1955a, 1956, 1964a), developed further by Nebylitsyn (Teplov and Nebylitsyn, 1963a and b; Nebylitsyn, 1972a), which are known as the methodological "credo" of the Moscow group, and which influenced to a high degree not only the research of the above-mentioned school but most of the investigations carried out in the Soviet Union in this area. The main theses of the "credo" may be characterized as follows:

(1) The initial exploration must be aimed at NS properties; only when these are established will it be advisable to deal with their configurations into TNS, the latter being merely an outcome of the relationships between strength, equilibrium, and mobility of nervous processes. This principle, as a rule, has been constantly adhered to by the Moscow group up to now.

(2) Rather than describing particular properties, the prime approach should consist of mathematical-statistical analysis enabling measurement of the exact interdependencies between the respective variables. Interestingly enough the factor-analysis method was first used for this purpose and Nebylitsyn was the first psychologist to apply this method in the Soviet Union (1960a).

(3) The principal approach should be through experimental laboratory studies rather than through the commonly used anamnesis and observation. Nothing short of an experiment can yield the essential data on the substance and structure of the basic properties of the NS.

(4) It is essential to investigate experimentally, in the laboratory, the general properties of the NS by reference to involuntary movements, in which the properties of nervous processes are clearly manifested, undisguised by the individual's experience (as is the case with all voluntary movements). The diagnostic methods based on involuntary reactions (e.g. photochemical, pupillary, vascular, and galvanic-skin reflexes) enable the elaboration of new conditioned reactions not influenced by the so-called "second signal system" (see also Saprykin and Mileryan, 1954). However, this position has been criticized (see Strelau, 1969; Eliasz, 1972). This critique has been grasped correctly by Peysakhov (1975) who stated that the diagnosis of TNS on the basis

of CR activity or involuntary reactions evokes many doubts if one accepts the fact that the individual constitutes a part of a highly developed social and ecological system.

(5) The diagnosis of NS properties should deal not only with CR procedures but with other psychophysiological measures as well, including sensory reactions and bioelectrical activity. In the last 10 years these psychophysiological indicators have become the most important ones in the research of the Moscow group due to the fact that the EEG indices enable the partiality phenomenon to be avoided (see Nebylitsyn, 1972b; Rusalov, 1975, 1977).

(6) The student of TNS must renounce any evaluative attitude and take the view, that NS properties are neither good nor bad, each being simply associated with a specific form of the organism's adjustment to the environment.

(7) The manifestation of each of the basic properties of the nervous system create a so-called "syndrome", understood as a complex of interrelated indicators of the given property. That indicator which characterizes the property most directly is treated as the basic, referent one (Teplov, 1963a, 1964b) and serves as the main criterion in the validation procedure (see also Belous, 1976). In most cases the first method elaborated in Teplov's laboratory to diagnose a given NS property was used as the validation criterion for other methods. For example, in the case of strength of excitation the induction method (see p. 79) or the extinction with reinforcement method (see p. 77) were used as referent methods; which seems problematical because these methods, like other ones used in the first period of research in the Teplov–Nebylitsyn school, are very highly influenced by the partiality phenomenon, as exemplified on p. 49.

One of the most important contributions of the Teplov–Nebylitsyn group is the elaboration of several methods used for the diagnosis of NS properties. These have been discussed in detail in English by Gray (1964) and Nebylitsyn (1972a). Many of my own publications have been devoted to describing these methods with some critical remarks (see Strelau, 1962, 1964b, 1965a, 1969). To get some idea of the work done by this group on the development of laboratory methods for the investigation of basic NS properties the reader is referred to Chapter 2, where many practical methods are described.

## Strength of Excitation as a Dimension Characterized by Two Poles: Endurance and Sensitivity

As mentioned before, the strength of the NS was treated by Pavlov as the most important property of the nervous system. This also seems to be true of the Moscow group which has conducted hundreds of experiments with this feature controlled. On the basis of data collected over several years (e.g. Nebylitsyn, 1956, 1957; Rozhdestvenskaya, 1959a; Turovskaya, 1963; Ippolitov, 1966) Teplov and Nebylitsyn concluded that there is a strict dependence between the strength of NS as regards excitation understood as the capacity to work (endurance) and sensitivity (i.e. response threshold) (Teplov and Nebylitsyn, 1963b). This relationship is expressed by the following formula:

$R/r \approx$ const.

where $R$ is endurance (the upper threshold of reaction, measured by the maximum intensity of the stimulus to which there is still an adequate response) and $r$ is sensitivity (lower threshold of reaction).

Both the endurance of nerve cells and their sensitivity can be viewed as two facets of one nervous property, namely strength of the nervous system. Hence, Teplov and Nebylitsyn came to consider excitatory strength of nervous processes as a bipolar property that can be designated in terms of either endurance or sensitivity. The correlation between strength as determined by measures based on endurance phenomenon, on the one hand, and sensitivity on the other, is about 0.7 (Nebylitsyn, 1972a). This conception of NS strength differs strongly from Pavlov's, who limited the strength of excitation to the upper threshold (functional capacity) only.

The differentiation of endurance (efficiency) and sensitivity, which has been discussed in detail by Nebylitsyn (1972a) was of great importance for further investigations in this area. The assumption that sensitivity had to be treated as one of the poles of the strength of excitation dimension enabled the development of new methods for diagnosing the strength of NS without having to use strong or long-lasting stimuli, a procedure criticized by many investigators for ethical reasons. It also helped to link the concept of strength of NS and some dimensions of personality where the phenomenon of sensitivity is used as one of the indicators of the given dimension, as, for example, extraversion–introversion (Eysenck and Levey, 1972), activation or arousability (Gray, 1964) or the dimension of stimulus intensity modulation (Barnes, 1976). These links will be discussed later (see Chapter 4).

The acceptance of sensitivity, measured by sensory threshold, as one of the two main facets of the strength of NS is a very attractive idea, since sensitivity can be easily measured. On the other hand, however, it may lead to complications which were not considered by Teplov's students. First of all, sensitivity is strongly influenced by the partiality phenomenon as will be shown later (see p. 49). Thus the question arises as to whether the nervous processes measured on the basis of the visual, auditory, or other sensory systems reflect the general properties of the nervous system or the specificity of the modality under investigation (see Strelau, 1965a). On the other hand sensitivity seems to be strongly influenced by the peripheral mechanism involved in ongoing information processing. For example, the structure and function of a sensory receptor must be taken into account when considering the final magnitude of excitation evoked by given stimulation (Thomson and Schaefer, 1961; Strelau, 1969). Haslam (1972) noted that there is no correlation between the strength of NS as measured by sensory threshold to pain and changes in the magnitude of this threshold under caffeine. According to the Teplov school caffeine should increase sensitivity by increasing the excitability of nervous processes. This means a subthreshold-stimulus may become a threshold-stimulus under caffeine. The individual differences in the amount of caffeine needed to cause this change are used as an indicator of the strength of nervous system. A high increase in sensitivity to a small dose of caffeine, as well as a decrease of sensitivity (caused by the development of protective inhibition) to large doses of caffeine, indicates a weak NS (see Nebylitsyn, 1959a).

One may ask to what degree NS strength so conceptualized remains within the framework of Pavlov's typology, but this question will be discussed when other NS properties have been presented.

## The Mobility of the Nervous System Subdivided into Two Properties: Mobility and Lability

Teplov, having analysed many works devoted to this property of the nervous system concluded that

> mobility, in the widest sense, refers to all the temporal characteristics of the functioning of the nervous system, i.e. all aspects of this functioning to which the category of speed is applicable (Teplov, 1964a, p. 75).

Mobility of the nervous processes is manifested in:
(1) the speed with which the nervous processes are initiated and terminated;
(2) the speed with which inhibition is replaced by excitation and excitation by inhibition;
(3) the speed of formation of new positive and negative conditioned connections;
(4) the speed of response modification when external conditions change.

## 1. Traditional Research and Current Approach

The statement that all these aspects of nervous system activity constitute one general property of the nervous system called mobility was an assumption which had to be changed in the face of evidence collected in Teplov's laboratory.

Ravich-Shcherbo (1956) ascertained that no concordance existed between the various indices used in the procedure of photochemical conditioning ascertained to investigate mobility. The speed of alteration of the signal value of a pair of stimuli did not correlate with the speed of evoking the trace conditioned reflex nor with the duration of the visual after-image. On the basis of her own experiment and reports published by other authors, Ravich-Shcherbo concluded that the functional patterns of mobility could be divided into two groups: (i) the active collision of the opposing nervous processes—excitation and inhibition (alteration of the signal value of stimuli), and (ii) the duration of nervous processes (trace reflex and visual after-image).

Taking into account these results as well as other data collected by his collaborators Teplov (1963a) concluded that mobility consists of two independent factors: first, mobility in the narrow sense, which might be characterized by the speed of alteration of the signal value of a pair of stimuli (so-called "alteration"); and, secondly, lability, which is manifested in the speed with which nervous processes are initiated and terminated.[8]

Teplov's collaborators conducted an experiment in which 36 different indices of mobility understood as temporal characteristics of the nervous processes were used. Factor analysis of the data supports the notion of two independent properties of mobility: mobility and lability (Borisova *et al.*, 1963). This view has also been represented by Nebylitsyn (1972a).

There is, however, an inconsistency in the understanding of mobility of the nervous system. Several results show that mobility correlates positively with the strength of the NS (see e.g. Melikhova, 1964; Kozlova, 1977; Troshikhin *et al.*, 1978). This has also been replicated many times in our laboratory (see Table XXI, p. 133). On the other hand several basic indices of lability, e.g. the speed of elaboration of inhibitory reflexes, delayed conditioned reflexes (Teplov, 1964a), and trace conditioned reflexes (Ravich-Shcherbo, 1956) were later used as standard methods for diagnosing the dynamism of nervous processes as regards inhibition (see Nebylitsyn, 1972a).

As has been stated (p. 23) Ivanov-Smolensky used the speed of positive CR formation as the basic index of mobility of nervous processes while at the same time the same technique has been used by several authors as an index of strength (see pp. 5, 20) and in Teplov's laboratory as the index of dynamism in excitation (Nebylitsyn, 1972a).

Probably this rather intricate situation in the research on mobility led Teplov (1963b) to forward doubts as to whether mobility is a property of the NS. He made the supposition that mobility should preferably be understood as a feature of behaviour. So, after many years of investigation, he reached a conclusion which is close to the starting-point of Pavlov's own research. Up to the beginning of the 1930s Pavlov distinguished the mobile and low types of NS on the basis of animal behaviour only (1951–52).

This pessimistic opinion about mobility has been supported by several other authors. Vasilets (1978), for example, using Khilchenko's RT method (see p. 105) to diagnose mobility, obtained 25 indices of mobility in a twin study. Her results suggest that only the critical time interval between exposed stimuli, necessary to produce an adequate reaction to their signal value, is under any gentic control.[9] The "alteration" method (see p. 104) as well as the after-effect of positive and negative stimuli used as mobility indices did not intercorrelate, and, moreover, did not show genetic determination, this being treated in Teplov's laboratory as one of the main criteria for considering behaviour as a manifestation of NS properties.

Carlier (in press), in a factor analytical study on NS properties investigated by Strelau's Temperament Inventory (see Chapter 3) showed that mobility cannot be isolated as an independent factor.

Troshikhin *et al.*, conscious of the difficulties in understanding (and investigating) the mobility of NP, proposed to use the term "functional mobility", by which they meant the ability to react to quickly-changing stimuli. The efficiency of reactions to high-speed stimuli depends on the speed of nervous process movements, on the reverberation (after effect) of nervous processes, the functional readiness of the CR apparatus to new reactions, and on the ability of the NS to assimilate a given rhythm (1978, p. 29). The above-mentioned authors thus suggest a rather compound physiological mechanism underlying mobility. Kozlova (1977), summarizing the discussion of the physiological mechanism of mobility, mentions two. One, traditionally, is the speed of change of nervous processes and the second, proposed by Nebylitsyn (1972a), is the speed of NP movements. Chuprikova writes in her analysis of the physiological mechanisms of NS system properties that

> the structural neural transformations which occur during alteration should, to some degree, depend on the success and efficiency in suppressing the old connections, which in turn should be causally related to the strength and equilibrium of nervous processes (1977, p. 139).

There is yet another overlooked problem in the Russian literature. If we assume that the alteration of the signal value of a pair of stimuli is the standard method for diagnosing the mobility of nervous processes in its narrow sense, then mobility thus conceptualized has very little in common with behaviour labelled temperament, since the ability to transform positive CRs into negative ones and vice versa is used as one of the basic criteria for judging the level of evolved intelligence in different species (c.f. Bitterman, 1965) and therefore lies within the domain of learning (Gagné, 1967; Konorski, 1967). The same has been suggested in the case of the speed of CR formation used as an index of NS properties (see p. 22). The question arises as to the degree to which these measures shed light upon the physiological mechanisms underlying temperament as was the case in Pavlov's attempts to explain the TNS concept.

## Dynamism of Nervous Processes as the Fourth Property of NS

When Nebylitsyn (1963a) analysed the numerous experimental studies aimed at diagnosing the strength of the NS (e.g. those of Barkhudaryan, 1956; Fedorov, 1961; Chebykin, 1961) along with his own results he came to the conclusion that the speed of positive and negative (inhibitory) conditioned response formation does not correlate with the established indices of strength of NS. In NS strength investigation two different functions of the nerve tissue have been muddled: first, the generation of nervous processes in the neural structures during formation of positive and negative temporal connections; and, secondly, the efficiency of the NS, i.e. its ability to work.

According to Nebylitsyn the first function can be measured by evolving positive CRs along with their differentiation, extinction, and delay. In the case of the second function the method of repeatedly applied, strong, or prolonged stimuli is used. Nebylitsyn also acknowledged the fact that in several studies, some of which were conducted in Teplov's laboratory (e.g. Borisova *et al.*, 1963; Yermolayeva-Tomina, 1963; Ravich-Shcherbo, 1956), no correlation was found between the accepted indices of mobility and the speed of CR formation.

On the basis of these facts, Nebylitsyn put forward the hypothesis that the property of the NS which is manifested in the formation of temporal connections, i.e. in the ability to learn in the broad sense of this concept, should be treated as an independent one, and he called it *dynamism* (Nebylitsyn, 1963a, p. 26).

Dynamism should be understood as the facility and speed with which the processes of excitation and inhibition are generated during the formation of CRs. The main index of this property is the efficiency of positive (dynamism of excitation) and negative (dynamism of inhibition) classical CR formation (Nebylitsyn, 1963a; Teplov and Nebylitsyn, 1963a, Teplov, 1964b, 1972). The notion of dynamism has been discussed in detail in Nebylitsyn's fundamental monograph (1972a).

Probably taking as a starting-point the well-known fact that the formation of CRs depends among other things on the level of activation, Nebylitsyn hypothesized that the dynamism of nervous processes, especially the balance between the dynamism of excitation and inhibition, is a function of cortico-reticular interaction.

> The balance of both nervous processes as regards dynamism, their equilibrium, should be considered as the equilibrium of the reticular formation system and the cortex, i.e., as the balance between the activating influence of the reticular structures of the subcortex on the one hand, and the regulatory, inhibitory action of the cortex on the other (Nebylitsyn, 1963a, p. 18).

Such a position with regard to dynamism gave rise to an upsurge of EEG utilization in the first stage of investigating the above-mentioned NS property. However, following Golikov's (1956) suggestions that the types of bioelectrical activity are related to the types of higher nervous activity, this direction of research was further extended to the other properties of the nervous system.[10]

I have set down several doubts (Strelau, 1969) as to whether dynamism may be treated as an independent property of the NS. Nebylitsyn's argument that the strength of the NS does not correlate with the speed of CR formation has no more experimental evidence than does the opposite statement; it depends on the attitude with which the literature is viewed. As I have already mentioned, the speed of conditioning was, and still is, used as an indicator of all the properties of the NS (see also Belous, 1976; Mangan, 1982); which, of course, testifies against its use as an appropriate index for this purpose as it does against the idea that the separate NS properties are orthogonal.

Even in Nebylitsyn's laboratory there have been data collected which show that the speed of CR formation depends on the NS strength (see Ippolitov, 1969, Rozhdestvenskaya *et al.*, 1969a). Yermolayeva-Tomina (1969), summarizing the results of seven experiments which had been conducted over about ten years in Teplov's laboratory on more than 250 subjects and had been aimed at estimating the speed of GSR conditioning as an index of dynamism, concluded that the speed of CR formation cannot be used as an indicator of dynamism with regard to excitation, because the speed of conditioning is highly influenced by the type of unconditioned reinforcement used in the GSR procedure (thereby supporting the data obtained in our study) (Strelau, 1964a). This means, practically, that changing the UCS causes changes in the diagnosis of dynamism of excitation [Yermolayeva-Tomina, 1969).

Golubeva and Rozhdestvenskaya (1969) stated, in a study devoted to the investigation of the dynamics of bioelectrical activity as a function of the individuals' dynamism and lability of nervous processes, that dynamism measured by the speed of GSR conditioning, and lability estimated by the duration of alpha-blocking after visual stimuli exposition and by click-fusion frequency (see p. 100) have many elements in common. They also quote several studies where a significant and negative correlation between dynamism in excitation and lability was established. In the same study the authors stated that individuals differing in dynamism of excitation diagnosed on the basis of the CR procedure did not differ in the characteristics of their alpha rhythm, the latter having been used by Nebylitsyn (1972a) as the main criterion of dynamism (see p. 37).

The concept of dynamism has been criticized by Ilin (1978) who stresses that the dynamism of nervous processes as interpreted by Nebylitsyn covers two qualitatively different phenomena: the speed of generating nervous processes and the speed of CR formation, both being governed by different mechanisms, whereas Nebylitsyn treats them as identical.

Powell (1979) concludes that there is an analogy between the term conditionability, introduced by Eysenck, and dynamism, which of course supports our suggestion that this NS property is directly related to the sphere of learning and ability rather than temperament.

Gray's (1967) comparison between the excitation-inhibition balance in Eysenck's former concept of extra-introversion and the balance of dynamism in excitation and inhibition, both measured by the speed of CR formation, shows some correspondence between these concepts. However, as has been stated several times, extra-introversion seems to be related more to NS strength (see Gray, 1967; Eysenck and Levey, 1972; Strelau, 1970a).

Summarizing, although the treatment of dynamism of nervous processes as an independent property is an interesting approach, the issue has never been unequivocally resolved. The most fruitful outcome of research on this property seems to be the growing interest in individual differences in EEG phenomena, especially concerning the cortico-reticular loop. The latter is in turn, interpreted by many authors as a physiological mechanism underpinning several personality dimensions (Eysenck, 1967; Gray, 1972a; Powell, 1979; Zuckerman, 1979).

### Balance as a Secondary Property of the Nervous System

Following Kupalov's suggestion (see p. 16) Teplov (1957, 1960, 1961, 1972) stated very clearly that the strength and mobility of nervous processes constitute the primary properties of the NS whereas balance, also called equilibrium, being a secondary feature, should be considered only in relation to strength or mobility. However, in some of his papers Teplov, referring to Pavlov's first considerations on nervous system properties, changed his mind when writing about the essence of balance (see e.g. Teplov, 1963a, 1963b). He put forward a rather doubtful hypothesis that the balance of NP should be considered as an independent property. As he states: "strength of the nervous system with regard to excitation and equilibrium—these are two separate features of the nervous system, independent of each other" (Teplov, 1963a, p. 34).

In the literature there are but few studies of balance in relation to mobility (e.g. Ivanov-Smolensky, 1953; Rokotova, 1954; Popescu-Neveanu, 1954; Leites, 1956a).

The most systematic and consequent view as regards the balance of nervous processes has been introduced by Nebylitsyn (1963a, 1972a). According to him the balance of NP comprises strength, mobility, lability, and dynamism of NP. The notion "balance" has a broader and more general sense than had been previously assumed, and has attributed to it the role of general principle of organization of NS properties. According to the author the whole programme of NS properties investigation consists of twelve quantitative indicators, eight of which are basic, such as strength, mobility, lability, and dynamism, with regard to excitation and inhibition (the latter is treated separately). The balance of these four properties consists of the remaining features, which are secondary since they relate to the separate basic properties. Any of the given indices may be an object of investigation. Nebylitsyn also proposes a general estimation of balance which might be quantitatively expressed as the difference between the general value of excitation and inhibition, these being the sums of the indices of excitation and inhibition of the separate basic properties. This index enables an estimation of whether excitation predominates over inhibition, or vice versa, without describing to which of the basic properties—strength, mobility, lability, or dynamism—it refers. This understanding of balance is reminiscent of Eysenck's concept of excitation–inhibition balance which he had formerly treated as the physiological mechanism of extra-introversion (Eysenck, 1970).

Such a conceptualization of equilibrium, where one does not know to which NS properties it relates, may be found in many publications, causing several misunderstandings (see Nebylitsyn, 1963a; Leites, 1963; Golubeva, 1963, 1980a; Golubeva and Shwarts, 1965; Gurevich, 1965, 1970; Utkina, 1964). In most cases if the term "equilibrium" ("balance") is used without referring to any of the given properties of the nervous system it means equilibrium of dynamism. Usually it is measured directly, without comparing the dynamism of excitation and inhibition (see Gurevich, 1970; Nebylitsyn, 1972a; Ravich-Shcherbo and Shibarovskaya, 1972; Golubeva, 1980a), e.g. by means of the alpha index. As Nebylitsyn writes: "alpha index similarly reflects both dynamism of inhibition and dynamism of excitation" (1972a, p. 92). The low alpha-index is treated as an indicator of the predominance of excitation over inhibition as regards dynamism, whereas the high value of this index is a measure of the predominance of inhibition over excitation.

Despite Teplov and Nebylitsyn's statement that balance of dynamism should be directly considered as a secondary feature, measurement of equilibrium, without comparing dynamism of excitation with dynamism of inhibition (see also Chapter 2), leads us to the conclusion that the authors, in using this kind of method, are treating the balance in dynamism as a primary property counter to their own intentions.

The confusion as to how equilibrium is to be understood has been shown by Golubeva (1980b) in her classification of NS properties (see p. 41).

## Attempts at Extracting other Independent Properties of the Nervous System

Borisova (1959), a student of Teplov, considered the ability of the nervous processes to concentrate, which she termed "concentratability", to be an independent property of the NS, as suggested earlier by Kupalov (1954) and Teplov (1957).

In a series of experiments conducted systematically over a period of 20 years Borisova (1969a, 1972, 1977, 1978) showed that two main indices of concentratability, i.e. the discrimination threshold and the latency period of choice RT do not correlate with referent indices of the other properties of the NS, especially with the strength and lability of NP. Strength was measured by the sensory threshold and the slope of RT curve (see p. 86). Lability was established on the basis of critical frequency of flicker-fusion and click-fusion frequency (see p. 98).

Borisova quotes data which show that concentratability or the "tendency of the nervous processes to concentrate" (1972, p. 38), which is manifested first of all in sensory discrimination, has a high degree of stability and people differ vastly in this respect. These are additional reasons why concentratability should be considered as an independent property (1977, 1978). To testify to what degree concentratability may be regarded as a general feature of the nervous system the author compared results based on the visual system with those obtained in the auditory system, other variables being constant. Borisova found a satisfactory correlation between these which convinced her that concentratability ought to be treated as a cross-modal property. The author assumes that the psychological content of concentratability is not limited to sensory discrimination but spreads to perception, motor reactions, and habits (Borisova, 1977).

It is a pity that there are no other studies in the literature concerned with extracting concentratability as an independent property. Even Teplov and Nebylitsyn's students did not emphasize this problem. Thus the hypothesis that concentratability may be treated as an independent feature of the nervous system still seems to have little supporting evidence.

Paley, a Leningrad psychologist who stems from the Ural temperament group, has acknowledged the fact that Teplov's notion of sensitivity (see p. 29) seems to be a core concept in neurotypology (1976). The indicators on the basis of which the properties of the NS are diagnosed, e.g. the speed of CR formation, its alteration, and so on, depend on the intensity of the nervous process evoked by the acting stimulus. This intensity correlates with sensitivity. The statistical concentration of the indicators of dynamism, lability, and mobility of the nervous processes around "sensitivity-strength" may be regarded as a neurodynamic manifestation of individual differences. The facility and accuracy with which the individual receives weak signals, elaborates CRs, and alters them, reveals invariant individual differences.

> The "intensity" of nervous processes characteristic of any individual, which depends on sensitivity, constitutes the physiological basis of this invariability (Paley, 1976, p. 17).

On the basis of these considerations the author presents a hierarchical concept of NS properties. The initial and most general level of this hierarchy constitutes the norm for a given individual "intensity" of nervous processes dependent on sensitivity. Individual features of other neurodynamic aspects, e.g. the formation of CRs, alteration etc., appear largely as different partial facets of this general factor and are therefore on a lower level of this hierarchy (ibid.).

In 1972 Paley and Gorbachevsky introduced the concept of "activat-

## 1. Traditional Research and Current Approach

ability" (aktivirovannost) to replace the notion of sensitivity (see Paley, 1976). It characterizes not only the energy of the organism but also the organization of the nervous processes. According to Paley, the essence of activatability, understood as the most general organization of the energetic characteristic of the NS, is the balance between excitation and inhibition processes. This concept of balance, as interpreted by Paley, was used as the first criterion in Pavlov's typology and it appears as the only "penetrating" indicator in Nebylitsyn's scheme of typological properties.

This very interesting though equivocal concept of activatability has been studied by Teplov's student, Golubeva and her collaborators. The Moscow group collected data which show that such classical indices of dynamism of NP as speed of positive and negative CR formation do not correlate with the basic indices of dynamism distinguished by Nebylitsyn on the basis of EEG indices (see Nebylitsyn, 1963b, 1972a), e.g. alpha index and amplitude and frequency of alpha rhythm, used primarily as measures of balance of nervous processes as regards dynamism.

Golubeva (1975, 1980a, 1980b) ascertains that sufficient data have been accumulated to permit the division of equilibrium of nervous processes, as formerly understood by Pavlov, into two separate properties, namely equilibrium between conditioned excitation and inhibition (constituting balance in dynamism as interpreted by Nebylitsyn) and equilibrium between the unconditioned[11] excitation and inhibition processes, i.e. activatability.

Activatability thus conceptualized refers to stable and inborn individual differences in activation (see Leites *et al.*, 1980), the physiological substrate of which is based on the activating functions of the reticular formation. Since the EEG method is the only one used in Teplov–Nebylitsyn's school for diagnosing this property Golubeva also calls it "EEG balance" (1980a).

The syndrome of activatability as a property of the NS has been found to comprise the following indices of the brain's unconditioned bioelectric activity: amplitude, frequency, and total energy of alpha waves; the alpha index; and the energy of theta waves (Golubeva *et al.*, 1974; Golubeva, 1975; Izyumova *et al.*, 1977).

Individuals scoring high on activatability display low overall energy of the alpha and theta rhythms, and low amplitude and high frequency of alpha waves. Individuals scoring low on activatability display the opposite characteristics.

It is evident that Golubeva's concept of activatability differs from Paley's. For him activatability was the most general property of the NS, closely related to strength (sensitivity) of the NS; whereas Golubeva considers this feature as a particular case of equilibrium as understood by Pavlov. She also writes that activatability may to some degree determine balance of dynamism (1975). Paley's understanding of activatability resembles Gray's (1964) original concept of arousability,[12] which is a determinant of individual differences in activation level. As long as all other determinants are held constant, this level is indeed a function of arousability thus conceived. The term has been coined by Gray in an effort to point out the convergences between the concept of nervous system strength and the theory of activation level. Gray states that

> the weak nervous system is more easily or more highly "aroused"; and the personality dimension known as "strength of the nervous system" could be described as a dimension of "levels of arousal" or of "arousability" (1964, p. 289).

Activatability is also considered to be by others the most general property of the NS. For example, Ilin (1978) writes that, when discussing the essence of strength of NS understood as a primary property, one is referring to the basic property of the excitable substance where physiology ends and biochemistry begins. However, the data collected during recent years force us to revise this position.

> There is serious evidence to assume that the property "activatability" in the resting state (basic activation) is a more primary property of the nervous substrates (Ilin, 1978, p. 45).

Activatability is the property which most generally characterizes the level of activation of the brain's functional systems.

This short review illustrates a tendency among the Russian investigators to distinguish a property of the NS which is directly related to individual differences in the level of activation, the indices of which, depending on the research conducted, are correlated with strength, or dynamism, or do not correlate at all with classical NS properties.

An experiment by Oderyshev (1975), aimed to establish the relations between activatability and vegetative indices of metabolism, illustrates how activatability can be understood as an outcome of all basic NS properties. Oderyshev diagnosed this property on the basis of:

(1) RT curve to stimuli of different intensity (which is a classical index of the strength of NS—see p. 86);
(2) basal skin resistance level at the beginning of the experiment (index of dynamism of excitation—see Nebylitsyn, 1972a);

(3) critical frequency of flicker-fusion and click-fusion frequency (used as classical indices of lability—see p. 98); and,
(4) electrodermal sensory threshold (used as a classical index of strength—see p. 84).

The arithmetic mean of all these indicators was used as the activatability index. According to Oderyshev, activatability, being a general and stable characteristic of the individual, should be considered as the energetic mobilization of cortical and subcortical regulatory centres of the nervous system (1975, p. 111). This position resembles the concept of energy mobilization introduced by Duffy (1951, 1957, 1962), the author of the "intensive dimension" of behaviour which seems to be one of the main sources of contemporary concepts of personality based on the energetic aspect of human activity.

It seems to me that the introduction of activatability, as a new independent property of the NS, should provoke the Pavlovian typologists to revise the list of NS properties. As the number of postulated features increases, the relation between them is going to become more complex and many experimental findings do not justify this increasing search for new NS properties.

An attempt to revise the essence of NS properties and relations between them has been made recently by Golubeva (1980a, 1980b). Taking as a starting-point the traditional properties distinguished by Pavlov and the methods of diagnosis of these properties (on the basis of unconditioned or conditioned reactions), the author proposes the following classification of nervous system properties:

A. Strength of nervous system, which should be divided into (i) strength of unconditioned excitation and inhibition, which is manifested by the endurance of the nervous system; (ii) strength of conditioned excitation and inhibition which, as follows from the text, should be treated both as dynamism of excitation and inhibition.[13]

B. The equilibrium of nervous processes. Taking the unconditioned–conditioned diagnostic methods as the criterion, Golubeva divided equilibrium into: (i) equilibrium of unconditioned excitation and inhibition, calling it, as aforementioned, activatability, and (ii) balance[14] of conditioned excitation and inhibition. The latter relates to the balance of dynamism as described by Nebylitsyn.

C. Mobility of nervous processes. Golubeva distinguished between (i) mobility of unconditioned excitation and inhibition (traceable to Teplov's lability), and (ii) mobility of conditioned excitation and inhibition, which, being measured by the alteration of the signal value of stimuli, corresponds with the notion of mobility in its narrow sense.

This classification, based on theoretical assumptions faithfully reflecting Pavlov's concept of three basic NS properties, does not seem to have resolved the growing confusion in NS property investigation. Rather, it supports my impression that we are now in a blind alley in this type of investigation and a new step must be taken to push the Pavlovian typology idea forward.

## Twin Studies on Inheritance of NS Properties

Pavlov's position as to the inheritance of the TNS was not very clear. When speaking of the TNS, he used the notion "genotype" but expanded its content to encompass both inherited and inborn properties of the NS. Teplov stressed in several publications (1963b, 1964b, 1972) that the NS properties were inborn, by which he meant that the inherited features may change in the early stage of ontogenesis including pre- and post-natal changes. For Teplov and his students the most important criterion for innateness was the stability of NS properties (Teplov, 1964a; Gurevich, 1970; Ravich-Shcherbo, 1977; Klyagin, 1974).

The assumption that stability is proof for innateness is not justified in psychology. There is evidence showing that certain attitudes shaped during ontogenesis may be very stable throughout life, although they are not inborn and vice versa. There may be many (psychological and biological) inborn traits which do change very considerably during ontogenesis under environmental influences (see e.g. Bloom, 1964; Tyler, 1978; Strelau, 1975b).

The only serious studies aimed to assess the role of genetics in shaping NS properties in humans have been conducted by the Moscow group, particularly by Ravich-Shcherbo and her students. Using the classical twin method in children and adults they conducted systematic research on the separate NS properties. I have summarized the results in Tables I–IV which show the general tendencies with respect to inheritance of strength of excitation, mobility, lability, and equilibrium of excitation and inhibition processes (activatability). Most of the studies are conducted on the basis of the EEG method, thus making the results more comparable. Since the only common index of heritability in the studies under review was a within-pairs correlation, only this measure will be used to show the regularities resulting from these studies.

The results testifying to the inheritance of strength of the NS with respect to excitation were obtained using four different indices of this

NS property, i.e. the extinction with reinforcement method, the photic driving reaction to stimuli of low frequency, the total energy of delta rhythm, and the RT curve to stimuli of different intensity.[15]

As far as the extinction with reinforcement method, used as one of the standard methods to diagnose the strength of excitation (see Teplov, 1964a, 1972) is concerned, it may be seen from Table I that the range of correlation coefficients varies from $-0.044$ to $0.933$ in MZ twins and from $0.026$ to $0.977$ in DZ twins, and generally, there is no difference between MZ and DZ twins in correlation values.

These results suggest that there is a considerable lack of coincidence in heritability estimation of the strength of excitation measured by extinction with reinforcement.

Taking into account the correlation coefficients of low-frequency photic driving indices we may state a lower range of coefficients for MZ twins ($0.325$ to $0.738$). In all cases the DZ correlations are lower than the MZ ones and they range from $-0.113$ to $0.466$. These results support the inheritance hypothesis more unequivocally.

The best evidence for genetic contribution has been provided by the total energy of delta-rhythm index where the correlations for MZ twins are consistently high ($0.608$ to $0.735$) and higher in all three studies than those of DZ twins ($0.573$ to $0.655$).

The classical index of strength—the slope of RT curve to stimuli of different intensity—supports the inheritance hypothesis if we focus on the MZ twins ($0.674$ to $0.937$). In two of the three studies reported in Table I there is no correlation between pairs of DZ twins ($0.087$ to $0.144$).

Concerning mobility of the NS we have less evidence on which to base any conclusions about the inheritance of this property. Moreover, both indices of mobility used in the twin study, i.e. the alteration of signal value of a pair of stimuli and the critical time interval of speed of stimuli exposition, are based on RT experiments.

The results (see Table II) for the standard alteration method are rather pessimistic. The correlations for MZ pairs vary from $0.005$ to $0.494$ and they do not differ from the coefficients for DZ twins ($0.011$ to $0.487$). There is, however, some evidence for genetic contribution if we consider the second index, i.e. the critical time interval. MZ twins had correlations between $0.520$ and $0.900$ in four studies. The data registered in DZ twins are quite different. In two cases there is no correlation at all ($0.028$ to $-0.164$) and in one study the correlation $-0.600$ suggests that there exists a negative relation between the DZ twins, which cannot be explained within the genetic hypothesis.

TABLE I. Genetic determination of strength of excitation

| Reference | Extinction with Reinforcement in EEG | | Low Frequency Photic Driving | | | | | | Total Energy of Delta Rhythm | | Slope of RT Curve | |
|---|---|---|---|---|---|---|---|---|---|---|---|---|
| | | | 4 Hz | | 5 Hz | | 6 Hz | | | | | |
| | MZ | DZ | MZ | DZ | MZ | DZ | MZ | DZ | MZ | DZ | MZ | DZ |
| Ravich-Shcherbo et al., 1969 | 726[e] | 977 | | | | | | | | | | |
| Shlakhta, 1972 | 933 | 883 | | | | | | | 608 | 583 | | |
| Ravich-Shcherbo, 1976 | 097[a] 791 | 428 380 | | | | | | | | | | |
| Shlakhta and Panteleyeva, 1978 | −044 to 791[b] | 026 to 560 | 690[c] 483 394 | 243 203 350 | 640[c] 738 325 | −113 375 235 | 528[c] 575 571 | 235 466 162 | 735 | 655 | | |
| Shibarovskaya, 1978 | | | | | | | | | 661 | 573 | | |
| Panteleyeva, 1975 | | | | | | | | | | | 905[d] 674 937 | 144 408 087 |

a. Two criteria were used.
b. Seven different criteria were used and the results reflect the dispersion between the lowest and the highest correlations.
c. Three different criteria were used: total energy, relative estimation, and frequency.
d. The measures are taken separately for 3 age groups: (1) 9–11 years, (2) 13–16 years, (3) 33–56 years.
e. For convenience the correlation coefficients are written without zero.

TABLE II. Genetic determination of mobility of nervous processes

| Reference | Indices of Mobility | | | |
|---|---|---|---|---|
| | Alteration in RT experiment | | Critical interval of speed of Ss exposition | |
| | MZ | DZ | MZ | DZ |
| Vasilets, 1978 | | | | |
| age 7–11 | 005[a,b] to 400 | 032 to 423 | 677 | 028 |
| age 33–35 | 078 to 494 | 011 to 487 | 896 | −164 |
| Ravich-Shcherbo, 1976 | | | | |
| age 7–12 | 101 | 138 | 520 | 370 |
| age 33–56 | 057 | 172 | 900 | −600 |

a. Four different criteria were used and this is the dispersion between the lowest and highest correlation coefficients.
b. See footnote e to Table I.

A substantial number of studies have been conducted to prove the genetic contribution to lability of the NS (see Table III). The often-used CFFF index shows genetic contribution if we look at the correlations for MZ twins (0.718 to 0.842) although DZ twin data are not consistent with them. There is no correlation at all (−0.008 to 0.160) or else it is negative (−0.311).

The after-effect of excitation and inhibition measured in RT experiments and used as index of lability does not support the genetic hypothesis. Most of the eight correlations are nil.

The other indices of lability are based on the EEG method. The correlations of the driving reaction of high frequency partially support the genetic hypothesis. In six measures the coefficients vary from 0.368 to 0.805 in MZ twins and from 0.135 to 0.296 in DZ twins. The best evidence for genetic contribution in lability of nervous processes is provided by the total energy of $beta_1$ and $beta_2$ rhythm indices. In MZ twins the correlations obtained for all nine measures are satisfactory (0.521 to 0.890) and in all but one case they are lower in DZ twins. Two coefficients from Shlakhta's study (1972) are rather peculiar. This author, taking into account the $beta_1$ index, recorded a correlation of 0.943 in DZ twins (0.687 in MZ) that cannot be explained by genetic contribution, as is also the case for the $beta_2$ index, where the correlation for DZ twins is 0.804 (0.866 for MZ twins).

The last property of the NS for which data have been collected to estimate genetic determination is equilibrium in dynamism, also recently called activatability (see p. 39). In Table IV, five studies are presented in which four indices were used to measure this property of NS, i.e. the alpha index, the total energy of alpha rhythm, alpha

TABLE III. Genetic determination of NS lability

| Reference | CFFF MZ | CFFF DZ | After-effect of Excitation MZ | After-effect of Excitation DZ | After-effect of Inhibition MZ | After-effect of Inhibition DZ |
|---|---|---|---|---|---|---|
| Panteleyeva, 1975 | 1/ 782[a,e] | 160 | | | | |
| | 2/ 842 | −008 | | | | |
| | 3/ 718 | −311 | | | | |
| Vasilets, 1978 | | | −045[b] | 184 | 094 | 463 |
| | | | −177 | −035 | 062 | −040 |
| Ravich-Shcherbo, 1976 | | | 040[c] | 160 | 400 | 210 |
| | | | 040 | 230 | 000 | 320 |

| | Photic driving reaction | | | | | | Total energy | | | |
|---|---|---|---|---|---|---|---|---|---|---|
| | 18 Hz MZ | 18 Hz DZ | 25 Hz MZ | 25 Hz DZ | 30 Hz MZ | 30 Hz DZ | beta$_1$ MZ | beta$_1$ DZ | beta$_2$ MZ | beta$_2$ DZ |
| Panteleyeva and Shlakhta, 1978 | 440[d] | 135 | 545 | 219 | 584 | 296 | | | | |
| Shlakhta, 1975 | 805 | 236 | 600 | 286 | 368 | 234 | | | | |
| Shibarovskaya, 1978 | | | | | | | 633 | 208 | | |
| Shlakhta and Pantaleyeva, 1978 | | | | | | | 890 | 793 | 712 | 180 |
| Shlakhta and Pantaleyeva, 1978 | | | | | | | 862 | 267 | 633 | 208 |
| Ravich-Shcherbo et al., 1969 | | | | | | | 751 | 221 | 521 | 291 |
| Shlakhta, 1972 | | | | | | | 687 | 943 | 866 | 804 |

a. Three different age groups were studied: (1) 9–11; (2) 13–16; (3) 33–56 years old.
b. Two groups aged: (1) 7–11 and (2) 33–35 years old were studied.
c. Two groups aged: (1) 7–12 and (2) 33–56 years old were studied.
d. The results stem from different criteria: total energy and relative estimation.
e. See footnote e in Table I.

TABLE IV. Genetic determination of balance in dynamism (activatability)

| Reference | Alpha Index | | Total Energy of Alpha Rhythm | | Alpha Amplitude | | Alpha Frequency | |
|---|---|---|---|---|---|---|---|---|
| | MZ | DZ | MZ | DZ | MZ | DZ | MZ | DZ |
| Shibarovskaya, 1975 | 555[a] | 066 | 781 | 476 | 822 | 376 | 873 | 483 |
| Shibarovskaya, 1978 | −035 | 025 | 807 | 528 | 804 | 332 | 754 | 622 |
| Shlakhta and Pantaleyeva, 1978 | | | 959 | 426 | | | | |
| Ravich-Shcherbo et al., 1969 | 603 | 742 | 918 | 700 | 918 | 700 | 806 | 727 |
| Shlakhta, 1972 | 727 | 974 | 721 | 947 | | | | |

a. See footnote e to Table I.

amplitude, and alpha frequency. These indices are also used in other kinds of investigation and many data reflecting their genetic determination may be found in Western literature. I will limit myself, however, to the studies which are concerned with NS properties.

All the fifteen coefficients of correlation for MZ twins, including the indices mentioned above, strongly support the genetic hypothesis (0.555 to 0.949), except for one based on the alpha index where one of the correlations is nil (−0.035). The picture is rather confused if we examine the correlation values for DZ twins. There are seven measures which strongly support the genetic contribution in shaping activatability (0.332 to 0.622) and they are distributed among all indices except the alpha index, for which the most contrasting results appear. In two studies conducted by Shibarovskaya (1975, 1978) there is no correlation at all among the DZ twins, whereas in two other studies using the alpha index the correlations are very high. In one case registered by Shlakhta it almost reaches 1.00 (0.974), a result which cannot be explained by genetic contribution. The same author obtained a similar correlation value for the same DZ twins taking as a measure the total energy of alpha rhythm (0.947), which suggests that the results are not accidental. The last three correlations for DZ twins, distributed among all indices except the alpha index, are also too high (0.700 to 0.727) to be explained by the genetic hypothesis.

This short review of results obtained in several twin studies at answering the question of the extent of the genetic contribution in shaping NS properties does not permit any unequivocal statement. The picture is much more confused than is the case in IQ studies, where the values of correlations are to a high degree related to the genetic relationship of the compared pairs (see Erlenmeyer-Kimling and Jarvik, 1963; Cattell, 1971). Except for a few studies (e.g. Panteleyeva and Shlakhta, 1978; Shlakhta and Panteleyeva, 1978) a limitation was introduced since no unrelated pairs were included.

Ravich-Shcherbo (1977), summarizing the research conducted by her collaborators on more than 300 MZ and DZ pairs aged 7–56 years, obtained results similar to those presented in Tables I–IV. In discussing the evidence collected in her laboratory she concluded that the syndrome of basic properties of the NS comprises indices of two different kinds: those that are genetically determined and those that are subject to environmental influences (Ravich-Shcherbo, 1978).

Golubeva (1980b) suggests that only the so-called unconditioned properties of the NS (see p. 41) are inborn; a statement only partly, however, supported by the data collected in Tables I–IV.

In conclusion, it would be an over-simplification to state that the NS properties are inherited, or, more cautiously, inborn, although there is some evidence that genetic factors contribute to some degree to the formation of NS properties. There is not enough evidence to establish the heritability estimation, which will probably be different for different properties and within a given property, as it ought to differ for the separate indices used to diagnose that property.

## Partiality Phenomenon in Investigation of Nervous System Properties

As already mentioned, Ivanov-Smolensky acknowledged the fact that the diagnosis of the type of NS based on CR experiments depends on the kind of UCSs used. The data collected in his laboratory led him to the conclusion that, apart from the general type of NS, there exist partial types which refer to different functions of the organism, depending on the kind of UCSs used in TNS investigation (Ivanov-Smolensky, 1935).

The concept of general and partial properties of the NS has been developed by Teplov and his students. Teplov (1964a) gave a general review of investigations conducted on partial NS properties and considered this type of research to be one of the main tasks in TNS properties investigation. According to him, the general NS properties which characterize the work of the brain hemispheres as a whole, constitute the physiological bases of temperament. In turn, the partial NS properties, characterizing the work of separate parts of the cortex, play an important role in shaping special aptitudes (Teplov, 1964a). Teplov seems to have been under the influence of Spearman's idea of general and special abilities; however, he never referred to Spearman.

The first experimental data supporting the idea of the existence of NS properties, depending on the sensory mechanism under investigation in human TNS research, were collected by Nebylitsyn. Using auditory and visual stimuli in experimental diagnosis of strength of NS based on different indices he stated that in 28% of diagnosed subjects the estimation of strength depends on whether visual or auditory stimuli were applied (Nebylitsyn, 1957).

Other authors, when diagnosing the strength of the NS on the basis of the sensory threshold, found, to an even higher degree than Nebylitsyn, a lack of correlation between characteristics of strength based on auditory and visual modalities. Turovskaya (1963), when comparing the results for visual threshold with the results for auditory threshold, obtained the correlation coefficient $\rho = 0.23$, which is statistically insignificant. Paley *et al.* (1966) found a practically zero correlation

($\rho = 0.08$) when comparing threshold values. Ippolitov (1966), when investigating the interdependence between the auditory, tactile, and visual thresholds, obtained the following results: tactile–auditory, $\rho = 0.05$; visual–auditory, $\rho = 0.49$ ($p < 0.01$); visual–tactile, $\rho = 0.05$. Our own experiments, where visual and auditory stimuli were used in diagnosing the mobility of NS on the basis of the alteration of the signal value of a pair of stimuli used in GSR conditioning, supported the lack of coincidence in the diagnosis of this property of the NS (Strelau, 1972a).

Nebylitsyn (1972a), summarizing the data collected in TNS investigations, especially those conducted by the Moscow group, concluded that the partiality phenomenon in NS properties is manifested in three ways:

(1) by registering different effector manifestations of CR activity (effector aspect);
(2) by using CSs of different quality (afferent or analyser aspect); and,
(3) by using different reinforcements (subcortical aspect).

He stated that the partiality problem involves only about 15–20% of subjects; however, he was inconsistent in making this conclusion. Doing so he concentrated only on interanalyser differences and did not refer to the divergence in TNS diagnosis following from the fact that different effectors and (or) different UCSs may be used in experimental investigation of NS properties.

In one of his later papers devoted to the partiality phenomenon, Nebylitsyn (1972b)—referring to Pribram's conception of the brain's functioning—distinguished two basic areas of the brain: (i) The frontal cortex together with the subcortex and the brain stem. This is the regulatory brain system which plays the role of general regulator of the individual's functioning and which controls planned and performed action. (ii) The second area, which covers the structures of separate sensory afferents, is the so-called perceptual brain system. Its function is to analyse and synthesize afferent signals, so it primarily performs gnostic functions. Nebylitsyn argued that there is no correspondence between the properties of both the regulatory and perceptual brain systems. Taking as a point of departure these considerations, he concluded thus upon the physiological bases of general and partial NS properties:

> if the structures of separate analysers are the neuroanatomical bases of partial properties, then the regulatory brain system, including the anterocentral cortex, together with the connected complex of paleocortex and subcortical nuclei, forms the morphological substrate of the general properties (Nebylitsyn, 1972b, p. 411).

## 1. Traditional Research and Current Approach

Sympathizing with Teplov's statement that general NS properties determine human temperament and partial NS properties play an important role in determining special aptitudes, Nebylitsyn argued that general NS properties also appertain to other important functions, like drives, motivation, attention, general abilities, etc.

Nebylitsyn's hypotheses about the physiological bases of general and partial NS properties again supports my position that he limited the partiality phenomenon to interafferent differences, an unjustified approach if one takes into account the many data which show large discrepancies in NSP diagnosis depending on the kind of effector and the kind of UCSs (when CR experiments are performed) under control (Strelau, 1965a, 1969, 1972a; see also p. 111). Umansky (1961), although only on the basis of theoretical considerations, mentioned six different sources of partiality in TNS investigation in humans, depending on the level of the organism's functioning on which the diagnosis is performed. He distinguished the following levels of partiality: subcortical (unconditioned), subcortical-cortical, afferent, interafferent (or so-called first signal system), and the second signal system. Without entering into any detailed discussion of the justification for Umansky's classification it illustrates the richness of sources which may cause discrepancies in TNS investigation.

Ilin (1978), a psychologist from Leningrad, proposed to distinguish horizontal and vertical partiality, when discussing the problem of partiality, with special emphasis on Ivanov-Smolensky, Teplov, Nebylitsyn, Merlin, and Strelau's concepts of this phenomenon. Horizontal partiality refers to different receptors and sensory afferents. The vertical is bound with different levels of the organism's functioning, e.g. unconditional, conditional, voluntary, and verbal. In his criticism of Nebylitsyn's neuro-anatomical principle of partial and general NS properties differentiation, Ilin stresses that Nebylitsyn's idea of general NS properties of the brain may be reducible to the activation concept of the brain and to the sensitivity phenomenon connected with this concept.

Rusalov (1975, 1977), who has paid special attention in recent years to the problem of partiality, provides evidence that different areas of the frontal cortex may be sources of differences in the diagnosis of strength of the NS if one employs EEG indices. He also cites data supporting the idea that there exist general EEG brain factors (amplitude and frequency) common to the frontal and posterior cortex. These facts, which show that the general properties may be more partial and the partial may be at the same time more general, to some degree weaken Nebylitsyn's concept of neuro-anatomical bases of general and partial NS properties.

Rusalov assumes that Anokhin's concept of functional sets of the brain would be the most appropriate for understanding the essence of general NS properties.[16]

According to Anokhin (1978) the functional set constitutes a wholly and, at the same time, multilevel integration with specificity at every given level. In correspondence with three basic levels of NS organization Rusalov distinguishes three levels of NS properties:

(1) General (systems) properties of the brain. They contain the whole brain and are manifested during human goal-directed activity. Only these properties, which are "supramorphological" and which constitute the most integrative functional characteristic of the brain, may be treated as general properties of the NS.

(2) Complex properties of the NS, bound primarily with nervous processes aroused on different levels of the NS during CR activity (e.g. sensory afferents, subcortex, frontal cortex). According to Rusalov, most traditionally understood properties of the NS belong to this level.

(3) Elementary properties of the NS, limited to separate morphological structures and not bound with each other. As Rusalov suggests we are concerned with properties of neuronal tissue, whereas with both former levels, especially with the first, the given properties constitute a stable, functional characteristic of the NS which does not follow unequivocally from the elementary properties.

As already mentioned, Rusalov's view of NS properties, including the relation between general and partial ones, is based mainly on Anokhin's theory of functional sets of the brain and corresponds with the systems approach in contemporary psychology. The empirical evidence supporting his point of view is at the same time rather unsatisfactory though promising.

As we can see from this very short survey, which has been limited mostly to the contribution of the Teplov–Nebylitsyn school to this area, the problem of the relation between general and partial NS properties is far from being solved, although its importance is significant not only for TNS investigation. It is closely related to one of the basic methodological questions in personality research, namely to what degree are we allowed to generalize our diagnosis of a given personality trait beyond the variables controlled in our investigation.

## Stimulation Level of Situations and Strength of the Nervous System

The Moscow group involved in TNS investigation has also been active in research, designed to show the significance of NS properties in human behaviour and in psychophysiological changes taking place

## 1. Traditional Research and Current Approach

under highly stimulating situations. As mentioned by Nebylitsyn (1972a) the role of temperament in human behaviour is particularly pronounced when the balance between the organism and environment is disturbed, this happening mostly under so-called stressful situations (see also Suvorova, 1975). Characterizing the individual traits of an operator acting in highly stimulating situations Nebylitsyn (1976) considered strength of the NS to be one of the main properties which co-determines the work performance.

A field study conducted by Gurevich and Matveyev (1966; Matveyev, 1965; Gurevich, 1970) might serve as a good exemplification of this line of research as developed by the Teplov–Nebylitsyn school. These investigators demonstrated an interrelation between strength of NS and efficacy of work performed by operators in the course of dealing with a (simulated) breakdown in a power plant, i.e. under extreme stress. The investigation revealed the behaviour of all persons with a weak NS to be disorganized during the breakdown emergency. This was reflected in numerous aspects of behaviour, and especially in disorders of perception, memory, and thinking. Subjects with a strong NS, on the other hand, displayed considerable endurance in the face of stress. The differences between these two groups were found to be statistically significant. In this study 26 operators were investigated. The strength of the NS was estimated on the basis of a rather rare indicator, i.e. the so-called critical frequency of flashing phosphene described in detail by Nebylitsyn (1972a). The observation of the operators' behaviour was conducted by experimenters who did not know the results of the strength of NS estimation. Similar studies as regards the relationship between NS properties and performance in real-life situations (professional activity, school performance etc.) have been conducted by Merlin and his students (see p. 70).

Many studies of the relationship between NS properties and behaviour, as well as psychophysiological changes under situations differing in stimulation level, have been conducted by the Moscow group under laboratory conditions. The most systematic research in this area was undertaken by Rozhdestvenskaya (1977a, 1977b) in collaboration with other students of the Teplov–Nebylitsyn group (Golubeva and Rozhdestvenskaya, 1969, 1978; Rozhdestvenskaya et al., 1969b, 1972; Rozhdestvenskaya and Levochkina, 1972). All these experiments, conducted during a period of over ten years, have been recently summarized by Rozhdestvenskaya (1980). Without going into details let me give a short description of this research project whose aim it was to examine the dependency between strength of the NS and the performance of subjects under monotonous and fatiguing conditions.

The author defined fatigue as a temporary decrease in working capacity evoked by intensive or prolonged activity. The decrease in efficiency, subjective feeling of weariness, and physiological changes were treated by Rozhdestvenskaya as indicators of fatigue. The monotonous situation evokes, according to Rozhdestvenskaya (1980), such symptoms as decrease of psychic activity and vigilance, and a subjective state of weariness.

In order to study the interrelations of strength of the NS and the individual's performance under both states described above (fatigue vs. monotony), experiments under five different conditions were conducted.

*Series 1:* heterogeneous and tension-producing mental activity performed under high motivation. The task consisted of memorizing three-digit figures over a period of four hours. The figures were placed on three successively presented tables differing in colour, each containing 50 figures dispersed randomly. The task of the subject was to remember the figures in order of presentation (see Rozhdestvenskaya *et al.*, 1969b, 1972).

*Series 2:* simple, homogeneous activity which consisted of verbal reactions to visual stimuli applied at a slow rate. Slides containing seven rows with fifteen letters in each row were presented on a screen. The presentation was changed every 27 s. The task was to count how often a given letter occurred on one slide (the number varied from 7 to 23). The experiment consisted of three phases, each of which lasted 80 min and in each phase the target letter was changed (Rozhdestvenskaya, 1980).

*Series 3:* the conditions were similar to series 2. The only difference was that the duration of presentation of the slides was shortened to 20 s and the experiment lasted three hours instead of four. In this situation the duration of stimulus presentation was too short for subjects to count the letters (see Rozhdestvenskaya *et al.*, 1969b, 1972).

*Series 4:* homogeneous, somewhat composed activity with moderate speed of performance. Auditory stimuli were applied at more or less optimal tempo. The subject was asked to count the number of auditory stimuli presented and, at the same time, to press a key as fast as possible for another stimulus applied at irregular intervals (varying from 1 to 1.5 min). After the presentation of 20–40 stimuli with 1 s interval a break of 5–6 s occurred to allow the subject to write the number of signals counted. This task was continued for a period of three hours (Rozhdestvenskaya, 1977a; Golubeva and Rozhdestvenskaya, 1978).

*Series 5:* continuous and homogeneous activity performed without external stimuli. The subject was instructed to press a key once every

5 s, and then to press the key three times every 30 s. The task was to count the signals until five presentations (corresponding to 30 s) had occurred where the subject had to react in a different way (three pressings of the key instead of one). The subject was informed that the experiment would last 2.5 to 3 hours, however, it actually lasted two hours (Rozhdestvenskaya, 1977a).

The strength of the NS was estimated in most of the experimental settings by using the induction method (see p. 79) and the photic driving reaction to stimuli of low frequency (see p. 92). The increase in RT and decrease of number of written letters were used as indices of fatigue. The indicators of a state of monotony varied from series to series and they included: decrease in critical frequency of flashing phosphene, in click-fusion frequency, and in critical frequency of flicker-fusion. Also, the total energy of delta, theta, alpha, and beta rhythms was usually recorded before and after the experiment. The subjective state of weariness was estimated after each series.

Reviewing the results of these experiments, Rozhdestvenskaya (1980) concluded, among others, that the efficiency of work measured by the number of mistakes and speed of task performance was higher in individuals with a strong NS only in series 1. According to the author this is due to the high tension and high motivation introduced by this experiment. The conditions in series 1 evoked fatigue in individuals with a weak NS, as opposed to the strong ones. The same regularities in a fatigue-generating experiment were found by Gorozhanin (1977).

In all remaining series, which could be characterized as monotonous situations, individuals with a weak NS prevailed over those with a strong NS with regards to the efficiency of performance. Also, the state of monotony registered by physiological indicators was higher in "strong" individuals as compared with the "weak" ones. The only exception was series 5 where the state of monotony was higher in the weak TNS than in the strong one. However, absolute efficiency was still higher in persons with a weak NS. As mentioned before, this series included a lack of presentation of any stimuli, the task being to react by pressing a key at regular intervals according to the instruction. Rozhdestvenskaya explains the exceptional results in this series as follows: individuals with strong TNS use internal stimulation here which allows them to increase their level of activation. Nothing of this sort happens in the weak TNS. This interpretation seems to be unsatisfactory since it does not explain why "strong" individuals do not use the same mechanism of self-stimulation in other monotonous situations. If we compare the "strong" individuals with extraverts and the "weak" ones with introverts, an issue discussed in detail in Chapter

4, we may see a close analogy between "strong" individuals and "response hungry" extraverts (evident in series 5 where no stimuli were applied) and between the "weak" individuals and "stimulus hungry" introverts (as displayed in series 2–4 where the reactions were regulated by the stimuli presented. The distinction between the response and stimulus-hungry individuals with respect to the extraversion dimension was introduced by Brebner and Cooper (1974, 1978).

In series 4 and 5 level of activation was measured before the onset of the experiment proper by using the frequency index of alpha rhythm. Because the strength of the NS was assessed in both series by the driving reaction to low frequency stimuli and the number of mistakes was transferred into standard deviation scores, it was possible to combine the results and to assess the interrelation between strength of the NS, level of activation, and level of performance. As regards the level of activation, all subjects, i.e. 63 adults of both sexes, were divided into five groups differing in frequency of alpha rhythm. The group with the lowest level of activation (group I) was characterized by frequency of alpha rhythm, 9.5–9.9. The alpha frequency of 11.5–11.9 was the criterion for distinguishing the group with the highest level of activation (group V). As regards strength of the NS two groups were distinguished: individuals with strong NS (29 Ss) and with weak NS (34 Ss).

When the whole sample (63 subjects) was assessed regardless of strength of NS, the interrelation between number of mistakes and level of activation, as measured in series 4 and 5, reflects the classical curvilinear dependency between efficiency of performance and level of activation; this is displayed in Fig. 3. As we can see, the largest number of mistakes were made by both extreme groups with regard to the level of activation.

This picture changes, however, when the dependency between level of activation and number of mistakes is presented separately for weak and strong TNS individuals. As seen from Fig. 4 the curvilinear dependency became even more expressed in the group with weak NS, which cannot be said for individuals with a strong NS. The latter reveal a linear dependency as regards the efficiency of work in relation to activation: the higher the level of activation the higher the efficiency measured by number of errors. The data presented in Fig. 4 suggest at the same time that the range of activation level, within which the individual functions efficiently, is larger in the strong type of NS than in the weak one.

The reults derived from the many series of experiments conducted by Rozhdestvenskaya and her collaborators are consistent with those observed many times in Pavlov's laboratory. As we know, Pavlov

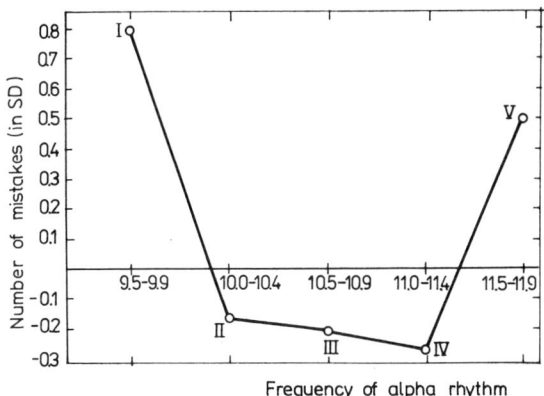

FIG. 3. Dependency between number of mistakes and level of activation (adapted from Rozhdestvenskaya, 1980).

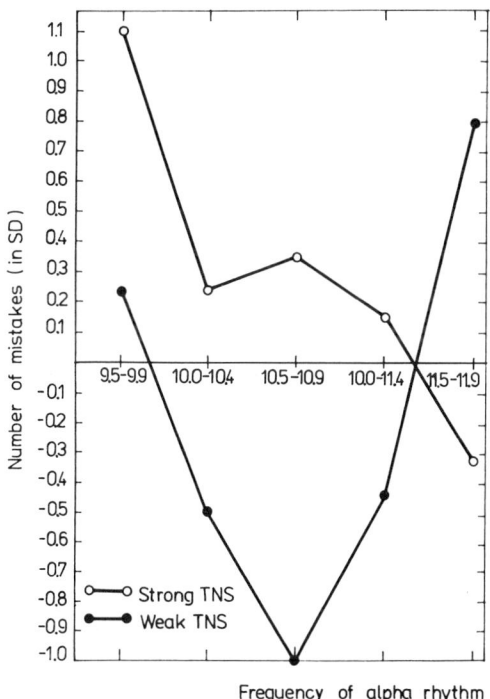

FIG. 4. Dependency between number of mistakes and level of activation in individuals differing in NS strength (adapted from Rozhdestvenskaya, 1980).

(1951–52) acknowledged the fact that the sanguine type of dog, when sited in experimental conditions of very low stimulative value (monotony, deprivation), manifests proneness to sleep. This state has been interpreted by Pavlov as caused by the development of inhibitory processes. Also Rozhdestvenskaya (1980) showed that the increase of monotony, developed under homogeneous conditions of rather low stimulation, is especially expressed in individuals with a strong NS (which includes the sanguine type). Making use of the inhibitory hypothesis in interpreting this fact, Rozhdestvenskaya introduced two types of inhibition: transmarginal and preventive inhibition; the latter being established by Simonov (1962, cited by Rozhdestvenskaya, 1980). Preventive inhibition develops when stimuli of low intensity are presented and it does not disturb the individual's functioning under high stimulation. Preventive inhibition, thus understood, should be especially pronounced in individuals with a strong NS due to their higher sensitivity threshold. In monotonous situations, characterized by low stimulative value, this stimulation is experienced as weaker in individuals with a strong NS and this may help to explain the regularity found in Rozhdestvenskaya's results. In situations with high stimulation level the state of fatigue develops (as shown in series 1) which is caused by transmarginal inhibition. The latter, as we know, is especially strongly pronounced in the weak TNS, due to its low endurance and high sensitivity.

The experiments conducted by Rozhdestvenskaya and her associates have much in common with Western psychologists' research on the level of performance in situations varying in stimulation level with respect to individual differences (see e.g. Fiske and Maddi, 1961; Zuckerman, 1979; Eysenck, 1981; Krohne and Laux, 1982) and it seems to me that this line of investigation may be used as one of the common links between the Western and Eastern approach to individual differences.

## Nervous System Properties and Memory

A further example of research conducted to investigate the degree to which TNS properties influence or co-determine cognitive activity may be mentioned. One area where the contribution of the Teplov–Nebylitsyn school seems to be of special significance is in the relationship between NS properties and different aspects of human memory.

It was Teplov (1964a) who, discussing the advantages and faults of the separate properties of the NS, set up the hypothesis that inertia of the nervous processes, understood as the opposite pole of mobility, seems to be one of the most important physiological mechanisms of memory. This hypothesis has been verified, with some limitations, by several studies. These limitations are, among others, concerned with the distinction between voluntary and involuntary memory.

Golubeva, who is the most productive researcher in the area of memory and NS properties, ascertained in several studies that the relations between memory and NS properties may be quite different depending on whether we refer to voluntary or involuntary memory (Golubeva, 1972a, 1980a; Golubeva and Guseva, 1972; Golubeva et al., 1977b). Studying the efficiency of voluntary and involuntary memorizing in relation to NS properties, Golubeva (1972a) found that lability,[17] measured by the driving reaction to stimuli of high frequency, correlates positively with efficiency of involuntary memorizing, whereas in voluntary memorizing the "labile" individuals are less efficient. Pictures, two- and three-digit figures, codes, syllables, and texts were used as material for memorizing. The same regularity was also found in other studies (Golubeva and Guseva, 1972; Golubeva and Rozhdestvenskaya, 1976; Golubeva et al., 1977a), where, regardless of the type of material memorized, individuals requiring high lability performed better in tasks with involuntary memorizing whereas individuals with low lability were more efficient in voluntary memorizing.

Izyumova (1976) studied the relation between lability and voluntary memory. She took as a starting-point the hypothesis that involuntary memorizing is based on the functions of the posterior brain whereas voluntary memorizing is mainly regulated by the frontal brain, recognized as the substratum of the individual's regulatory and control functions. Diverse material was used for memorizing, e.g. meaningless syllables, three-digit figures, pictures, words (concrete and abstract). The efficiency of memorizing was measured by the amount of correct material recalled. The driving reaction to visual stimuli of high frequency, registered separately from the frontal and posterior cortex, was used to measure lability. The highest efficiency in voluntary memorizing was found in subjects with high lability in the frontal cortex and/or low lability in the posterior cortex. Interpreting this data Izyumova suggests that the long-lasting traces in structures bound with perception and primary information analysing typical for "inert" (in posterior brain) individuals, cause growing efficiency in voluntary memorizing. Also, in contrast, high lability in frontal structures causes rapid organization and control processes in memory which are of special importance in voluntary memorizing.

The leading Russian psychologist in memory research, Smirnov (1966), discussing the relation between memory and NS properties, acknowledged the fact that strength of NS may influence the efficiency of memory depending on the volume of the material to be memorized as well as on the degree of difficulty. In experiments on memory where material of large volume or high degree of difficulty is used, individuals with a strong NS should perform better than weak ones. There may be no difference in the efficiency of memory between the "strong" and "weak" individuals when the given material is of lower volume and not difficult to remember.

This hypothesis has been partially supported by several experiments, conducted mainly in Teplov's laboratory. For example, Golubeva (1972a) found that individuals with strong NS reveal higher efficiency in memory tasks involving large quantities of material and a low degree of comprehension. The strength of NS was diagnosed on the basis of the driving reaction to stimuli of low frequency (see p. 92) and material for memorizing varied in volume and degree of comprehension.

In another experiment (Golubeva and Trubnikova, 1971) the degree of comprehension was the main variable which differentiated individuals with strong and weak NS in memory efficiency. Meaningless syllables exposed in large numbers were better recalled by the strong type of NS. However, when meaningful texts were considered, also of large volume, the "weak" type was more efficient in recall. Similar results, although based on a different methodological approach, were obtained by Trubnikova-Morgunova (1977).

Soleveva (1972) performed an experiment on memory in relation to strength of the NS, in which she manipulated the level of motivation and degree of emotional tension by introducing training and control (evaluated) tasks and found that:

(1) in all tasks highly motivated subjects reveal higher memorizing efficiency, independent of the level of strength of NS;
(2) in low and medium emotional tension situations, strong motivation causes an increase of memorizing in both strong and weak NS types; under high emotional tension conditions strong motivation increases performance, but only in "strong" individuals;
(3) differences in efficiency are strongly expressed in highly motivated individuals; low emotional tension increases memorizing efficiency in "weak" individuals whereas high emotional tension causes increments in performance in "strong" individuals.

The strength of NS was diagnosed on the basis of RT experiments and extinction with reinforcement in GSR.

All the above tasks involved visual or auditory material. However, similar results were obtained using different materials. Yusim (1975), who used motor tasks and controlled kinesthetic memory, showed that with easy, uncomplicated tasks (e.g. reproducing the length of a drawn line or shape of tangent geometrical figures), "weak" individuals performed better than "strong" ones, whereas in complicated situations (recognizing maze structures) individuals with strong NS dominated over those with weak NS. The strength of the NS was measured using EEG indices (mean energy of delta rhythm and driving reaction to stimuli of low frequency).

Concluding, one may say that Smirnov's hypothesis, suggesting that when the material to be remembered is of large quantity individuals with strong NS will be more efficient than weak ones, should be limited to meaningless material. Maybe the degree of meaninglessness, different for different materials, should be treated as a kind of difficult, overloaded situation (see Trubnikova-Morgunova, 1977). As we know from many studies (see the former section) in such situations individuals with strong NS reveal higher task performance efficiency than "weak" ones and this also seems to be the case when memory experiments are taken into account.

There are also studies in which the relation between equilibrium in dynamism or activatability (see p. 39) and memory has been examined (e.g. Golubeva and Rozhdestvenskaya, 1969; Golubeva, 1972a; Izyumova, 1976). Without going into details, let me repeat the conclusion reached by Golubeva in her monograph devoted to the area of memory in relation to NS properties (1980a). As she writes, in most studies of voluntary and involuntary memory, irrespective of the kind of verbal or symbolic material to be remembered, individuals with predominance of excitatory processes (high activatability) show higher efficiency of recall compared to individuals in whom inhibitory processes dominate over excitatory ones (low activatability). In contradistinction, when concrete material is used in voluntary memory, the efficiency is higher in individuals characterized as having low activatability.

This short review does not exhaust all the studies conducted in this area[18] although it reflects the main directions of research. Considering the number of experiments subjected to the relation of memory and NS properties one wonders about their small contribution to the explanation of the physiological mechanisms of memory. Our understanding of the physiological mechanisms underlying memory processes does not seem to have advanced. It seems reasonable, however, to look at the data collected by Russian typologists as yet another research approach to the study of memory functions in relation to the level of arousal or activation, with special attention to individual differences in the latter.

Space restrictions do not permit a full presentation of the contribution of the Teplov–Nebylitsyn school in the area of NS properties. Not all the data nor all the directions of research presented by this group have been discussed. However, on the basis of this short review, it can be convincingly concluded that Teplov and his students have influenced to a high degree the current status of Pavlov's typology. The essential contribution of the Teplov–Nebylitsyn school to this field justifies it for consideration as the founder of neo-Pavlovian typology.

## MAIN DIRECTIONS OF RESEARCH IN PAVLOV'S TYPOLOGY PRESENTED BY THE URAL GROUP

Almost simultaneously with the onset of Teplov's research on NS properties, Merlin, a psychologist from Perm, published his 1955 paper in which he showed school pupils react differently to their marks depending on type of nervous system. In the weak TNS unsatisfactory school marks evoke negative emotions and decrease the pupils' activity in school, whereas the same marks in pupils with a strong NS may have a positive effect, causing increased mobilization (Merlin, 1955). Without any attempt at evaluation of this project, which was a kind of case study, I mention it to stress that Merlin, from the very beginning, paid much attention in his research on Pavlov's typology to the significance of NS properties in human behaviour. It is no accident that the main research on the relation between NS properties and so-called style of action stemmed from his laboratory, with special contributions to this area by Klimov and Baymetov.

Merlin and his students did not pay much attention in their research to the understanding of the essence of NS properties, as was the case in Teplov's school. However, it was Merlin's group who devoted considerable attention to the relation between NS properties and temperament traits, thus bridging the gaps between Pavlov's typology and psychology. Contrary to Teplov's view, the Ural group paid attention not to single NS properties but to their configurations, making typological thinking one of the main elements of their approach to the study of temperament. This line of research has been developed especially by Merlin and Belous.

Being aware of the role of temperamental traits in everyday behaviour Merlin and his students have undertaken many studies in physical activity, school situations etc., with the aim of discovering if temperamental traits influence (and, if so, in what way and to what degree) the efficiency of functioning in these activities and situations. The studies conducted by Vyatkin and his students may serve as an example of this line of research.

The contribution of the Ural group, part of which is now scattered over many universities, has been largely distributed by rather peripheral publishers, in very low numbers, hence most of their research is completely unknown in the Soviet Union itself, not to mention other countries. Perhaps the only exception are those papers which were published in the journal *Voprosy Psikhologii*. Under Merlin's editorship at least ten volumes devoted to the problem of temperament and TNS have been published (Merlin, 1964a, 1967a, 1968, 1970a, 1971, 1973, 1974a, 1976a, 1977; Merlin and Nikityuk, 1976).[19] Klimov wrote the only monograph concerned with individual style of action in relation to type of nervous system (1969) and Vyatkin is author and editor of several books related to temperament and sports activity (1972a, 1974a, 1976, 1978). In my opinion those considerable numbers of scientific reports cannot be ignored simply because of their very local distribution.

## Style of Action and Type of Nervous System

Merlin (1973) stressed the importance of temperament in the process of adjustment of the individual to his environment, and mentions the three following ways within which this process may take place:

(1) Modification of temperament traits according to the requirement of the surroundings; not very effective due to the rather low susceptibility of temperamental traits to change.

(2) Choice of activity or environment by the individual, according to his temperament. Selection to professionals performed in extreme settings or conducive to strong physical or social threat may serve as an example here. Merlin assumes that the choice of activity or surroundings according to the individual's temperament has a limited value and is not the optimal way to adjust to the requirements of life and society.

(3) Individual style of action in accordance with one's temperament. As Merlin suggests, this is the basic form of adjustment which allows any individual with a given temperament to cope with the demands generated by his surroundings.

By individual style of action Merlin and his students (Merlin, 1973; Klimov, 1969; Mastvilisker, 1967) are referring to stable modes of action and forms of reaction, determined by the type of nervous system, on which efficient performance of activity depends. It develops by experience and on the basis of knowledge acquired by the individual during ontogenesis (Merlin, 1973; Klimov, 1969; Shtimmer, 1974;

Shchukin, 1977). The Ural group treats style of action as a manifestation of ability[20] (e.g. Merlin, 1973, Mastvilisker and Dikopolskaya, 1976). There is almost full agreement between Merlin's approach and the typical modes of action (style) proposed by Galperin as main components of the structure of activity with reference to orienting and executive actions (see Mastvilisker, 1967).

Since the classical experiment conducted by Klimov (1959) it has been shown that subjects differ in the amount of orienting activity performed during professional work depending on NS properties. In Klimov's first experiment, the relation between style of action and level of NS mobility in weavers working in the textile industry was studied. The emphasis on mobility followed from the fact that the rapid change from one loom to the other is one of the main requirements the individual has to follow to work efficiently. Among 60 women, 35 diagnosed as either "mobile" or "slow" were selected. Transformation of stereotype in an RT experiment and Leites' (1956a) after-effect RT method were used for diagnosing the mobility of nervous processes. On the basis of systematic observation, chronometric method and interview, the style of work was estimated. Among others, attention was paid to individual differences in: orienting activity, amount and speed of changes from one activity to the other, amount of preventive work, control activity, etc.

It was found that the level of the weavers' efficiency does not depend on the mobility of their nervous system; the latter, however, remains in relation to the style of work. The "mobile" weavers try to perform their tasks rapidly, and they succeed because of their high mobility. In turn, the "slow" weavers protect themselves against irregularity during work and employ much time in protective and orienting activity.

Most of the research on nervous system properties and style of action has been performed with regard to the strength of NS dimension. Let me again give an example of an experiment conducted in Merlin's laboratory by Kopytova (1964) who was interested in the relation between the strength of NS and the professional efficiency of operators, as well as in the ways the actions are performed during preservation and maintenance of machine tools. The strength of the NS was measured by the extinction with reinforcement method (in GSR) and by changes in RT during frequently repeated stimuli. The methods of controlling professional activity were similar to those used by Klimov. Kopytova (1964) found among other things that:

(1) Operators with a weak NS displayed significantly more control and prophylactic activity under non-stressful conditions than operators with a strong NS. Because of this activity the "weak" individuals work

efficiently and it allows them to avoid or to diminish threatening situations.

(2) In threatening situations the orienting, control, and executive activity is inhibited in individuals with weak NS; this is not the case with "strong" individuals, who, as a rule, do not manifest disorganized behaviour in such situations.

(3) In general the efficiency in professional performance does not differ in operators with strong and weak TNS, which is in accordance with Klimov's data related to mobility of NS.

Generalizing, the data of most experiments conducted in this area show that in individuals with strong NS the executive activity dominates over orienting activity or both of these are well-balanced. In subjects with weak NS a preponderance of orienting activity over executive activity occurs.

Most of the studies related to NS properties and style of action have been performed in children, especially in pupils (e.g. Mastvilisker, 1967; Prusakova, 1974; Shtimmer, 1974; Shchukin, 1977). In one of these studies Baymetov (1967) analysing the data concerned with style of action in school performance stated that three factors differentiating the individuals with strong and weak NS types may be distinguished. Let me give an abbreviated characterization of these factors.

(1) The dynamic of involvement in work and level of tiredness

| *"Strong" individuals* | *"Weak" individuals* |
|---|---|
| Low proneness to fatigue | High proneness to fatigue |
| Low need for relaxation | Tendency to relax |
| Tendency to do homework at a stretch | Need for silence and solitude during homework |
| Gradual involvement in work (need for warm-up) | Proneness to perform difficult tasks first, easy ones later |

(2) Range of intellectual activity

| *"Strong" individuals* | *"Weak" individuals* |
|---|---|
| Integration of preparatory, executive and control activity | Predominance of preparatory and control activity |
| Introduction of changes and corrections during performance of basic activity | Introduction of changes and corrections in task but during control activity |
| Efficient functioning without need for work drafts | Tendency to make plans and drafts for a day, week, etc. |

(3) Level of tension

| "Strong" individuals | "Weak" individuals |
|---|---|
| The range of intellectual activity may increase under tension | The range of intellectual activity narrows under tension |
| Performance duration shortens | Performance duration lengthens |

The data on the basis of which the described factors of activity style in pupils were distinguished were collected during observations, by chronometric method, and by using questionnaires and interviews given to teachers and parents. The following activity of 41 high-school students was controlled: reading, writing, solving mathematical tasks, summaries, compositions, dictation, reproduction texts. Some of the tasks were performed at school, others during experiments conducted separately with every individual.

Over the past few years special attention has been paid to the fact that the development of style of action in accordance with the individuals' NS properties takes place only when a given intellectual level (measured by IQ) is attained (e.g. Prusakova, 1974; Shtimmer, 1974). Without going into details let me give a short characterization of the results obtained by Mastvilisker and Dikopolskaya (1976) in a study of preschool children. The authors wanted to determine style of action and strength of NS in relation to IQ, measured by the WISC. The following three styles of action were distinguished:

(1) long preliminary orientation; orienting, executive, and control activities are separated, presence of control during the last stage of task performance;
(2) lack of preliminary orientation, executive, and control actions fuse, lack of control during the final stage of performance;
(3) blind trials, which lead randomly to the expected goal.

It was found that the rational kinds of task performance (styles 1 and 2) occur significantly more often in children with $IQ \geq 110$; however, the level of intelligence does not determine whether style 1 or style 2 dominates. In individuals with $IQ < 110$ the trials and errors method is the most typical. There is a strong relation between strength of NS and style of action. The "strong" individuals prefer style 2, whereas the "weak" ones style 1. Prolonged training may, to some degree, change the style of action in individuals with an intelligence level below IQ 110.

The above-mentioned research does not exhaust the whole scope of problems related to style of action and TNS. Several studies have been conducted by the Moscow group (e.g. Turovskaya et al., 1972;

Gurevich *et al.*, 1975; Klyagin *et al.*, 1977; Akimova, 1980) as well as by other psychologists in the Soviet Union (e.g. Danch, 1974; Gerasimov, 1976). In my opinion they do not, however, introduce any qualitatively new elements into this direction of research. Research conducted in our laboratory concentrates, among other things, on the relation between temperamental traits and style of action. Discussing this problem in Chapter 6, I will refer to the contribution of Soviet psychologists in this area.

## Links between TNS Properties and Temperament and New Approaches in Typological Thinking

Teplov and Nebylitsyn stressed in their "methodological credo" (see p. 27) that one of the most important tasks in research on Pavlov's typology is to investigate the separate NS properties; whereas searching for types which might be arranged on the basis of different configurations of these properties plays a secondary role. A quite opposite position has been taken by Merlin and his students, especially with regard to temperament which develops, according to them, on the basis of TNS. The former includes such traits as: anxiety, extraversion–introversion, rigidity, impulsivity, emotional excitability, and emotional stability[21] (Merlin *et al.*, 1967; Belous, 1976; Silina, 1977; Vyatkin, 1978).

According to Merlin, it is essential for any temperamental feature that it be included in given configurations with other features of temperament, thus forming a temperament type. "In temperament research one should avoid investigating the separate features which do not refer to given types" (Merlin, 1973, p. 11).

Taking as a starting-point the above-mentioned features of temperament, as well as the strength of NS with regard to excitation and dynamism in inhibition[22] Belous (1970, 1972; Belous and Palkina, 1974), using factor analysis, separated two factors—so-called "complexes of symptoms".

(1) Extraversion–introversion, based on strength of excitation. This includes: strength of NS (in its negative), anxiety, rigidity and introversion;
(2) Emotionality, determined by dynamism as regards inhibition and comprising: dynamism with regard to inhibition (negative), and emotionality measured by emotional excitability and stability.

Merlin (1967b) and Belous (1968) found also that strong and balanced TNS, both mobile and low, differ with reference to the temperamental features mentioned.

Silina (1977) who was interested in developmental changes in temperamental structure, compared thirteen to fourteen-year-old pupils with fifteen to sixteen-year-olds and stated that in both developmental stages the same two complexes of symptoms (factors) may be identified and they do not differ essentially from those found in adults. However, with age, the link between temperamental features and NS properties becomes closer (see also Mastvilisker, 1973). She also stated that the second factor, called emotionality, includes mobility of nervous processes.

This correlational approach in searching for types of temperament based on linear dependencies was only the starting-point in Merlin and Belous' typological thinking. They introduced the concept of type of temperament using the model of invariance, by which they mean such a mathematical relationship between the variables which are stable, irrespective of changes in the variables. According to these authors, the invariance expresses the causal interrelations between variables, thus explaining the process of creating whole systems of different degrees of complexity. Like any self-regulatory system the type too may be characterized by the invariance of relations between traits (Belous, 1970; Merlin, 1976b). In searching for the typological invariance of temperament Belous starts from the assumption that this is a result of features, correlating and non-correlating with each other, which are different from the point of view of biological function and which play different compensatory roles in human adjustment behaviour (Belous, 1976).

The configurations of temperamental traits based on the model of invariance have been studied by the Ural group using the concept of taxonomy and by parabolic modelling of relations between temperamental traits (equation of regression).

Silina's (1977) study may serve as an example of an approach to temperament based on the taxonomy model. She used, as initial material for analysis, the values of all distinguished temperament traits and the strength of NS estimated in two groups of subjects (13–14 years and 15–16 years of age) separately. Taking into account the most general features of the points in the multi-dimensional space which correspond with the notion of taxon, the author separated taxa, $S_1$ and $S_2$, common in both groups under investigation. Taxon $S_1$ included subjects with such features as strong TNS, low anxiety, low rigidity, extraversion, and high emotional excitability. This type has been labelled type A. Taxon $S_2$ incorporated subjects with: weak TNS, anxiety, rigidity, introversion, and low emotional excitability. The label "type B" is given to this configuration of features. Belous (1968), investigating adult subjects, obtained similar results.

The equation of parabola, reflecting the interaction of orthogonal variables of temperament, is another way of using the model of invariance in temperament studies. According to Merlin and Belous, it expresses better than any other equation the curvilinear functional dependency of temperamental traits. Psychologically, this model corresponds with functional dependencies of a different kind, such as compensation, co-operation, and equilibrium, thanks to which a constant level of adjustment to different needs of the surroundings may be ensured (Merlin, 1970b; Belous, 1970; Belous and Palkina, 1974).

The main question which gave rise to the development of this kind of approach to the configurations of temperamental features, was whether such functional relations exist between orthogonal complexes of symptoms which are common for different types and may be expressed by invariant quantitative characteristics of humankind. In several studies (Belous, 1970, 1972, 1976, 1977; Belous and Palkina, 1974) using the equation of parabola ($y = ax^2 + bx + c$) and taking into account all possible combinations of pairs of temperamental features it has been stated that, irrespective of individual or typological, sex, or age differences two pairs of temperamental features exist: (i) introversion–emotionality; and (ii) rigidity–emotionality, which are common for all individuals and which reflect the species-specific structure of temperament. These invariances exist as a result of the dependency between adaptational functions of different temperamental traits. The functional dependencies, as mentioned above, may be of a different kind.

This short outline of views on temperamental structure has been given to show that Merlin and his students represent a new systems approach in temperament study that is not common in Pavlov's typology research.[23] There are, however, some faults, which mean, among other things, that the contribution of the Ural group in this area cannot be assimilated by other researchers of temperament. I have found no study justifying the set of temperamental traits—anxiety, extraversion–introversion, rigidity, impulsivity, emotional excitability, and emotional stability—proposed by Merlin.[24] The Ural group should have estimated temperament traits by means of diagnostic methods accepted, or at least known to other psychologists, in order to be able to communicate with those engaged in temperament research. If not, their own methods should be described in detail, paying attention to all the necessary psychometric rules.

It is a pity that the Ural group has limited the curvilinear approach to temperamental traits, only fortuitously paying attention to one or another NS property, without explaining precisely why that NS property was chosen. It would be interesting to use this methodological background for studying the configurations of all the NS properties further.

Thus the question of the relations between the separate properties of the nervous system, as has been shown in the above section, remains unresolved.

One must say, finally, that the curvilinear approach with particular reference to the parabolic model only enables one to grasp the functional relations between two analysed traits. This limitation, stated by Merlin (1976b), means that we are still far from apprehending the whole richness of functional relations within the system created by humans and their surroundings.

## TNS Properties and Efficiency of Performance in Different Situations

As mentioned above (see p. 62) in the first half of the 1950s, Merlin conducted a case study, on the basis of which he was able to state that the strength of NS may influence the efficiency of school performance, a phenomenon especially prominent when a pupil with a weak TNS has to cope with difficult situations (in this case low school marks) which usually cause efficiency decrement. In such situations the opposite behaviour often occurs in the individual with the strong NS, where efficiency increase is observed (Merlin, 1955).

Utkina, measuring the relation between strength of NS and level of efficiency in normal and stressful school situations, observed a similar regularity in high-school (1964) and college (1968) students. In both groups, each containing over 30 subjects, the strength of NS was experimentally measured (extinction with reinforcement in GSR and RT experiments) and different school tasks were performed. Much attention has been paid to concentration and distribution of attention, used as one of the indicators of efficient behaviour. In high-school students social threat was posed by informing them that their final semester marks would depend mostly on experimental task results. In the control situation they were informed that the task results would have no essential influence on their final marks. It was found that high-school students with a weak TNS obtained significantly worse results under stress compared with the strong individuals (Utkina, 1964). In college students stress was evoked by informing them that their mathematical solutions were wrong, irrespective of the results they really got. In the control situation, performance was estimated using only positive reinforcement. Utkina (1968) stated that in the difficult situation the results did not differentiate between the "strong" and "weak" individuals, although there were differences in motor behaviour. Students with a weak TNS behaved in a more emotionally excited manner compared with "strong" individuals. In the control situation, where the students were encouraged to solve the tasks, significant differences in performance in favour of the individuals with the strong TNS were found. Utkina, interpreting this data, has suggested that for the difficult situation in both groups ("strong" and "weak") the optimal level of excitation was exceeded, thus differences are to be found at the motor behaviour level only. In the "encouragement" situation full manifestation of stress is observed in the "weak" individuals for whom this situation seems to evoke above-optimal excitation, not the case in "strong" individuals (Utkina, 1968).

Many studies have been conducted by Vyatkin and his students on sports activity, with the aim of finding out whether or not NS properties influence the efficiency of behaviour. Different kinds of competitions, levels of motivation, and task complexity were used as measures of difficult situations. In most cases the strength of NS, measured by standard methods used in Merlin's laboratory, and temperamental traits (see p. 67) were used as independent variables.

So, for example, Vyatkin (1972b, 1974b) conducting research on artistic gymnasts, aged between fifteen and twenty-three, showed that the efficiency of performance depended both on the degree of emotional tension (measured, among other things, by changes in tremor and estimation of short time-intervals) and the strength of NS, as well as on some temperamental traits (anxiety and emotional excitability). In competitions evoking high levels of emotional tension, the individuals with weak NS properties and with high levels of anxiety and emotional excitability reveal a decrement in their sports results. Training increases efficiency in "weak" individuals. The same effect may be evoked by manipulating the level of motivation to win the competition (measured on a 100-point rating scale). When motivation is very high, "strong" individuals are more efficient than "weak" ones. If the level is low an opposite regularity is found. Similar results were obtained in high-school students where gymnastic activity in training and competition was taken into account (Vyatkin, 1974b).

In a study conducted on fencers, where the speed and accuracy of movements with the duelling sword under different emotional states were measured, Suslov (1972) stated that in individuals with a weak NS the performed movements are of higher accuracy than in "strong" individuals. In the latter, the speed of performed reactions is higher under an elevated emotional state (e.g. evoked by blame) whereas in "weak" individuals the time is shorter than in "strong" subjects where emotional state is lower (e.g. under praise).

In several studies (Vyatkin and Markelov, 1974; Markelov, 1976;

Vyatkin, 1978), where different kinds of sportsmen were investigated, it was found that the most important effect on efficiency in sports activity is not caused by the separate properties of the nervous system or the temperamental traits, but by their different configurations. Using the method of discriminant analysis the authors were able to distinguish two sets of temperamental and NS traits, separately for individuals whose results improved under competition and for those in whom the performance decreased in such situations. The shortcoming of these studies consists, however, of the inability to indicate the specificity of configurations of NS and temperamental traits.

Studies have also been conducted in other areas of human activity to show the significance of NS properties in the efficiency of performance of different kinds of tasks. For example, Kopytova (1964) conducted a study to answer the question of whether strength of NS influences the efficiency of the operators' work when performed under threat. The answer was "yes". When unexpected work stoppage of the machine tools occurred there was a significant decrement of productive efficiency in individuals with weak TNS.

Samonov (1972, 1974) showed that strength of NS is a very important variable in firemen, who work under extreme conditions. The Moscow psychologist Gurevich (1970) distinguishes professions of two types: type I—professions usually involving extremely difficult situations, in which the professional performance requires given individual traits, especially properties of the nervous system; type II—professions which may draw upon any individual traits the person has, where the type of NS does not have any influence on the level of performance (see also Shchukin, 1977). Referring to this distinction one may say that firemen are representatives of professions belonging to type I, where, as has been argued by Samonov, a certain degree of strength of the NS is needed and where the strong TNS dominates over the weak TNS.

Although the Ural group started with this kind of investigation, which is still one of the main areas in their Pavlovian typology research, there are also many other studies in which the significance of NS properties in human activity, with special attention to different kinds of job and professional activity, has been illustrated (see Gurevich, 1970, 1974; Gurevich and Matveyev, 1966; Nebylitsyn, 1976; Klyagin, 1975; Gordeyeva and Klyagin, 1977; Troshikhin *et al.*, 1978).

# 2
# Laboratory Methods used by Neo-Pavlovian Typologists to Diagnose the Nervous System Properties

### INTRODUCTION

Research on nervous system properties in humans has mainly been based, in analogy with Pavlov's own studies conducted in dogs, on the CR phenomenon. This is in line with the methodological credo expressed by Teplov and Nebylitsyn (see p. 27) stressing the necessity to investigate NS properties on the basis of involuntary reactions, thus bypassing the masking effect of environmental influences. Such popular diagnostic methods as extinction with reinforcement or the alteration method may serve as examples. However, the estimation of NS properties based on the CR methods requires specific equipment and much time, so the use of these methods for practical purposes is not feasible. The diagnosis is highly influenced by the kind of UCS, CS, and effector used in the conditioning procedure. Additionally, it is important to ask to what degree CR activity may be treated as a specific human behaviour.

The phenomenon of voluntary motor reaction, accepted as a typical human form of behaviour, was introduced relatively early in laboratory experiments aimed to diagnose NS properties. It inspired many new methods, which developed partly along the lines of classical RT experiments. As examples, the following methods may be mentioned: change of RT during repeatedly applied stimuli, slope of RT curve, or speed of reaction change to rapidly changing stimuli. However, this kind of psychological method, though easy to use, has several disadvantages. Results are strongly influenced by the kind of stimuli (visual or auditory) used for diagnosing the given NS property. It may be asked how close the use of voluntary methods take us to understanding the essence of the basic properties of the NS in relation to cortical and subcortical centres of the brain? These doubts stimulated neo-Pavlovian typologists to adapt EEG methods for diagnosing the afore-mentioned properties.

There is a strong belief expressed by most Russian researchers involved in NS property investigation (e.g. Nebylitsyn, 1972a; Rusalov, 1979), that the EEG method enables us to characterize general NS properties, in contradistinction to the partial properties revealed by most other methods used in this area. Nebylitsyn was the first to use EEG indices and since the mid-1960s these methods have become the methods of choice in diagnosing NS properties in laboratory conditions by the Moscow group. As mentioned by Klyagin (1974) the EEG technique seems to be of special importance for diagnosing NS properties for at least three reasons:

(1) the biopotentials of the brain constitute the most informative index of CNS activity;
(2) the EEG record is highly stable; and
(3) the EEG activity reveals substantial individual differences.

The review of methods given in this chapter has been limited to those which, in the author's opinion, are the most relevant in diagnosing NS properties or those which gained most popularity among Pavlovian typologists. Those methods which are out of date or have not been empirically validated will not be presented here. For example, in order to diagnose the strength of the NS with regard to excitation, the change in sensitivity threshold under caffeine (Teplov, 1959; Nebylitsyn, 1957, 1959a; Rozhdestvenskaya *et al.*, 1960), the critical frequency of flicker phosphene (Nebylitsyn, 1972a; Gurevich, 1970; Rozhdestvenskaya, 1971), or the change of sensitivity threshold under additional stimuli, known also as the action of distractors (Teplov, 1959; Nebylitsyn, 1972a; Borisova *et al.*, 1969; Rozhdestvenskaya *et al.*, 1960; Golubeva, 1972b) have been used as measures of this NS property. It would, however, be difficult to find a study conducted during the last ten years in which these methods have been used.

On the other hand, there have been attempts to introduce new diagnostic techniques to estimate the strength of the NS. These are mostly related to the EEG. For example, Klyagin (1974) proposes to use the variance of EEG amplitude as a measure of the strength of the NS. As Klyagin argues, individuals with a strong NS differ from those with a weak one not only in the endurance of the NS, as proven in

## 2. Laboratory Methods used by Neo-Pavlovian Typologists 75

classical experiments, but also in the scope and level of an energy store which manifests its physical characteristic in the variance of the EEG amplitude. The author has found that individuals with a strong NS have a significantly higher variance of EEG amplitude than subjects with a weak NS. Strength was measured by such methods as slope of RT curve and extinction with reinforcement (EEG variant). The variance of EEG amplitude has also been used in other studies aiming to diagnose the strength of the NS (Gurevich *et al.*, 1975; Alexsandrova, 1977).

Another example is the attempt to use evoked potentials (EP) to diagnose the strength of NS. As known from the literature (see Regan, 1972) the evoked potential amplitude has been found to be related to the intensity of sensory stimuli. Bazylevich (1974b), taking as point of departure the fact that the strength of NS is manifested when the increasing stimulus intensity ceases to evoke increased reaction (the "law of strength"), used somatosensory evoked potentials (SEP) to measure this NS property. As the author concludes:

> The property of strength of the reticular brain system is directly reflected in the SEP understood as a function of the intensity of proprioceptive stimulation (Bazylevich, 1974b, p. 91).

Chuprikova (1977) proposed using the amplitude of the $N_1$ and $P_{200}$ components of the auditory evoked potentials (AEP) to stimuli of different intensity for diagnosing NS strength. However, there are also EP studies conducted by neo-Pavlovian typologists without attempts to relate this phenomenon to the well-known basic NS properties (e.g. Maryutina, 1974, 1978; Rusalov, 1974; Golubeva *et al.*, 1977b; Pasynkova *et al.*, 1980). For example, Rusalov, taking into account the polarity–amplitude assymetry of the AEP and the SEP (both of these recorded from the frontal, occipital, and vertical brain areas) stated that this phenomenon, being consistently independent of the variables under control, reflects a general brain factor which might be identified as a general property of the NS (Rusalov, 1974, 1979). Evolution in diagnostic methods may also be observed with regard to other NS properties.

This review of diagnostic methods does not include those aimed at diagnosing the strength of the NS in relation to the inhibitory process. Some attempts have been made to measure the strength of inhibition by the endurance of conditioned inhibition which is manifested in CR activity (e.g. Ilina, 1959; Yermolayeva-Tomina, 1963; Rozhdestvenskaya, 1963b). However, as far as I know, for the last 20 years nobody has tried to measure this feature of the NS under laboratory conditions.

The concept of equilibrium of the NS, which was interpreted by Pavlov as the relation between the strength of excitation and strength of inhibition, has been transferred in research conducted on humans to dynamism of the nervous processes. Research initially aimed at separately diagnosing dynamism of excitation (mostly measured by the speed of orienting response (OR) extinction, or speed of CR formation) and dynamism of inhibition (also measured by the speed of OR extinction, and the speed of CR extinction and differentiation) (cf. Nebylitsyn, 1972a; Yermolayeva-Tomina, 1969, 1971; Ravich-Shcherbo and Shibarovskaya, 1972), has given way to investigations concentrating on diagnosing the balance of dynamism of nervous processes. For this reason, the review does not include diagnostic techniques devoted separately to dynamism of excitation and dynamism of inhibition.

The description of methods contained in this chapter is primarily informative. Nebylitsyn's book (1972a), translated into English, was published in Russian in 1966 and Gray's *Pavlov's Typology* in 1964. Since then no systematic review of the methods used to diagnose NS properties has been published. Psychologists in the West usually refer to the two above-mentioned publications when characterizing the state of NS properties investigation, which do not reflect the current status of this area. For example, Powell (1979), summarizes five methods for diagnosing NS strength:

(1) threshold of transmarginal inhibition;
(2) threshold of concentration and irradiation of excitation;
(3) absolute sensory threshold;
(4) reaction time and stimulus intensity; and
(5) attention and distractability.

The second and fifth methods mentioned by the author belong more to the history of NS property investigation, whereas other methods discussed in this chapter are not on Powell's list.

It is the author's belief that acquaintance with the most popular methods used in NS property investigation will help psychologists in Western countries to find more links between their own research and ideas and those developed by neo-Pavlovian typologists. The first steps have already been taken by, among others, Gray (1964, 1967, 1972a, 1981), Eysenck (1966, in press), Mangan (1982; also Mangan and Farmer, 1967), Strelau (1969, 1978, 1981), Powell (1979), Loo (1979), Sales (Sales and Throop, 1972; Sales *et al.*, 1974), Buchsbaum (1976), Paisey and Mangan (1980), and Levey and Martin (1981).

## METHODS FOR DIAGNOSING THE STRENGTH OF THE NERVOUS SYSTEM WITH REGARD TO EXCITATION

### Extinction with Reinforcement

This method is based on Pavlov's (1951–52) assumption that NS strength is manifested primarily in the ability of the nerve cells to work, i.e. the capacity to endure prolonged and concentrated excitation. Pavlov argued that the endurance of the NS might be measured by repeating stimuli that have been used in the extinction with reinforcement method. Frequently repeated stimuli evoking exhaustion of the NS cause protective inhibition to develop. Depending on the strength of NS this phenomenon, measured by changes in magnitude or intensity of reaction, may occur under different amounts of stimulation. The weaker the NS the more prone it is to developing protective inhibition.

The extinction with reinforcement method was first used in Pavlov's laboratory in research on dogs. Rozhdestvenskaya (1959b) introduced this method for diagnosing the strength of NS in humans.

The essence of this method consists in comparing the magnitude of CR before and after intense stimulation. The procedure is illustrated schematically in Fig. 5. First the CR has to be evoked (stage I). The procedure of differentiation to similar stimuli is used in order to promote maximal CR development. When the CR is consolidated, its amplitude is measured (stage II–$CR_1$). Next, a series of CS–UCS pairings are presented (stage III). Depending, among other things, on the modality of the CR the number of pairings may vary from ten (e.g. in photochemical reflexes) to almost a hundred (conditioned EEG alpha-blocking). The exhaustion of the NS and the occurrence of transmarginal inhibition depends not only on NS strength but on the number of CS–UCS pairings used, the inter-trial interval, and the intensity of the CS and UCS. The greater the number of stimuli

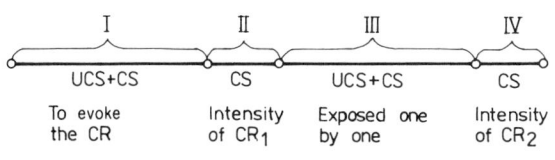

$CR_1 > CR_2 \rightarrow$ weak TNS
$CR_1 \leqslant CR_2 \rightarrow$ strong TNS

FIG. 5. Extinction with reinforcement.

applied, the shorter the time interval, and the higher the intensity of stimuli used, the more easily the endurance of the NS decreases. CR amplitude is measured after the final pairing has been presented (stage IV–$CR_2$).

An increase or lack of change in CR activity following intensive stimulation indicates high endurance of the NS ($CR_1 \leq CR_2$) and is used as the index of strong TNS, whereas a decrease or disappearance of CR activity under strong stimulation, caused by protective inhibition, indicates the weak NS ($CR_1 > CR_2$). The magnitude of change in CR activity, used as a criterion of strength of the NS, differs from study to study and is not based on statistically significant differences between the intensity of $CR_1$ and $CR_2$. Another criterion for diagnosing the NS strength, based on the extinction with reinforcement method, is also used from time to time (see Nebylitsyn, 1972a). This consists of recording solely the number of CS–UCS pairings required to diminish CR activity. The number of pairings (stage III) needed to evoke protective inhibition indicates the strength of the NS. The more presentations required to decrease the CR the stronger the NS, and vice versa.

Primarily, the extinction with reinforcement method was used for photochemical conditioned reflexes[1] (Rozhdestvenskaya, 1959b; Rozhdestvenskaya et al., 1960; Teplov, 1959, 1963a; Nebylitsyn, 1959a, 1972a; Turovskaya, 1963; Borisova and Ravich-Shcherbo, 1967; Ippolitov, 1969, 1972). Nebylitsyn (1972a) introduced this method to conditioned EEG alpha-blocking version, where it has been used by many of Teplov's students (Nebylitsyn et al., 1965; Shlakhta, 1972, 1975; Ravich-Shcherbo, 1976; Shlakhta and Panteleyeva, 1978). This index of strength is also frequently used by the Ural group which has improved the GSR method in this CR procedure. Muscular contraction evoked by pressing a special key (with 5–10 kg pressure strength) is used as UCS (see Merlin, 1964b; Merlin and Mastvilisker, 1971; Kopytova, 1964; Utkina, 1964; Vyatkin, 1968; Suslov, 1972; Kapustin, 1976; Kolchina, 1976).

The extinction with reinforcement method is still one of the most popular techniques for diagnosing the strength of the NS. According to Teplov it is used as one of the referent, basic methods in determining the strength of nervous processes with regard to excitation. The estimation of strength based on this method has been compared with several other indices used for diagnosing this NS property. As may be seen from Table V, which gives a short review of correlations between extinction with reinforcement and other methods, they vary from near 0.0 to 0.84, depending on the indices compared.

There is not much evidence regarding the reliability of the extinction with reinforcement procedure. Nebylitsyn (1965) using this method in EEG obtained a retest reliability of 0.661 ($p < 0.001$). Using the same criterion of reliability for extinction with reinforcement in the photochemical version, Borisova and Ravich-Shcherbo (1967) obtained a similar result (0.74). As a kind of equivalent form of reliability, the correlation between extinction with reinforcement in EEG recorded simultaneously from the left and right hemispheres may be used. As has been shown in our own study (Strelau, 1969) the correlation coefficient is satisfactory and varies from 0.758 to 0.822, depending on which of the three criteria used for estimation of extinction was taken into account.

## The Induction Method

Teplov, while studying visual sensitivity, discovered that a point of light in peripheral vision changed the sensitivity threshold to the target stimulus (test point of light). Depending on the intensity of the peripheral stimulus the sensitivity to the test point may increase or decrease (see Rozhdestvenskaya, 1955). Low peripheral stimulation (from the subthreshold to three to five times above the threshold) increases sensitivity to the target stimulus; additional stimuli of medium intensity (20–100 times above threshold) causes a decrease in visual sensitivity; and strong light in peripheral vision (about 120–160 times above threshold) again increases visual sensitivity (Rozhdestvenskaya, 1969).

These empirical findings confirm the so-called "law of induction" established by Pavlov, which states that "given a weak excitatory process, irradiation takes place, given a medium one—concentration, and under a very strong one, again, irradiation" (Pavlov, 1951–52, p. 329). Teplov put forward the hypothesis that the shifts from irradiation to concentration (threshold of concentration of excitation) and from concentration to irradiation (threshold of irradiation of excitation) will be different depending on the strength of the NS. This hypothesis has been empirically supported by Rozhdestvenskaya (1955, 1959a) who is the author of the so-called "Induction Method" for measuring the strength of the NS. The method has been used and described many times by Rozhdestvenskaya (1955, 1959a, 1969, 1971, 1980), Nebylitsyn (1959a, 1972a), and other collaborators from Teplov's laboratory (e.g. Rozhdestvenskaya et al., 1960; Turovskaya, 1963; Golubeva, 1972a). The most penetrating analysis of the theoretical assumptions underlying this method may be found in Gray's monograph (1964).

TABLE V. Extinction with reinforcement compared with other indices of strength of the NS

| Indices of Strength of the NS | Photochemical | Extinction with Reinforcement EEG | GSR |
|---|---|---|---|
| Induction method | 0.45++–0.69++ Rozhdestvenskaya et al., 1960[a] 0.12–0.26 Rozhdestvenskaya et al., 1960[b] | | |
| Slope of RT curve | 0.653++ Nebylitsyn, 1972a | 0.591++ Nebylitsyn et al., 1965 0.444+; 0.278 Danch, 1974 0.78++ Ryabinina, 1977 | 0.31++ Kolchina, 1976 |
| Visual sensitivity threshold | 0.19 Borisova and Ravich-Shcherbo, 1967 0.103 Strelau, 1969 0.38+; 0.69++; 0.29 Ippolitov, 1972[c] | 0.472+ Nebylitsyn et al., 1965 0.025 Strelau, 1969 | |

| | | |
|---|---|---|
| Change of RT under repeated stimulation | $0.73^+$ | Kopytova, 1964 |
| | $0.67^{++}$ | Vyatkin, 1968 |
| | $0.62^{+++}$; $0.80^{+++}$ | Soloveva, 1970 |
| | $0.51$–$0.87$ | Merlin and Mastvilisker, 1971[d] |
| | $0.84^{+++}$ | Suslov, 1972 |
| | $0.648^{++}$ | Kapustin, 1976 |
| Driving reaction in theta band | $-0.44^+$ | Golubeva, 1972b |
| | $-0.351^+$ | Shlakhta, 1975[c] |
| | $-0.486^{++}$; $-0.332$; $-0.387$ | Guseva and Shlakhta, 1974[f] |
| | $0.59$ | Rozhdestvenskaya, 1980 |

$^+ p < 0.05$; $^{++} p < 0.01$; $^{+++} p < 0.001$.

a. Four variants of the method were used and the correlations varied within this limit.
b. In this case auditory stimuli were used as CSs whereas previously visual stimuli were applied.
c. Three types of CS were used: auditory, kinesthetic, and visual.
d. In thirteen experiments conducted by different authors between 1964–70 all the correlations were significant.
e. Only 4 Hz were used as indicator of strength.
f. Consecutively the driving reaction to 4, 5, and 6 Hz has been applied.

The procedure resembles the experimental conditions for measuring visual sensitivity. After adaptation to darkness (about 45–50 min) the visual threshold to a point of light (test point) is measured. The fixation point (red light) presented during sensitivity measurement is 2°17′ above the test point and its intensity is ten to fifteen times greater than the sensitivity threshold value. Below the test point (at an angular distance of 45′) the peripheral stimulus may be applied and its intensity varies from subthreshold values to 180× threshold. In order to measure the effect of peripheral stimulation on visual sensitivity, the ratio of sensitivity in the presence of peripheral stimulus ($VT_s$) to initial sensitivity measured without peripheral stimulus (VT), is calculated ($VT_s/VT$). Gray (1964), reinterpreting Rozhdestvenskaya's data, showed that in subjects with strong NS, characterized by low sensitivity (r) and high endurance (R) the threshold of concentration (decrease of sensitivity under additional stimulation) is reached with lower intensity stimuli than is the case with individuals with weak NS. This regularity, as well as other relationships between the strength of NS and the manifestation of the "law of induction" is shown in Fig. 6. It is also stressed by Rozhdestvenskaya (1955) that in "strong" individuals the irradiation is soon replaced by concentration, and in some individuals with strong NS irradiation may be not observed at all. One must state, however, that the concentration threshold has not been used in further investigations concerned with the induction method.

It has been shown in Rozhdestvenskaya's first experiments (1955, 1959a) that it is rather difficult to reach the threshold of irradiation of excitation by simply manipulating the intensity of additional visual stimuli. This author, summarizing the results of 184 subjects, showed that this threshold (expressed in increasing sensitivity) can only be observed in 2.7% of cases (Rozhdestvenskaya, 1969). According to Teplov the threshold of irradiation of excitation is the most important for characterizing the strength of the NS. As might be seen from Fig. 6 this threshold is lower in individuals with weak NS, i.e. the shift from concentration to irradiation develops in these subjects at a lower intensity of peripheral stimuli (Teplov, 1961). The induction curve derived from changes in sensitivity under peripheral stimuli only, is known as the "shape of the curve" version of the induction method and is not normally used for diagnosing the strength of the NS.

To intensify the effect of the peripheral stimulus, which has been fixed at an intensity of 100× threshold value, different versions of the induction method have been developed. The first consists of administering different doses of caffeine (e.g. 0.005 and 0.2 g). According to the Teplov school caffeine increases the excitatory process, thus inten-

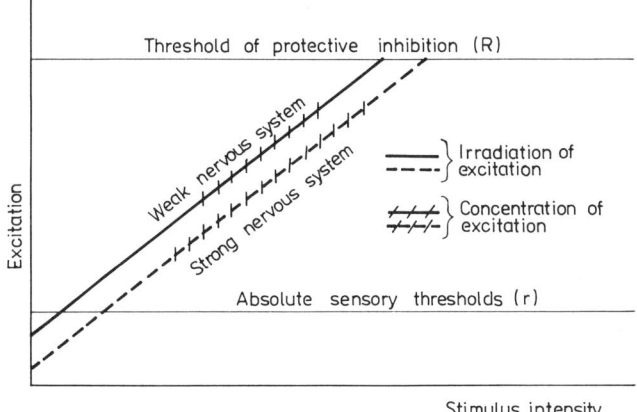

FIG. 6. Strength of the NS and four response thresholds (taken from Gray, 1964).

sifying the peripheral stimulus. In "weak" individuals the irradiation threshold appears under strong caffeine doses (e.g. 0.2 g). This version of the induction method, called "caffeine", has not been used since the beginning of the 1960s, however, because of the conflicting results obtained with this procedure.

Two other versions were developed—so-called "repetition" and "exhaustion". The "repetition" version consists of measuring the sensitivity threshold many times (usual 20×) in the presence of a peripheral stimulus (with intervals of 1 min between applications). The cumulative effect of additional stimuli intensifies the excitatory process. As suggested by Rozhdestvenskaya (1959a, 1969), the same effect may be attained by using the "exhaustion" version. In this case the sensory threshold is measured in very short time-intervals (10–15 s) without additional stimuli for about 15–20 min.

The following procedure (according to Rozhdestvenskaya, 1969, p. 206–207) is normally used in experiments which intensify the effect of the peripheral stimulus.

(1) Sensory sensitivity to the test point (without additional stimulus) is measured.
(2) The sensory sensitivity threshold to the test point in the presence of a peripheral stimulus is measured; the additional stimulus being 100× the threshold value.
(3) The magnitude of negative induction is determined; the percentage

of the decrease in sensitivity under situation (2) in relation to situation (1) is calculated.
(4) One of the procedures for intensifying the effect of the peripheral stimulus is applied.
(5) Visual sensitivity without additional stimulus (repetition of situation 1) is measured.
(6) Visual sensitivity in the presence of the peripheral stimulus is again measured. The intensity of the latter stimulus is 100× the threshold value determined in situation 5.
(7) The influence of the peripheral stimulus on sensitivity under conditions of the intensified effect of the additional stimulus is determined.

The higher the visual sensitivity under these conditions the weaker the NS, i.e. the more the threshold of irradiation in excitation is surpassed. The decrease of sensitivity, caused by the extension of concentration developed under these conditions is taken as the index of strength.

Rozhdestvenskaya et al. (1960) compared the diagnoses of strength of NS using all four versions of the induction method and obtained correlation coefficients ranging from 0.52 to 0.73 ($p < 0.01$). Similar correlations have been reported by Turovskaya (1963) and Borisova (1965). We may thus conclude that there is moderate agreement in diagnosis of strength of the NS obtained with different versions of this method.

The induction method which, together with the extinction with reinforcement method, is considered the most robust method for diagnosing the strength of the NS (Teplov, 1961; Nebylitsyn, 1972a) and has often been compared with other techniques for measuring the strength of NS. Most of these studies are presented in Table VI along with content validity data of the respective methods.

It has been stressed several times by Rozhdestvenskaya (1969, 1971, 1980) that the induction method enables measurement of the strength of NS of the visual system only, thus greatly limiting its usefulness, since it thus only measures partial rather than general NS strength and, since the procedure is extremely complex and time-consuming, it has only been used in Teplov's laboratory and, in fact, now been virtually abandoned.

## Sensitivity Threshold

Teplov, following Pavlov's suggestion that cortical cells are highly reactive (Pavlov, 1951–52), put forward the hypothesis that individual differences exist in cortical cell reactivity as a function of the strength of

## TABLE VI. Induction method and other indices of strength of the NS

| Indices of NS Strength | Version of Induction Method | | | |
|---|---|---|---|---|
| | "Exhaustion" | "Repetition" | "Caffeine" | "Slope of induction curve" |
| Extinction with reinforcement in photochemical CR | 0.45++ and 0.24 Rozhdestvenskaya et al., 1960[a] | 0.56++ and 0.26 Rozhdestvenskaya et al., 1960[a] | 0.69++ and 0.18 Rozhdestvenskaya et al., 1960[a] | 0.54++ and 0.23 Rozhdestvenskaya et al., 1960[a] |
| Visual sensitivity threshold | 0.44++ Rozhdestvenskaya et al., 1960<br>0.36+ Turovskaya, 1963<br>−0.21 Rozhdestvenskaya et al., 1969a | 0.41++ Rozhdestvenskaya et al., 1960<br>0.51++ Turovskaya, 1963 | 0.42++ Rozhdestvenskaya et al., 1960 | 0.45++ Rozhdestvenskaya et al., 1960<br>0.31+ Rozhdestvenskaya et al., 1969a |
| Auditory sensitivity threshold | 0.45++ Rozhdestvenskaya et al., 1960<br>0.03 Turovskaya, 1963 | 0.24 Rozhdestvenskaya et al., 1960<br>0.08 Turovskaya, 1963 | 0.37+ Rozhdestvenskaya et al., 1960 | 0.42++ Rozhdestvenskaya et al., 1960 |
| Slope of RT curve | 0.11 Rozhdestvenskaya et al., 1969a | 0.35 Borisova, 1965[b] | | −0.26 Rozhdestvenskaya et al., 1969a |
| Driving reaction to stimuli of low frequency | 0.46+ Rozhdestvenskaya et al., 1967[c]<br>−0.13; −0.15; −0.09; −0.05 Rozhdestvenskaya et al., 1969a[d] | | | 0.44++; 0.40++; 0.13; 0.09 Rozhdestvenskaya et al., 1969a[d] |

a. In the first case visual CSs were used; in the second—auditory CSs.
b. The ratio RT max/RT min has been taken as index of strength.
c. The total energy of driving reaction to stimuli: 2–12 Hz was measured.
d. Separate reactions to stimuli: 4, 6, 8, and 10 Hz were taken into account. For significant data see Table V.

the NS. The weak type of NS results from high reactivity of the nerve cells and this should be revealed in high sensory sensitivity (Teplov, 1955b). On the basis of several studies Teplov and Nebylitsyn concluded that there is a reciprocal relation between sensory sensitivity (lower threshold of reaction) and the endurance of the NS (upper threshold of reaction). This has been discussed in the previous chapter 1.

Nebylitsyn (1956) was the first to support the hypothesis concerning the relation between sensory sensitivity and strength of the NS understood as the working capacity of the NS. Since then the sensory threshold of different modalities has often been used to diagnose the strength of NS (see e.g. Teplov, 1959; Yermolayeva-Tomina, 1960; Nebylitsyn, 1963b, 1972a; Ippolitov, 1966, 1972; Turovskaya, 1963; Paley et al., 1966; Borisova, 1969a; Borisova et al., 1969). There is even a strong recommendation to use this method as one of the referent indicators of strength of excitation (Nebylitsyn, 1972a; Teplov, 1972).

There is no need to describe the procedures for measuring the sensory threshold, because they do not differ, in general, from those used in psychophysics. The sensory threshold index, on the basis of which subjects with high sensitivity thresholds are considered to have strong NS and subjects with low thresholds to have weak NS, has been compared with several other methods used for diagnosing strength of NS. This comparison is presented concisely in Table VII which is an illustration of very diverse estimations of validity if one regards comparison with sensory threshold as a criterion of validity.

It has already been stated that strength–sensitivity correlates poorly across modalities (see Chapter 1). For this reason, this index for diagnosing strength of NS has been eschewed since the 1970s.

## Slope of RT Curve

As follows from elementary knowledge of psychology, the law of strength predicts that simple RT decreases (to a given limit) with the increasing intensity of stimuli. In individuals with low sensory thresholds, a stimulus of low intensity evokes higher excitation than in individuals whose sensory threshold is high. This is due to the high reactivity of the NS of the former, who might be characterized, according to Nebylitsyn, as individuals with a weak NS. Because of their high reactivity, the RT to stimuli of low intensity is significantly shorter as compared with the RT to the same stimuli applied to individuals with strong TNS, who have high sensitivity thresholds. This has been proven several times by Nebylitsyn (1960b, 1972a) and other investigators (e.g. Nebylitsyn et al., 1965; Ravich-Shcherbo,

TABLE VII. Sensitivity threshold and other indices of NS strength

| Indices of NS Strength | Visual Sensitivity | Auditory Sensitivity |
|---|---|---|
| Extinction with reinforcement in photochemical reflexes | 0.32$^+$ and 0.49$^{++}$ Rozhdestvenskaya et al., 1960$^a$ 0.29 Ippolitov, 1967 0.19 Borisova and Ravich-Shcherbo, 1967 0.10 Strelau, 1969 | 0.17 and 0.33$^+$ Rozhdestvenskaya et al., 1960$^a$ 0.38$^+$ Ippolitov, 1972 |
| Extinction with reinforcement in EEG | 0.472$^+$ Nebylitsyn et al., 1965 0.03 Strelau, 1969 | 0.20$^+$–0.63$^{++}$ Nebylitsyn, 1963b$^b$ |
| Induction method | 0.41$^{++}$–0.45$^{++}$ Rozhdestvenskaya et al., 1960$^c$ 0.36$^+$ and 0.56$^{++}$ Turovskaya, 1963$^d$ −0.21 Rozhdestvenskaya et al., 1969 −0.36$^{++}$–−0.46$^{++}$ Rozhdestvenskaya et al., 1969$^e$ | 0.24–0.45$^{++}$ Rozhdestvenskaya et al., 1960$^c$ |
| Slope of RT curve | 0.319 Nebylitsyn et al., 1965 −0.40$^{++}$ Rozhdestvenskaya et al., 1969 | |
| Driving reaction to stimuli of low frequency | 0.29$^+$ and 0.14 Rozhdestvenskaya et al., 1969$^f$ | |

*a.* Consecutively, auditory and visual CSs were used.  *b.* Three different situations for the EEG version of extinction with reinforcement method were applied.  *c.* Four versions of the induction method were used: "shape of curve", "exhaustion", "repetition", and "caffeine".  *d.* Consecutively, the "repetition" and "exhaustion" versions were used.  *e.* The correlation between both indices of strength was measured in five different studies.  *f.* The frequencies of 4 and 6 Hz were taken into account. For significant data see Table V.

1969; Olshannikova and Alexsandrova, 1969; Zyryanova, 1970; Bazylevich, 1974a).

The higher the intensity of the applied stimuli the lower the differences in RT between "strong" and "weak" individuals. At a given intensity of stimuli the differences totally disappear. Nebylitsyn (1972a) interpreting this fact, argued that under high-intensity stimulation in both types (strong and weak NS), the limits functional capacity of the NS may be reached. Nebylitsyn (1960b, 1972a) drew curves of RT to stimuli of different intensity, separately for individuals with strong and weak NS diagnosed by the extinction with reinforcement method, and found that the RT curve for individuals with strong TNS is deeper, with an evident decline, as compared with the slope of RT curve for individuals with weak TNS (see Fig. 7).

The procedure for diagnosing the strength of NS on the basis of the slope of RT curve, described in detail by Nebylitsyn (1972a) and Peysakhov (1974) may be characterized in general as follows.

Auditory or sometimes visual stimuli of different intensity are applied in a simple RT experiment. For example, in experiments with auditory stimuli the intensity may vary from 20–120 dB. Usually 4–6 different intensities are used.[2] A stimulus of each intensity is applied about 15–25 times in random order with time-intervals of about 12–30 s (longer for visual stimuli). Usually a warning signal (light, sound, or the signal "attention") is given about 2 s prior to presentation. The whole experiment may last from about 20 to 60 min, depending on the number of stimuli presented. Mean RT is calculated for separate intensities of stimuli.

Different criteria are used as indices of strength of the NS; however, two are most popular. The simplest is the ratio of the longest to the shortest RT (RT max/RT min). As has been shown by Olshannikova and Aleksandrova (1969) in a study conducted on 49 subjects, using auditory stimuli, this ratio varies from 2.34 to 1.04. The higher the value (mainly caused by long RT to low intensity stimuli, RT max) the stronger the NS. The RT max/RT min index is a simplified indicator of the slope of RT curve because it comprises only the extreme values of the curve. The most popular index of the slope of RT curve which reflects quantitatively the slope of the curve is the so-called coefficient $b$, calculated from the equation of regression: $y = a + bx$ (Nebylitsyn et al., 1965; Ravich-Shcherbo, 1969; Olshannikova and Aleksandrova, 1969). When drawing the RT curve the ratios of RT for a stimulus of given intensity to RT to the stimulus of highest intensity (t/t min) are taken into account (see Fig. 7) rather than absolute values of RT to separate intensities of stimuli. Nebylitsyn (1972a) has shown that the

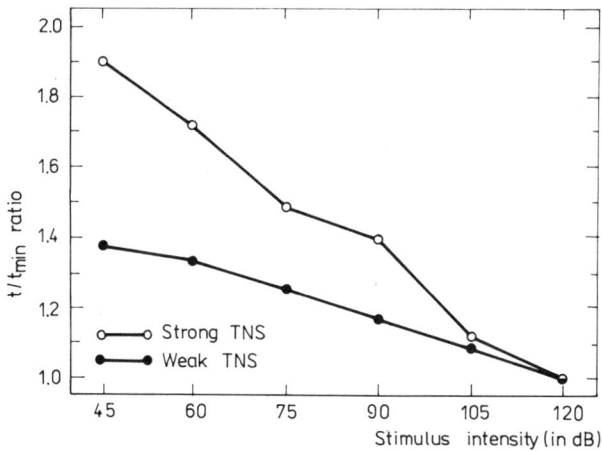

FIG. 7. Curves of $t/t_{min}$ ratios as a function of intensity of the auditory stimulus for individuals with strong and weak NS (adapted from Nebylitsyn, 1972a).

curves derived from the relative values differentiate better between the strong and weak types of NS than curves based on absolute RT. Ravich-Shcherbo (1969), summarizing results collected in four separate studies (altogether 264 subjects) were coefficient $b$ was used as an indicator of strength of the NS, stated that the distribution of results was almost normal, with a slight right-hand skew. In this study 61% of the subjects had $b$ coefficients ranging from 2.22 to 4.32. The higher the value of $b$, i.e. the deeper the slope of the RT curve, the stronger the NS. It has been shown that both indices, RT max/RT min and coefficient $b$, intercorrelate very highly. For example, Olshannikova (1967), using auditory stimuli, found a correlation of 0.915 ($p < 0.001$).

In our laboratory Klonowicz (1974c) introduced another index reflecting the slope of the RT curve. Taking into account a simplified curve extracted from the extreme points of the empirical curve, the angle of slope was calculated as the angle formed by a right-angled triangle, its verticles portraying the RTs to the extreme (weakest and strongest) stimuli applied in the experiment.

There is some evidence of the reliability of this method. In Olshannikova and Aleksandrova's study (1969) the retest reliability was estimated, taking into account four measures, for auditory and visual stimuli separately. The $b$ coefficient was used for the auditory stimuli and RT max/RT min was applied for visual stimuli to indicate strength of the NS. Very high correlations varying from 0.810 to 0.910 were found for auditory stimuli. Similar results were obtained for visual stimuli (0.843 to 0.901). Split-half reliability was also measured. The four correlation coefficients in the RT experiment using auditory stimuli range from 0.941 to 0.994. When visual stimuli were used the correlations attained a level of 0.843 to 0.934. Ryabinina (1977), using the slope of RT curve for auditory stimuli, diagnosed the strength of the NS twice, three months apart, and obtained a stability coefficient similar to the above-mentioned reliability estimations ($0.85; p < 0.01$). The simplicity of the procedure and the relatively low technical requirements have facilitated attempts to standardize this method for use in applied psychology (Peysakhov, 1974).

The slope of RT curve has often been used by Nebylitsyn and his students, together with other standard techniques of measuring strength of the NS (see Tables V, VI, and VII). However, because it is almost exclusively designed to measure the strength of the NS within the auditory or visual analyser, and cannot be treated as a measure of general NS property (Nebylitsyn, 1972b; Golubeva, 1980a; Rusalov, 1979), the popularity of this method has decreased during the last years giving way to EEG methods.

## Change of Simple RT Under Repeatedly Applied Stimuli

A phenomenon similar to that of intensity of reaction to given stimuli may be observed with reaction time. When stimuli are frequently repeated, protective inhibition may develop. This type of inhibition is manifested not only in the decrement or disappearance of a reaction but also in extension of the RT (Boiko, 1961). This phenomenon has been used by Kopytova (1963) for diagnosing the strength of NS with regard to excitation.

The procedure is reminiscent of the extinction with reinforcement method to some extent (see Fig. 8) and is based on the same theoretical assumptions. A series of stimuli (visual or auditory) is presented to the subject who reacts to them by pressing a key. Simple RT is measured. The number of stimuli may vary as well as their intensity and interstimulus interval. Kopytova (1963, 1964), for example, used only 50 presentations with an inter-stimulus interval of 19 to 20 s. In our experiment (Strelau, 1967b) 240 presentations were used with a inter-stimulus interval of 5 to 7 s. Peysakhov (1974), who proposed to standardize conditions in order to make comparable the results obtained by different authors, used the following arrangement: 150 presentations of light stimuli, applied for a duration of 2000 ms; inter-stimulus

## 2. Laboratory Methods used by Neo-Pavlovian Typologists

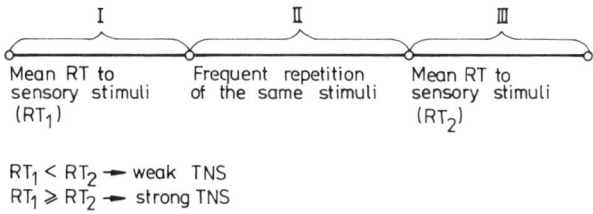

FIG. 8. Change of RT under repeated stimuli.

interval of 6 s, presentations preceded (2 s) by sound (80 dB) as a warning signal. In analogy to the extinction with reinforcement procedure, one may assume that the exhaustion of the NS, which reveals itself in the lengthening of RT (Boiko, 1961), depends not only on the strength of NS, but is also a positive function of the strength, number and brevity of the inter-stimulus interval (Vasilev, 1960).

The mean RT to first applications of stimuli is measured (stage I) and compared with the mean RT to the last applications (stage III). Usually 10 to 30 presentations are taken into account for comparing the mean RTs. The assumption is made that with frequently repeated stimuli (stage II) protective inhibition may occur (lengthening of RT) and depending on the strength of NS individual differences in RT changes occur under these conditions.

The ratio of the mean RT of the final applications ($RT_2$) to the mean RT of the first applications ($RT_1$) is used as the index of strength of NS with regard to excitation. If the mean RT to the last stimuli is longer than the mean RT to the first, according to the Pavlovian law of strength, this indicates a weak NS and vice versa. If mean RT to the last stimuli is equal to, or shorter than, the mean RT to the first applications, this indicates a strong NS (Kopytova, 1963; Merlin and Mastvilisker, 1971). Peysakhov (1974) introduced the following criterion as an indicator of strength of the NS:

$$A = \frac{\text{mean RT to 30 Ss exposed at the end}}{\text{mean RT to 30 Ss exposed at the beginning}} \cdot 100$$

When standardizing the results of 222 subjects the latter author proposed to classify as weak TNS those individuals whose A criterion is $\geq 105.0$. Individuals whose A criterion is $\leq 95.2$ are classified as having a strong TNS.

The change of simple RT under repeated stimuli has been used as indicator of strength of the NS almost exclusively by the Ural group (Kopytova, 1963, 1964; Merlin, 1964b; Merlin and Mastvilisker, 1971; Vyatkin, 1964a, 1964b; Utkina, 1964; Paley et al., 1966; Kapustin, 1976; Kolchina, 1976) and it still remains one of the most popular experimental procedures for diagnosing strength of the NS. This method has been validated, above all, by comparing it with the extinction with reinforcement procedure (GSR variant) and the results are shown in Table V.

Merlin and Mastvilisker (1971) have quoted three studies in which retest reliability was measured. The correlations are as follows: (a) 0.65 ($p < 0.001$); (b) 0.82 ($p < 0.001$); and (c) 0.46 ($p < 0.01$). A summarizing review with some critical remarks on considerable arbitrariness in using this method has been published by Peysakhov (1974).

## Photic Driving Reaction (PDR) to Stimuli of Low Frequency

The "law of strength", which states that the magnitude of reaction depends on the intensity of stimuli, has often been used by neo-Pavlovian typologists for diagnosing the strength of the NS, the slope of the RT curve being the best example (see p. 86). In EEG investigation it has been stated that the photic driving reaction is subjected to the same law, i.e. the expression of the driving reaction grows, to a given degree, with the increasing intensity of rhythmic exposure of light stimuli (e.g. Livanov, 1940; Danilova, 1961). Nebylitsyn, taking advantage of the fact that PDR depends on the intensity of stimuli applied, made use of this phenomenon in investigating the strength of the NS (Nebylitsyn, 1964b). As has been shown many times, individuals with a weak NS, because of high sensitivity, react to stimuli of given intensity with more expressed (higher, larger) reactions compared with individuals with a strong NS. This regularity is especially pronounced when stimuli of low intensity are applied.

Nebylitsyn, in an experiment conducted on 25 subjects, showed that the power value of photic driving reaction to stimuli of different flash frequencies (5–22 Hz) is higher for individuals with a weak NS, irrespective of the brightness of the light (25–1000 lux). Figure 9 drawn by Nebylitsyn (1964b) illustrates the mean total power value for all frequencies investigated. The correlation coefficient ($0.723; p < 0.01$) between strength of NS diagnosed by extinction with reinforcement (EEG version) and the shape of PDR curve obtained by Nebylitsyn

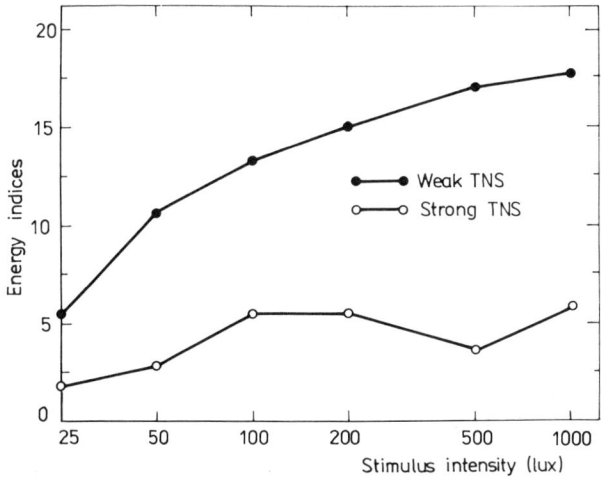

FIG. 9. Relationship of PDR to stimulus intensity depending on NS strength (taken from Nebylitsyn, 1972a).

supports the hypothesis regarding the relation between the strength of NS and magnitude of the photic driving reaction.

On the basis of curves drawn separately for mean power values of theta, alpha, and beta bands, the author stated that the differences between "strong" and "weak" individuals are most expressed in the beta band and there is no clear relationship between strength of the NS and PDR in alpha frequency. In a study published one year later Nebylitsyn *et al.* (1965), taking into account 22 indices of driving reaction (including total power indices as well as indices for separate frequencies: 2–80 Hz), ascertained that PDR in the alpha band correlated significantly with the referent indices of strength of the NS. They therefore concluded that PDR in the alpha band is the best indicator of strength measured on the basis of the EEG record. This frequency has also been recommended by Golubeva (1965) as the most sensitive PDR indicator of strength of the NS.

In further investigations it has been argued that the photic driving reaction in the theta band or in given frequencies within this band are the most sensitive indicators and in most EEG studies related to NS properties this index has been used for diagnosing the strength of NS (e.g. Golubeva and Guseva, 1972; Rozhdestvenskaya and Levochkina,

TABLE VIII. Photic Driving Reaction (PDR) and other indices of NS strength

| PDR Indices | Extinction with Reinforcement (EEG) | Slope of RT Curve | Visual Sensitivity[f] | Induction Method |
|---|---|---|---|---|
| Total power value of PDR | 0.723[++] Nebylitsyn, 1964b[a] −0.470[+] Nebylitsyn et al., 1965[b] | −0.364 Nebylitsyn et al., 1965[b] −0.41 Golubeva, 1972b[a] | −0.409[+] Nebylitsyn et al., 1965[b] 0.45[+] Golubeva, 1965[a] | 0.46[+] Rozhdestvenskaya et al., 1967[c] |
| Theta band | −0.275 Nebylitsyn et al., 1965 | −0.361 Nebylitsyn et al., 1965 −0.63 Golubeva, 1972b | −0.390 Nebylitsyn et al., 1965 0.19 Golubeva, 1965 | |
| Alpha band | −0.562[+] Nebylitsyn et al., 1965 | −0.404 Nebylitsyn et al., 1965 −0.27 Golubeva, 1972b | −0.424[+] Nebylitsyn et al., 1965 0.30 Golubeva, 1965 −0.43[+] Golubeva, 1972b | |
| Beta band | −0.451 Nebylitsyn et al., 1965 | −0.204 Nebylitsyn et al., 1965 −0.43[+] Golubeva, 1972b | −0.473[+] Nebylitsyn et al., 1965 0.40[+] Golubeva, 1965 | |

| 4 Hz | −0.189 Nebylitsyn et al., 1965 | −0.314 Nebylitsyn et al., 1965 | −0.404 Nebylitsyn et al., 1965 | −0.13 and 0.44++ Rozhdestvenskaya et al., 1969a[d] |
| --- | --- | --- | --- | --- |
| | −0.486++ Guseva and Shlakhta, 1974 | | 0.29+ Rozhdestvenskaya et al., 1969a | |
| 5 Hz | −0.239 Nebylitsyn et al., 1965 −0.332 Guseva and Shlakhta, 1974 | −0.468+ Nebylitsyn et al., 1965 | −0.341 Nebylitsyn et al., 1965 | |
| 6 Hz | −0.387+ Guseva and Shlakhta, 1974 | | 0.14 Rozhdestvenskaya et al., 1969a | −0.15 and 0.40++ Rozhdestvenskaya et al., 1969a[d] |
| 7 Hz | −0.372 Nebylitsyn et al., 1965 | −0.386 Nebylitsyn et al., 1965 | −0.451+ Nebylitsyn et al., 1965 | −0.09 and 0.13 Rozhdestvenskaya et al., 1969a[d,e] |
| | | | 0.00 Rozhdestvenskaya et al., 1969a[d] | |

*a.* Flash frequencies of 5–22 Hz were used.
*b.* Flash frequencies of 2–80 Hz were used.
*c.* Flash frequencies of 2–12 Hz were used.
*d.* The variations: "exhaustion" and "shape of curve" were used.
*e.* Flash frequency of 8 Hz was used.
*f.* The differences in signs of coefficients of correlation (+ or −) derive from the fact that either sensitivity threshold or visual sensitivity have been taken into account.

For significant data see Table V.

1972; Bazylevich, 1974a; Golubeva *et al.*, 1974; Turovskaya, 1974; Rozhdestvenskaya, 1977a; Ravich-Shcherbo, 1977; Shlakhta and Panteleyeva, 1978; Trubnikova-Morgunova, 1977; Golubeva, 1980c).

Izyumova *et al.* (1977), using photic driving reactions to flash frequencies of 4 and 6 Hz argued in favour of this method as follows:

> The most determined relations with NS properties occur in indicators of the reactive potentials—in the photic driving reaction. It has been stated that the driving reaction of low frequency is unequivocally connected with strength of nervous system (p. 82).

One must, however, remark that this strong statement is not corroborated by equally strong empirical evidence. The data collected in Table VIII support my opinion. The highest correlation coefficient between PDR frequencies of 4 and 6 Hz and the referent indices of strength of NS is rather low (0.486; $p < 0.01$), if one is to take this as a measure of validity. Moreover, there is no empirical evidence for stating that the driving reaction within the theta band should be a more sensitive indicator of strength than, for example, the PDR in alpha or beta bands (see Table VIII). The only fact which I was able to find in the literature and which gives support to such a conclusion is the factor-analytic study by Rozhdestvenskaya *et al.* (1969), where it was found that the driving reaction of flash frequencies 4 and 6 Hz was included in the strength factor with loadings: 0.66 and 0.58. One must add, however, that mostly theta band frequencies were used in this study. In the Soviet literature there is no satisfactory theoretical explanation for the statement that PDR in the theta rhythm, which seems to be mainly determined by the hippocampus (see Numan, 1978), is the most sensitive frequency for diagnosing the strength of NS as regards the EEG phenomenon (e.g. Golubeva, 1980a).

The procedure for diagnosing the strength of NS on the basis of PDR does not differ, in general, from standard measures of PDR used in EEG laboratories. Very often the driving coefficient, understood as the ratio of the number of assimilated waves to the number of visual stimuli presented for a 10-second period (100×), is used. The higher the coefficient the weaker the NS, which is understandable if one refers to Nebylitsyn's theoretical assumption given above. Other quantitative measures of PDR are also used, e.g. the ratio of power value under exposed flash frequencies of a given band to power value of the same band recorded during rest. Sometimes only the power value of a given frequency (or frequency band) derived under stimulation is used. In both cases the higher the value the weaker the NS.

The PDR to stimuli of low frequency is used for measuring the strength of NS almost exclusively by Nebylitsyn's students and it seems to be the most popular index of this NS property currently in use.

## DIAGNOSTIC METHODS FOR LABILITY OF THE NERVOUS SYSTEM

### Adequate Optical Chronaxie (AOC)

In former studies (see Teplov, 1963a, 1964a) the Adequate Optical Chronaxie (AOC) was used as a measure of mobility understood generally as the temporal characteristic of reactions (see p. 30). Since lability was separated from mobility as an independent NS property, which is manifested in the speed with which the nervous processes (NP) are initiated and terminated, the AOC was used as the measure of lability. AOC, which was introduced as a measure of mobility of NP by Asratyan (cited by Teplov, 1964a) has been accepted by the Teplov school as an indicator of the speed of initiation of NP limited to the visual system (see Ravich-Shcherbo and Shvarts, 1959; Borisova *et al.*, 1963; Turovskaya, 1963).

The procedure for measuring lability on the basis of the AOC does not differ from standard measurements of this optical phenomenon. After adaptation to darkness (30–50 min) the visual sensitivity threshold is determined. Afterwards the brightness of the light spot is increased to double the visual threshold. The experimenter changes the duration of the light spot, by increasing and decreasing exposure time until it is barely visible. Finally, the minimal duration, with brightness double the value of the visual threshold, is determined. This duration time, which is an indicator of the speed of initiation of the visual sensation, has been accepted as a measure of lability. The smaller the AOC the higher the lability of the nervous system.

The AOC, used almost exclusively in Teplov's laboratory (Teplov, 1964a; Rozhdestvenskaya, 1963b; Golubeva, 1965; Golubeva and Vasilenko, 1965; Nebylitsyn, 1972a), was a especially popular index of lability in the 1960s. In Table IX there is some evidence for the validity of this method. Because of the disproportionate influence of the visual system in determining lability of the NS on the basis of AOC Teplov's students discarded this method in later investigations.

TABLE IX. Adequate Optical Chronaxie (AOC) and other indices of lability

| Indices of Lability | AOC | Reference |
|---|---|---|
| Photic driving reaction | $-0.426^+$<br>$-0.53^{++}; -0.441^+$ | Golubeva, 1965, 1972b[a]<br>Nebylitsyn, 1972a[b] |
| Critical frequency of flicker-fusion (CFFF) | $0.57^{++}$<br>$0.63^{++}$<br>$0.64^{++}$ | Turovskaya, 1963<br>Borisova et al., 1963<br>Ravich-Shcherbo and Shvarts, 1959 |
| Speed of visual sensitivity restoration | $0.57^{++}$ | Borisova et al., 1963 |

a. Photic driving reaction in gamma band (35–80 Hz) was measured.
b. The photic driving reaction to 60 and 80 Hz was measured.
For significant data see Table V.

## Critical Frequency of Flicker-Fusion (CFFF)

The critical frequency of flicker-fusion (CFFF) introduced to NS property investigation by Shvarts (1959; Ravich-Shcherbo and Shvarts, 1959) has been the most popular index of lability, measured by the speed of termination of NP. This method, like some other methods of diagnosing lability, is based on a concept introduced in 1892 by the Russian physiologist Vvedensky (cited by Golubeva, 1972b, p. 22). According to Vvedensky "lability is manifested by a considerable speed of the elementary reactions which accompany functional activity". This method, like the AOC, is highly influenced by the so-called partiality phenomenon (see p. 49) and thus measures of NP lability are limited to the visual system only.

The procedure measuring CFFF is standard. After adaptation to darkness (35–50 min) the visual sensory threshold is measured. Hereafter, the intensity of the light spot is increased, depending on the given experiment, 2–70× in comparison with the threshold value. The duration of the stimulus is held constant (10–25 ms), with the interstimulus interval varying from 5–475 ms (Shvarts, 1963). Kashin (1974) and Bundych (1974) proposed light stimuli of frequencies varying from 7 to 60 Hz. In further investigations of lability experimenters excluded preliminary adaptation to darkness to save time (Nebylitsyn et al., 1965; Kashin, 1974). The stimuli are presented in increasing and descending series, with the aim of establishing the time-interval at which the subject just begins to perceive the applied visual stimuli as a continuous light (increasing frequency of presentation); and

TABLE X. Critical frequency of flicker-fusion (CFFF) in relation to other indices of lability

| Index of lability | CFFF | Reference |
|---|---|---|
| AOC | 0.64[++] | Ravich-Shcherbo and Shvarts, 1959 |
|  | 0.57[++] | Turovskaya, 1963 |
|  | 0.63[++] | Borisova et al., 1963 |
|  | 0.137 | Nebylitsyn et al., 1965 |
| Speed of visual sensitivity restoration | 0.86[+++] | Borisova et al., 1963 |
|  | 0.87[+++] | Shvarts, 1963 |
|  | 0.80[+++] | Shvarts, 1965 |
| Photic driving reaction of high frequency | 0.33; 0.54[+] | Golubeva and Shvarts, 1965[a] |
|  | −0.080; −0.082 | Nebylitsyn et al., 1965[b] |
|  | −0.002—−0.058 | Nebylitsyn et al., 1965[c] |
|  | 0.594[++] | Golubeva and Guseva, 1972[d] |

a. The following frequency bands were used: 16–30 and 35–80 Hz.
b. Frequencies of 18 and 28 Hz were applied.
c. Four different frequencies in gamma band (35–80 Hz) were used.
d. The PDR to stimuli 25 Hz was measured.
   For significant data see Table V.

conversely, when the subject is able to perceive the exposed stimuli as separate flashes (descending frequency of application). These moments are recognized as the critical frequency of flicker-fusion (CFFF). The higher the frequency of the separate presentations of the light spot at which the subject perceives the stimuli as separate presentations the higher the CFFF and the higher the lability of NP. Low CFFF is an index of low lability (inertia) of the NS. The CFFF has been used by many Teplov and Nebylitsyn students as the referent method for diagnosing the lability of NS (Shvarts, 1960, 1965; Turovskaya, 1963; Golubeva, 1972b, 1980a; Golubeva and Shvarts, 1965; Golubeva et al., 1977a; Ravich-Shcherbo, 1976; Rusalov, 1979; Panteleyeva, 1975). Table X presents consistency data for this indicator of lability as compared with other measures used to diagnose this NS property.

Kashin (1974) who, together with Bundych (1974), has made efforts to standardize the techniques for measuring NS properties, gives some evidence for the reliability of the CFFF. The split-half reliability is 0.967 ($p < 0.001$), whereas stability is 0.878 ($p < 0.001$). Bundych (1974) computing thresholds of flicker differentiation and flicker fusion separately, obtained similar results: internal consistency—0.969 and 0.866; stability—0.898 and 0.722, all of these highly significant.

Click-fusion frequency (CFF) is sometimes used instead of CFFF (Golubeva and Rozhdestvenskaya, 1969; Bundych, 1974; Kashin, 1974; Kozlova, 1974; Rusalov and Kotov, 1980). Critical frequency of flashing phosphene (CFFP) is sometimes though very seldom recommended for diagnosing the lability of NS (Nebylitsyn, 1972a; Bundych, 1974). Both latter methods are based on exactly the same principle except that acoustic stimuli are used for CFF and electric stimuli for CFFP. The correlation between CFFF and CFF is very low (0.18) and insignificant (Kashin, 1974), thus exemplifying the extent to which the diagnosis of lability based on these methods is affected by the specificity of the modality (visual–auditory) under control.

## Speed of Visual Sensitivity Restoration

There are individual differences in the speed with which the magnitude of visual sensitivity threshold is reinstored after a presentation of strong light. Shvarts (1959) hypothesized, that this speed depends on the lability of given nerve centres; on the ability of the nerve cells to change rapidly their functional state. The speed of termination of nervous processes in the visual analyser is in this case again treated as a function of individual lability. High speed of visual sensitivity restoration after application of a light stimulus is taken as an index of high lability of the NS and vice versa. In individuals with inert nervous systems the restoration of baseline (initial) visual sensitivity after light stimulation takes longer.

The experiment which enables the speed of visual sensitivity restoration to be measured runs as follows: after adaptation to darkness (about 50 min) the visual sensitivity threshold is measured; next, a bright light (20–25 lux) is applied for a period of 10 s; again, the visual sensitivity threshold is measured several times (5–6) with a time-interval of 1 min. It has been stated that the speed of visual sensitivity restoration varies from 1 to 4.5 min.

Tables IX and X present data on the construct validity of this lability index as compared with AOC and CFFF. In further investigations the speed of visual sensitivity restoration was also compared with EEG indices of lability. Golubeva (1972b) found that the speed of visual sensitivity restoration correlated with the photic driving reaction measured by total energy in 1.5–80 Hz band (0.54; $p < 0.02$) and in 35–80 Hz band (0.58; $p < 0.02$).

This index of lability used for the first time in Teplov's laboratory in the 1960s (Shvarts, 1963, 1965; Golubeva, 1965, 1980a; Golubeva and Shvarts, 1965) lost its popularity in favour of EEG indices which are not biased by peripheral phenomena as is the case with visual sensitivity restoration.

## Photic Driving Reaction (PDR) in Beta Band

The photic driving reaction (PDR) discovered by Adrian and Matthews (1934) and used since the early 1950s as an indicator of several temperamental features (e.g. Mundy-Castle, 1953) has also been used by neo-Pavlovian typologists as an indicator of NS properties (in diagnosing NS strength—see p. 92). Golikov (1950) and Kopylov (1956), taking as a point of departure the operational definition of lability given by Vvedensky, according to which

> lability (functional mobility) is the largest number of electric waves which the given physiological apparatus can reproduce per second in accordance with the rhythm of maximum stimulation (cited by Golubeva, 1972b, p. 22)

have shown that PDR to high frequency may be treated as a measure of lability.

In the Teplov–Nebylitsyn school this index was first propagated by Golubeva and her students (Golubeva, 1965, 1972b, 1980a; Golubeva and Guseva, 1972; Golubeva et al., 1974, 1977a). The first evidence collected in Teplov's laboratory (Nebylitsyn et al., 1965; Golubeva, 1965; Golubeva and Shvarts, 1965) showed that among the photic driving reactions for frequencies varying from 2–80 Hz the only ones which correlate significantly with referent indices of lability are high-speed frequencies (35–80 Hz) belonging to the gamma band, and the total energy of all frequencies used (see Table XI). The adequate optical chronaxie (AOC), the critical frequency of flicker fusion (CFFF), and the visual sensitivity restoration were used as indices of lability. According to Golubeva and Shvarts (1965) the evidence collected in Teplov's laboratory supports Kopylov's (1965) statement, that

> the upper limit of the driving reaction, i.e. the greatest amount of local electric responses of the brain synchronized with the rhythm of the afferent stimuli should be treated as a measure of lability of the nerve centres (p. 136).

The first study (and as far as I know the only one published) in which a significant correlation between lability, as measured by CFFF, and PDR in beta band (25 Hz) was found, was conducted by Golubeva and Guseva (1972). These authors used the frequency 25 Hz on the ill-founded premise that this frequency had been used as the index of lability in other studies, which does not follow from the literature. Since then only the photic driving reaction in beta band frequencies has been accepted as the indicator of lability. Golubeva et al. (1974) as well as Guseva and Shlakhta (1974) factor analysed the results of many EEG indices, including PDR to frequencies varying from 4–30 Hz and were able to separate the PDR to 18, 25, and 30 Hz frequencies as an independent factor which they called lability of nervous processes.

Several studies in which PDR to beta band frequencies were used as indices of lability can be mentioned. Golubeva et al. (1977a) used the PDR to 25 Hz as index of this NS property, Izyumova (1977)—to 18, 20, and 25 Hz, Izyumova et al. (1977)—to 18 and 25 Hz. In Ravich-Shcherbo (1976, 1977) as well as in Panteleyeva and Shlakhta's (1978) studies the PDR to frequencies of 18, 25, and 30 Hz was used as the index of lability. After careful study of almost all the papers published by Soviet neo-Pavlovian typologists up to the end of 1981, I did not find any empirical evidence to support the validity of the PDR to frequencies in beta band as an indicator of lability. All coefficients of correlation between PDR to high frequency and the referent indices of lability which I was able to extract from the studies conducted by Nebylitsyn's students are present in Table XI. Regardless of its rather dubious validity, PDR to frequencies in the beta band has been the most popular index of this NS property for the Moscow group over the last 15 years or so.

The procedure used in Teplov's laboratory to measure the photic driving reaction to high frequencies is exactly the same as the one used to measure the strength of the NS on the basis of PDR to stimuli of low frequency (see p. 92). The same is true of techniques for calculating the value of assimilated reactions. The higher the driving coefficient of beta band frequencies the higher, in accordance with the Pavlovian typologists' theory, the lability of the individual and vice versa.

## Total Energy of Beta Rhythm

Golubeva et al. (1974) conducted a study in which 20 different indices of EEG activity were investigated. Frequencies in delta, theta, alpha, beta-1, and beta-2 bands were measured during background activity by total energy indices, photic driving reactions to 4, 6, 18, and 25 Hz, and frequency of alpha rhythm. All measures were recorded from the left and right hemispheres. The results were factor analysed and the authors were able to extract a factor comprising the PDR to 18 and 25 Hz as well as both indices of the total energy of beta rhythm: beta-1

TABLE XI. Photic Driving Reaction (PDR) to high frequencies and standard indices of lability

| PDR | CFFF | AOC | Speed of Visual Sensitivity Restoration |
|---|---|---|---|
| 18 Hz | −0.080<br>Nebylitsyn et al., 1965 | −0.202<br>Nebylitsyn et al., 1965 | |
| 25 Hz | −0.082<br>Nebylitsyn et al., 1965<br>0.594[++]<br>Golubeva and Guseva, 1972 | −0.081<br>Nebylitsyn et al., 1965 | |
| 35 Hz | 0.056<br>Nebylitsyn et al., 1965 | −0.260<br>Nebylitsyn et al., 1965 | |
| 45 Hz | 0.002<br>Nebylitsyn et al., 1965 | −0.382<br>Nebylitsyn et al., 1965 | |
| 60 Hz | −0.002<br>Nebylitsyn et al., 1965 | −0.530[++]<br>Nebylitsyn et al., 1965 | |
| 80 Hz | −0.058<br>Nebylitsyn et al., 1965 | −0.441[+]<br>Nebylitsyn et al., 1965 | |
| Beta band<br>16–30 Hz | 0.33<br>Golubeva and Shvarts, 1965 | ?<br>Golubeva, 1965[a] | |
| Gamma band | 0.54[+]<br>Golubeva and Shvarts, 1965 | −0.426[+]<br>Golubeva, 1965<br>−0.43<br>Golubeva, 1972b[b] | 0.58[+]<br>Golubeva, 1972b |
| Total energy of<br>2–80 Hz | 0.53[+]<br>Golubeva and Shvarts, 1965 | ?<br>Golubeva, 1965[a] | 0.54[+]<br>Golubeva, 1972b |

[a]. The author correlated both variables. The amount of correlation is not given in the table but, as she states, it is not significant.
[b]. It is not clear from the text but it might be the same coefficient quoted in the author's previous study (Golubeva, 1965).

(13–20 Hz) and beta-2 (20–30 Hz). All four indices, separate for left and right hemispheres, had very high factor loadings, varying from 0.898 to 0.994. Since the driving reaction to frequencies 18 and 25 Hz has been recognized as one of the referent methods in diagnosing the lability of NPs (see p. 101) the authors concluded that the total energy values of beta-1 and beta-2 bands might also be treated as indices of lability.

Guseva and Shlakhta (1974) who used 24 different indices of EEG activity, including all those investigated in the above-mentioned study, confirmed, in general, the results of Golubeva *et al.* (1974). The total energy in beta band frequencies (beta-1 and beta-2) measured as background activity has been used thereafter as an index of lability (Golubeva *et al.*, 1977a; Izyumova, 1977; Izyumova *et al.*, 1977; Golubeva, 1980a).

The theoretical justification for the acceptance of the total energy beta band as an indicator of lability is not quite clear. Nebylitsyn (1972b), who tended to equate beta rhythm with the dynamism of excitation, has suggested that it reflects the functioning of activating reticular structures. Golubeva *et al.* (1974) refer to Golikov who had suggested that the beta frequency was directly related to the "impulsive activity of the nerve cells, to the conductance of excitation and the lability of neurons" (p. 172). There are also some data (e.g. Krupnov, 1970) which show that there is a positive correlation between the total energy of beta-2 band and such behavioural indices as speed and variety of reactions.

The procedure applied by neo-Pavlovian typologists to evaluate the total energy of beta band frequencies is standard in EEG investigation. The higher the value of total energy of the beta band (beta-1 and beta-2) the higher the individual's NS lability.

## DIAGNOSIS OF MOBILITY OF THE NERVOUS PROCESSES

### Alteration of the Signal Value of Applied Stimuli

As has been mentioned in Chapter 1 the alteration of the signal value of applied stimuli seemed to be the most classical index of mobility, understood in the Pavlovian sense as the speed with which the NS responds to changes in the surroundings. Teplov, who subdivided the Pavlovian concept of mobility into mobility in its narrow sense and lability of nervous processes, has accepted the position, that "in practice mobility is that property of the nervous system which is characterized by alteration of stimulus signs" (1963a, p. 37).

The procedure for measuring mobility by the alteration of the signal value of applied stimuli has been directly transferred from Pavlov's laboratory to human studies. The essence of this technique consists of evoking a positive CR to one stimulus and a negative CR (inhibitory response) to another. Both stimuli are presented alternately. When both of the CRs (positive and inhibitory) to a stimuli are consolidated

## 2. Laboratory Methods used by Neo-Pavlovian Typologists

the experimenter changes the signal value of the pair of stimuli. The positive stimulus, no longer reinforced, becomes negative, and the negative stimulus, now reinforced changes its value into positive. The speed with which the subject is able to react adequately to the reversed value of the pair of stimuli, usually measured by the number of presentations needed, is the most popular index of mobility of the nervous system. The fewer stimuli with changed signal value that are needed to evoke adequate changes in the individual's conditioned responses, the higher his mobility. In the experimental procedure different UCSs and CSs have been used and different reactions have been investigated (e.g. GSR, photochemical reflex).

The classical alteration paradigm has been transferred to RT experiments, where sensory (visual and/or auditory) or verbal stimuli are used (Rokotova, 1954; Gurevich, 1959a, 1959b; Kolchenko, 1965; Borisova, 1969; Kashin, 1974; Strelau et al., 1974; Vasilets, 1978; Troshikhin et al. 1978). Two or more stimuli are presented to the subject. To one (or more) of these he has to press a key (or different keys) and to the other (or more) the subject is asked not to react. After adequately consolidating the motor reactions to the stimuli, the subject is instructed to react in an opposite way, i.e. the subject has to press the key (keys) to stimuli which were formerly negative and to stop pressing the key (keys) to stimuli which were of positive value before the new instruction. Changes in RT after alteration in relation to RT before the instruction and/or the number of presentations needed to react adequately to the changed signal value of applied stimuli are used as indices of mobility.

The alteration method, alongside the speed of elaboration of CR with delay is the only method for measuring mobility in animals. In the last few years it has lost its popularity in human investigation. As has been shown in Chapter 1, the speed of alteration is influenced by the strength of the NS and, moreover, it is questionable whether mobility measured by the ability to transform positive CRs into negative (inhibitory) ones, and vice versa, may be treated as a manifestation of temperament or whether this ability belong to the domain of learning ability, as illustrated by Bitterman (1965).

### Speed of Reaction Change to Rapidly Changing Stimuli

Functional mobility which is manifested, according to Vvedensky, in the largest number of units of excitation which a given nerve tissue can reproduce, in accordance with the rhythm of maximum stimulation (see p. 101). Correspondingly, in Pavlov's view on mobility, which is manifested in the speed with which the NS responds to changes in the surroundings, these units have been used as starting-points for several techniques applied in TNS investigation.

One of the most popular groups of methods which refer to this conceptualization of mobility are the motor or verbal reaction techniques based on the principle of increasing speed of stimuli presentation. The maximum speed of applied stimuli to which the subject reacts faultlessly or with minimal mistakes provides an index of mobility. Troshikhin *et al.* (1978) emphasized that the activity of subjects in this experimental situation consists of differentiation of stimuli in time-deficit conditions in which functional mobility may occur. As stressed by the authors the value of the mobility index in this procedure depends on several variables, i.e. speed of motion, after-effect of NP, speed of functional readiness of the CR apparatus to perform a new reaction, ability of the NS to assimilate the enforced rhythm. For these reasons the authors prefer to speak of functional mobility instead of mobility of nervous processes, a term used by Pavlov and most Pavlovian typologists.

As far as I know, Saprykin and Mileryan (1954) were the first to try to diagnose the mobility of the NS in experimental conditions based on the above principles. A series of eight differently coloured bulbs were presented to the subject at random, with the task of pressing one of the eight buttons of the same colour as the stimuli. The experimenter modified the intervals between stimuli and seven different speeds of presentation were used. Malkov (1957), measuring mobility with this method, used stimuli with changes in frequencies ranging from 30 to 120 per minute. The shorter the interval between the stimuli to which the subject was able to react adequately, the higher his mobility.

The experimental procedure developed by the Ukrainian psychologist Khilchenko (1958) and improved by his students (Troshikhin *et al.*, 1978) became the most popular psychological technique for diagnosing mobility of the NS. Three hundred different words are presented on a screen with intervals from 0.5 to 4.0 s. The words belong to three groups: animals, plants, or inanimate objects. After checking if the words are familiar to the subject, he is asked to press the left key with the left hand to words which belong to the animal category, the right key with the right hand to words from the plant category, and not to react to words belonging to the inanimate object category. Reactions to unfamiliar words are not taken into account. The presentation starts with the largest interval which is reduced until the subject begins to make mistakes. More than 5% of mistakes during 50 presentations of the same frequency is the criterion for accepting a given time-interval as the index of mobility. If one refers to Pavlovian terminology it could be said that this method primarily enables measurement of the mobility of the second signal system (on the level of verbal behaviour). There are also some variants of this method. One elaborated by Khilchenko (1958; Khilchenko et al., 1966) consists of using different geometrical figures—circles, squares, and triangles—other conditions being the same as described above.

Borisova (1969b), developed Khilchenko's idea into a relatively standardized choice RT procedure. In her experiment three different sounds are presented to the subject, at which he has to press the right key with the right hand (400 Hz) and the left key with the left hand (3000 Hz), or not react at all (1200 Hz). The duration of presentation is 200 s. The interval varies from 2600 ms to 600 ms, with systematic changes of 200 ms after 60–80 randomly presented stimuli.

To eliminate the influence of the strength of NS in diagnosing the mobility, Vasilets (1974) used the Khilchenko–Borisova method but held constant the intensity of stimuli. Auditory stimuli with intensity of 50 dB above the individual's sensitivity threshold were used. As mentioned in Chapter 1, the same author (Vasilets, 1978) investigating 25 different indices of mobility based on RT experiments, has shown that the speed of reaction change to rapidly changing stimuli, as measured by the Khilchenko–Borisova method, is the only one to be strongly determined by genetic factors determined in a twin study.

In the Pavlovian typology literature many studies are described in which the Khilchenko method is used, sometimes with different modifications (Rabinovich, 1961; Khlebutina, 1962; Gorbunov, 1973; Shevko et al., 1973; Akimova, 1974; Kozlova, 1975, 1977; Ravich-Shcherbo, 1976; Kordyukova, 1977). The most systematic study using the Khilchenko method to diagnose mobility has been conducted by Troshikhin et al. (1978). They measured the stability of this index in six groups of subjects differing in age from 5 to 30 years, and with an interval between two successive measures ranging from two to four years. All of the six correlation coefficients were statistically significant ($p < 0.01$) and ranged from 0.54 to 0.95. In several studies (e.g. Vasilets, 1974, 1978; Troshikhin et al., 1978) it has been found that the speed of reaction change to rapidly changing stimuli does not correlate with the alteration of the signal value of exposed stimuli. This may be because in the former method, the subject is familiar with both the stimuli, and the relevant reactions and the ability to react to rapidly changing stimuli is the most important factor to influence the efficiency of behaviour. As stressed several times, learning is involved in the alteration method and the ability to learn how to react to changes in the signal value of stimuli (without time-limits between applications) is the main factor to determine the final behavioural outcome.

For the reader interested in measuring mobility by the Khilchenko method the monograph by Troshikhin and his collaborators may serve as the most solid source of information.

## BACKGROUND ALPHA RHYTHM CHARACTERISTICS AS INDICES OF EQUILIBRIUM OF EXCITATION AND INHIBITION (ACTIVATABILITY)

By definition, dynamism of excitation is manifested in the efficiency of elaborating positive CRs, whereas dynamism of inhibition is reflected in the formation of negative classical CRs, e.g. extinction or differentiation (Nebylitsyn, 1972a; see also Chapter 1). At the beginning of the 1960s Nebylitsyn (1963b) using the EEG procedure, found that the speed of conditioning (positive and negative), as well as the speed of habitation of the orienting response (which he used as one of the referent methods for measuring dynamism of the inhibitory process), correlates with indices of background alpha activity. This relationship was especially vivid in the alpha index. Since it correlated with both the efficiency of elaborating positive CRs and with the speed of extinction of both CRs and OR, the alpha index became the principal measure of balance of excitation and inhibition in dynamism. As quoted in Chapter 1 "alpha index similarly reflects both dynamism of inhibition and dynamism of excitation" (Nebylitsyn, 1972a, p. 92). Nebylitsyn (1963b) also factor analysed 18 different indices of dynamism of the NS and found that all characteristics of background alpha activity used in the study—alpha index, amplitude, and frequency of alpha rhythm—constitute one factor together with the referent CR indices of dynamism and with the indices characterizing the speed of OR extinction. As a rule, they did not have statistically significant factor loadings in any of the three other factors extracted by Nebylitsyn. This allowed him to label this factor "balance of nervous processes".

The existence of the background alpha activity syndrome in the factor called "balance in dynamism", or just "balance" has been supported by several other studies conducted in Nebylitsyn's laboratory (see Ravich-Shcherbo and Shibarovskaya, 1972; Guseva, 1975; Izyumova, 1980). The interrelation of background alpha rhythm indices was found many years ago in the West (e.g. Roget, 1960), and Gastaut (1954) and Werre (1957), taking into account the alpha index and the amplitude and frequency of the alpha rhythm, elaborated a typology, dividing subjects into hyper- and hypo-excitable individuals.

## 2. Laboratory Methods used by Neo-Pavlovian Typologists 109

Since the mid-1960s (Nebylitsyn, 1965), the total energy of the alpha rhythm has also been used as the indicator of balance in dynamism. As Nebylitsyn writes:

> Insofar as summed energy of alpha-rhythm is concerned, this index, which seems to be a product of alpha amplitude and alpha-index, correlates with indices of dynamism at approximately the same or somewhat higher level than does amplitude; at the same time the correlations show the same trend as that with alpha-index (1972a, p. 90).

The CR procedure for diagnosing the balance of the NS gradually lost its popularity and has been subsequently replaced by indices of background alpha rhythm. Most of the studies concerned with dynamism use more than one index of rest alpha rhythm. Some authors have taken the whole background alpha activity syndrome into account (Ravich-Shcherbo and Trifonova, 1967; Aleksandrova, 1969; Ravich-Shcherbo and Shibarovskaya, 1972; Zhorov and Sitkovskaya, 1974; Guseva, 1975; Shibarovskaya, 1978; Izyumova, 1980). Sometimes only two EEG indices of balance in dynamism are used (Rozhdestvenskaya et al., 1967; Golubeva et al., 1974; Golubeva, 1980c; Pasynkova et al., 1980). If only one index of rest alpha rhythm activity is applied to measure balance in dynamism it is usually the alpha index which is generally accepted as the most valid criterion for diagnosing balance in dynamism (Nebylitsyn, 1965; Nebylitsyn et al., 1965; Golubeva, 1965; Gurevich, 1965; Shlakhta, 1972; Halmiova and Uherik, 1972). Sometimes, however, only alpha rhythm frequency is used to diagnose this NS property (Golubeva and Guseva, 1972; Leites et al., 1980).

Balance in dynamism measured by the speed of positive and inhibitory CR formation, proposed by Nebylitsyn, should be regarded as classical indices of dynamism of excitation and inhibition. Balance in dynamism understood as the equilibrium of unconditioned excitation and inhibition measured by background EEG indices of alpha rhythm, is proposed by Golubeva (1980b) to be labelled as equilibrium of dynamism. It has been also argued in Chapter 1 that equilibrium of excitation and inhibition has often recently been replaced by the notion of activatability, a term introduced to Pavlovian typology at the beginning of the 1970s (see p. 38).

According to Nebylitsyn and his students high alpha index, high amplitude, high scores of total energy of alpha rhythm, and its low frequency reflect the predominance of inhibition over excitation; in other words, low activatability. Low alpha index, low amplitude, low scores of total energy, and high frequency of alpha rhythm on the other hand, are used as indicators of the domination of excitation over inhibition, i.e. high activatability.

The procedures for measuring the alpha index as well as the other indices of background alpha rhythm are standard ones, therefore there is no reason to describe them here. As is well known, the same indices of EEG background activity may be found in many publications as indicators of other psychophysiological phenomena, especially as indices of activation understood as a state or a trait, and as correlates of several personality dimensions (Moruzzi and Magoun, 1949; Lindsley, 1952; Gastaut *et al.*, 1951; Mundy-Castle, 1957; Becker-Carus, 1971; Gale, 1973, 1981).

# 3
# The Temperament Inventory as a Result of Studies in Methods for Diagnosing Nervous System Properties

Since 1956, I have been strongly involved in Pavlovian typology, with a special interest in the laboratory methods used to diagnose nervous system properties. It is not my purpose here to give an exhaustive description of my own research in this area because it has been published in detail in two previous books (Strelau, 1965a, 1969) and in several papers, including one written in English (Strelau, 1972a). In general I must conclude that this research convinced me of a large discrepancy in the diagnosis of the separate nervous system properties (NSP) depending on the kind of variables under investigation in laboratory conditions. This is the so-called partiality phenomenon which has been studied especially by the Teplov–Nebylitsyn group (see Chapter 1). However, at the experimental level, this group has limited the partial NSP almost exclusively to inter-modality differences.

## DISCREPANCIES IN THE ESTIMATION OF NERVOUS SYSTEM PROPERTIES DIAGNOSED IN LABORATORY CONDITIONS

Nebylitsyn (1957), who stated that the diagnosis of strength of the NS (based, among other things, on the extinction with reinforcement method) may vary depending on the kind of CS (auditory versus visual) employed in the experiment, provoked me to conduct a study the aim of which was to see if the diagnosis of mobility showed similar regularities. In that study the alteration of the signal value of a pair of stimuli in a GSR procedure was used as the main index of mobility. The UCS was an electric shock, visual and auditory stimuli were used as CSs. It was found that mobility in the visual system provided no indication of the mobility of these processes in the auditory system and vice versa (Strelau, 1960).

The aim of the next study was to see if the diagnosis of NSPs depends on the kind of UCS used in the CR procedure (Strelau, 1964a, 1965a). The following indices of nervous system properties were used: speed of positive CR formation (dynamism in excitation), speed of negative CR formation (dynamism in inhibition), and the "alteration" method (mobility of nervous processes). Different bulbs served as CSs to the galvanic skin response. Three kinds of UCSs were used: electric shock, high temperature, and strong voluntary distraction of the muscles of the right hand (see Merlin, 1958). The data of this experiment, which seems to be the only one in Pavlovian literature aimed directly at determining the role of reinforcement procedure in the diagnosis of the type of nervous system (TNS), show without doubt that there is a divergence in the diagnosis of NSPs depending on the type of UCS used in the CR procedure. The analysis of data showed that the physiological strength of UCSs, with regard to which there are individual differences, codetermines the stated divergencies in NSP diagnosis. As measures of the physiological strength of the UCSs the RT and magnitude of GSR to these stimuli were used, along with their emotional value estimated on a 5-point rating scale.

In order to obtain a more complete picture of the variables which may influence the diagnosis of NSP I conducted a series of experiments aimed at showing the degree to which the kind of effector, or more generally, the kind of reaction (used as dependent variable) influences the diagnosis in question. This type of investigation has not been undertaken by the Pavlovian typologists. Nebylitsyn, discussing the influence of the effector on NSP estimation wrote:

> Unfortunately such studies have not yet been undertaken with human or animal Ss. Thus the question of the influence of the effector response characteristics on the measurement of nervous system properties remains unanswered (1972a, pp. 275–276).

The studies I have conducted in this area (see Strelau, 1969, 1972a) do not encourage optimistic conclusions. Let me give a short report.

Taking as a point of departure the assumption that the strength of the NS as regards excitation is manifested in efficiency of performance under long-lasting stimulation, two experimental settings were arranged:

(1) the strength of the NS was estimated using the method called "change of simple RT under repeatedly applied stimuli" (see p. 90).

RT was measured to a series of visual stimuli (green light), presented 240 times at 5–7 s intervals;
(2) as an analogous task for measuring strength on the basis of mental activity the Kraepelin test was applied; the subjects worked at this for 80 min. Strength of the NS was measured by comparing the mean number of correctly completed additions at the end of the experiment with the number in the first stage of the experiment.

The comparison study conducted on 25 subjects showed that there is no statistically significant correlation ($r = 0.38; p < 0.1$) between both of these methods aimed at diagnosing the strength of the NS and those based on mental and motor activity.

The next experiment was designed to show whether the kind of reaction measured in the CR procedure influences the diagnosis of strength of the nervous system. As an index of strength the well-established method "extinction with reinforcement" (see p. 77) was used in two variants: photochemical and EEG. In both procedures the same type of UCSs (light) and CSs (sounds) were presented. The results for 24 adult subjects indicate that the diagnosis of strength on the basis of the photochemical reaction does not coincide with the estimation of this property based on the extinction with reinforcement method applied in conditioned alpha blocking ($\rho = -0.142$).

A critical analysis of both above-mentioned experiments led me to conclude that they do not fulfil the methodological requirements necessary to infer effector specificity in diagnosing NSPs. In the first experiment the variables not only differed as to kind of activity (mental versus motor) but also as to criteria used to diagnose strength (RT versus amount of performed mental work). The duration of both experimental procedures was also different. As regards the second experiment the question rises as to the nature of the effector in EEG activity. Taking this critique as a point of departure I conducted one more experiment to determine whether the diagnosis of strength based on the change of simple RT under repeatedly applied stimuli would differ if we took into account two different motor reactions. The RT of the following two responses was measured:

(1) pressing the response key with the forefinger of the right hand (all Ss were right-handed);
(2) making the sound "puff" into a microphone.

In both cases the same stimulus was used (sound of 1000 Hz, 70 dB). 240 applications were presented with a time-interval of 5–7 s, and after every 10 consecutive stimuli the subject was ordered to respond differently—pressing the key, then vocal response etc. or vocal response, then pressing the key. These interchangeable presentations enabled measurement of the strength of the NS on the basis of the two different responses during the same period. The comparison of diagnosis of strength based on two different motor reactions—finger pressing and vocal response—in 34 adult subjects gave a negative result. There was no correlation ($r = 0.043$) between both these estimations differing only in the kind of motor reaction measured.

As may be seen in all three experiments, described in detail elsewhere (Strelau, 1969), attention is focused on diagnosing the strength of the NS. In one of our studies (Strelau *et al.*, 1974) we investigated whether the temporal characteristic of behaviour, measured by motor reaction indices, corresponds with the same characteristic assessed at the level of verbal responses. The following measures were taken:

(i) simple RT;
(ii) choice RT to six different stimuli;
(iii) choice RT with handicap (among six stimuli two of them required altered reactions to every third application);
(iv) alteration of the signal value of a pair of stimuli.

Both series differed not only as regards required reactions (motor versus verbal) but also as to the kind of stimuli used. In one experimental setting verbal stimuli were used and non-verbal ones were used in the other (different bulbs). The results collected from 35 adult subjects are displayed in Table XII. The data are rather pessimistic, irrespective of what behavioural traits these measures indicate. In none of the compared indicators is any correlation between motor and verbal temporal characteristics to be found.

The discrepancy in diagnosis of NSPs stated by the Teplov–Nebylitsyn group as well as by our own studies should not be so surprising if one takes into account the similar results of other investigations where

TABLE XII. Temporal characteristic of behaviour measured on the level of verbal and motor reactions

| Indices of Verbal Reactions | Indices of Motor Reactions | | | |
|---|---|---|---|---|
| | (1) | (2) | (3) | (4) |
| (1) Simple RT | 0.199 | | | |
| (2) Choice RT | | 0.196 | | |
| (3) Choice RT with handicap | | | 0.069 | |
| (4) Alteration | | | | −0.038 |

psychophysiological indices are used as indicators of different states or traits of behaviour (see e.g. Lacy, 1950, 1956; Franks, 1956; Fahrenberg, 1980). Summarizing the results of all the studies mentioned here in a very abbreviated form, one may conclude that the partiality phenomenon is much broader than has been stated by Nebylitsyn (1972a) and can definitely not be limited to the inter-modality differences stressed by that author. Thus my own experience in TNS investigation discouraged me to continue this research and caused growing interest in methods which are not concerned with psychophysiological reactions or laboratory conditions, but which are aimed at diagnosing NSP on the basis of more molar behaviour.

## INTERVIEW AND OBSERVATION AS DIAGNOSTIC METHODS IN PAVLOV'S TYPOLOGY

The diagnosis of TNS or its separate properties on the basis of non-experimental techniques has become especially popular since the beginning of 1950s. One of the methods since developed is the interview, used primarily for diagnosing the TNS in clinical settings (see Birman, 1951; Lang-Belonogova and Kok, 1952; Bakulev and Busalov, 1957; Ilina and Paley, 1959; Cytawa, 1959; Pervomaysky, 1964). The interview proposed by Cytawa (1959), who summarized the investigation of TNS based on this technique and conducted until the end of 1950s, may be mentioned. His interview draft includes 57 questions concerned with different life situations in which NS properties may be revealed. For example, the questions aimed to diagnose the strength of the nervous system deal with such categories of behaviour as:

(a) endurance to strong stimuli;
(b) endurance to long-lasting stimuli;
(c) resistance to external inhibition;
(d) behaviour in highly stimulating social situations.

The interview methods used in Pavlov's typology investigation enable users to make a qualitative characterization of the type of NS. Some attempts have been made by Pervomaysky (1964) to introduce quantitative descriptions; however, they are very global and fall far short of psychometric requirements.

Almost simultaneously the observation method gained considerable popularity in Pavlovian typology research. This method was applied primarily in studies aimed at diagnosing the TNS in children (Davydova, 1954; Gorbacheva, 1954; Samarin, 1954; Basan, 1960;

Gerstmann *et al.*, 1961; Ilina, 1961; Chudnovsky, 1963). Observational techniques were used to diagnose the TNS over a long period, taking into account behaviour in all possible life situations (see Umansky, 1960). Leites' (1956b) study, the purpose of which was to give a psychological characteristic of temperament to three high-school students who differed in TNS, may serve as an example. The unstructured observation was conducted over a period of two years. The diagnosis of the separate NSPs was formulated among others, on the basis of the following indices:

(1) strength of excitation—ability to do long-lasting and intensive work, speed of recovery after fatigue and intensive activity, persistence and ease in coping with obstacles;
(2) strength of inhibition—ability to regain control, ability to refrain from given activity, restrained speech;
(3) mobility of the NS—ease of passing from one activity to another, ability to organize behaviour in situations requiring different kinds of activity, uninhibited social contacts

In some child studies the observation method was used in natural experiments in which the given situations and behaviours provoked by the experimenter's instruction enabled a diagnosis of the TNS within a short period. In most cases games were organized for the children, e.g. block-building (Samarin, 1954), "signalman" (Umansky, 1958), or "driver" (Chudnovsky, 1963).

Without going into details, most of the studies in which the TNS was diagnosed using observation in natural experiments were based on the assumption that the typological features of the child are manifested primarily in motor reactions, in habit formation and modification, habit stability, and speed and strength of motor reactions. Emotional reactions evoked during play and social interaction were also generally taken into account, especially their strength, stability, and duration.

The observation method has also been used to diagnose NSP in adults, especially in natural settings such as sports or professional activities (Biryukova, 1961; Matveyev, 1965; Klimov, 1969). Almost all the interview and observation methods used permit only qualitative characterizing of the TNS or the separate NS properties. Matveyev (1965) attempted to develop a kind of rating scale or rather an observation chart. Behaviour, in which the NSPs are revealed, was estimated on four-point scales (0–3). When a given trait was especially expressed in the behaviour he used the estimation 3!; so, in practice, a five-point scale was really used. This ambiguity in the rating system leads to difficulty in statistical data analysis.

None of the above-mentioned interview and observation methods aimed at diagnosing the NSPs have to my knowledge, any reliability or validity data. Thus no clear-cut conclusions concerning given properties of the NS, or relations between them and different kinds of behaviour, can be derived from the analysis of studies based on these methods.

Dissatisfied with such solutions, mainly because the interview and observation methods used till the mid-sixties could not give a quantitative appraisal of basic NSPs, while such appraisal seemed to be necessary in research on individual differences, I designed a behaviour observation chart with rating scales that did allow quantitative measurement of strength, mobility, and balance of nervous processes.

At this point one should naturally ask how physiological phenomena, among which basic NSPs (i.e. strength, mobility, and balance of nervous processes) must be undoubtedly included, can be measured by observing behaviour—one of psychology's principal assessment methods. I approached this issue—as far as TNS are concerned—in the late 1960s, in an answer to Witoszek's (1967) question as to why typology of the nervous system is studied by psychologists (Strelau, 1969).

The answer still adhered to can be put briefly as follows. Pavlov was interested, above all, in objective examination of the activity of the cerebral hemispheres in animals, i.e. connected external events (stimuli), with various reactions of an animal according to his own conditioning procedure. That is why Pavlov used the term "behaviour" as a synonym of "higher nervous activity" in the title of one of his fundamental works (1952). This fact is pregnant with meaning and I believe that, in a way, it gives a reason for treating Pavlov's "physiology of higher nervous activity" as a "study of behaviour". Refusal to do so is probably caused mostly by prejudiced assumptions with which the study of behaviour in its behaviouristic edition is saturated.

The point made by the Pavlovian theory of behaviour which has influenced contemporary psychology to such an extent as to become its integral part, is that the relationship between stimulus and response is formed at the central nervous system level. Speaking in more general terms, the equilibrium between the organism and its environment is regulated through conditioned reflex activity, with its anatomical basis located in the cerebral hemispheres.

The "physiological" approach to the problem of TNS consists of interpreting certain forms of behaviour, supposed to express temperamental features, by referring to a hypothetical physiological mechanism; namely, to a certain combination of strength, mobility, and balance of nervous processes. The latter are explanatory concepts which we relate to functions of the CNS (see also Gray, 1964; Powell, 1979; Mangan, 1982). It seems Pavlov conceived the matter in a similar way. When he defined strength of excitation, the amount of "excitable substance" in a neuron did not seem to be as relevant as the cell's working or functional capacity. Without going into detail, we must say that Pavlov described such concepts as strength, mobility, and balance of nervous processes in terms of the relation between a given set of stimuli and behaviour (reaction). Thus, the answer to the question of why typology of the nervous system is studied by psychologists depends on how we relate basic NSPs to temperament. Temperament is a psychological concept, circumscribing the field of reality investigated by a psychologist in a general way. Instead, if we use the concept of TNS, conceived here in Pavlovian terms, we should point out that the phenomena composing temperament are based upon a hypothetical physiological mechanism, related by Pavlov and his followers to a set of basic NSPs, i.e. strength, mobility, and balance of nervous processes, constituting the TNS.

After this digression, without which a correct picture of the role and part of psychological methods in research on basic NSPs would not be possible, I shall return to my observation chart, based upon four-point rating scales, which served as a starting point for developing the Strelau Temperament Inventory (STI).

A full description of the observation chart is presented elsewhere (Strelau, 1965b, 1969). I shall only generally mention here that the chart, a kind of standard programme of investigation, comprises 75 questions referring to various kinds of behaviour and different situations. The instrument permits diagnosis of strength of excitation, strength of inhibition, and mobility of nervous processes, with 25 questions for each property. In accordance with Pavlov's conception, balance of nervous processes is determined by comparing strength of excitation scores with strength of inhibition scores. Situations and behaviours (supposed to indicate particular properties) were selected upon an analysis of other methods for diagnosing the TNS in humans (used and described in the literature) and after examining the Pavlovian concepts of strength, mobility, and balance of nervous processes. The procedure for final scoring is described in the above-mentioned books.

## THE STRELAU TEMPERAMENT INVENTORY (STI)

Since the observation chart turned out to be very time-consuming and, thus, impractical, I decided to construct an inventory. For all the reasons discussed above and also considering the fact that an inventory allows measurement of overt behaviour, and not estimation of physiological properties, I named my new technique "The Temperament Inventory". The inventory is designed in such a way that it allows diagnosis of temperament in Pavlovian terms, according to which the physiological mechanism of temperament is built upon hypothetical properties of nervous processes: strength, mobility, and balance of excitation and inhibition; their combination forming the TNS.

The first stage of research on the Temperament Inventory, its reliability and validity, have been presented elsewhere (Strelau, 1969, 1972b). Originally, the inventory listed 50 items for each NSP (strength of excitation, strength of inhibition, and mobility of nervous processes) giving 150 items in all. The items were composed by formulating two parallel questions to each item from the observation chart. This procedure was adopted in order to check the inventory's internal reliability.

Items were arranged and assigned to one half of the inventory or the other at random. A three-point rating scale was employed: "Yes", "No", and "Don't know". Strength of excitation, strength of inhibition, and mobility of nervous processes were calculated from the total scores obtained in each category. As in the observation chart, balance of nervous processes was indicated by the quotient of strength of excitation index divided by the strength of inhibition index.

The internal reliability of the first version of the Temperament Inventory was tested twice and appeared fairly high (see Table XIII). The correlation coefficients computed between the two equivalent parts of the questionnaire were satisfactory; they ranged from 0.72 to 0.93 and were statistically significant.

Validity of the first version of the Temperament Inventory was tested by comparing scores with ratings made with the observation chart.

TABLE XIII. The internal reliability of the first version of the temperament inventory

| Study | Subjects | Strength of Excitation | Strength of Inhibition | Mobility of the NS |
|---|---|---|---|---|
| 1 | N = 27 (15F and 12M) Age: 18–30 | $\rho = 0.85$ | $\rho = 0.81$ | $\rho = 0.82$ |
| 2 | N = 100 (68F and 32M) Age: 17–42 | $r_{tt} = 0.86$ | $r_{tt} = 0.93$ | $r_{tt} = 0.72$ |

All coefficients significant at the 0.01 level

TABLE XIV. The diagnostic validity of the first version of the temperament inventory

| Study | Subjects | Strength of Excitation | Strength of Inhibition | Mobility of the NP |
|---|---|---|---|---|
| 1 | N = 14 (8F and 6M) Age: 21–61 | $\rho = 0.75^a$ | $\rho = 0.84^b$ | $\rho = 0.66^a$ |
| 2 | N = 27 (15F and 12M) Age: 18–30 | $r = 0.49^a$ | $r = 0.17$ | $r = 0.53^a$ |

a. $p < 0.05$
b. $p < 0.01$

Since behaviour was rated on the chart for three months, during which time a subject was observed in various life situations (considerable differences were noted from person to person in this respect), only a small sample could be examined. Diagnostic validity was assessed twice. Results are presented in Table XIV.

Results of the first study, though derived from a small sample, speak for sufficient validity of the inventory. However, results of the second study are quite different, especially when strength of inhibition is considered. This discrepancy was mainly attributed to the fact that as many as six observers were employed for rating the behaviour of 27 subjects from the second study (each observer evaluated four to five subjects during a three-month period), while only two observers participated in the first study. The larger number of evaluators was undoubtedly an undesirable factor. Sanocki (1976) interpreted the low correlation coefficients from the second study by pointing to the fact that the observation chart and the inventory are based upon different types of indicators, and thus, they probably measure different variables, which might indeed be one reason for the weak correlations.

### General Description of the Current Version of the STI

The next stage of investigation, bringing the Temperament Inventory to its present shape, was mainly devoted to an analysis of particular questions. In some cases, the answers given within a paired question were inconsistent with each other. Where 50% or more subjects answered in this manner, those questions were deleted. In total, six questions (three pairs) had to be excluded. Also, those questions which tended to be answered "Don't know" were removed, since these were unclear or ambiguous. In this way, ten questions to which more than

# 3. The Temperament Inventory

25% of subjects gave the answer "Don't know" had to be deleted; five questions were reformulated.

In all, 16 items were excluded, leaving the current version of the Strelau Temperament Inventory (STI) with 134 items—44 for strength of excitation, 44 for strength of inhibition, and 46 for mobility of nervous processes.

Items for diagnosing particular properties of nervous processes are listed below. Each item is represented by two parallel questions (series A and B) with their ordinal position in the inventory indicated in parentheses. The STI is presented in its full form in Appendix 1.

## *Strength of excitation*

1. A(3)    Does a brief rest remove your work fatigue?
   B(56)   Does a night's sleep remove the fatigue caused by a hard day's work?
2. A(7)    Can you forget your fatigue when immersed in work?
   B(82)   Are you capable of working uninterruptedly for a long time?
3. A(15)   Do you easily fall asleep after a strong emotion?
   B(107) Do you find it difficult to fall asleep after a full day of strenuous and fatiguing brainwork?
4. A(19)   In the face of hardships, do you still feel in control of the situation?
   B(106) Can you suppress momentary moods of dejection?
5. A(21)   Do you readily assume responsible jobs?
   B(134) Do you like assignments involving responsibility?
6. A(24)   Do you talk as freely as usual in the presence of a person whom you want to impress?
   B(123) Does your voice fail you in a critical situation?
7. A(39)   When reading a book etc., do you find it easy to follow the author's line of argument from start to finish?
   B(73)   Are you able to concentrate on your work for any length of time?
8. A(47)   Do you often give up plans because of some difficulty?
   B(66)   Are you quick in overcoming obstacles?
9. A(58)   Do you solve your problems by yourself, as a rule?
   B(97)   Are you self-reliant in a critical situation?
10. A(51)   Does noise disturb you at your work?
    B(4)     Can you work in adverse circumstances?
11. A(61)   Can you work (or study) hard?
    B(114) Can you work with great intensity?
12. A(72)   Do you like strenuous occupations?
    B(13)   Do you like occupations which involve mental exertion?
13. A(81)   Can you work as usual when you have had little sleep at night?
    B(45)   Can you work at night after a full day's work?
14. A(94)   Do you preserve your composure having witnessed a road accident?

122          Temperament, Personality, Activity

     B(78)    Having witnessed an unpleasant or distressing sight, can you carry on with your customary efficiency?
15. A(98)    Do you feel at ease in numerous or unknown company?
    B(18)    Do you behave in your customary manner in the presence of strangers?
16. A(105)  Would you question a generally accepted view if you were sure you were right?
    B(122)  Do you consider yourself a person of courage?
17. A(113)  Do you easily submit to painful medical or surgical treatment?
    B(83)    Does a headache or toothache seriously interfere with your work?
18. A(117)  Do you eagerly offer your help in an accident?
    B(102)  In an accident, do you feel an urge to show initiative?
19. A(124)  Are you able to overcome despondency after failure?
    B(23)    Do you easily survive a defeat?
20. A(130)  Do you like to make public addresses?
    B(32)    Do you readily take the floor at meetings or other gatherings?
21. A(132)  Do you feel an urge to rescue people in danger even if this were to endanger your own life?
    B(60)    Would you jump into the water to rescue a drowning person, provided you could swim?
22. A(133)  Are your movements vigorous?
    B(121)  Do you like occupations which require you to perform vigorous movements?

*Strength of inhibition*

1. A(5)    In a discussion, can you resist the temptation to resort to non-substantial, emotional arguments?
    B(110)  Are you able to argue calmly in a heated debate?
2. A(10)   Can you easily keep a confidence?
    B(67)    Do you have difficulty in restraining your curiosity when an opportunity arises to take a look at someone's things or notes?
3. A(16)   Can you refrain from showing your superiority when necessary?
    B(36)    Are you hot-tempered?
4. A(27)   Do you keep calm when waiting for some important announcement which could change the course of your life?
    B(53)    Can you control yourself when waiting for an exam, an unpleasant confrontation, etc.?
5. A(34)   Do you have difficulties in disengaging yourself from a job when engrossed in it?
    B(99)    Can you interrupt a conversation at once when time has run out?
6. A(37)   When working with partners, can you easily fall in step with them?
    B(89)    Are you patient?
7. A(41)   Can you refrain from arguing with someone who is wrong, when such argument is bound to be ineffective?

## 3. The Temperament Inventory

    B(109)  Can you abstain from lodging complaints when these are obviously useless?
8. A(50)  Can you restrain the impulse to react without forethought?
    B(48)  Can you keep calm when the situation requires it?
9. A(52)  Can you resist the temptation to tell people the truth, when restraint is desirable?
    B(62)  Can you refrain from making comments when these are out of place?
10. A(59)  Do you put forward your own arguments before the other party has stopped presenting his?
    B(2)  Are you capable of restraining yourself from doing something until you are given the signal to do it?
11. A(65)  When facing a crucial decision, do you weigh carefully all the "pros" and "cons"?
    B(38)  Do you always think twice before deciding on a course of action?
12. A(69)  Is it easy for you to heed the rules of conduct in public places?
    B(129)  Is it easy for you to heed the rule of conduct accepted in your milieu?
13. A(75)  Do you preserve your calm in difficult situations?
    B(96)  Do you keep calm when seeing the suffering of a person dear to you?
14. A(77)  Having done a job, can you wait patiently for the others to finish theirs, if necessary?
    B(8)  Having asked someone to perform a job, can you wait patiently until it's finished?
15. A(87)  Are you able to work while waiting for guests?
    B(84)  When there is a need to finish a job, do you proceed with it despite the fact that your colleagues are enjoying themselves or waiting for you?
16. A(90)  Are you able to adapt to someone else's tempo of work if it is slower?
    B(30)  Can you easily adjust your gait or eating habits to someone who walks or eats much slower than you?
17. A(103)  Can you restrain a smile when it is out of place?
    B(126)  Are you able to control your mirth if this could hurt someone?
18. A(108)  Are you able to wait quietly in a long queue?
    B(12)  Do you show patience in supplying explanations?
19. A(112)  Can you behave quietly when asked to do so?
    B(35)  Can you refrain from talking when this disturbs someone?
20. A(120)  Can you control your mimicry (pulling faces, smiling ironically, etc.)?
    B(70)  Can you refrain from superfluous gesticulation etc. while talking, addressing a gathering, or passing an oral test?
21. A(125)  Are you able to sit or stand quietly for a long time, when asked to do so?

B(118) Do you refrain from excessive shouting or gesticulation at a sports event?
22. A(128) Are you easily thrown out of gear?
    B(17) Do you have difficulties in controlling irritation or anger?

## Mobility of nervous processes

1. A(6)   Is it easy for you to resume work after a long break (caused by a holiday, or the summer vacations)?
   B(11)  Is it easy for you to resume a task you interrupted some weeks or months ago?
2. A(14)  Do you feel bored or sleepy when performing monotonous work?
   B(68)  Do you get bored when performing stereotyped operations?
3. A(22)  Is your mood usually influenced by your surroundings?
   B(33)  Are you easily upset?
4. A(26)  Do you have a ready answer to every argument?
   B(85)  Are you quick in responding to unexpected questions?
5. A(29)  Are you quick in reacting to unexpected stimuli?
   B(111) Do you react at once to a sudden change in the situation?
6. A(31)  Do you fall asleep quickly when in bed?
   B(9)   Do you easily fall asleep, irrespective of the hour of day, once in bed?
7. A(40)  Are you quick to join in a conversation with fellow travellers?
   B(1)   Do you make friends easily?
8. A(43)  Do you change your mind when confronted with new arguments?
   B(88)  Do you easily change your opinion in the face of cogent arguments?
9. A(46)  Do you read novels quickly?
   B(79)  Are you quick in looking through the day's newspapers?
10. A(54)  Do you quickly get accustomed to a new environment?
    B(28)  Are you quick in settling down when on holiday?
11. A(55)  Do you like frequent changes and diversions?
    B(71)  Do you like to stay in a place full of hustle and bustle?
12. A(63)  Do you prefer to have your permanent seat at work, at the table, in the lecture hall, etc.?
    B(115) Do you readily change your place of entertainment or rest?
13. A(74)  Do you like those occupations which call for quick movements?
    B(42)  Do you like work requiring manual dexterity?
14. A(76)  Do you rise immediately upon wakening when necessary?
    B(49)  Do you wake quickly and without difficulty?
15. A(80)  Does it ever happen that your speech is so fast that it becomes incomprehensible?
    B(86)  Do you speak rapidly?
16. A(92)  Does good-humoured company help you to recover from depression?
    B(127) Do you easily switch from sadness to good humour?

## 3. The Temperament Inventory

17. A(93)  Can you perform several operations at a time without much exertion?
    B(91)  Can you plan your work in such a way as to perform more than one assignment at a time, when this is possible?
18. A(95)  Do you like a job that calls for performing diverse operations?
    B(57)  Do you shun those occupations which involve different operations in quick succession?
19. A(100) Do you easily adapt to the way other people work?
    B(44)  Do you easily get accustomed to a new job routine?
20. A(101) Do you like to change your occupation frequently?
    B(64)  Do you easily switch from one occupation to another?
21. A(116) Do you have difficulties in adapting to a new daily schedule?
    B(25)  Do unexpected changes in your day's schedule irritate you?
22. A(119) Do you like work that involves talking to many people?
    B(20)  Are you capable of adapting your conduct to the behaviour of others in a group when necessary?
23. A(131) Are you quick in starting your work, without tedious preparation?
    B(104) Starting your work, do you get in high gear right at the beginning?

All questions concerning strength of excitation were formulated congruently with the Pavlovian approach stating that this property simply consists in the neuron's working capacity, expressed mainly by functional capacity of the nervous system, i.e. endurance of long-lasting, or short but intense excitation, without passing into protective inhibition. Its measure is the resistance to intensive, long-lasting, or repeated stimulation (Pavlov, 1951–52).

In the STI, such resistance can be determined by ratings on the following categories of questions:

(a) readiness for an action (activity) in highly stimulating situations;
(b) carrying on activity in highly stimulating situations;
(c) lack of emotional disturbances in stress situations (high load of stimulation);
(d) lack of evident changes in efficiency during conditions of intensive or long-lasting stimulation.

Since Pavlov often changed his views on strength of inhibition, especially on the relation between unconditioned and conditioned inhibition (see Chapter 1), certain difficulties were met when formulating questions referring to this property. It seems however, that Pavlov and other investigators dealing with the problem of TNS speak of strength versus weakness of inhibition mostly in terms of conditioned, or learned inhibition. Even the term "weak type" would suggest so, as being chosen by Pavlov to underscore the denoted type's weak excitation and weak conditioned inhibition.

Therefore, we here conceive strength of inhibition after Teplov (1964a) and Nebylitsyn (1972a), i.e. as functional capacity of the NS for conditioned inhibition. In his description of basic indicators of inhibition strength, Pavlov originally mentioned the persistence of inhibition i.e. the amount of time a neuron can remain in an uninterrupted state of conditioned inhibition (Pavlov, 1951–52). In his animal studies, Pavlov noted that weak inhibitory subjects cannot withstand prolonged conditioned inhibition, and may show disturbances of action and even neurosis.

Strength of inhibition defined in the above way is manifested in the following types of behaviour:

(a) restraining from reaction (motor, verbal, emotional);
(b) delay of action;
(c) interruption of action.

All questions referring to strength of inhibition were divided into these categories.

Items for diagnosing mobility of nervous processes perfectly correspond to Pavlov's conception.

> Since the environment undergoes continuous, frequently extreme and abrupt changes, both processes [says Pavlov] have to follow, so to speak, these changes. They should show considerable mobility, capacity for giving way quickly, giving priority to one impulse or another, to excitation or inhibition—as demanded by the situation. (1952, p. 540)

At the level of behaviour, mobility is revealed in capacity for reacting quickly and adequately to changing conditions. All questions for diagnosing mobility referred to this capacity.

Concluding, Pavlov's theory of basic properties of nervous processes served as a criterion for selecting items. Thus, the STI shows high content validity as far as strength of excitation, strength of inhibition, and mobility of nervous processes are conceived in accordance with Pavlov.

The STI does not incorporate the more recent developments in the study of basic features of the NS (e.g. Teplov, 1961; Nebylitsyn, 1972a; and their co-workers). As mentioned before (see p. 29) sensitivity was distinguished by these authors as an opposite pole to working capacity on the strength of excitation dimension. I believe that the sensitivity factor should be included in the future in the STI, the more so because it is one of the links between the conception of NS strength and several other dimensions which refer to biologically determined individual differences in behaviour.

Moreover, the STI does not pretend to diagnose dynamism of nervous processes—a feature assumed by Teplov and Nebylitsyn (1963a) to be independent of strength and mobility (see p. 33). Balance of nervous processes was also conceived in the STI according to the Pavlovian tradition, i.e. as a secondary feature depending on the relation between strength of excitation and strength of inhibition (see p. 8).

## A Psychometric Characteristic of the STI

In contrast with the majority of temperament and personality inventories, the proposed diagnostic tool did not develop from factor analysis, but instead was generated from a definite theory of basic NSPs, as developed by Pavlov and his followers and verified over several decades.

I was very much surprised with the popularity of my inventory, used in its above-described form for many years. As I have already mentioned, there is no other inventory, as far as I know, for measuring basic NSPs and, hence, temperament, according to Pavlovian theory. Perhaps, that is the reason for the STI's popularity.

The Temperament Inventory has been translated into English, Russian, German, French, Spanish, and Slovakian. It has been used abroad mostly by psychologists trying to relate the conception of TNS to those personality dimensions that are largely biologically determined (see Chapter 4).

Under such circumstances, I decided to set aside my main interests, focused on psychophysiological individual differences, and present some data from my co-workers' and my own studies that could tell us something about the psychometric value of the STI.

### Distribution of scores

I shall start the psychometric description by discussing the distribution of STI scores. The normality of distributions of scores on particular NSPs was tested in male and female students aged 18–24 years. Results are presented in Table XV.

As can be seen in Table XV, the distributions of strength of excitation and mobility are fairly close to normal, which cannot be said about strength of inhibition, and less so about balance of nervous processes. Distributions of the two latter properties do not meet the parameters of a normal curve. Certainly, the non-normal distribution of strength of

TABLE XV. Distribution of scores for basic nervous system properties obtained by students of both sexes

| NSP | N | M | SD | Me | Approximation to Normal Distribution |
|---|---|---|---|---|---|
| Strength of excitation (E) | 235 | 49.8 | 11.8 | 49 | Close (55%) |
| Strength of inhibition (I) | 241 | 60.6 | 11.3 | 62 | Distant (15%) |
| Mobility (M) | 242 | 56.0 | 10.7 | 56 | Moderate (30%) |
| Balance (B) | 234 | 0.85 | 0.3 | 0.8 | No resemblance (below 0.01%) |

inhibition accounts for the distribution of balance which, as we know, is secondary to strength of excitation and inhibition.

It is often remarked that temperamental features differ in value across sexes. In order to verify this statement, the distributions were examined separately for males (aged 18–34) and females (18–30). The subjects were students and white-collar workers with higher education. Results are presented in Table XVI.

The approximation to normal distribution did not change significantly after dividing the total sample. Distribution of balance again did not meet the parameters of the normal curve in either sex group. Distribution of strength of inhibition was even more deviated from normality in females. Moreover, the distribution of mobility was skewed in females, giving a poor resemblance to the normal curve.

Our distributions characterized in Tables XV and XVI are not all consistent with the results obtained by Stawowska. Her study included 2520 subjects (1255 females and 1265 males) aged 17–60 and yielded normal distributions for all four NSPs (see Stawowska, 1973, 1977). In a comparative study of strength of excitation and mobility of nervous processes in Warsaw and Moscow female students, Klonowicz (1979b) also obtained normal distributions in both groups. Vyatkina (1976) investigating strength of excitation and mobility in teachers (35–45 years) obtained a normal distribution of these traits.

Considering all the studies aimed at testing the normal distribution of basic nervous properties, we must state that such a distribution is at least true for strength of excitation and mobility of nervous processes. These two properties have especially drawn our interest.

Looking at Table XVI, we can notice that distribution of basic NSPs differs across sexes. All the four properties, i.e. strength of excitation,

TABLE XVI. Distributions of scores for basic NS properties obtained by females and males

| Sex | NSP | M | SD | Me | Approximation to Normal Distribution |
|---|---|---|---|---|---|
| F | E | 48.0 | 12.94 | 48 | Close (50%); $X^2 = 20.96; df = 22$ |
|   | I | 55.7 | 15.91 | 58 | No resemblance (about 0.05%); $X^2 = 37.35; df = 19$ |
|   | M | 57.1 | 12.43 | 58 | Distant (about 15%); $X^2 = 25.97; df = 20$ |
|   | B | 0.94 | 0.40 | 0.86 | No resemblance (about 0.01%); $X^2 = 55.32; df = 23$ |
| M | E | 57.7 | 15.92 | 60.5 | Moderate (40%); $X^2 = 20.27; df = 20$ |
|   | I | 60.9 | 15.85 | 62 | Close (80%); $X^2 = 10.06; df = 15$ |
|   | M | 59.4 | 13.13 | 61 | Moderate (20%); $X^2 = 24.79; df = 21$ |
|   | B | 0.99 | 0.39 | 0.95 | No resemblance (about 0.01%); $X^2 = 34.49; df = 16$ |

strength of inhibition, mobility, and balance, are significantly more marked in males. Stawowska (1973) also found males to show higher strength of excitation and inhibition in her mass testing mentioned before, while mobility and balance did not differ between the two groups. As has been indicated by Goryńska (1982; see p. 202), the distribution of the temporal characteristic of behaviour differs between sexes, depending on whether reaction persistence or reaction recurrence, and mobility, speed and tempo are considered. All the presented findings suggest that research with the STI should pay attention to sex specificity. Also, separate norms for males and females should be established, as done by Stawowska (1977).

*Reliability of the STI*

Some information on the reliability of the STI has also been gathered. Reliability was tested by two principal methods. Namely, internal reliability was measured by correlating the two equivalent series (A and B) of the STI (split-half reliability), and retest reliability was examined. Results of the internal reliability testing are presented in Table XVII.

We have to admit that the internal reliability is not very high, particularly in the case of mobility and strength of inhibition, where correlation coefficients fell below 0.707, taking this quantity as the critical coefficient of determination (Guilford, 1956). Scores were obtained from the same sample that served for distribution testing (see Table XV). Since the study was conducted in the early 1970s, I cannot

TABLE XVII. Internal reliability of the STI

| NSP | N | r |
|---|---|---|
| E | 235 | 0.70 |
| I | 241 | 0.68 |
| M | 242 | 0.63 |
| B | 234 | 0.73 |

All coefficients significant at the 0.001 level

present any extra information about the subjects, which could perhaps explain the reason for these fairly low correlations.

Stability of scores was tested twice in students and white-collar workers, the sample consisting of males and females aged 18–34. Table XVIII contains results obtained in the two testings: one covering a 6–15 month lapse between measurements, and the other covering a 13–15 month lapse.

Considering the fact that the lapse between measurements was relatively long, exceeding even one year in the second testing, the obtained stability indices seem to be sufficiently high.

Terelak (1982) has measured the retest reliability of the STI in 20 subjects (men, 23–52 years old) sampled in an Antarctic expedition group. The results of retest estimation after a year of isolation are presented in Table XIX.

As may be seen there is no significant change in the estimation of strength of the NS (as regards excitation and inhibition) whereas mobility of the NS showed some increase, a result rather difficult to explain. Taking as a point of departure Eliasz's (1981) hypothesis concerned with the active and passive physiological mechanism of

TABLE XVIII. The stability of measurement of NS properties

| NSP | Test 1 (6–15 months) | | Test 2 (13–15 months) | |
|---|---|---|---|---|
| | N | r | N | r |
| E | 216 | 0.677 | 129 | 0.632 |
| I | 241 | 0.692 | 136 | 0.700 |
| M | 241 | 0.594 | 136 | 0.586 |
| B | 195 | 0.610 | 127 | 0.660 |

All coefficients significant at the 0.001 level

TABLE XIX. Changes in NS properties during one year of Antarctic isolation
(taken from Terelak, 1982)

| Measure | Strength of E | | Strength of I | | Mobility of NP | |
|---|---|---|---|---|---|---|
| | $M$ | $SD$ | $M$ | $SD$ | $M$ | $SD$ |
| Before expedition | 68.20 | 9.03 | 72.6 | 10.67 | 61.7 | 10.97 |
| | | | | | $\updownarrow p < 0.05$ | |
| After expedition | 66.9 | 9.68 | 70.1 | 13.48 | 65.5 | 11.96 |

regulation of stimulation (see p. 182) one could assume that the Antarctic environment, rather devoid of variation and novelty, may cause a kind of sensitization of this kind of behaviour revealed, among other things, in the increase of mobility features.

*Validity testing*

As I have already mentioned, I have never factor analysed the basic NSPs distinguished by Pavlov, although such analysis has been accomplished at the level of psychophysiological measurement at Teplov's laboratory (see Nebylitsyn, 1972a), suggests that Pavlov's traits are virtually independent. One hundred and thirty-four items from the STI in its French version were factor analysed by Carlier (in press) yielding four factors:

*Factor I*, comprising items referring exclusively to strength of excitation and mobility;
*Factor II*, including items referring almost exclusively to strength of inhibition;
*Factor III*, saturated mostly with items for strength of excitation;
*Factor IV*, containing items concerning mobility and strength of inhibition.

Carlier did not obtain any independent factor that could correspond to Pavlov's mobility of nervous processes. Table XX presents correlations between the four factors distinguished by Carlier and STI scales.

Similar results were obtained by Paisey and Mangan (1980) who factor analysed the English version of the STI. The higher-order analysis which emerged from sixteen obliquely-rotated factors yielded six second-order factors. The authors showed that the first second-order factor combines strength of excitation and mobility of the nervous system, the second reflects strength of inhibition, the third represents the negative pole of strength of inhibition. Most interesting is the fact,

TABLE XX. Correlations between NS properties and factors distinguished in factor analysis of STI items (taken from Carlier, in press)

| NSP | Factors | | | |
|---|---|---|---|---|
|  | I | II | III | IV |
| E | 0.72[a] | 0.29[a] | 0.52[a] | 0.07 |
| I | −0.08 | 0.89[a] | 0.18[a] | 0.28[a] |
| M | 0.66[a] | −0.13 | 0.06 | 0.47[a] |

a. $p < 0.05$

Carlier did not include balance, a secondary feature of the NS, in her analysis. Data were collected from 202 subjects, including 30 males (aged $Me = 20$) and 172 females (aged $Me = 21$).

which appears in both factor analysis studies, that mobility does not seem to be an independent factor and cannot be separated from the strength of excitation—a finding also supported by our intercorrelation analysis (see Tables XXI and XXII) based on several studies conducted in our laboratory.

Terelak (1974) obtained similar data in his study on pilots. For certain research purposes, he distinguished pilots with high alpha indices (N = 95) and low alpha indices (N = 115). The subjects were males aged 20–45.

Zarzycka (1980) intercorrelated the same properties in her study of determinants of accidents caused by train drivers. She distinguished 59 male accident makers in a random sample of train drivers (N = 174). Results obtained in the two studies are combined in Table XXI.

The Table contains correlation coefficients computed between the four basic NSPs. Correlations were obtained in four samples representing different populations. Some general regularities can be noted. In all four samples, significant positive correlations were obtained between strength of excitation and strength of inhibition (coefficients ranging from 0.448 to 0.614), and between strength of excitation and mobility (0.564–0.713). Positive, though weak correlations were also found between strength of inhibition and mobility (0.198–0.405) in each sample. The remaining intercorrelations were discordant across samples. For instance, while Terelak found positive correlations between certain properties (e.g. mobility and balance), Zarzycka noted negative ones. In contrast, negative coefficients in Zarzycka's study (e.g. between excitation strength and balance) were positive according to Terelak.

TABLE XXI. Correlations between scores on particular NS properties

| NSP | Terelak (1974) | | | | Zarzycka (1980) | | | |
|---|---|---|---|---|---|---|---|---|
| | E | I | M | B | I | | M | B |
| E |  | 0.589[c] | 0.595[c] | 0.282[b] |  | 0.522[b] | 0.564[b] | −0.579[b] |
| I | 0.448[c] |  | 0.283[b] | −0.555[c] | 0.405[b] |  | 0.198[b] | 0.180[a] |
| M | 0.713[c] | 0.305[b] |  | 0.266[b] | −0.249 |  |  | −0.388[b] |
| B | 0.535[c] | −0.465[c] | 0.385[c] |  |  |  | −0.398[b] |  |

(Sectors marked on the table: A, B, C, D)

Sector A — pilots with low alpha indices
Sector B — pilots with high alpha indices
Sector C — random sample of train drivers
Sector D — train drivers, accident makers

a. $p < 0.05$
b. $p < 0.01$
c. $p < 0.001$

TABLE XXII. Pearson's correlations ($r$) between strength of excitation, strength of inhibition, and mobility of nervous processes

| Number of Subjects and Sex | NSP | E | NSP I | M |
|---|---|---|---|---|
| 159 67M and 92F | E | | $0.390^a$ | $0.597^a$ |
| 159 67M and 92F | I | $0.390^a$ | | 0.088 |
| 159 67M and 92F | M | $0.597^a$ | 0.088 | |

$a. p < 0.01$

Results of my own research (with balance excluded) presented in Table XXII confirm the regularities stated by Terelak and Zarzycka with regard to correlations between strength of excitation and strength of inhibition, and between strength of excitation and mobility.

Considering now only those results that appeared to be consistent in all four samples and were confirmed by our own data, we must say that strength of excitation and strength of inhibition are not orthogonal properties at all, as could be expected. In a way, the above-stated relation between strength of excitation and strength of inhibition supported Pavlov's (1951–52) assumptions, according to which both these processes should be strong in the strong type, weak in the weak type, and a relative predominance of excitation over inhibition should exist in the unbalanced type.

Interesting is the comparatively high and positive correlation between strength of excitation and mobility of nervous processes which is in line with the factor analysis studies. I have already expressed earlier my doubts about the orthogonality of these two properties (Strelau, 1969; see also p. 31).

The fact that both these NSPs—strength of excitation and mobility—are not so independent as thought by most Pavlovian typologists, including Pavlov, was stressed by several authors in animal studies (e.g. Davidenkov, 1947; Fedorov, 1961; Krasusky, 1971) as well as in research conducted in humans (see Nebylitsyn, 1972a, 1976; Turovskaya, 1963; Kozlova, 1977). It is especially evident when mobility is measured by the most referent "alteration" method, applied since the very beginning in animal and human typology research. Troshikhin et al. (1978), in a study conducted on 225 subjects aged from 5–24 years, divided into seven separate groups differing in age, stated that in all groups mobility of the NS correlates positively

(0.51–0.83) with the strength of excitation. In this case mobility was measured by the "alteration" method and strength of the NS by a variant of the method proposed by Kopytova (see p. 90). Kordyukova (1977), discussing the convergence between strength of mobility estimation, suggests that both these NSPs are co-determined by the reticular formation. It also has been suggested (p. 197) that behavioural mobility, where the ability of switching behaviour in response to changes in the surroundings is most essential and which at the level of indicators may be compared with mobility of the nervous system, cannot be separated from the energetic characteristic of behaviour. "Mobile" individuals are expected to cope more efficiently with novel and variable situations which cause high stimulative value (Fiske and Maddi, 1961). On the other hand we know that individuals with a strong NS are more resistant to intensive stimulation.

In the literature some data may be found which yield information about the construct validity of the Strength of Excitation scale derived from the STI. This is the scale most important to us, because, as will be seen later (see p. 198) this scale has been used in our laboratory to diagnose the reactivity dimension. Most of the data which inform about construct validity were collected by Russian psychologists who compared the estimation of strength as diagnosed by STI with the diagnosis of this NSP based on one of the most popular methods known as the "change of simple RT under repeatedly applied stimuli" (see p. 90). As may be seen from Table XXIII, in all four studies the correlations are positive and statistically significant and they range from 0.544 to 0.864, in accordance with the theoretical assumption.

Khalik (1972) measured the construct validity of the Strength of Excitation scale of the STI by correlating the results with the referent extinction with reinforcement method as regards the GSR (see p. 77)

TABLE XXIII. Strength of excitation measured by STI and by change of simple RT under repeated stimuli

|  |  | Subjects | |  |
| --- | --- | --- | --- | --- |
| Author | N | Age | Sex | $r$ |
| Khalik, 1972 | 50 | 18–25 | M | $0.58^b$ |
| Samonov, 1974 | 173 | College-age | M | $0.68^b$ |
| Dorfman, 1976 | 34 | 18–21 | M | $0.544^a$ |
| Vyatkin and Chekirov, 1976 | 45 | 18–26 | M | $0.864^b$ |

a. $p < 0.01$
b. $p < 0.001$

and supported the validity of this scale ($r = 0.67$; $p < 0.001$). In his study 50 sportsmen aged 18–25 were investigated. However, this result contradicts the data referred to by Carlier (in press). In her study the strength of excitation was measured in a CR eyelid procedure which consisted of determining the threshold of transmarginal inhibition to CSs of different intensity. To some degree this method is comparable with the extinction with reinforcement method where, instead of manipulating the intensity of stimuli, the repetition of application is used to measure the endurance of the NS. Carlier divided 18 subjects (first-year psychology students) into two groups—high and low NS strength—and found no significant differences in the excitation factors (Factor I and Factor III) which she derived from the STI (see p. 131).

To validate inventory techniques by relating the psychometric results to psychophysiological data one must treat the results, whether positive or negative, with great caution. This is because of the partiality phenomenon or, in other words, strongly expressed intra-individual differences biasing most of the psychophysiological procedures (see pp. 1–49 and 111). It has been also stated with reference to other personality dimensions that diagnosis based on inventory estimation does not correlate with psychophysiological indices of the given dimension, special attention having been given to extraversion–introversion (see Franks, 1956, 1957; Willett, 1960; Gale, 1973; Gale *et al.*, 1969).

The application of the STI may evoke several doubts concerned with fulfilling all necessary psychometric requirements and with the crucial question as to whether this method allows measurement of the Pavlovian features of the NS. Referring to the first question I may say in self-mitigation that the construction of the Temperament Inventory sprang initially from my "hobby" and was not a professional enterprise, and I meant to use it only for our own purposes. As regards the second doubt, I have partly discussed it before, but let us look at it from another point of view.

Pavlov's typology has been subjected to several changes and, depending on the problem being solved, different evolutions resulted, from which it is not easy to decide what is and what is not Pavlovian typology. As Eysenck (in press) correctly writes

> Pavlov's theory has undergone several stages of evolution and hardly any two exponents agree completely in their interpretation . . ., what we are dealing with is Gray's, or Strelau's, or Mangan's interpretation of Pavlov's theory, which is quite a different matter.

The same remark, however, must also be made for other interpretors of Pavlov's typology, including Teplov, Merlin, and Nebylitsyn, because the research which stems from their laboratories, as from many others, has little in common with the old-fashioned Pavlovian typology. If we call all this research performed after Pavlov and derived from his studies on TNS neo-Pavlovian typology and if we try to establish what kinds of changes and modifications have been introduced in comparison with the primary concept, we may avoid much misunderstanding in this area. This remark also concerns the studies using the STI.

# 4
# Pavlovian Typology and Some Personality Dimensions Based on Biological Endowment

## INTRODUCTION

Eysenck (1965), when discussing the concepts of personality in which classical conditioning plays the crucial role, mentioned two main theories: the anxiety theory of the Iowa school and his own concept of extraversion–introversion. As is well known, the anxiety dimension, derived from Hull's learning theory paradigm, was elaborated by Spence (1953, 1956; Spence and Taylor, 1951) in experiments with eyeblink conditioning. Due to Taylor (1953) who constructed the Manifest Anxiety Scale (MAS) based on Spence's theory it is possible to measure this dimension in group investigations. The theory of extraversion–introversion, primarily developed by Jung (1960), gained new shape due to the conditionability concept and physiological interpretation introduced by Eysenck (1957, 1967, 1970). The many experiments conducted by himself and his students (known as the Maudsley group), aimed at understanding the essence of extraversion–introversion, were based mainly on the classical conditioning paradigm. Here too, the eyeblink phenomenon was the one most commonly subjected to investigation. Parallel to laboratory studies, Eysenck worked intensively at the construction of inventories enabling measurement of the basic dimensions of his personality theory. His psychometric approach interlaced with laboratory studies threw new light on the nature of the main personality dimensions—extraversion–introversion, neuroticism, and psychoticism—introduced to his personality concept.

One of my own studies (Strelau, 1969) drew attention to the fact that Eysenck, in characterizing the concepts of personality linked to classical conditioning, forgot to refer to Pavlov's basic and fundamental theory of types of nervous systems and temperaments. This theory should definitely be treated as primary for both above-mentioned personality dimensions: anxiety and extraversion–introversion. Even granted that Pavlov's original theory of types of nervous system was developed for animals only, Ivanov-Smolensky's typology and Krasnogorsky's research on temperament conducted since the 1930s, and described in Chapter 1, as well as Teplov–Nebylitsyn and Merlin's studies on type of NS and temperament, initiated in the second half of the 1950s (see Chapter 1), should be regarded as convincing arguments that Pavlov's typology of the nervous system can hardly be omitted when discussing personality dimensions linked to conditioning. This omission has been overcome by Eysenck's co-workers, Levey and Martin (1981), who when discussing the personality dimensions linked to conditioning depart from Pavlov's typology and its modifications.

In my opinion, at least two basic facts led to the growing popularity of Pavlovian typology in the West and stimulated some psychologists to search for links between the concept of TNS and selected personality dimensions. The first was Gray's fundamental book *Pavlov's Typology* (1964). Some papers of the Pavlov–Nebylitsyn group published in that volume gave a broader outlook on Pavlov's typology pertaining to human beings. But, most important from the point of view mentioned above are the chapters written by Gray himself where he was able to show some similarities between the concept of nervous system properties, especially the strength of the NS and the arousal theories on which several personality dimensions developed in Western psychology are based. So the first bridge between Pavlov's typology and some biologically determined personality dimensions built by Gray facilitated a two-way transmission of ideas in this area.

The second basic fact to stimulate increasing interest in searching for links between the research conducted on NS properties and personality dimensions was the Symposium "Physiological Bases of Individual Psychological Differences" organized at the meeting of the XVIII International Congress of Psychology, Moscow, 1966. In his paper given at this symposium Eysenck (1966) pointed to similarities between the NS strength and extraversion–introversion. The papers delivered at this symposium also served as a starting-point in collecting material for the book *Biological Bases of Individual Behaviour* edited by Nebylitsyn and Gray (1972) in which several links between Pavlovian typology and some personality dimensions are demonstrated on the bases of theoretical considerations as well as empirical facts to which I will refer mainly in the next sections.

Cattell (1972), discussing the relation between NSP investigation and personality research in the West, ascertained that one of the main differences results from the fact that Western personality psychologists concentrate on a multidimensional approach whereas in Pavlovian typology only one dimension is taken into account, i.e. the strength of the nervous system. This erroneous opinion was probably derived from the fact that Cattell based his conclusion on Gray's (1964) publication only, where all but Teplov's chapters are indeed devoted to the strength of NS. But at the same time that Cattell made his conclusion there were already hundreds of publications devoted to the investigation of such nervous system properties as: mobility, lability, dynamism, balance of these NS properties, and concentratability, as has been shown in Chapter 1.

Comparing the strength of NS with his personality concept Cattell (1972) hypothesized that there may be some relations between the strength of the NS and such dimensions as assertive ego, general inhibition, hypomanic temperament, exuberance, cortertia, capacity to mobilize vs. regression and exvia vs. invia. Special attention has been paid by Cattell to cortertia which has a lot in common with Gray's (1964) concept of arousability. Gray uses this concept to show the similarities between the strength of the NS and the concept of arousal (see p. 40).

Cattell's theoretical considerations about the relations between strength of the NS and the personality dimensions he himself distinguished requires empirical verification. A study conducted by Orlebeke (1972) does not support Cattell's idea. The former author administered Cattell's 16 PF Questionnaire to 60 subjects (college students) in whom the strength of NS was diagnosed on the basis of the RT max/RT min index (see p. 86). The only factor, among the sixteen measured, which correlated positively with strength of the NS was surgency vs. desurgency, not mentioned by Cattell when he hypothesized about the links between strength and his personality dimensions. Another study conducted by Orlebeke (1972) on a group of 30 subjects gave a similar result. The only statistically significant correlation was between surgency and strength of the NS ($r = 0.48$; $p < 0.05$). Surgency includes such features as: cheerful, sociable, energetic, humorous, talkative, and placid (see Cattell, 1965). People characterized as sociable, energetic and talkative should reveal activity of rather high stimulative value, such as could be expected in individuals with strong NS, and this, in turn, suggests that Orlebeke's results are consistent with the concept of strength of the NS.

Stimulation-seeking behaviour in relation to strength of the NS was

## 4. Personality Dimensions Based on Biological Endowment

subjected to study by Sales *et al.* (1974). These authors took as a point of departure Gray's (1964) statement that in individuals with a weak NS the arousal mechanism enhances stimulation and in "strong" individuals it depresses stimulation. On this basis the authors hypothesized that individuals with a strong NS are effective in dealing with intensive stimulation whereas subjects with a weak nervous system are relatively sensitive to faint stimuli. The need for stimulation was measured in two experiments differing in kind of stimulation: sensory and social. In the first experiment two settings were arranged. In one, the subjects (24 persons) pressed a button to receive simple visual and auditory stimuli applied at 2-s duration. The number of applications was regulated by the subjects themselves who were allowed to press the button during a 20-min session as many times as they wished. In the second setting, more complex stimuli were presented (bulbs of different colours and sounds of different compositions). In this setting, which did not differ in other variables from the first one, 27 subjects were studied. The authors found a significant interaction between the strength of NS and the conditions of the experiment. The "strong" individuals pressed the button more frequently than the "weak" ones in the more complex situation whereas in the experimental setting, where simple stimuli were presented, there was a predominance of button-pressing in the weak NS subjects.

In the second experiment need for stimulation was measured by the subject's preferences as to the number of people to be put in two fictitious rooms without making them overcrowded. Models of an airport waiting-room and a lounge in which a cocktail party was being held were provided. The results of this experiment (30 Ss) were consistent with the previous ones. It was found that there is a positive correlation between the strength of the NS and the number of people placed in the model rooms. Analysis of variance confirmed the significant interaction between social setting and strength of NS—"strong" individuals allotted more people in both social settings.

In another study Sales and Throop (1972) using the kinesthetic figural after-effect (KFA) as a measure of stimulus intensity modulation (see Petrie, 1967), showed it to correlate significantly with strength of NS. Reducers, who underestimate the size of the measurement block after stimulation, tend to have a strong NS. Most individuals with a weak NS, on the other hand, are augmenters who, in turn, overestimate the size of the measurement block. This result is in agreement with Gray's (see p. 40) enhancing/depressing hypothesis with regard to the strength of NS. Also Barnes (1976), when reviewing research concerned with stimulus intensity modulation and strength of the NS, concluded that a relationship exists between these dimensions. Individuals with high stimulus intensity modulation (augmenters) should be regarded as having weak NS whereas individuals with low stimulus intensity modulation (reducers) may be compared with the strong type of NS.

It has to be mentioned, however, that Buchsbaum (1976) who borrowed the notions "augmenter" and "reducer" from Petrie (1967) posits an opposite relation between strength of the NS and the augmenting/reducing dimension. According to Buchsbaum augmenters have strong NSs and reducers have weak ones. This difference can mainly be attributed to the measurement procedure: Buchsbaum, when measuring the amplitude of average evoked responses (AER) to increasing intensity of stimuli, taken as an index of the augmenting/reducing dimension, took into account changes in AER amplitude to stimuli of high intensity (Buchsbaum, 1976, 1978; Buchsbaum *et al.*, in press). In this case, using the Pavlovian conceptual NS terminology, transmarginal inhibition leads to a stronger decrease of reaction to high intensity stimuli in weak NS individuals and this in turn leads to the decrease in reaction magnitude. In strong individuals the "increasing" phenomenon is due to the fact that they react according to the growing intensity of stimuli. Of course, there are substantial differences between Petrie and Buchsbaum's concepts of the augmenting/reducing dimension which are not without influence on the mentioned discrepancy, but it is not the aim of this chapter to discuss this problem.

Zuckerman (1979, 1980), in discussing his concept of sensation seeking referred also to the analogy with the Pavlovian types of NS. As he writes:

> The sanguine dog, characterizable as a strong nervous system type with mobile processes, may be equated with high-sensation seekers and the phlegmatic type with low-sensation seekers (Zuckerman, 1979, p. 38)

Zuckerman's comprehension of types is, however, not quite adequate for what he really had in mind. Presenting Pavlov's typology in cubic form the author erroneously ascribed the phlegmatic type to the weak type of nervous system, with weak excitatory and inhibitory processes. According to Pavlov and all Pavlovian typologists, these are characteristics of the melancholic type. There is no doubt that Zuckerman, when referring to low-sensation seekers, had in mind the weak type of the NS, i.e. the melancholic. Our data (Oleszkiewicz, unpublished report) on 171 subjects (men, 16–20 years old) support Zuckerman's hypothesis to some extent. Strength of the NS measured by the STI had a low but significant correlation with the following subscales of the Sensation

Seeking Scale (SSS, Form IV): General Scale ($r = 0.25$; $p < 0.01$), Thrill and Adventure Seeking ($r = 0.36$; $p < 0.001$), and Boredom Susceptibility ($r = 0.25$; $p < 0.01$). These results are not consistent with the factor analytic study conducted by Paisey and Mangan (1980). These authors administered Eysencks' EPQ, Zuckerman's SSS, and Strelau's STI to 277 subjects and on basis of the items from these questionnaires identified the following four factors:

I. extraversion/strength of excitation/mobility;
II. self-control of affect/stability/caution;
III. strength of inhibition/verbal control/motor expressiveness/non-manipulativeness; and
IV. sensation-seeking/nervousness.

This data suggest that sensation seeking should be treated as a dimension unrelated to the strength of the NS and to mobility and balance of the NS as regards strength of nervous processes. The authors explain the lack of correlation by the fact that sensation seeking has pathological components.

Since the 1960s I have been interested in searching for interrelations between NSPs as measured by STI and such dimensions of personality as extraversion–introversion, neuroticism, and anxiety. These dimensions have also been subjected to research in relation to NSPs by several psychologists in other countries, especially in the West. The data and discussion concerned with the interrelation between NSPs and the above-mentioned personality dimensions are presented in the next two sections.

## EXTRAVERSION–INTROVERSION AND NERVOUS SYSTEM PROPERTIES

### Review of Studies

Eysenck(1947, 1957, 1970) seems to be the first personality theorist in the West to have paid attention to Pavlovian typology when referring to physiological mechanisms underlying temperament dimensions. As mentioned before, Eysenck advanced the hypothesis that extraversion–introversion (E/I) has some elements in common with the strength of the nervous system: "The 'weak' personality type appears to resemble the introvert, the 'strong' personality type the extravert" (1966, p. 33). This analogy put forward and developed by Eysenck in his later studies (Eysenck, in press; Eysenck and Levey, 1972) was facilitated by Gray's (1964) theoretical considerations regarding the similarities between the concept of strength of the NS and arousability; the latter concept serving to explain relatively stable individual differences in level of arousal. One of the clauses of his arousability theory states that

> Individuals who are low on the dimension of arousability (i.e. who, in any given stimulus situation, show relatively low levels of arousal) correspond to individuals with a strong nervous system; individuals who are high on the dimension of arousability (i.e. who, in any given stimulus situation, show relatively high levels of arousal) correspond to individuals with a weak nervous system. (Gray, 1964, p. 306)

Discussing the differences between the strong and the weak NS Gray argues that

> the weaker the nervous system, the greater is the degree of non-specific bombardment of the cortex by the ascending reticular system for any given stimulus situation. (1964, p. 305)

This is exactly what Eysenck states when interpreting the difference between the extravert and the introvert using his reticulo-cortical arousal loop theory, introduced in the second half of the 1960s to explain the physiological basis of E/I (Eysenck, 1967, 1981). According to this conceptualization the introvert and the weak TNS should be regarded as having generally higher levels of arousal as compared with the extravert and the strong TNS. Paisey and Mangan (1982), when comparing the E/I dimension with strength of the NS, put forward the hypothesis that:

> In behavioural terms, extraversion and strength of excitation are dimensions of goal-directed behaviour expressed, on the one hand, through social activity, and, on the other, through work.

Gray (1964) hypothesized that strength of the NS should be related primarily to neuroticism; however, a few years later, he rejected this position in favour of Eysenck's view as regards the relation between extraversion–introversion and strength of the NS (Gray, 1967), and he provided evidence in support of this position. The main supporting data are presented in Table XXIV.

As seen from the Table there is no full agreement as to the analogy between the weak TNS and the introvert; this is especially true as regards susceptibility to fatigue and the phenomenon of reactive inhibition. Gray drew attention to the fact that experiments investigating fatigue must be unified from the point of view of the stimulation value of the situation, in order for any conclusion about the relation between E/I and strength of the NS to be valid. This contention has strong support in Rozhdestvenskaya's (1980) studies. The latter author con-

TABLE XXIV. Experimental data presented by Gray (1967) illustrating the relation between the strength of the NS and the extraversion–introversion

| Data | E/I | Strength of NS |
|---|---|---|
| 1. Low sensitivity threshold | introvert | weak TNS |
| 2. Positive influence of additional stimuli | extravert | strong TNS |
| 3. Enhancement of stimulation | introvert | weak TNS |
| 4. High flicker-fusion | introvert | weak TNS[a] |
| 5. Direction of stimulant drugs' operation | introvert | weak TNS |
| 6. High susceptibility to fatigue | extravert | weak TNS |
| 7. High reactive inhibition ($I_R$) | extravert | weak TNS |

*a*. In Pavlovian typology the flicker-fusion phenomenon is used rather to diagnose the lability of the NS (see p. 98)

ducted a series of experiments from which she was able to show that under prolonged monotonous conditions individuals with a weak NS perform better and display lower fatigue as compared with individuals with a strong NS. Exactly the opposite is true, however, when the stimulative value of the situation is high. In this case the weak type of NS is especially prone to fatigue.

Eysenck's experimental evidence to show that reactive inhibition ($I_R$) is higher in extraverts than in introverts is in strong contradiction to the Pavlovian concept of strength of NS. One of the reasons may be that the notion of reactive inhibition introduced by Hull (1943) is somewhat confused and this is probably one of the reasons why Eysenck (1967) refused to use it in his physiological interpretation of extraversion–introversion. According to the latter author $I_R$ should be treated as conditioned inhibition corresponding with his temporal inhibition. If Pavlov were able to interpret Hull's position as regards $I_R$, he would, no doubt, consider it to be unconditioned inhibition since Pavlov (1951–52) treated all kinds of innate inhibition as unconditioned inhibition (see Footnote 1 on p. 330). When Hull described the state he described as reactive inhibition, he wrote:

> Whenever any reaction is evoked in an organism there is left a condition or state which acts as a primary negative motivation in that it has an *innate* [*my italics*] capacity to produce a cessation of the activity which produced the state. (1943, p. 278)

But more important than the confusion in terminology are the facts. As is well known from the literature, Eysenck (1957, 1970) designed a series of experiments to study reminiscence, a phenomenon tested in relation to the accumulation of (reactive, temporal) inhibition in the course of amassed practice, as a result of which performance deteriorates until a break is made, after which it is greatly improved due to dissipation of inhibition during rest. The data collected in the many studies conducted in Eysenck's laboratory shows reminiscence to be much stronger in extraverts than in introverts. From the point of view of Pavlov's conceptualization the decline in performance, the reduction of the response or lowering of level of functioning under the influence of prolonged practice (fundamental for reminiscence) mean precisely the same as Pavlovian exhaustion of nervous cells as a result of prolonged or repeated stimulation. As such they are classic examples of protective or transmarginal inhibition. As is well known from the entire Pavlovian literature, the appearance of transmarginal inhibition is considered as the main index of strength of the NS as regards excitation—the weak type being more prone to develop this state compared with the strong one. This basic discrepancy between E/I and strength of the NS shown by Gray (1967) has also been observed by other authors (Strelau, 1969, 1970a) when discussing the similarities and discrepancies between both of the dimensions in question.[1]

There are some data in the literature which support Eysenck and Gray's position as regards the relation between strength of the NS and E/I. For example, Frigon (1976), using the criterion of one $SD$, selected (on the basis of Eysenck's EPI) four groups of subjects differing in the level of E/I and neuroticism (N = high; n = low): EN, En, IN, and In. Altogether 36 male subjects were investigated, nine in each group. In all subjects the EEG variant of the extinction with reinforcement (see p. 77)) was applied to assess the strength of the NS. Analysis of variance revealed that introverts show a gradual significant decrease in response magnitude in the extinction with reinforcement method, a result typical for the weak TNS ($F = 8.47$; $df = 4/128$; $p < 0.001$). Similar results were obtained by Gilliland (in press), who used the EEG variant of the extinction with reinforcement method and the STI for diagnosing the strength of NS. Karpova (1974), using the slope of RT curve (see p. 86) and change of simple RT under repeatedly applied stimuli (see p. 90) as measures of strength of the NS, was able to show that strength of the nervous system correlated positively with extraversion; however, the diagnosis of this dimension described in her paper is not quite clear.

There are also some factor analytic studies which underline the correspondence between extraversion and strength of the NS (Orlebeke, 1972; Paisey and Mangan, 1980, 1982; Mangan, 1982). Paisey and Mangan (1980), in a study described briefly on p. 143, separated, among others, a factor which comprises, with highest loadings, extraversion, strength of excitation, and mobility (see also Paisey and Mangan, 1982). Carlier (in press) who used the STI to diagnose NS properties, and the EPI to diagnose extraversion and neuroticism in a sample of 202 psychology students (173 women and 29 men) stated, among other things, that the Extraversion scale correlates positively with the Strength of Excitation scale (0.38; $p < 0.05$). When factor analysing the items of the STI using the Varimax method, Carlier distinguished four factors:

*Factor I* with highest loadings in Excitation and Mobility scales items;
*Factor II* which includes mostly the items of the Inhibition scale;
*Factor III* which comprises first of all those items which are related to working situations; and
*Factor IV* including above all Mobility, and Strength of Inhibition scales' items, all with rather low loadings.

In order to answer the question of correspondence between E/I and NS properties Carlier correlated the four factors with the Extraversion scale of the EPI. She found that Factor I, which includes strength of excitation and mobility, correlated positively with extraversion (0.66; $p < 0.05$), thus supporting Paisey and Mangan's (1980) data. However, Factor III, also regarded as an excitatory factor, when correlated with the Extraversion scale is not consistent with the result given above ($-0.15; p < 0.05$).

The fact that mobility of the NS is positively correlated with extraversion, as stated in Paisey and Mangan's as well as in Carlier's study, has support in other studies (Mangan, 1967c, 1978; Vasilenko, 1967; Troshikhin *et al.*, 1978). However, Loo (1979) who factor analysed the indices of basic NS properties diagnosed in motor RT tasks with the scales of EPQ found no support for the former authors' position as regards the relation between E/I and mobility of the NS. In Loo's study mobility constituted one factor together with paranoia as one of sixteen factors extracted from the EPQ items.

In the literature there are some data which contradict Eysenck and Gray's position as regards the correspondence between E/I and strength of the NS. Mangan (Mangan and Farmer, 1967), who should be considered as one of the pioneers in studying the interrelations of Pavlovian typology and personality dimensions, presents a list of data which show that extraversion correlates negatively with strength of the NS. The authors, who probably considered the strength (intensity) of excitation and inhibition as processes, as was typical of Eysenck's former physiological interpretation of E/I (see Strelau, 1970a), hypothesized that the introvert (predominance of excitation over inhibition) corresponds with the strong type of NS. In turn, extraverts, with predominance of inhibition over excitation should be regarded as having a weak NS.[2] As stressed before (see p. 3), in Pavlovian typology strength of excitation and inhibition are considered as traits (see also Nebylitsyn, 1972a) and there is a reverse relationship between both strength as a trait and strength (intensity) of nervous processes as a state. This means that introverts with predominance of excitation over inhibition (understood in Eysenck's theory as a state) should be compared with the weak type of NS in whom, because of his weak (sensitive) excitatory processes (understood in Pavlovian typology as a trait), the intensity of excitatory processes (considered as a state) is rather high. In spite of the incoherence in the theoretical justification of the hypothesis as regards the negative relation between extraversion and strength of the NS, Mangan and Farmer (1967) obtained results which they felt supported their hypothesis. Strength of the NS was diagnosed in this experiment on the basis of the slope of RT curve (see p. 86). Extraversion was estimated by the MPI, administered to 20 subjects (men, ranged from 18 to 24 years). A peculiar positive correlation (0.55; $p < 0.05$) between both the indices measured was obtained. As we know, the higher the score for the Extraversion scale of the MPI, the higher the extraversion. Exactly the same holds for the strength index derived from the slope of RT curve. The higher the value of this index the higher the strength of the NS. The conclusion from this study suggests that either the authors forgot to add the minus to their correlation coefficient or their conclusion about the negative relation between strength of the NS and extraversion is wrong.

Data supporting a negative correlation between E/I and strength of the NS have also been collected by other authors (see Zhorov and Yermolayeva-Tomina, 1972; Loo, 1979). Zhorov and Yermolayeva-Tomina, when correlating the Extraversion scale of the MPI with the strength index of the slope of RT curve on the basis of results from 25 subjects (14 men and 11 women), found a negative though insignificant correlation (−0.344). The strongest support for the view opposite to that of Eysenck and Gray is given by Loo (1979). The latter author measured the strength of NS using the slope of RT curve and the mean RT to low intensity stimuli (35 dB). He showed that extraversion, estimated by the EPQ, comprised one factor, together with the negative pole of strength (weak NS). His data were collected on 80 subjects (40 males and 40 females, ranging from 18 to 25 years).

As seen from this review there is no unequivocal evidence for the correspondence between the extraversion–introversion and the strength of NS and mobility of nervous processes.

In the research devoted to search for links between E/I and Pavlovian typology some studies may be found in which extraversion–introversion was compared with dynamism of the nervous system. Nebylitsyn (1966, 1972a), the author of the latter dimension, was the first to draw attention to the fact that this NS property resembles Eysenck's E/I dimension to some extent. However, the conceptualization of inhibition in Eysenck's former theory (1947, 1957), where conditioned inhibition in the Pavlovian sense (extinction of CRs) was considered together with Pavlovian unconditioned inhibition (e.g. the investigation of reminiscence which expresses the $I_R$) as one phenomenon does not, in Nebylitsyn's opinion, permit such an analogy. In the case of dynamism we have to make do with the elaboration of positive and negative CRs and the latter are indicators of conditioned inhibition only (Nebylitsyn, 1972a).

Gray (1967) also shared the opinion that E/I and dynamism of NP have several elements in common. For example, conditionability (one of the crucial notions in Eysenck's theory of E/I) understood as the ease with which CRs are evoked, relates directly to the dynamism of nervous processes. The speed of formation of CRs is used as the measure of both phenomena in question. However, Gray (1967) drew attention to the fact that, in Nebylitsyn's concept, dynamism of excitation and dynamism of inhibition were two independent dimensions; meaning in practice that they might be positively, negatively, or not at all correlated with each other. This is not the case with the E/I dimension. According to Eysenck the interaction between excitation and inhibition takes place in one dimension only. In extraverts inhibition dominates over excitation and the reverse holds for introverts, where excitation prevails over inhibition.[3] This means that there is always a negative correlation between excitation and inhibition (see also Loo, 1979).

According to Gray, the common denominator of both dimensions in question is the physiological mechanism. Nebylitsyn (1972a), when referring to the physiological bases of dynamism, drew attention to the reticular formation and the same is true when Eysenck considered the physiological mechanism of extraversion–introversion (Gray, 1967). Gray also noted some similarities between E/I and dynamism, taking as point of departure his own physiological interpretation of extraversion–introversion according to which introverts are, among other things, more susceptible to punishment and extraverts are more susceptible to rewards (1972a, 1981).

> The question of the relation between sensitivity to reward and sensitivity to frustrative nonreward is much the same as the problem described in the neo-Pavlovian work on personality dimensions (. . .) as that of the relation between «dynamism in excitation» and «dynamism in inhibition». (Gray, 1972a, p. 382)

The hypothesis that E/I and dynamism of nervous processes are related has been experimentally proven by Marton (1972; Marton and Urban, 1966). The author, taking the extinction of the orienting response (OR) in EEG and electro-dermal activity (EDA)[4] as an index of dynamism, found that extraverts differ significantly from introverts in the speed of extinction of the OR. Extinction was quicker in extraverts than in introverts. This, according to Marton, supports both Eysenck's hypothesis of the predominance of inhibition over excitation in extraverts as well as the hypothesis which argued for the correspondence between E/I and dynamism.

Loo (1979), who studied the interrelations between NSPs as measured in RT experiments (for description see Loo, 1978) and Eysenck's personality dimensions, diagnosed by the EPQ, was not able to confirm Marton's data. The factor analysis conducted by Loo showed that dynamism of inhibition (measured by the consolidation of an inhibitory motor response) constituted one factor, together with neuroticism, in line with data found by Cazzullo *et al.* (1970, cited by Loo, 1979). In turn, dynamism of excitation (measured by the speed of consolidation of a motor response to auditory stimuli) was included in one factor together with low co-operative sociability. The latter was one of the 16 primary orthogonal factors extracted from the EPQ items.

## The Inventory Data

This short review shows that among psychologists concentrating on research on the extraversion–introversion dimension, a growing interest in searching for various links with Pavlovian typology can be found (see also Halmiova and Uherik, 1972; Haslam, 1972; White and Mangan, 1972; Powell, 1979; Brebner, 1980).[5] The results of these comparisons are often contradictory and not always quite clear. Thus stimulated to search for links between E/I and the basic NSPs we collected data in our laboratory which brought us nearer to answering the question of the correspondence between both these concepts under discussion.

In all of our studies, the first of which I conducted myself in 1965, Strelau's Temperament Inventory (STI) was used to diagnose the NS properties, i.e. to assess the strength of excitation (E), strength of inhibition (I), their balance, and the mobility of the NS. Some doubts as to the use of this technique for measuring the NS properties in the Pavlovian meaning have been presented in Chapter 3. But to answer Eysenck's crucial question—are we still investigating Pavlovian typology? I may answer that most of the research reviewed in this chapter has little in common with Pavlovian typology in its classical sense for

## 4. Personality Dimensions Based on Biological Endowment

several reasons. Either nobody (except Frigon and maybe one or two more) used the notions of NS properties strictly in line with Pavlov's interpretation (e.g. dynamism, mobility of excitation, mobility of inhibition etc.) or the indices of these properties used are quite distinct from those used in Pavlov's laboratory. However, these studies, along with those conducted in the laboratories of Soviet psychophysiologists, reflect the present status of neo-Pavlovian typology which has its roots in the classical approach conducted by Pavlov and his early students.

There are at least two reasons which, in my opinion, justify the application of inventory techniques for measuring NSPs in relation to other personality dimensions also diagnosed by questionnaires. First, it is important that different personality dimensions, when compared with each other, be measured at the same level of behaviour organization. This is because the differences between them may derive not only from the fact that we are concerned with indices of different dimensions, but also due to the differences in the level of behaviour (reactions) under investigation (e.g. self-reports about the speed of reaction vs. RT measured in an experimental setting). Secondly, almost all laboratory methods used for diagnosing NS properties are heavily biased by the partiality phenomenon discussed in detail in Chapters 1 and 3. This means, in practice, that a given statement about the correspondence between NS properties and some personality dimensions is of low value if the properties of the NS were diagnosed in laboratory conditions (e.g. on the basis of RT experiments or CR procedure) and the compared personality dimensions using inventory techniques. This is due to the fact that exactly the same experimental conditions arranged for diagnosing the NS properties lead to different results when we change the kind of sensory stimuli (e.g. visual vs. auditory), unconditioned stimuli (e.g. electric shock vs. food), or the reaction under control (verbal vs. motor, voluntary vs. involuntary). Extraverts may have a strong TNS when the latter is assessed by the slope of RT curve to auditory stimuli but at the same time they may be characterized as weak TNS when using visual stimuli. As we see, when we use the inventory technique to estimate the properties of the NS, however removed from the physiological mechanism underlying these properties, this technique has some assets, especially in comparison studies in personality.

Turning back to our research the E/I dimension was diagnosed by the MPI in all our studies, mainly for technical reasons. The MPI has been adapted to Polish conditions by Choynowski (1977) and has since been used in our country for diagnosing E/I. The EPI and the EPQ have not been adapted to the Polish population. Some preliminary trials have been conducted in our laboratory by Toeplitz (1982); however, this author's serious (theoretical and practical) doubts concerning the psychoticism scale in EPQ led her to abandon further adaptation of the EPQ. The main inconvenience in using the MPI lies in the inability to separate the two main components of E/I—sociability and impulsivity. As mentioned by Eysenck and Levey (1972) it is above all impulsivity which has much in common with strength of the NS.

Our results concerning comparison of the dimension of extraversion–introversion with NS properties are presented in Table XXV.

A short glance at the correlations gathered in the table will suffice to show certain regularities. In brief, all eight studies yielded positive correlations (ranging from 0.349 to 0.548) between excitation strength and extraversion. Such correlations correspond with Eysenck and Gray's hypothesis (Eysenck, 1966; Eysenck and Levey, 1972; Gray, 1967, 1972a) and they support the data of Frigon (1976), Karpova (1974), Gilliland (in press), as well as those of Paisey and Mangan (1980) and Carlier (in press) in their factor analytic studies.

Mobility of nervous processes correlates positively with extraversion (0.448–0.692) in all studies. These correlation coefficients, the highest in Table XXV, cannot be accidental. As far as I know, the relation between mobility of nervous processes and extraversion has never been subject to profound theoretical analysis. The task is also quite difficult at the physiological level, since we have not yet come to the core of the physiological mechanism of mobility. However, considering the fact that mobility is behaviourally manifested mainly as the capability of reacting quickly and adequately to changing conditions, it can be assumed that this property should appear in individuals who are externally-oriented, i.e. focused on events occurring in the environment. Such orientation corresponds to extravert patterns of behaviour (Eysenck, 1970; Brebner and Cooper, 1974, 1978). Perhaps, the two properties can also be linked by the fact that individuals with high mobility of nervous processes are marked by a high need for a specific kind of stimulation, i.e. stimulation resulting from changes (of surroundings, conditions, behaviour). As we know, extraverts require more stimulation compared with introverts (Eysenck and Zuckerman, 1978).

These results which show that both properties of the nervous system—strength of excitation and mobility—correlate systematically and positively with extraversion, indirectly confirm the fact stated in Chapter 3 (see p. 134) that these properties are not so independent as most researchers think. Their lack of orthogonality has been stated in factor analytic studies conducted by Paisey and Mangan (1980) and by Carlier (in press).

TABLE XXV. Basic NS properties as measured by STI and extraversion–introversion

| References | Strength of E | Strength of I | Mobility of NP | Balance of NP |
|---|---|---|---|---|
| (1) Strelau, 1969<br>N = 78; M,F | 0.449[a] | −0.007 | 0.667[a] | |
| (2) Strelau, 1970a<br>N = 159; M,F | 0.476[a] | 0.028 | 0.652[a] | |
| (3) Strelau, 1971[u]<br>N = 171; M,F | 0.444[a]<br>0.381[a] | −0.080<br>N = 183; M,F<br>0.052 | 0.694[a]<br>N = 178; M,F<br>0.563[a] | 0.350[a]<br>N = 199; M,F<br>0.356[a] |
| (4) Terelak, 1974<br>N = 115; M | | | 0.536[a] | −0.413[c] |
| (5) Zarzycka, 1980<br>N = 174; M | 0.504[a] | 0.160 | 0.536[a] | −0.413[c] |
| (6) Zarzycka, 1980<br>N = 59; M | 0.548[a] | 0.156 | 0.448[a] | −0.504[a] |
| (7) Ciosek and Oszmiańczuk, 1974<br>N = 70; M | 0.349[b] | 0.165 | 0.517[a] | |
| (8) Carlier, in press*<br>N = 202; M,F | 0.38[c] | −0.21[c] | 0.54[c] | |

$a = p < 0.001$
$b = p < 0.01$
$c = p < 0.005$

M = Males
F = Females
N = Number of subjects

$u$ = Unpublished data
* The EPI was used to diagnose the E/I dimension

Considering in turn the relation of strength of inhibition to extraversion, we must admit that results suggest almost unequivocally the lack of relation between these two factors. As I have pointed out (see p. 145), conditioned inhibition as interpreted by Pavlov (and we have only such inhibition in mind when we speak of strength of inhibition measured by STI) differs very much from Eysenck's understanding of inhibition (see also Strelau, 1969, 1970a). Thus, the lack of correlation between the two variables should not be taken as a surprise. Our data in this respect are also in accordance with Paisey and Mangan's (1980, Mangan, 1982) study where it was shown that strength of inhibition constitutes, along with motor and verbal control, a separate factor, orthogonal to the factor which includes extraversion, strength of excitation and mobility.

The relation between balance of nervous processes as regards strength of excitation and inhibition, and extraversion–introversion seems to be the least clear one. In two studies, significant and moderately high positive correlations were obtained, while in two other studies, even higher, but negative correlations were found. Such results are not conclusive. These data can hardly be compared with any in the literature where balance understood by Pavlov's original meaning as the equilibrium between strength of excitation and strength of inhibition (see p. 8) was altogether very rarely subject to human research and never before compared with extraversion–introversion.

Closing the discussion about the correspondence between NS properties and E/I, I should make the remark that, in our laboratory, many studies (especially M.A. theses) have been conducted with the aim of correlating these dimensions in question, although mostly on smaller numbers of subjects. None of these studies unequivocally contradicts the regularity portrayed in Table XXV, suggesting that the stated dependencies cannot be regarded as accidental.

## ANXIETY AND NEUROTICISM AS RELATED TO THE BASIC PROPERTIES OF THE NERVOUS SYSTEM

### Anxiety and NSPs

Since his first papers devoted to the problem of types of the nervous system Pavlov (1951–52) drew attention to the fact that one mode of behaviour which distinguishes the weak type of NS from the strong type is fearfulness and cowardice. The weak type often exhibits the so-called passive–defensive reflex, i.e. fear, which marks its whole behaviour. Pavlov gave several examples of animal and human behaviour in highly-stimulating, dangerous, and threatening natural situations showing that individuals with a weak nervous system are more prone to react with fear in such situations compared with individuals with a strong TNS; and these reactions may become consolidated, constituting a relatively stable characteristic of the weak type of NS.

Ivanov-Smolensky conducted a study in 1932 (cited by Teplov, 1964a) in which he was able to show that a strongly expressed fear reaction and a clear-cut passive–defensive reflex may also appear in dogs with strong and well-balanced NSPs. The conviction that anxiety reactions are not only typical for the weak TNS has been confirmed by experimental evidence collected by Vyrzhikovsky and Mayorov (1954). Their experiment, conducted in the 1930s, consisted of rearing two groups of dogs during a period of two years under two extremely different conditions. One group of puppies was bred in a natural setting whereas the other group was placed (every dog individually) in isolated cages. After two years the behaviour of the dogs changed completely, independent of their type of NS (assessed in laboratory conditions) but depending on the kind of experimental settings. In dogs reared in "prison" conditions the passive–defensive reflex was strongly developed and they could be characterized as high-anxiety individuals. A similar experiment conducted by Krasusky (1959) led to analogous conclusions.

A study aimed at relating strength of the NS and the intensity of the passive–defensive reflex was conducted by Krushinsky (1947) on 51 dogs. The well-known standard (see p. 14) was used to diagnose the strength of the NS whereas the expressiveness of the passive–defensive reflex was assessed by a special method, developed by the author, which permitted a quantitative differentiation. The correlation between both variables compared ($-0.34$; $p < 0.05$) suggests that there is an interdependency between the strength of NS and the expressiveness of the passive–defensive reflex which might be regarded as the behavioural component of the anxiety trait. Analysing the dependency between both variables in question, separately for individuals with strong and weak NS, the author was able to show that in all but one of the 17 individuals with the weak nervous system the passive–defensive reflex is well expressed. In the case of strong TNS individuals (34 dogs) this reflex was also present in 19 dogs, whereas in 15 dogs the passive–defensive reflex did not appear at all. Similar results were obtained in a study of 10 dogs conducted by Kolesnikov (1953).

In some studies devoted to investigating the TNS in humans authors have occasionally drawn attention to the fact that anxiety reactions are above all typical for individuals with weak NS (Teplov, 1964a; Leites, 1956b; Merlin, 1964b). Nebylitsyn (1959b, 1972a) taking into account the speed of conditioning suggested that there exists an analogy between the weak type of NS and the anxiety dimension as conceptualized by Spence. A similar analogy has also been made by Marton and Urban who stated that "the weak, sensitive type of the nervous system reveals resemblance to personality traits characteristic of 'anxiety' individuals as studied in the Iowa Group" (1966, p. 92).

A theoretical analysis, justifying the relation between strength of the NS and the anxiety dimension according to Spence (1956, 1960), is contained in one of my earlier publications (Strelau, 1969). Just let me concentrate on some similarities between both these dimensions, with the assumption that the reader is familiar with Spence's concept of anxiety.

Taking into account the speed of conditioning to negative stimuli which, in Spence's model, is regarded as one of the main criteria differentiating high-anxiety individuals from low-anxiety ones, we are now able to state that the formation of CRs progresses more quickly in the weak NS than in the strong one (see p. 22), as is the case in high-anxiety individuals as compared with low-anxiety ones. This is explained by the higher sensitivity of the weak type. It follows that stimuli having the same objective physical strength should be regarded as physiologically stronger for the weak type of NS. This is in agreement with the enhancing/depressing hypothesis developed by Gray (1964) and applied to the strength of NS concept. According to the law of strength elaborated by Pavlov (1951–52) CRs should be formed more easily and earlier to stimuli of higher intensity.[6]

A weak aversive stimulus which does not yet evoke pain reactions and, in consequence, state anxiety in individuals with a strong NS may attain an above-threshold value in individuals with a weak NS causing negative emotional reactions ($r_e$), the latter construct ($r_e$) introduced into Hull's (1943) learning theory by Spence (1956, 1960). In consequence, the range of stimuli perceived as harmful (noxious), i.e. evoking anxiety reactions, will be broader in the weak TNS than in the strong one.

Noxious stimuli which evoke weak emotional reactions of negative connotation (anxiety) in individuals with a strong TNS may lead to strong negative emotional reactions in weak TNS individuals. Because the speed of conditioning as well as the range of stimuli which serve as signals of noxious (pain-generating) situations have higher values in individuals with a weak NS as compared with strong ones, we may expect fear reactions and anxiety states to appear more frequently in the former type and to be much stronger.

Taking these considerations as point of departure we conducted

## 4. Personality Dimensions Based on Biological Endowment

several studies which were aimed at comparing the NS properties measured by the STI with the anxiety dimension. As regards anxiety, Taylor's (1953) Manifest Anxiety Scale (MAS) was used in most of the studies since this inventory derives from Spence's concept of anxiety to which I have referred in my theoretical considerations. Because of the growing popularity of Spielberger's (Spielberger *et al.*, 1970) State-Trait Anxiety Inventory (STAI), some comparison studies have also been conducted in which trait anxiety was measured by this inventory. As shown by Spielberger *et al.* (1970) there exists a high positive and statistically significant correlation between Taylor's MAS and the Anxiety Trait Scale of the STAI (in females: 0.80, N = 126; in males: 0.79, N = 80). Spielberger equates trait anxiety with individual differences in anxiety proneness, which is manifested in the frequency of experiencing state anxiety over a long period and in the tendency to perceive situations as dangerous (Spielberger, 1972). The results of the comparison studies conducted in our laboratory are presented in Table XXVI.

As seen from the table, negative correlations were found in all the studies between strength of excitation and anxiety (ranging from $-0.394$ to $-0.72$). As mentioned before, dog experiments had earlier indicated that it is the weak type of NS which tends to exhibit high anxiety in behaviour, expressed by strong passive–defensive reactions. In four of the eight studies presented in the table the correlation is almost $-0.6$ or more, suggesting a moderately strong interrelation between both dimensions studied here. A similar result was obtained by Belous (1970). In his study the strength of the NS was diagnosed by the GSR variant of the extinction with reinforcement method and by the change of simple RT under repeatedly applied stimuli (see Chapter 2). Anxiety was measured in laboratory settings incorporating behavioural and physiological indices. All correlation coefficients between the indices of strength of the NS and anxiety were negative and statistically highly significant.

Looking now at the relation between strength of inhibition and level of anxiety we find that correlation coefficients are negative (except for one study), ranging from $-0.202$ to $-0.581$. Thus, the regularity stated for strength of excitation is repeated here; however, the values of coefficients are lower than those for strength of excitation. Yet in this case, no easy interpretation can be found. More extensive investigation is required—the positive relation between excitation strength and inhibition strength (see Table XXI) not being of much help. An analysis of STI items referring to strength of inhibition suggests that this property, revealed in overt behaviour, has many features in com-

TABLE XXVI. NS properties and anxiety as measured by MAS and STAI

| References | Strength of E | Strength of I | Mobility of NP | Balance of NP |
|---|---|---|---|---|
| (1) Strelau, 1969; MAS N = 75; M,F | −0.595[a] | −0.412[a] | | |
| (2) Strelau, 1971[a]; MAS | −0.481[a] N = 148; M,F | −0.202[c] N = 159; M,F | −0.177 N = 157; M,F | −0.190[c] N = 200; M,F |
| (3) Strelau, 1973[a]; MAS N = 159; M,F | −0.554[a] | 0.359[a] | 0.289[b] | |
| (4) Terelak, 1974; MAS N = 115; M | −0.617[a] | −0.581[a] | −0.282[b] | 0.002 |
| (5) Sosnowski and Wrześniewski, in press; MAS; N = 48; M | −0.63[a] | −0.45[b] | −0.41[b] | |
| (6) Zarzycka, 1980; STAI N = 174; M | −0.467[a] | −0.489[a] | −0.226[c] | 0.043 |
| (7) Zarzycka, 1980; STAI N = 59; M | −0.394[b] | −0.332[c] | −0.224 | 0.140 |
| (8) Sosnowski and Wrześniewski, in press; STAI; N = 48; M | −0.72[a] | −0.52[a] | −0.60[a] | |

Designations as in Table XXV.

mon with self-control. Paisey and Mangan's (1980) factor analysis study supports this hypothesis. One of the factors derived from Eysenck's EPQ, Zuckerman's SSS and Strelau's STI includes strength of inhibition and conscientiousness, the latter being interpreted by the authors as the willingness to uphold social rules. As follows from Kofta's (1979) detailed review of research conducted on self-control as related to other personality dimensions, most of the studies seem to support the hypothesis that the physiological components of anxiety are negatively related to self-control, i.e. the higher the self-control the lower the level of anxiety. This is in agreement with our data, if one makes the assumption, which has been suggested above, that high strength of inhibition might be positively correlated with high self-control.[7]

The results of correlating mobility of the nervous system with anxiety do not vary essentially from the regularities stated in the case of strength of excitation and inhibition. The coefficients of correlation are all (except one) negative, although most of them (5 in the total number of 8) do not reach the value of 0.3. It might be suggested with some caution that the negative interrelation between both dimensions in question is due to the fact that mobility is positively correlated with strength of the NS (see Table XXI on p. 133).

As regards the balance of the NS our data presented in Table XXVI allow us to conclude that there is no relation between anxiety and the balance of nervous processes as measured by the STI. Comparing all the results in Table XXVI we may observe a general regularity, i.e. that anxiety is negatively correlated with strength of excitation, strength of inhibition and mobility. Exactly the same was stated by Carlier (in press) who used Cattell's IPAT Anxiety scale[8] to diagnose anxiety.

## Neuroticism and NSPs

One of the personality dimensions which has often been compared with the Pavlovian concept of basic nervous system properties is neuroticism, which has much in common with anxiety (see Eysenck, 1970; Cattell, 1965; Gray, 1981). It was Eysenck (1947) who first drew attention to the fact that there is a link between the strength of the NS and neuroticism, however, he later abandoned this position. Until the mid-1960s he regarded neuroticism "as an inherited psychophysical disposition linked with the lability of the autonomic system, which governs a person's emotional reactivity" (Eysenck, 1963, p. 192). Under the burden of evidence, Eysenck (1967) changed his mind as regards the physiological basis of his personality dimensions, and the limbic system (visceral brain) took over the role of the physiological mechanism of the neuroticism dimension. Relating neuroticism to anxiety the author (Eysenck, 1970) regarded anxiety as a mixed concept, derived from both neuroticism and introversion. Anxiety, which is a conditioned fear reaction, is particularly characteristic of individuals who are introverts with a high position on the neuroticism scale.

An opposite position as regards the relation between neuroticism and anxiety has been taken by Gray (1972b, 1981), to whom anxiety and impulsivity (the latter regarded by Eysenck as one of the two components of extraversion) should be considered as primary dimensions, whereas extraversion–introversion and neuroticism are treated as secondary traits, being the outcome of interaction of the physiological mechanisms of anxiety and impulsivity. The behavioural inhibition system (BIS) which resides in the septo-hippocampal system and its neocortical projection in the frontal lobe, constitutes the physiological basis of anxiety. Neuroticism reflects, according to Gray (1981) the joint increment in sensitivity of the BIS and in the physiological mechanism which controls impulsivity, i.e. the so-called behavioural activation system (BAS).[9] From this it follows that neuroticism is the result of high anxiety and high impulsivity.

Gray's view as regards the relation between neuroticism and nervous system properties has fluctuated, probably due to the fact that his modification of Eysenck's theory took a long time to mature. In his first considerations concerned with the relation between NS properties and personality dimensions Gray (1964) hypothesized that strength of the NS corresponds with neuroticism or with manifest anxiety. Both these dimensions have some connections with the level of arousal which, in turn, when considered from the point of view of individual differences, has much in common with the strength of NS (Gray, 1964). Gray (1967) rejected this position with the argument that neuroticism is not related to the sensory threshold which is regarded as one of the main indices of strength of the NS. Eysenck (1972) mediated in this discussion with the suggestion that there is no reason why the weak NS should not correspond with both of his orthogonal dimensions—neuroticism and introversion. Neuroticism, as well as manifest anxiety which is highly (as measured by Taylor's MAS) correlated with this dimension, has much in common with such indices of the weak nervous system as distraction and overload, whereas introversion is characterized by, among other things, low sensory thresholds, as is the case with the weak TNS. Marton and Urban (1966) also share the opinion that neuroticism is linked to the strength of NS.

There are several data, collected in the literature, which throw some light on the relations between the neuroticism dimension and nervous system properties, especially strength of the NS. The first derive from Mangan and Farmer's (1967) study conducted on a small number of students (20 men aged 18–24) in which the authors used the slope of RT curve to assess the strength of NS and the MPI for diagnosing extraversion and neuroticism. They stated that neuroticism does not correlate with Nebylitsyn's index of strength of the NS. However, a negative correlation between strength and neuroticism was found in Mangan's later studies. Using caffeine as a factor inducing onset of transmarginal inhibition in the after-image duration phenomenon White and Mangan (1972) diagnosed the strength of nervous system in 16 men (students) selected from a group of 150 subjects for having extreme values on both dimensions—extraversion and neuroticism. The analysis of variance showed that there is a significant interaction between the after-image slope under caffeine and neuroticism, and the authors thus concluded that low strength of the NS was related to high neuroticism. Mangan (1978) gave additional evidence for this conclusion in a factor analytic study, where he was able to show that transmarginal inhibition, which is an index of the weak TNS, constitutes one factor together with neuroticism, measured by the EPI. However, the weakness of this study, as of the former one, lies in the fact that the transmarginal phenomenon was measured on the basis of the after-image slope under the administration of caffeine (for description see White *et al.*, 1969)—a method which is not used by Soviet psychologists for diagnosing the strength of the NS. A study conducted by Kulagin (1975) on rats confirms that emotional reactivity, which shows some analogies to neuroticism, correlates negatively with strength of the nervous system ($r = -0.514$; $p < 0.05$). Emotional reactivity was measured in open-field behaviour and the change of CR magnitude under caffeine was used as index of strength of NS.

There are some studies which support Mangan's first data, i.e. which suggest that there is no correspondence between NS strength and neuroticism (Orlebeke, 1972; Kovač and Halmiová, 1973; Karpova, 1974; Frigon, 1976). Izyumova and Aminov (1978), correlated the strength of NS, lability and activatability with emotional stability as diagnosed by the Cattell's 16 PF,[10] and stated that there is no relation between the strength of NS and emotional stability. Strength of NS was assessed on the basis of the photic driving reaction to low stimuli (see p. 92). At the same time the authors found that individuals with high emotional stability have a statistically significantly higher level of lability as measured by the photic driving reaction to high frequency (see p. 101) compared with individuals characterized as emotionally unstable. There is also a predominance of activatability in the group with high emotional stability. Activatability was measured by the alpha index (see p. 108). Orlebeke's (1972) study aimed at relating Eysenck's basic dimensions of personality to NS properties allowed him to collect some data which suggest that there is a relation between neuroticism and dynamism of the NS, the latter being measured by the speed of extinction of the orienting response (in EDA). The speed of OR extinction and introversion constitute one factor.

As may be seen from this review it is impossible to give any unequivocal answer to the question of the relation between neuroticism and strength of NS. As regards other NS properties, the evidence is so meagre that any conclusion about their correspondence with neuroticism is almost impossible. Here again, we have collected some results over the last decade which throw light on the relations in question. In our studies neuroticism was measured by the MPI as was extraversion–introversion. The STI was used to measure the properties of the nervous system. The results of our comparison studies are displayed in Table XXVII, which also contains data collected by Carlier (in press) and Paisey and Mangan (1982). These authors also diagnosed NS properties using the STI, whereas neuroticism was measured by the EPI (Carlier) and EPQ (Paisey and Mangan).

It is not difficult to find some regularities in the table. In all nine studies it was found that neuroticism correlates negatively with strength of excitation ($-0.378$ to $-0.557$), strength of inhibition ($-0.246$ to $-0.588$; except the study conducted by Mangan and Paisey) and, to a lesser degree, with mobility. In the latter case all coefficients of correlation are negative; however, only five of the total eight, are statistically significant ($-0.209$ to $-0.300$). There is no correlation between neuroticism and the balance of nervous processes. This configuration of interdependencies exactly resembles that showing the relations between NS properties and anxiety (see Table XXVI). The high agreement between the nine studies in question (of which the last three were conducted outside our laboratory) is probably due to the use of the same technique for diagnosing the properties of the NS. Neuroticism was almost always measured by the same technique (except studies 8 and 9—see above).

As regards the relation between neuroticism and the strength of NS, we were able to show in two independent studies that both of these dimensions are related, as shown in Table XXVII (Strelau, 1978). Defining neuroticism as emotional hyperactivity (which seems to be consistent with Eysenck's conception), we tested its relation to strength of the NS in 34 second-grade pupils, ranging in age from 8 to 9 years. Emotional hyperactivity was diagnosed on the basis of a standard

TABLE XXVII. NS properties and neuroticism

| References | Strength of E | Strength of I | Mobility of NP | Balance of NP |
|---|---|---|---|---|
| (1) Strelau, 1969<br>N = 78; M,F | −0.478[a] | −0.450[a] | −0.300[c] | |
| (2) Strelau, 1970a<br>N = 159; M,F | −0.557[a] | −0.526[a] | −0.215[c] | |
| (3) Strelau, 1971[a]<br> | −0.378[a]<br>N = 169; M,F<br>−0.538[a] | −0.246[b]<br>N = 178; M,F<br>−0.588[a] | −0.174<br>N = 177; M,F<br>−0.209[c] | −0.080<br>N = 197; M,F<br>0.108 |
| (4) Terelak, 1974<br>N = 115; M | −0.442[a] | −0.496[a] | −0.141 | 0.112 |
| (5) Zarzycka, 1980<br>N = 174; M | −0.426[b] | −0.545[a] | −0.173 | −0.020 |
| (6) Zarzycka, 1980<br>N = 59; M | −0.504[a] | −0.396[b] | −0.296[c] | |
| (7) Ciosek and Oszmiańczuk, 1974<br>N = 70; M | −0.49[c] | −0.48[c] | −0.21[c] | |
| (8) Carlier, in press<br>N = 202; F,M | −0.53 | −0.14 | | |
| (9) Paisey and Mangan, 1982<br>N = 174; no information about sex | | | | |

Designations as in Table XXV.

clinical interview. Strength of the NS was measured by the change of simple RT under repeatedly exposed stimuli (see p. 90). As it turned out, there were significantly more emotionally hyperactive subjects, compared with other children, among the individuals with weak NS. The same regularity was noted in another sample (39 subjects of the same age) where the relation between strength of the NS and motor hyperactivity was examined (Strelau, 1978).

The interpretation of dependencies between neuroticism and strength of inhibition and mobility does not depart, in general, from the one given regarding anxiety. I must repeat again, however, that our knowledge of the physiological mechanisms and explanatory concepts of strength of inhibition and mobility of the NS is highly unsatisfactory, making any understanding of the attained relations much more difficult.

## GENERAL CONCLUSIONS

Summarising our empirical findings as regards the relations between extraversion–introversion, neuroticism, and anxiety on the one hand, and the properties of the nervous system on the other, it is possible to make several conclusions which are illustrated in Table XXVIII.

In general, strength of excitation correlates positively with extraversion, but negatively with anxiety and neuroticism. Strength of inhibition is not related to extraversion; however, it correlates negatively with both neuroticism and anxiety. As far as mobility of the NS is concerned it is positively correlated with the E/I dimension and slightly and negatively with neuroticism and anxiety. Balance of NS (as regards strength of excitation and strength of inhibition) is not related to anxiety and neuroticism and its correspondence with extraversion is not unequivocal. Some studies support the positive relation between these dimensions, others are contradictory to these results.

The above regularities seem to be consistent with the factor analytic study conducted in our laboratory by Terelak (Terelak, 1974; Strelau

TABLE XXVIII. General characteristic of NS properties in individuals differing in extraversion–introversion, neuroticism, and anxiety

| NSPs | Extraversion | Neuroticism | Anxiety |
|---|---|---|---|
| Strength of E | high | low | low |
| Strength of I | no relation | low | low |
| Mobility of NP | high | rather low | rather low |
| Balance of NP | contradictory results | no relation | no relation |

and Terelak, 1974). Taking as point of departure the temperament dimensions measured by Eysenck's MPI, Taylor's MAS, the Guildford-Zimmerman Temperament Survey (GZTS), Thurstone's Temperament Schedule (TTS), and Strelau's STI, we were able to separate six factors using the method of principle components and Kaiser's Varimax.

*Factor I*, called vigorousness, comprises (with high factor loadings) such traits as extraversion, strength of excitation, mobility, ascendance, sociability, and impulsive, dominant, and sociable.[11]

*Factor II*, which we called emotionality, has its highest loadings in such traits as: manifest anxiety, neuroticism, strength of excitation, strength of inhibition, emotional stability, and emotional stable—the last four traits all with negative signs.

*Factor III* (thoughtfulness) comprises such traits as restraint, thoughtfulness, and reflective.

*Factor IV*, characterized as sociability, comprises personal relations, objectivity, and friendliness.

*Factor V*, which has been called "equilibrium of nervous processes", has, as follows from its label, the highest loading in the balance of nervous processes.

*Factor VI* contains (with high loading) the masculinity trait only.

The above temperament structure was derived from results collected in a group of 190 men with ages ranging from 20 to 40 years, selected for high alpha index. In another group, equivalent to the former one, except for the fact that the subjects were selected for a low alpha index, a similar factor analysis procedure was applied and in general the results obtained in this group do not differ significantly from those of the high alpha index group. The main difference consists of separating an additional Factor (VII) which has the highest factor loadings in activity traits (as measured by GZTS and TTS). In a study conducted by Kłodecka (1982) on high-school students, in which exactly the same traits were measured and subjected to factor analysis with the same method, very similar regularities were found.

Comparing the results of our factor analytic research with the data we obtained in the correlational studies, high convergence can be seen. This concerns Factors I, II, and V. The structure of Factor I convinces us that extraversion is positively correlated with strength of excitation and mobility, whereas Factor II gives evidence that anxiety and neuroticism correlate negatively with the strength of excitation and inhibition. In turn, Factor V, the equilibrium of nervous processes, which contains no other traits than the balance of NP, also corresponds with correlational data. Similar regularities have also been found by

Paisey and Mangan (1980, 1982) when comparing Eysenck's personality dimensions and the NS properties diagnosed by STI. As the authors write:

> This pattern of correlations strongly suggests that these questionnaire scales may be combined to produce three major clusters of personality/temperament characteristics: extraversion/strength of excitation/mobility, stability/strength of excitation/strength of inhibition/mobility, and strength of inhibition/impulse control (low P).

When formulating conclusions about the relations between extraversion–introversion, neuroticism, and anxiety on the one hand, and properties of the NS on the other, one has to bear in mind that such conclusions must be limited to studies where the nervous system properties are estimated by the STI. A comparison study between two given dimensions (e.g. extraversion and strength of the NS) diagnosed in laboratory conditions may completely change the picture of the dependencies in question, as has been shown in this chapter.

# 5
# Regulative Theory of Temperament

## THE PAVLOVIAN CONCEPT OF NERVOUS SYSTEM PROPERTIES AND ITS CRITICAL ANALYSIS AS A STARTING-POINT FOR THE REGULATIVE THEORY OF TEMPERAMENT

My thinking on temperament has been greatly influenced by Pavlov's functional approach, evidenced in his definition of nervous system properties in which he revealed their most important role to be their ability to adapt to the environment. This functional paradigm was further developed by the Teplov–Nebylitsyn school and the Merlin group (see Chapter 1) in contrast with the traditional, static temperament approach. The latter was limited to the description of temperament types, with no reference to real-life situations.

In all studies of NSPs, special attention has been paid to those aspects of behaviour revealed in energy level and temporal features. When reviewing temperament concepts, from the time of Kant and the founder of experimental psychology, Wundt, I came to the conclusion (Strelau, 1969) that vigorousness and temporal characteristics may be found in almost all concepts regardless of their idiosyncrasies. This convinced me that Pavlov's typology dealt with important temperament features.

Important to a proper understanding of temperament and its physiological basis was Pavlov's development of the idea that individual differences in behaviour, primarily involving CR activity, should be explained by features of the CNS. This changed the traditional thinking about the physiological mechanisms of temperament, which were mostly restricted to the endocrine system or to the functioning of the autonomic NS.

Most fascinating was the concept of NS strength with regard to excitation as modified by Teplov and Nebylitsyn. They treated it as one dimension, with one pole consisting of sensitivity and the other endurance. Although this feature, like all other NSPs, was considered by Teplov and Nebylitsyn to be a physiological phenomenon, most of the methods by which both the poles of strength have been measured (see Chapter 2) support my belief that this very important dimension should be of fundamental interest to psychologists.

I have drawn on all the ideas mentioned as well as on the tremendous amount of data from studies diagnosing the NSPs. However, after twelve years of research conducted within the framework of Pavlov's typology, under the influence of the Teplov–Nebylitsyn school,[1] I moved away from the Pavlovian concept of TNS and notions of the separate NS properties of strength, mobility, dynamism and balance of excitation and inhibition. The main reasons for this may be summarized as follows:

(1) Though treated as physiological bases of temperament, the NSPs are in fact explanatory notions, as mentioned before (see p. 117). Pavlov's original conceptualization is limited to hypothetical features of the cortex. This was a position taken by most Pavlovian typologists, but in my opinion, it did not take account of the considerable data in the literature showing that temperament features are co-determined by other physiological mechanisms, e.g. several centres in the subcortex, especially the reticular system, by the autonomic nervous system and the endocrine system (Strelau, 1969). Strelau *et al.* (1972) collated a great deal of data from the literature in support of this opinion. For several years Soviet psychologists have been emphasizing the importance of the subcortical area (Nebylitsyn, 1972a; Rusalov, 1979; Golubeva, 1980a). Some studies have even attempted to construct a typology for which the main criterion is the balance between the sympathetic and parasympathetic nervous systems; however, its relation to the NSPs or to temperament is rather unclear (Suvorova, 1974; Turovskaya, 1977).

(2) My own aim was to develop a psychological concept of temperament, the core of which was human behaviour. Pavlov's typology, no matter how it is evaluated, should be treated as more of a physiological concept. As mentioned before (see p. 62) Merlin attempted to link Pavlov's typology more closely with psychology by showing the interdependencies of NSPs within given temperament types. When referring to the "psychologicalization" of Pavlov's typology I therefore mean

the psychological reinterpretation of this conceptual system.

(3) As shown in Chapter 1, Pavlov (1951–52) considered the TNS as equated with temperament in humans, to be the genotype. Although he erroneously extended its meaning to include inborn traits, it does not alter the fact that his direct reference to the constitutional tradition was the weakest part of the theory. As a result of this way of evaluating types, Pavlov contended that (see p. 12) the weak type (melancholic) was destined by nature to be maladapted to life and to be more or less vitally defective. However, Teplov (1964a) and Nebylitsyn (1972a) abandoned the evaluation of NSPs, sharing the view that these are inborn and stable traits (for stability as a proof of innateness—see p. 42). This position can hardly be accepted if one takes into account the rich evidence for the influence of the environment on any psychological and physiological human trait, including temperament. In a further discussion we will return to this problem and to other arguments presented in this section.

(4) As mentioned before, according to Pavlov, the physiological concept of TNS referred to temperament in psychology. This position has been seriously challenged by Teplov and Nebylitsyn. Teplov (1964a) considered the partial NSPs to be physiological bases of special abilities or aptitudes. However, according to Nebylitsyn (1972b), the general NSPs should be regarded as a physiological mechanism underlying not only temperament but also general abilities, motivation, and several other psychological phenomena. Nebylitsyn's statement that NSPs should be extended to psychological features other than temperament is fully justified if one considers that he strongly advocated the existence of dynamism of the nervous processes. Nebylitsyn accepted speed of CR formation to be the main index of dynamism (1963a, 1972a). Chapter 1 argues that dynamism, as thus understood, should be treated as a physiological basis of learning ability and has little to do with temperament. However, the speed of conditioning which should be considered primarily as a domain of learning ability, appears to be an index of almost all NSPs such as strength, mobility, and dynamism.[2] This suggests either that the index is a bad one and/or that the properties of the NS are not as independent as the typologists of the NS have been arguing. Having no doubt that several relations exist between temperament and other psychological dimensions, I was primarily interested in developing a theory of temperament.

Taking this critique as a point of departure we developed our theory of temperament. I would like to stress that this concept does not only result from my own research but is a product of the contributions of many of my students and associates. At the end of the 1960s there were only three faculty members in the Department of Psychophysiology and Psychology of Individual Differences, now there are ten, excluding the many undergraduate and graduate students who are continuously working on dissertations in this field of psychology. The research conducted by Eliasz, Klonowicz, Matysiak, Matczak, and Sosnowski is of special importance. However, there are still differences among us in our approach to temperament. If there were no such discrepancies it would mean the death of our theory. For this reason, by using the phrase "we" I mean that my own position has been shaped by the vast amount of data and concepts collected and developed by many of my students.

Our theory of temperament stems from several sources, but it could not have developed in this direction without the basis of Pavlovian typology. In this sense our theory may be considered within the neo-Pavlovian typology area. We went further in our conceptualization and in searching for facts, making use of several other theories and concepts in psychology, which is why this so-called "regulative theory of temperament" can hardly be recognized as a neo-Pavlonian approach.

In developing our temperament theory, of considerable influence was the theory of action developed in Poland by my mentor, Tomaszewski (1963, 1978), the roots of which may be found in Russian psychology (Rubinstein, 1946; Vygotsky, 1962; Leontev, 1978). This theory forced me to look at temperament features from the point of view of reciprocal relations between humans and their environment, where human activity plays the most important role in regulating these relations (Tomaszewski, 1978) and the main philosophy in pursuing psychology consists in looking at humans within their environment.

To develop our theory we took advantage of the vast amount of data collected within the framework of research on arousal and/or activation, with special reference to the individual differences approach. Of most importance to us were the concept of the intensity dimension developed by Duffy (1951, 1957, 1962), the idea of the optimal level of arousal (activation) proposed by Hebb (1955), and the arousability concept evolved by Gray (1964, 1972a). Of course, many other theories and names should be mentioned here; however, I would rather refer to them when presenting our own theory based on the significant data collected in the laboratory, the knowledge gathered from many publications devoted to temperament, and, finally, on my 25 years' experience in temperament research.

## THE UNDERSTANDING OF TEMPERAMENT

In order to describe the regulative theory of temperament let me start with the definition of the notion in question. By *temperament* I mean relatively stable features of the organism, primarily biologically determined, as revealed in the formal traits of reactions which form the energy level and temporal characteristic of behaviour.

### Temperament as Comprising Relatively Stable Features

The designation "relatively stable features of the organism" takes several aspects into account. First, when comparing temperament features with any other psychological traits most psychologists agree that the former are very stable (e.g. Merlin, 1973; Buss and Plomin, 1975; Thomas and Chess, 1977; Strelau, 1978; Mangan, 1982). Secondly, temperament, like all other psychological and physiological features, can change during the course of development (Chudnovsky, 1963; Troshikhin *et al.*, 1971; Leites, 1972; Thomas and Chess, 1977; Strelau, 1978). This is due to the process of maturation under which progressive and regressive changes occur in the physiological mechanism underlying temperament. However, in spite of these changes, high consistency in the temperament characteristic may be observed (Thomas and Chess, 1977) implying a kind of stability in the face of this changeability.

Thirdly, temperament features are subject to changes under environmental influences. Speaking about such changes of NSPs Pavlov (1951–52) and other Pavlovian typologists (e.g. Teplov, 1964a; Merlin, 1973) restricted these to the effect of extraordinary conditions, such as trauma, disease, or severe disturbances in the surroundings. We have accepted the assumption that temperament features are more readily prone to changes, that might be caused by such factors as different kinds of prolonged stimulation or deprivation. Noise, nutrition, climate, population density, and several other features of the surroundings are examples of the variables which influence the shaping of temperament. This idea has been extensively developed in our laboratory by Eliasz (1979). He conducted several studies in order to discover if there were any relations between one of our main temperament features, reactivity (see p. 176), and the stimulative value of the environment in which one lives for a longer period (Eliasz, 1981).

Traffic noise and population density were the main sources of stimulation controlled for these studies. Reactivity was measured by STI (see p. 198). Studies were conducted in 225 male subjects aged

14–15 years and in 192 male subjects aged 25–50 years, each living in the same flat for at least five years. The author found several interesting statistically significant dependencies between the stimulative value of the environment and reactivity level. However, they differed in youth and adult populations. Because of housing problems in Poland, it is very difficult to move home according to one's desires or needs, which in practice means that people have to remain in one place. Eliasz hypothesized that changes in reactivity were mostly caused by the specificity of the stimulative value of the environment. However, to make this hypothesis more probable longitudinal studies are needed and are suggested by the author.

The general observations concerning the existence of a so-called national temperament (e.g. Brzezicki, 1946) coincide with Eliasz's conclusion. Such national differences, like all other temperament differences which refer to the specificity of the country or social groups, cannot be explained by differences in the genotype. This would support the role of environmental influences in shaping temperament. Environmental factors can probably change temperament features to such a degree as to cause structural changes in the physiological bases of temperament. When referring to temperament changes caused by the environment it must be realized that these changes do not take place from day to day, so the features of temperament being dealt with are relatively stable.

## Temperament Revealed in the Formal Aspect of Behaviour

By definition, temperament features are manifested in the formal features of behaviour. This needs explanation. Any object has its content and form. The content refers to the meaning of the object, i.e. the substance of the object. But any object has a shape, fashion, mode or style within which it exists and in which the content reveals itself. This is what I understand when using the notion "form". If this reasoning is transferred to behaviour it may be stated that temperament constitutes the formal aspect of behaviour. At least two important conclusions follow from this statement.

(1) Any form of behaviour has its mode or style within which it exists (see also Thomas *et al.*, 1968; Buss and Plomin, 1975; Burks and Rubenstein, 1979). The individual differences in respect to this mode (style), which I have limited to the energetic and temporal characteristic of behaviour, should be treated as temperament features. It must be stressed that there is no form of behaviour in which both these characteristics cannot be distinguished. This assumption is of great

importance because it means that temperament is not only expressed by emotions, as many psychologists assume (Allport, 1937; Eysenck, 1970; Levitov, 1969; Kreutz, 1966). In fact, Wundt seemed to be the initiator of this tradition when he stated that excitability is to sensory sensitivity what temperament is to emotions (Wundt, 1911).

Going against tradition, it is assumed that temperament features manifest themselves in all kinds of mental activities, including intellectual ones, as supported by Leites (1956b, 1972), Malkov (1966), and Merlin (1973) as well as by our own studies (Strelau, 1978; Klonowicz, 1979a; Matczak, 1982, in press). In summary, one can say that temperament features constitute an inherent attribute of every form of behaviour, which is the main reason why they have been labelled "formal traits". Consequently, one of the methodological paradigms resulting from this statement is that temperament features may be measured on the bases of all kinds of behaviour and they appear, as a rule, only in given behaviour and reactions because they do not exist as such, i.e. as isolated phenomena.

(2) Temperament, as constituting the formal aspect of reactions, should be distinguished from the content (substance) of behaviour which reflects the specificity of reactions, the relation of the humans to themselves, to each other and toward the world, their motivations, desires, and other psychological phenomena; all features that often appear under the label "personality". Since temperament is not a content of behaviour, it does not determine it directly; however, as will be shown in Chapter 7, temperament features, among many other variables, influence and determine the content of behaviour traditionally labelled "personality". This statement clearly breaks away from the views of many constitutional temperament typologists (Kretschmer, 1944; Conrad, 1963; Sheldon and Stevens, 1942), as well as from some of the popular psychometric concepts of temperament (Guilford and Zimmerman, 1956; Lovel, 1945; Thurstone, 1951) where the content of behaviour, which should be treated mainly as the result of social interaction, is directly derived from temperament or its physiological mechanisms.

## Temperament as being Primarily Biologically Determined

If temperament is defined as being primarily biologically determined it should be understood first of all that it is a result of biological evolution (see Leontiev, 1978) and this phenomenon called temperament may be found in animals as well as in humans. This means, among other things, that an individual at birth has a given temperament which is determined by the physiological mechanism shaped during prenatal life on the basis of a particular genetic endowment. This inborn physiological mechanism forms the initial basis of the individual's temperament, which is in turn subjected during ontogenesis to changes due to maturation and environmental influences.

## THE ENERGETIC LEVEL OF BEHAVIOUR AS ONE OF THE MAIN COMPONENTS OF TEMPERAMENT

As said before, temperament is manifested in energetic level of behaviour and its temporal characteristic. Let us concentrate on the energetic level. Most temperament theories have initially referred to the energetic level of behaviour. For example, Kant (1943) reveals the importance of "Lebenskraft" (energy life) which may vary from excitation to drowsiness. Wundt (1911), when characterizing temperament, mentioned intensity of emotions as one of the main criteria. Kretschmer (1944) acknowledged four main facets of temperament, among which the "Psychästesie" (mental sensitivity to stimuli) and "Psychomotolität (energetic aspects of motor behaviour) play an important role. His colleague, Ewald (1924) introduced the concept of biotonus, understood as a feature which depends on the individual's metabolism and which determines individual differences in the strength and tempo of psychic life. As one of the three dimensions in the old, but still popular, typology of temperament developed by Heymans and Wiersma (1906–09) the "activity–passivity" dimension should be mentioned. Many more examples can be found (see Diamond, 1957; also Strelau, 1969).

Several contemporary concepts also refer to the energetic level of behaviour, examples of which are the studies devoted to the strength and activatability of the nervous system described in Chapter 1. Based on research into the level of activation (Duffy, 1951, 1957, 1962; Freeman, 1948; Malmo, 1957, 1959) the concept of the "intensive dimension" has been developed which stresses individual differences in behaviour caused by the level of activation. According to Duffy, the intensive dimension should be regarded as a temperament characteristic. Gray (1964), analysing the level of activation data in relation to the strength of NS, formed the concept of arousability which refers to individual differences in activation level. He states that:

> the differences between the strong and weak nervous system can be accounted for on the hypothesis that the weaker the nervous system, the greater is the degree of non-specific bombardment of the cortex by the ascending reticular system for any given stimulus situation. (p. 305)

Thomas and Chess (Thomas *et al.*, 1968; Thomas and Chess, 1977) described temperament as comprising nine basic traits, and included at least three dimensions closely related to the energetic level of behaviour (activity, strength of reaction, and discrimination threshold). In Buss and Plomin's temperament typology (1975), which derived from the Thomas and Chess' conception, four dimensions are distinguished, among which activity and emotionality belong to the characteristic in question.

A study by Terelak (1974; see also Strelau and Terelak, 1974) on the structure of temperament in two independent populations (groups with high and low alpha index)[3] showed that out of six (seven in the second group) distinguishable temperamental factors, the factor which contributed most to the controlled variance of behaviour measured in this study was the energy factor. This brought together the following traits: impulsiveness, extraversion, sociability, leadership, dominance, NS strength (in excitation), and activity. This factor was provisionally called vigorousness (see Fig. 10), since a comparative analysis showed that the common denominator for all these traits are those forms of behaviour based on stable individual differences in the energy level of the organism.

This review of theories and concepts, in which the importance of traits referring to the energetic level of behaviour has been revealed, is far from exhaustive; it shows, however, that there is a great deal of

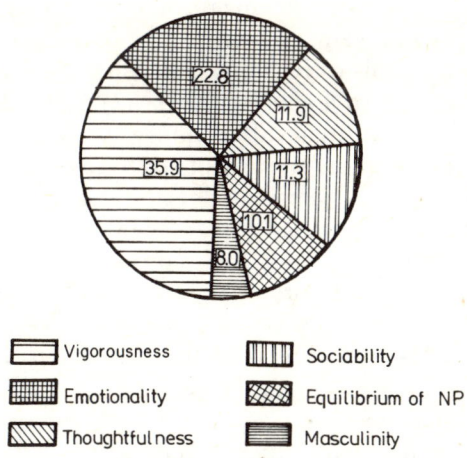

FIG. 10. Factors making up the structure of temperament (adapted from Strelau and Terelak, 1974).

interest in this phenomenon. The growing concern with the energy level of human behaviour, and particularly with relatively stable individual differences in this respect, stems mostly from the fact that the current conditions formed by our civilization consist, among other things, of a high frequency of situations involving highly stimulating qualities (overload, deprivation, monotony or various kinds of stress). The individual trait which causes the stimulative value of same objective settings to be perceived in differing degrees from one person to another, seems to be an important regulator of human actions, especially in extreme situations.

We assume that there are two basic dimensions of temperament responsible for individual differences in the energetic level of behaviour—reactivity and activity. Both these terms have had different meanings in the literature; however, it will be shown that they acquire a specific meaning in our conception.

## Reactivity as a Primary Feature of Temperament

The concept of reactivity developed in our laboratory since the end of the 1960s (Strelau, 1969, 1970b, 1974, 1978; Eliasz, 1974, 1981) is supported by experimental evidence, showing that people differ in the intensity or magnitude of their reactions to stimuli (situations) and that these differences remain relatively stable. The sensitivity threshold may be mentioned as the most common phenomenon (Duffy, 1962; Petrie, 1967; Nebylitsyn, 1972a; Teplov, 1972; Haslam, 1972; Eysenck, 1981). Although the magnitude of reaction in sensitivity threshold experiments seems to be constant (it is the minimal reaction to be stated), individuals differ in the intensity of stimuli at which the threshold is attained. In Pavlov's (1951–52) laboratory it has been frequently shown that animals differ in magnitude of CRs to stimuli of given intensity. In humans, the law of strength established in the CR procedure by Pavlov, is manifested differently, depending on the strength of their NS. Semagin (1971), in experiments on CR activity in rats, found evidence to support high consistency in the intensity of reaction. Using nine indicators of the magnitude of CR activity, for which altogether 45 coefficients of correlation were computed, he obtained correlations oscillating from 0·257 to 0·869. In 35 cases these correlations were statistically significant.

It has been stated that, depending on the temperament dimension under control in RT experiments individuals differ in response amplitude to stimuli of different intensity. Castaneda (1956) observed differences between high and low anxiety individuals, and Ratanova

(1975) was able to show that subjects with strong NS differ from "weak" ones in this respect. The magnitude of the orienting response (as measured by GSR and EEG techniques) to different kinds of stimuli has often been used an an index of NSPs (see Nebylitsyn, 1972a) and, as stated by Zuckerman (1979), also differentiates high and low sensation seekers.

Individual differences in the amplitude of evoked potentials of stimuli of different intensity were established many times and, being stable, have been used as indicators of several traits, e.g. augmenting/reducing (Buchsbaum, 1978, 1979; Buchsbaum and Silverman, 1968; Buchsbaum et al., in press), sensation seeking (Zuckerman, 1979, 1980) or NS strength (Bazylevich, 1974b; Chuprikova, 1977). Many examples in the psychological literature support our assumption that individual differences in intensity (magnitude) of reaction are rather common phenomena. Duffy, who acknowledged this fact and who linked differences in reaction strength with stable individual differences in the level of activation hypothesized that individuals who react strongly in one situation will often also react more strongly in different situations than other individuals might (1957, p. 268).

We assume that reactivity is that feature of the organism which determines the relatively stable individual differences in question. The notion "reactivity" has been used in physiology and psychology by several authors. It has its rather unequivocal meaning in physiology where it is understood to refer to the ability of the nervous system to react to excitation of receptor systems (Konorski, 1967; see also Kavetsky et al., 1961). Reactivity was one of the main concepts in Thomas et al.'s (1968) theory of temperament, where this notion was used as a synonym for temperament. However, in order to stress that temperament is revealed not only in the passive behaviour suggested by the term "reactivity", but also in interaction of the individual with the surroundings, the authors rejected this concept (Thomas and Chess, 1977). Nebylitsyn (1972a) assumed reactivity to be a synonym for sensitivity of the NS.

Our theory treats reactivity as a psychological concept. *Reactivity* is a temperament feature which determines the relatively stable and characteristic intensity (magnitude) of reactions for a given individual. It is a dimension in which individuals differ and these differences can be characterized quantitatively. Taking as a point of departure the well-known law of strength, which states that the intensity of reaction grows to a given limit in accordance with the increasing intensity of stimuli, we may state that there are individual differences in the way the law of strength is revealed: individuals differ in the degree as well as in the

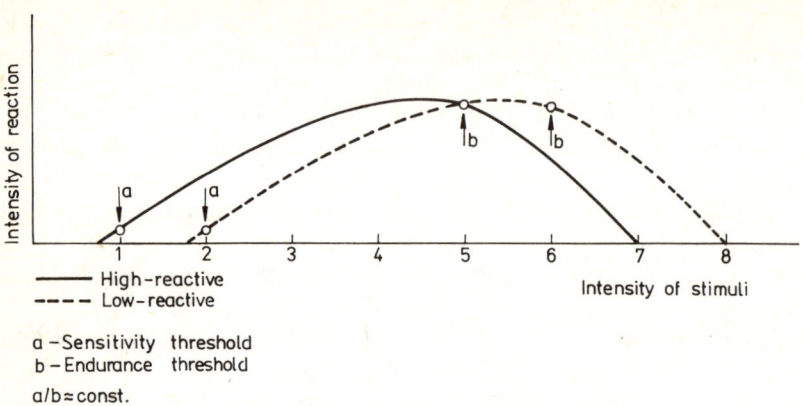

FIG. 11. Model of intensity (magnitude) of reactions in high- and low-reactive individuals.

range in which the intensity (magnitude or amplitude) of reaction is expressed (see Fig. 11). Figure 11 shows that reactivity may be manifested in reactions to stimuli of any intensity. However, crucial to our understanding of reactivity is the fact that it co-determines sensitivity (sensory and emotional), as measured by sensory threshold, and the organism's capacity to work (its endurance), as manifested in reactions to strong or prolonged stimulation. It is revealed in the breakdown of the law of strength, when increasing stimulation causes a decrease or disturbance in the reactions, induced by protective inhibition.

When considering persons who occupy extreme positions with respect to the reactivity dimension, we can distinguish between high- and low-reactive individuals. High-reactive individuals might be characterized as highly sensitive (low sensitivity threshold) and with low endurance. The converse is true of the low-reactive individuals—their sensitivity is low but their endurance is high. Teplov and Nebylitsyn (1963b) have stated that the ratio between sensitivity (r) and endurance (R) is reasonably stable (see p. 29). Ilin (1975) has argued that in individuals with a strong NS, who should be compared with low-reactive ones, the distance between sensitivity and endurance is greater because of their high endurance capacity. This hypothesis has not been verified, however, and the question of the R/r ratio is still open.

*The physiological mechanism of reactivity*

The physiological mechanism determining reactivity is a very complex one and probably includes all anatomic and physiological systems responsible for the accumulation, as well as the release of, stored energy. In determining the individual differences in reaction intensity, the significance of the receptor has been revealed by several authors (e.g. Fiske and Maddi, 1961; Palmer, 1970). Researchers in temperament have often stressed the role of the endocrine system in determining the energetic level of behaviour (Furukava, 1927; Kretschmer, 1944; Frankenhaeuser et al., 1971). Special attention has recently been paid to MAO (monoamine oxydase) as a co-determiner of neurotransmitter conductance (Zuckerman, 1979). Individual differences in the functioning of the autonomic NS, with special emphasis on the balance between the sympathetic and parasympathetic system, have also been linked with the differences in the intensity and expressiveness of human reactions, especially with regard to emotional states (Wenger, 1942; Terry, 1953; Eysenck, 1966; Helson, 1964; Suvorova, 1974).

There is an abundance of facts that show the significance of subcortical areas in determining individual differences in the intensity of reaction; the reticular system is of special importance in determining the differences in this respect (Hebb, 1955; Berlyne, 1960; Duffy, 1962; Gray, 1964). Finally, the entire Pavlovian typology research is based on the assumption that certain features of the cortex play the most important role in determining the phenomena of sensitivity and endurance. In one of our studies (Strelau et al., 1972) considerable data collected from the literature show that the energetic level of behaviour may be co-determined by many systems. On this basis we argued that all these closely interconnected systems operate as a block (unit) which possesses a fairly stable structure. A concept of biochemical individuality was developed by Williams (1956) who not only pointed to the universality of stable individual differences in human anatomy and physiology, but also stressed that the configurations between the given systems are relatively stable. This is close to our understanding of the physiological mechanism of temperament, especially reactivity. However, we would stress neuroendocrine rather than biochemical individuality as constituting the physiological basis of temperament.

The question arises whether any system can be distinguished as playing a specially significant role in determining the intensity of reactions. As most human behaviour is controlled by the cortical-subcortex mechanisms (Konorski, 1967; Anokhin, 1969; Numan, 1978) it seems reasonable to assume that the reticular formation-cortex loop should be mentioned here. However, the question still remains open. The role of the separate systems co-determining the intensity of reaction is especially evident when pathological changes in their functioning occur.

This is frequently argued to be the importance of a given system in determining temperament differences. For example, Kretschmer (1944) used as the main argument for the endocrine system determining human temperament the increased excitability caused by the hyperfunctioning of the thyroid gland and revealed by reaction incommensurate with stimuli strength.

The separate systems co-determining intensity of reaction may also be of differing importance depending on the kind of reaction being investigated. It seems probable that in measuring the magnitude of the GSR to given stimuli, the autonomic NS is of special importance. In the case of EP amplitude it will be reasonable to concentrate on the reticular formation-cortex loop. The so-called partiality phenomenon referred to many times in NSP investigations (see Nebylitsyn, 1972b; Strelau, 1972; Rusalov, 1979; see also p. 49) is probably derived to a certain extent from the fact that different physiological systems co-determine the intensity of reaction, depending on the variables under control.

*Stimulation processing coefficient (SPC)*

Taking as a starting-point the fact that individuals differ in the intensity (magnitude) of reactions to stimuli, we assume that this is because in some individuals this complex physiological mechanism either enhances or suppresses stimulation. This enhancing–suppressing notion has been taken from Gray (1964) who introduced it when discussing the individual differences in activation level. When the value of a stimulus (situation) operating upon the organism (O) is denoted as $S_n$ and the magnitude (intensity) of response (behaviour) as $R_n$, the above-mentioned regularity can be presented as follows:

$$S_n \longrightarrow O \longrightarrow R_{n \pm x}$$

This means that the same stimulus evokes a stronger reaction (more intensive behaviour) in some individuals, while in others the response is decreased.

In high-reactive individuals (with high sensitivity and low endurance) the physiological mechanism is assumed to enhance stimulation ($S_n \longrightarrow O \longrightarrow R_{n+x}$). This means that (external and internal) stimuli evoke stronger responses in these individuals than in low-reactive individuals. However, this regularity should be limited to intensity of stimuli below the endurance threshold. Using the terminology introduced by Matysiak (1980) high-reactive individuals may be characterized as having a high stimulation processing coefficient (SPC). On the other hand, in low-reactive individuals representing the opposite pole of the reactivity dimension (low sensitivity and high endurance) the physiological mechanism of reactivity suppresses exteroceptive and interoceptive stimulation ($S_n \longrightarrow O \longrightarrow R_{n-x}$). It is revealed in a lowered intensity (magnitude) of reactions as compared with high-reactive individuals. Low-reactive individuals can be said to have a low SPC.

The enhancing or suppressing phenomenon, as mentioned above, may be caused by different peripheral and central mechanisms involved in the process of energy storage and release and it seems to be the role of physiologists to bring us closer to an understanding of this interaction. What is most important, however, is the final effect of the mechanisms in question, which is revealed in the relatively stable individual differences in the intensity (magnitude) of reactions.

*Trait- and state-reactivity*

Since intensity (magnitude) of reaction is considered as the main index of reactivity, we should differentiate between state- and trait-reactivity. State-reactivity, not being a temperament phenomenon, is the result of such variables as strength of stimuli acting on the organism, their meaning (which often changes from situation to situation), the current level of activation (regulated by the CNS) and arousal (peripheral regulation), motivation, the whole state of the organism, and, finally, individual reactivity understood as the temperament dimension. It is trait-reactivity which, irrespective of the many factors which co-determine the magnitude (intensity) of reaction, is responsible for observed individual differences in this respect. Thus trait-reactivity, being the subject of our considerations, should be treated as a relatively stable tendency to react to stimuli (situations) with a given intensity or magnitude.[4]

There is a tremendous amount of data collected in the literature which show that, under given conditions (such as deprivation or overload), the organism may be subjected to changes which might be limited from the point of view of our interests) to the process of sensitization and desensitization. Sensitization of the organism, caused mainly by different kinds of deprivation, as a rule enhances stimulation; whereas desensitization, which occurs under overloaded situations, suppresses stimulation. These adaptation processes have been discussed extensively in Helson's (1964) adaptation-level theory. Insofar as they are reversible in accordance with environmental requirements they should be treated as functional changes co-determining state-reactivity. However, as has been shown by Eliasz (1981), who discussed in detail the system of regulation of stimulation within the framework of optimal level of activation, opposite changes may occur under long-lasting stimulation or deprivation. In most situations, deficient or surplus stimulation in relation to the optimal level of activation causes negative feedback in the functional states of the physiological mechanisms taking part in the regulation of the optimal level of activation. Eliasz calls this "active regulation", examples of which are the above-mentioned processes of sensitization caused by deprivation and desensitization developed under strong stimulation. However, long-lasting stimulation may lead to sensitization, caused by the exhaustion of physiological mechanisms taking part in stimulus regulation. This leads to a collapse of the discussed regulation level. Consequently, positive feedback in the physiological mechanisms occurs, which Eliasz calls passive regulation of stimulation. The same process may take place in deprivation which, if very prolonged, may cause desensitization instead of sensitization. The interplay between active and passive forms of regulation of stimulation is shown in Fig. 12.

Eliasz (1981) concludes that the speed with which active regulation changes into passive is a product of the degree of discrepancy between the desired and the given stimulation, and the duration of this discrepancy. One may assume that long-lasting passive regulation of stimulation, i.e. changes in the organism caused by positive feedback, may then lead to structural changes in the physiological mechanism of temperament, i.e. changes in temperament referred to as trait-reactivity.

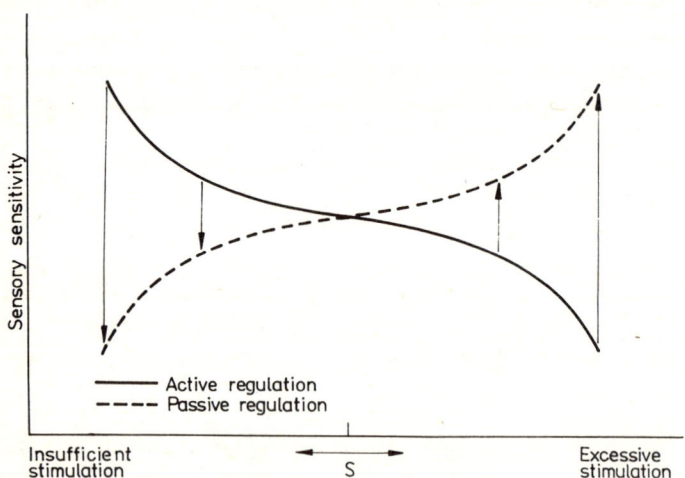

FIG. 12. Active and passive form of regulation of stimulation under different stimulation load (taken from Eliasz, 1979).

## Reactivity and strength of the nervous system

As may be seen from the given characteristic of reactivity this temperament dimension has much in common with NS strength. In both concepts the sensitivity/endurance ratio plays a crucial role. Many studies to which we refer are taken from the investigations of NS properties. Moreover, the STI in Chapter 3, aimed at diagnosing the basic NS properties, is also used in our laboratory for diagnosing the reactivity dimension (see p. 198). It concerns the Strength of Excitation scale which is mainly aimed at measuring the individual's endurance expressed by different kinds of behaviour to intensive, long-lasting, or repeated stimulation. We also use other methods developed primarily to investigate the strength of NS in order to diagnose reactivity (see p. 205).

However, there are differences between both concepts. As previously stated, reactivity as we view it is a psychological phenomenon. NS strength should be treated as a physiological property.

When characterizing the strength of the NS as one property of the NS with two facets—endurance of the nerve cells and their sensitivity (see p. 29)—Teplov and Nebylitsyn treated both these poles of strength as physiological phenomena. However, they were not very consistent since they also used these terms as psychological concepts (Teplov and Nebylitsyn, 1963a). By both sensitivity and endurance we mean psychological phenomena which are co-determined by reactivity. Co-determined, because sensitivity and endurance, which may vary in different situations, depend on the same variables which characterize state-reactivity (see p. 181). Sensitivity and endurance probably do not occur as extreme poles of the reactivity dimension because reactivity may determine reaction intensities below the sensitivity threshold understood as the phenomenon measured by subjectively estimated sensory threshold. When the endurance threshold is surpassed it does not mean that reactivity has disappeared; it exists as a property of the individual organism. Nebylitsyn (1972a) used the term reactivity interchangeably with sensitivity of the NS. Schematically both these dimensions can be presented as shown on p. 184.

Finally, it should be noted that the physiological mechanism of reactivity shown above (see p. 178) does not correspond with strength of excitation. Strength of the NS is a much narrower concept when compared with our understanding of the physiological bases of reactivity, where features of the cortex are one of the elements co-determining the temperament dimension.

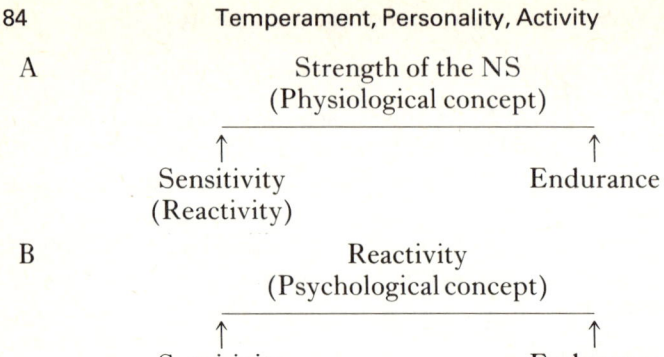

To a great extent the concept of activatability introduced by Paley (1976), understood as the factor responsible for the most general organization of the energetic characteristic of the NS, has some elements in common with our own concept of reactivity (see p. 38). However, the idea of arousability introduced earlier by Gray (1964) which was not without influence on our theory, is much less ambiguous.

### Activity as a Temperament Trait

The second feature of temperament related to the energetic level of behaviour is activity. This has been used by many authors as one of the main temperament dimensions, although with different connotations. For example, in Heymans and Wiersma's (1906–09) theory of temperament it was one of three dimensions to be distinguished. According to these authors activity is revealed in the way people perform tasks in school, at home or at work, when using free time (active or passive), in relation to duties (immediate performance of tasks or with delay), etc. Among the fourteen dimensions of temperament distinguished by Guilford (Guilford and Zimmerman, 1956) general activity occupies the first position. An active individual might be characterized as being energetic, sometimes impulsive, having speedy movements, with a tendency to work quickly and to undertake actions. A similar characterization of this dimension was given in Thurstone's (1951) concept of temperament.

Activity also occupies the first place in Thomas *et al.*'s (1968) theoretical concept of temperament. Activity is characterized by the level, tempo, and frequency with which the motor component reveals itself in behaviour. Buss and Plomon (1975) interpret activity, which is one of the four main temperaments (in our understanding, features of temperament), as total energy output. An active person is busy, often in a hurry and likes to keep moving. Nebylitsyn (1976) also refers to activity, together with emotionality, as one of the two main features of temperament. He interprets activity as a set of personality traits which determine the individual's need for external activity and self-expression toward the external world.

As may be seen from this condensed and selective review, researchers in temperament can hardly avoid the concept of activity. However, when referring to this trait of behaviour they often mean different things. Our first ideas about activity as a temperament dimension developed at the beginning of the 1970s (Strelau, 1969, 1970b, 1974; Eliasz, 1974). As will be shown later, activity has been given special significance as a regulator of stimulation need which derives, in turn, directly from the individual's reactivity. By *activity* I understand a temperament feature which determines the amount and range of activities of a given stimulative value which are undertaken. It is conceived as a property in which individuals show relatively constant differences.

*Optimal level of activation as a standard for the regulation of stimulation*

To understand the role of activity in our temperament theory let us invoke the concept of optimal level of arousal (activation)[5] (Hebb, 1955). According to this concept, the individual stimulates himself until he attains an optimal level of activation. An individual who is excessively stimulated initiates activities in order to reduce the activation evoked by this stimulation to an optimal level. Maintenance of such a level becomes a need which develops in ontogenesis. Disturbance of the individual's equilibrium elicits the impetus to act in such a way as to ensure (provide or maintain) an optimal level of activation. According to our conception, activity is the feature of the organism which plays the basic regulatory function in providing or maintaining the optimal level of activation.

The regulatory role of activity in maintaining a given level of stimulation, which, according to Hebb (1955), enables the optimal level of activation to be ensured, is also described by other concepts that refer to the regulatory functions of energy in the human organism. In the first place, the concept of optimal stimulation elaborated by Leuba (1965) should be mentioned. Here the focus is not on the changes of internal processes taking place in the nervous system but on the agents causing these changes. Consequently, there is a strong analogy between both concepts: one treating the optimal level from the point of view of activation (Hebb), the other (Leuba) from that of stimulation. Fiske and Maddi (1961) referring to the normal level of activation, by which they understand one typical of each stage of the sleep–wakefulness cycle of activation, stress the role of human activity in maintaining this normal level. This is in line with our own understanding of the role of activity.

The adaptation-level theory elaborated by Helson (1964) should also be mentioned. Helson describes the role of human activity in increasing or decreasing the stimulative value of situations and its significance for maintaining the organism at a given distance above or below the so-called zero or origin of the adaptation level (divergence from this zero level being the source of stimulation). He states:

> Although the flow of energy is from the environment to the organism, our powers of selection, our ability to "gate" stimuli as Bruner has put it, and our ability to change the environment by moving about in it allow us to determine to a large extent the nature and degree of stimulation that we receive" (Helson, 1964, pp. 52–53).

Finally, Haber's (1958) concept of optimal discrepancy, in which he refers directly to Helson's adaptation-level theory, demonstrates the regulating function of activity understood as a temperament trait.

It seems that all the above-mentioned concepts have something in common, i.e. a specific standard to which stimulation delivered from the interior and exterior of the organism has to be regulated. We have ascribed a special role in this regulation of activity. Since Hebb's concept of optimal level of activation (arousal) seems to be the primary one, and also a starting-point for most of the other theories mentioned, it seemed reasonable to adapt it for our own purposes. This has been done by Eliasz (1974). This author has shown that, like reactivity, the role of optimal level of activation forms a part within the whole system of the regulation of stimulation (Eliasz, 1979, 1981). Following Berlyne's (1960) considerations, Eliasz argues rightly that the optimal level of activation, in being a standard for the regulation of stimulation, has to be treated as a band situated mainly in the central part of the activation continuum.

> This is the optimal level of activation as regards the comfort of the subject, and it is of special significance when the subject does not have to perform any task. This is the organism's optimal level of activation also because of the readiness to cope with tasks of broad-ranged difficulties, and it especially favours solving fairly difficult tasks at a relatively low psychophysiological cost (Eliasz, 1981, p. 9).

We may ask whether individuals have equal optimal levels of activation maintained by different stimulation levels because of differences in reactivity, or whether the optimal level itself differs in each individual, so that different degrees of stimulation are needed to ensure different individual optimal levels (Łukaszewski, 1975). However, this is a rather academic question since, regardless of the answer, individuals in the same situation and under approximately equal psychophysiological conditions do differ in the amount of stimulation needed to maintain an optimal level of activation. This fact forms the core of our theory. Nevertheless, faced with the enormous amount of data showing the significance of different physiological mechanisms in enhancing or suppressing stimulation (including the receptor–effector level) it cannot be denied that stimulation is modulated before it is finally manifested in the level of activation.

Eliasz (1981) hypothesized differences in the width of the band of optimal activation in which individuals differ, depending on the level of reactivity, with low-reactive individuals having broader bands than high-reactive ones. His main arguments are based on Gray's (1964) analysis of reaction magnitude for "strong" and "weak" individuals with the so-called "induction" method (see Fig. 6). Eliasz's hypothesis cannot yet be treated as being empirically true. However, it corresponds with Ilin's (1975) suggestion concerning NS strength that the sensitivity/endurance ratio is larger in low-reactive individuals (see p. 178). It seems that the optimal level of activation should depend to some degree on the distance between sensitivity and endurance. The Teplov–Nebylitsyn arguments suggest that the R/r ratio is more or less stable.

*Activity as regulator of stimulation need*

Many sources of stimulation by which the individual satisfies his need to maintain an optimal level should be mentioned and they are discussed by several authors (e.g. Fiske and Maddi, 1961; Helson, 1964). However, we would like to emphasize the role of activity in regulating stimulation. The individual's own activity may be a direct source of stimulation for at least two reasons.

(1) The individual's physical (motor) activity, which is manifested in all kinds of movements, results in activation of the receptors which pass on this activation to higher nervous centres (Fiske and Maddi, 1961). This type of stimulation arises on the basis of the well-known mechanism of afferent feedback. Reactive behaviour is manifested in reactions to given stimuli or as a result of increased activation, and aims mainly to reduce over-excitation, as often found in children. It should also be treated as a source of stimulation based on the mechanism of afferent feedback. However, its primary function is to release energy.

Freeman (1948) discussed the main ways in which the tension of the nervous centres may be released and he mentions motor, mental, and visceral reactions. People differ in the ways they prefer to release the excitatory state. To differentiate between the manifestation of reactivity in a given behaviour and activity as a temperament feature, we have to know whether the main goal of this behaviour is to supply stimulation (activity) or to reduce the state of increased activation (reactivity).

(2) The performed actions themselves possess particular stimulative value, since most human behaviour has emotional connotation. In this case, the emotional state accompanying the given activity comprises the excitation-inducing factor. Activities may thus be a source of stimulation, chiefly because they generate certain emotions which, in turn, elicit a particular state of activation. Good examples are different activities which carry varied aspects of threat, risk, pleasure, which cause tension and are sources of discomfort or satisfaction. This type of activity seems to be particularly efficient in delivering stimulation, mainly because of the physiological mechanisms of emotions which have a high impact in regulating the level of activation. In cases (1) and (2) activity should be treated as a direct source of stimulation.

Many sources of stimulation surround the individual: situations, settings, tasks, all kinds of environmental stimuli which might be characterized by a given degree of variation, novelty, intensity, complexity, and meaningfulness (Fiske and Maddi, 1961; Zuckerman, 1979). Any sensory event, as shown by Hebb, has two different effects: "One is the *cue function*, guiding behaviour; the other, less obvious but no less important, is the *arousal* or *vigilance function*" (1955, p. 249). Activity has a special position among these sources of stimulation. It "organizes" these sources of stimulation. Through activity the individual may approach different kinds of situations, surroundings etc. of a given stimulative value, or might be led to avoid the impact of stimulation from a given situation, task, or other element of the environment. This means that activity as the "organizer" of type and amount of stimulation should be treated here as an indirect source of stimulation. The function of activity in regulating the stimulative value of the surroundings has been stressed by Helson (see p. 186).

In high-reactive individuals, whose physiological mechanism enhances stimulation (with high SPC), the need for stimulation to ensure the optimal level of activation is lower than in low-reactive individuals. Therefore, their activity, as far as it serves as a direct source of stimulation, is also low. Low-reactive individuals, on the other hand, with a physiological mechanism suppressing stimulation, i.e. with low SPC, have a greater demand than high-reactive individuals for stimulation, in order to reach their optimal level of activation. As a result of this interdependency the activity of low-reactives as a direct source of stimulation is also high.

However, the relation between activity and reactivity changes, if we take into account activity which itself serves as an indirect source of stimulation, i.e. plays the role of "organizer". In a study conducted on rats, Matysiak (1980) found that highly-reactive animals[6] manifested a great deal of activity in their behaviour, provided the aim of their activity was to reduce or avoid stimulation. On this basis the author differentiated between positively and negatively oriented activity. The aim of the former was to seek stimulation; therefore, it would be found more frequently in low-reactive individuals. On the other hand, negatively oriented activity aimed at avoiding stimulation, would be found in high-reactive individuals. For the above reasons, we may state that both these activities aimed at "organizing" stimulation, may be labelled as stimulation-seeking and stimulation-avoiding activities.

It follows from our conceptualization, that activity understood as a temperament feature acts, independently of its specificity and direction, as the main regulator of the amount of stimulation needed for the individual to maintain, or attain, an optimal level of activation. To stress the importance of regulatory mechanisms of stimulation, among which temperament activity plays the crucial role, our theory was labelled the "regulative theory of temperament" and this seems basically to differentiate our theory from the Pavlovian concept, as well as from other conceptualizations of temperament. Mangan and Paisey (1980), labelled it a "behavioural model of temperament", probably to stress the importance of activity in our theory.

We assume that any kind of activity, regardless of the main goal of the individual's behaviour, may result in regulating his stimulation need. All kinds of activities, irrespective of their specificity, have a given stimulative value and this is one of the most important statements of our theory. Playing with a rattle, swimming, football-playing, driving, solving mathematical tasks, engaging in research, searching for friends, escaping from the city, raping, bank-robbing etc., are examples of activities, which although primarily serving the satisfaction of specific individual needs, are also aimed at regulating the amount of stimulation the individual requires in order to ensure the optimal level of activation. Using Hebb's words one may say:

> The drive (to ensure the optimal level of activation—J.S.) is an energizer, but not a guide; an engine but not a stearing gear. These are precisely the specifications of activity in the arousal system (1955, p. 249).

Temperament does not determine what kind of behaviour the individual performs or prefers; this is mainly determined by social factors, particularly education. However, temperament is an important factor in the sense that it determines to a large extent whether the individual prefers activities of high or low stimulative value, stimulation-seeking or stimulation-avoiding activities.

In early ontogenesis, activity, understood as a regulator of stimulation need, is non-specific and only under learning and socialization processes does the individual acquire special kinds of activities which play the role of stimulation regulators. This means that it is the environment, especially the family and educational system, which determines whether the individual will satisfy his need for stimulation by playing football or by rowdy actions. Once these activities are consolidated, however, they might become chosen activities, preferred for satisfying the need for stimulation; this would then affect, to a certain degree, the development of personality. Some of the studies presented in Chapters 6 and 7 show that, depending on their level of reactivity, individuals may prefer activities of different stimulation levels.

## Reactivity and Activity

The question arises as to the difference between reactivity and activity and the degree to which the two may be treated as independent dimensions. Above all, it must be stated that they have not been distinguished by factor analysis or any other statistical techniques. They are more a result of theoretical considerations based mainly on numerous theories of temperament already known and on the theory of action (Tomaszewski, 1978). Their distinction has been proved in several of our studies. We are conscious of the need to formulate a quantitative analysis to support our assumption that reactivity and activity are two independent dimensions of temperament that cover the energetic characteristic of behaviour. To do this a diagnostic tool must be developed to measure the stimulative value of different activities as direct and indirect sources of stimulation. This is one of the main tasks we have to solve in the near future.

Relating both dimensions to each other I would like to point out two main differences between dimensions of reactivity and activity.

(1) Reactivity should be treated as a primary temperament feature, which is directly determined by the physiological mechanism modulating the value of stimulation. This mechanism is only a starting-point for activity and it provides the individual with a biologically determined

tendency to develop activity that ensures satisfaction of the need for stimulation. When activity develops in accordance with the above tendency, a specific relationship between both these temperament dimensions is observed: the higher the reactivity, the lower the highly stimulating activity and vice versa. Low-reactive individuals prefer highly stimulating activity.

Since it is mainly the social environment which determines specific forms of human activity, the stimulative value of the individual's activity might not develop in accordance with his reactivity level. This may result in different behaviour disorders and disturbances (Eliasz, 1974; Strelau, 1978). Thomas and Chess (1977; Thomas *et al.* 1968), provide much evidence of disorders in children's behaviour that are caused by lack of understanding of the child's temperament, particularly by members of the family, or by an anomalous interaction within the family.

(2) Reactivity, directly determined by physiological mechanisms, is manifested primarily in the intensity (magnitude) of reactions in response to given stimuli or resulting in energy release caused by overexcitation. Using Skinner's terminology one should say that reactivity is revealed primarily in reactive behaviour. According to his terminology, activity involves operant behaviour which serves as a source and regulator of stimulation need and ensures the optimal level of activation. Activity as goal-directed behaviour is often directly contingent upon current stimulation.

In most theories concerning temperament where reactive and operant behaviours have been substituted under the common label "activity" it is impossible to prove the importance of the stimulative value of activity (as understood in our theory) as a regulator of human behaviour. This is because, within the system of stimulation regulation, reactivity, which is manifested in reactive behaviour, plays a different role from activity, which is manifested in operant behaviour.

## Energetic Level of Behaviour as Common Denominator of Selected Personality Dimensions

Individual differences in the energetic level of behaviour, which play such a crucial role in our theory and which have been reduced to reactivity and activity, are also revealed in several contemporary theories of personality, and, in some areas, their biological roots are acknowledged. Thus our theory is not isolated and cannot pretend to be completely original; hopefully the differences are clear. Similarities are highlighted by two phenomena in which individuals differ. These are acknowledged in several theories, although with different emphases, as being sensitivity, measured by the sensory threshold, and activity, understood and measured in various ways.

Taking into account individual differences in sensitivity, it should be possible to distinguish individuals with strong and weak nervous processes (Teplov, 1964a; Nebylitsyn, 1972a); extraverts and introverts, as in Eysenck's (1970) personality theory; and reducers and augmenters, as in Petrie's (1967) dimension of stimulus intensity modulation. People differing in sensitivity should also have different positions on the arousability scale (Gray, 1964). The importance of activity as a source of stimulation is particularly emphasized by Zuckerman's (1979) sensation-seeking drive; on this basis sensation seekers and sensation avoiders are differentiated. Brebner and Cooper (1974, 1978) stress the importance of activity within the extraversion–introversion dimension and they label extraverts "response hungry" and introverts "stimulus hungry".

Irrespective of their differences, two common denominators, sensitivity and activity, can be used to illustrate the interdependence of the above personality dimensions (see Table XXIX, and Strelau, 1982).

Others have also attempted to describe similarities between strength of the NS and other personality dimensions (see Powell, 1979; Paisey and Mangan, 1980; Mangan, 1982; see also Chapter 4). Klonowicz (1982) took as a point of departure such items as sensory deprivation, monotony, stimulation overload, and the subject's potential for regulating stimulation influx, and was able to show, in a comparative study,

TABLE XXIX. Sensitivity and/or activity as common denominators of selected personality dimensions

| Dimension | High Sensitivity and/or Low Activity | Low Sensitivity and/or High Activity | Author |
| --- | --- | --- | --- |
| Strength of NS | Weak TNS | Strong TNS | Pavlov, Teplov–Nebylitsyn |
| Extraversion–introversion | Introverts "Stimulus hungry" | Extraverts "Response hungry" | Eysenck Brebner and Cooper |
| Arousability | High-arousable | Low-arousable | Gray |
| Stimulus Modulation intensity | Augmenters | Reducers | Petrie |
| Sensation-seeking | Sensation avoiders | Sensation seekers | Zuckerman |
| Reactivity | High-reactive | Low-reactive | Strelau |

interdependencies between: extraversion–introversion, NS strength, stimulus intensity modulation, Witkin's cognitive styles, and reactivity. These are generally compatible with the data shown in Table XXIX. Klonowicz's comparison indicates similarities between the field-independent type and high-reactive individuals, weak TNS individual, and augmenters. She concludes that the common denominator is the need for stimulation (Klonowicz, 1982).

## TEMPORAL CHARACTERISTICS OF BEHAVIOUR

This section is devoted to that part of the definition of temperament presented on p. 171 which includes the so-called temporal characteristics of behaviour. Starting with an analysis of different temperament theories and typologies, while still concentrating on the formal aspect of behaviour (in line with our understanding of temperament), I was able to extract several features of temperament concerning the temporal characteristics of behaviour (Strelau, 1969, 1974).

### Preliminary Selected Traits Referring to Temporal Characteristics

Based on theoretical considerations the following traits were separated: speed of reaction, mobility, durability, reaction tempo, and rhythmicity.

Speed of reaction, traditionally measured by RT, has long since been recognized as a relatively stable temperament trait. It may be found in the old temperament typologies of Kant (1943), Wundt (1911), and Ewald (1924). Another way of conceiving speed of reaction, is the adequate optic chronaxie (AOC) used in Teplov's laboratory for measuring the lability of the NS (see p. 97). In contemporary temperament theories this feature tends to be included as an element in different behaviour characteristics, not distinguished as an independent dimension.

Another temporal property of behaviour is mobility, referring to the ability to shift from one reaction (activity) in response to changes in the surroundings. Mobility is considered here to be a behavioural trait similar to the others under discussion and should not be confused with the mobility of nervous processes (although on the level of some indicators used, these two concepts are comparable). Mobility thus understood may be measured by the smallest time-interval between two or more different stimuli required for an adequate response to both those stimuli. Mobility of the NS, when calculated by such indices as rhythmic reinforcement and non-reinforcement of the same stimulus presented at varied time intervals (used in Pavlov's laboratory—see p. 9), corresponds with our interpretation of mobility. Khilchenko's method for diagnosing mobility of the NS designated as "speed of reaction change to rapidly changing stimuli" (see p. 105) could be directly used to measure mobility within our framework. Similarly, studies of rigidity (see Kounin, 1943; Eysenck, 1970) are related to mobility thus defined. The role of this temperamental feature seems particularly important for those human activities for which the ability to adjust quickly to changing situations is essential.

Durability refers to individual differences in maintaining (preserving) a reaction after the stimulus has terminated. It is manifested in the continuance of a given activity when the conditions that evoked the activity, as well as the need to continue it, are removed. Its measure is the duration of the reaction after cessation of the stimulus. In Pavlov's typology durability corresponds with lability and is estimated by methods aimed at measuring the termination of nervous processes, e.g. critical frequency of flicker-fusion (see p. 98), speed of visual sensitivity restoration (see p. 100). According to Heymans and Wiersma (1906–09), durability of reaction is a basic component of the tri-dimensional typology of temperaments. This is the so-called secondary function also known as perseveration. Perseveration interested many psychologists, such as Spearman (1927), who referred to it as the P factor, corresponding to the degree of cognitive inertia. Cattell (1948) equates this factor with the ability to discard a behaviour pattern acquired by learning, since degree of perseveration is associated with rigidity or plasticity of habits.

Reaction tempo is the ability to produce homogeneous reactions within a given time-unit, and is measured as the maximum number of reactions, e.g. number of words, or motor responses, per time-unit, derived mostly from the tapping test. Together with rhythmicity, this trait formed part of Kretschmer's (1944) general concept of mental tempo. Reaction tempo also has something in common with the lability of the NS when measured by the photic driving reaction (PDR) to high frequencies (see p. 101). However, the latter is concerned with specific electro-biological phenomenon. For Buss and Plomin (1975), tempo of reaction is one of the components of their activity temperament.

To complete the review of temporal features of temperament, so far identified in the literature, rhythmicity should be mentioned. This has been characterized by regularity of intervals between homogeneous reactions. The more regular the intervals between particular reactions,

# 5. Regulative Theory of Temperament

the greater the rhythmicity. As mentioned above, Kretschmer considered rhythmicity to be a feature of so-called mental tempo. More recently Thomas *et al*. (1968; Thomas and Chess, 1977) included this trait in their nine-dimensional temperament theory, particularly emphasizing the regularity of basic biological functions.

## Psychometric Studies on Temporal Features of Temperament

To see how our theory of the temporal characteristics of behaviour corresponded with empirical data, Goryńska (1979; Goryńska and Strelau, 1979) analysed all kinds of temporal characteristics measured by an inventory technique. First, all types of behaviour which included temporal characteristics were recorded. Only those forms of behaviour concerned with the speed of learning were omitted, since these phenomena belong to the domain of learning ability and not to temperament, as has been argued in Chapter 1. After categorizing all recorded types of behaviour, six traits were distinguished: reaction persistence, reaction recurrence, reaction mobility, reaction regularity, reaction speed, and reaction tempo. All of these were operationally defined and inventory items were selected in accordance with the operational definitions. The list of empirically separated traits coincides to a large extent with the traits distinguished on the basis of theoretical considerations similarly defined. There is one extra trait among the empirical categories because the trait which I term "durability" has been divided in two: persistence and recurrence of reaction. Reaction persistence has been defined by the length of time over which a particular reaction is maintained after the original stimulus has ceased, irrespective of the operation of competitive stimuli.

Reaction recurrence was measured by the length of time over which the particular reaction was repeated and by the number of repetitions after cessation of the original stimulus, similarly irrespective of competitive stimuli. The trait earlier known as rhythmicity we retitled regularity, though retaining its previous meaning.

These six traits were included in an inventory called the "Temporal Traits Inventory" (TTI) (see p. 201 and Appendix 5). On the basis of a study conducted on adult subjects we were able to separate two factors[6] which are introduced in Table XXX.

Factor I shows that the highest loadings were obtained for two traits, persistence and occurrence of reaction, and a moderate loading with opposite sign for mobility. Since traits with the highest loadings are related to a certain rigidity of the perseverative kind we labelled it perseverance of behaviour. For practical purposes, it may be treated as

TABLE XXX. Matrix of isolated factors of the temporal characteristic

| Trait | Before Rotation | | After Rotation | |
| --- | --- | --- | --- | --- |
| | Factor I | Factor II | Factor I | Factor II |
| (1) Persistence | 0.856 | 0.302 | 0.855 | −0.307 |
| (2) Recurrence | 0.624 | 0.374 | 0.720 | −0.104 |
| (3) Mobility | −0.720 | 0.017 | −0.547 | 0.468 |
| (4) Regularity | 0.325 | −0.114 | 0.179 | −0.294 |
| (5) Speed | −0.460 | 0.285 | −0.176 | 0.512 |
| (6) Tempo | −0.568 | 0.550 | −0.092 | 0.785 |

a synonym for the former durability trait based on theoretical considerations. All the dimensions previously compared with durability could be mentioned again to indicate the similarities between Factor I with traits identified in the literature.

Factor II is closely related to reaction tempo, which obtained the highest factor loading, and to a lesser degree to reaction speed. Although having an opposite sign, mobility, with a moderate loading in Factor I, is represented by a similar loading in Factor II. After analysing the psychological aspects of the two traits with the highest loadings—tempo and speed of reaction—this factor was named liveliness of behaviour. If one was to refer to the Pavlovian typology properties, liveliness, like Factor I (perseverance) is to some extent comparable with lability, when measured by PDR in beta band frequencies (see p. 101) and by AOP (see p. 97). The fact that both Factors I and II have some elements in common with different indicators used for measuring lability might suggest that lability, comprising different phenomena, is not as homogeneous as assumed by the Teplov-Nebylitsyn school.

Interestingly enough, regularity (formerly called rhythmicity) is represented in neither of the factors. It thus constitutes a different phenomenon and ought to be considered within the framework of individual differences in circadian rhythms (see Colquhoun, 1971).

Mobility of behaviour, which shares its factor loadings with both extracted factors, should be treated as a secondary trait contingent on speed and tempo of reaction, on the one hand, and perseverance of behaviour on the other. Measured this way, mobility is a temperament feature understood to mean the capacity to switch behaviour in response to changes in the surroundings. However, it should be limited to changes within the former acquired repertoire of reactions in order to separate it from learning ability. It mostly resembles so-called functional mobility—a notion introduced a long time ago by Vvedensky, psychologically interpreted by Khilchenko (1958) and Troshikhin *et al.* (1978) and understood by them to be the ability to react to quickly changing stimuli (see p. 105). Troshikhin acknowledged the fact that functional mobility results from a rather compound physiological mechanism in which the receptor-reaction systems, as well as the centres in the CNS, take part. Our data convince us that the above-mentioned authors were correct in stressing the manifold determination of mobility as a psychological phenomenon.

On the basis of research Goryńska's two factors were distinguished: perseverance and liveliness of behaviour, which should be treated as primary temperament features referring to the temporal characteristic of behaviour. Mobility of behaviour, which plays an important role in contemporary human life, should be treated as a secondary temperament feature. As shown from the data in Chapter 3, mobility of behaviour probably cannot be entirely separated from reactivity. This has been confirmed by Carlier (in press) who showed that items from the Strength of Excitation scale and from the Mobility scale taken from STI run into one Factor (see p. 131). Considering that novelty and variation in the surroundings are of high stimulative value (Fiske and Maddi, 1961; Zuckerman, 1979) and that individuals with high mobility should cope better with such situations, the finding that high-reactive subjects have rather low mobility and vice versa should not be so surprising.

The physiological mechanism of the separate temperament features in question should not be reduced to mobility and/or lability of the nervous system since the use of these hypothetical constructs makes no progress towards understanding the essence of the separated features as related to the temporal characteristic of temperament. The physiological mechanism of these features remains an open question.

Our contribution to the understanding of temporal characteristic of behaviour in relation to temperament, and its significance in regulating the interactions of humans and their surroundings, is far from satisfactory and does not pretend to be highly original. However, since publication in English (Strelau, 1974) of the theoretical consideration of the current research, a step forward has been made.

## METHODS USED FOR DIAGNOSING TEMPERAMENT FEATURES

From studying the history of psychology, it is evident that in order to survive, any theory must provide methods and tools for its verification. A deductive approach, of which this chapter is an example, has to be supported by data collected in real-life settings or in the laboratory to assure us that we are going in the right direction. This section describes typical methods for diagnosing the temperament features under investigation.

Most studies of temperament conducted in our laboratory have used the Strelau Temperament Inventory (STI) to diagnose two traits (see Appendix 1). The STI scale "Strength of Excitation" has been used to estimate reactivity, whereas the scale "Mobility of the Nervous Processes" has been used to measure mobility of behaviour. As shown in Chapter 3, the Strength of Excitation scale deals with the endurance of behaviour (see p. 125) in highly stimulating situations, in line with both reactivity and strength of excitation. In these areas attention has been paid to the sensitivity/endurance ratio. As described in Chapter 3, the higher the estimation on this scale the higher the strength of the NS. Therefore when using this scale to measure reactivity it must be remembered that, conversely, the higher the score on this scale the lower the reactivity level.

As for mobility, the items on the scale Mobility of Nervous Processes refer to those features of behaviour which are manifested in speed and adequacy in reacting to changing situations (see p. 126), which corresponds not only with one of the main aspects of the Pavlovian interpretation of mobility but also exactly fits our concept of mobility of behaviour. The higher the score on this scale the higher the level of both mobility of the nervous system and of behaviour.

Other techniques have recently been developed in our laboratory to diagnose temperament features. Particularly significant are Friedensberg's Reactivity Rating Scales and Goryńska's Temporal Traits Inventory.

## Reactivity Rating Scales (RRSs)

For diagnosing reactivity in children and adolescents three 5-point rating scales have been developed by Friedensberg (1982). The first Reactivity Rating Scale ($RRS_1$) is intended for pre-school children (see Appendix 2), and the second $RRS_2$ for primary school children. A separate Reactivity Rating Scale ($RRS_3$) has been developed for secondary school pupils (Appendix 4). The aim when constructing the RRSs was to make them comparable on the one hand and to take into consideration developmental differences on the other. The RRSs are applied by school and nursery teachers and are based on samples of typical behaviour in pre-school and school situations. The types of behaviour selected are concerned with tasks and social situations, and

## 5. Regulative Theory of Temperament

the main difference between the three RRSs that deal with the same kinds of behaviour is the age-specific descriptions of selected categories.

The scales also differ in the number of items included. The $RRS_1$ consists of nine items, in $RRS_2$ ten items are included, and $RRS_3$ has eleven items. Within items 1–9 the scales are comparable. The higher the total score in each RRS the lower the level of reactivity. Because the number of items is different in each RRS the distribution of scores in the separate scales varies as follows: $RRS_1$—9 to 45 points; $RRS_2$—10 to 50 points; and $RRS_3$—11 to 55 points.

Three different criteria were used to assess reliability of the RRSs: inter-item consistency, coefficient of stability, and scorer reliability (Anastasi, 1961). The reliability of $RRS_1$ was tested in a group of 80 6-year-old boys, and that of $RRS_2$ in a group of 106 pupils aged 8 to 13. The reliability of the third scale ($RRS_3$) was estimated on a sample of 82 16-year-old high-school students. Only male subjects were under investigation, following on from the aim of the experiment for which these scales were primarily constructed.

Table XXXI shows the inter-item consistency evaluated separately for the three RRSs. For $RRS_1$ where nine items were included, the inter-item consistency was calculated separately in three subgroups, since the pre-school children were from three different kindergartens. As the table shows, item 9 does not reach the critical coefficient of determination established at 0.707 (see Guilford, 1956). Only one correlation reached this criterion in item 1. In all other items at least two coefficients gained the required criterion.

For $RRS_2$ four separate correlation coefficients were computed. Children from four different classes were studied; only in item 6 did two

TABLE XXXI. Inter-item consistency of the reactivity rating scales (RRSs) (Adapted from Friedensberg, 1982)

| Items | Reactivity Rating Scale | | |
|---|---|---|---|
| | $RRS_1$ | $RRS_2$ | $RRS_3$ |
| 1 | 0.446–0.767 | 0.272–0.946 | 0.689–0.822 |
| 2 | 0.734–0.881 | 0.429–0.921 | 0.803–0.842 |
| 3 | 0.554–0.769 | 0.728–0.926 | 0.876–0.923 |
| 4 | 0.644–0.925 | 0.484–0.918 | 0.805–0.874 |
| 5 | 0.504–0.829 | 0.799–0.897 | 0.834–0.877 |
| 6 | 0.652–0.854 | 0.629–0.896 | 0.759–0.894 |
| 7 | 0.659–0.887 | 0.760–0.950 | 0.833–0.918 |
| 8 | 0.501–0.804 | 0.787–0.925 | 0.827–0.918 |
| 9 | 0.469–0.642 | 0.659–0.817 | 0.802–0.871 |
| 10 | — | 0.810–0.929 | 0.882–0.935 |
| 11 | — | — | 0.691–0.871 |

coefficients reach the critical coefficient of determination. In all other items at least three results satisfactorily supported the internal consistency requirements of the scale.

Where three separate estimations were taken into account (in boys from three different classes), $RRS_3$ also reached required internal consistency demands. The only exception was item 11 which only reached the necessary criterion once. However, the two other correlation coefficients are close to the critical value. Except in item 1, where two coefficients are satisfactory, in all other items all coefficients are higher than the critical coefficient of determination. All three RRSs showed satisfactory inter-item consistency, except item 9 in $RRS_1$.

To estimate the retest reliability two separate measures of reactivity were conducted with a one-month interval. For each of the three scales the coefficients of stability were calculated using Pearson's stability coefficient $(r)$ and by the Scott-Wertheimer coefficient of absolute stability $[r_{sb}]$. The results of these stability estimations may be found in Table XXXII.

TABLE XXXII. Retest reliability of the RRSs (adapted from Friedensberg, 1982)

| RRS | Stability coefficients | |
|---|---|---|
| | Pearson's $(r)$ | Scott-Wertheimer's $(r_{sb})$ |
| $RRS_1$ | 0.800–0.983 | 0.791–0.970 |
| $RRS_2$ | 0.669–0.985 | 0.667–0.984 |
| $RRS_3$ | 0.688–0.944 | 0.553–0.874 |

Because pre-school children were from three kindergartens and every subgroup was estimated by two teachers independently, six correlation coefficients were computed for $RRS_1$. As the table shows, all reached the accepted critical coefficient of determination in both statistical tests. With the elementary school children, as mentioned before, the sample consisted of four subgroups from different classes. In two classes of 8-year-old boys, two teachers in each class estimated the reactivity of the pupils; in two other classes of 10 and 13-year-old boys, three teachers in each class were asked to estimate the reactivity level. Altogether 10 coefficients of correlation were obtained for $RRS_2$ for both statistical tests separately. The two measures of stability show high reliability of $RRS_2$. Among the ten coefficients only one did not reach the accepted criterion in both statistical tests $(r; r_{sb})$. In high-school pupils nine coefficients of correlation were obtained (three classes and three scorers in each class). Except for one correlation all Pearson's coefficients show satisfactory reliability of $RRS_3$. As far as the absolute stability measurement ($r_{sb}$) is concerned two of the nine correlations calculated did not reach the critical determination coefficient. In general, one should conclude that all three RRSs have a high stability.

Scorer reliability was assessed as the third criterion of reliability of RRSs. In each group the same subjects were assessed twice and so the number of correlations is double the number of combined pairs of scorers. The data for scorer reliability was displayed in Table XXXIII.

TABLE XXXIII. Scorer reliability of the RRSs (adapted from Friedensberg, 1982)

| RRS | Number of Correlations | Dispersion of Coefficients |
|---|---|---|
| $RRS_1$ | 6 | 0.639–0.961 |
| $RRS_2$ | 16 | 0.340–0.943 |
| $RRS_3$ | 18 | 0.509–0.909 |

For $RRS_1$ six coefficients were calculated, three of which did not reach the accepted criterion. Scorer reliability for $RRS_2$ is somewhat higher. Among sixteen correlation coefficients eleven reached the level of the critical coefficient of determination (0.707). Scorer reliability of $RRS_3$ as of $RRS_1$, was found for 50% of the coefficients. Out of 18 correlations nine were below the accepted criterion. The data analysis showed that with almost all teacher pairs, the compared diagnosis of reactivity did not reach the critical value where the teachers had been working with a given class for no longer than six months, and so did not know the assessed pupils well enough.

Taking into account the three criteria of reliability used in this study we may conclude that all three Reactivity Rating Scales have a satisfactory level of reliability, though this conclusion should be limited to males only.

## The Temporal Traits Inventory (TTI)

The Temporal Traits Inventory (TTI) has been developed by Goryńska (1982; Goryńska and Strelau, 1979; see Appendix 5) to diagnose the temporal features of temperament. The procedure used to calculate six temporal traits of reactions—(persistence, recurrence, mobility, regularity, speed, and tempo)—as well as their definitions are discussed on pp. 193–195).

After a pilot study an experimental version of the inventory was constructed. It comprised 122 items arranged within six scales, of 20–21 items each, according to the six traits. The normal distribution, index of multiple deviation, item analysis, and the subject evaluation (as regards imprecise or repetitive questions), separately for each item, were tested in a sample of 200 subjects (100 female and 100 male, aged 20 to 22). On the basis of these results the third and final version of the TTI was constructed to consist of 108 items, the number of items varying in the six scales from 14 to 21. Again a group of 200 subjects, 100 of each sex, aged 20 to 22 years was tested for further evaluation of the inventory. As can be seen from Table XXXIV the distribution data combined for male and female are very close to normal.

On inspecting the data for male and female subjects separately, women scored higher on reaction persistence and reaction recurrence than men; whereas on the scales of mobility, speed and tempo, male subjects scored higher than females. No statistically significant differences were recorded for the regularity scale.

Reliability of the inventory was tested by measuring its internal consistency and stability. The former was estimated by means of

TABLE XXXIV. Male, female, and combined inventory scores for six temperament traits

| Trait | Sex | $M$ | $SD$ | $Mo$ | $Me$ | Skewness | Curtosis |
|---|---|---|---|---|---|---|---|
| Persistence | M | 12.09 | 6.47 | 12.51 | 12.23 | 0.13 | −0.79 |
| (1) | F | 16.82 | 6.00 | 15.10 | 16.24 | 0.37 | 0.23 |
|  | M+F | 14.46 | 6.66 | 13.72 | 14.21 | −0.22 | −0.66 |
| Recurrence | M | 18.20 | 9.67 | 17.86 | 18.08 | −0.07 | −1.10 |
| (2) | F | 23.40 | 7.76 | 21.72 | 22.84 | −0.43 | −0.31 |
|  | M+F | 20.80 | 9.12 | 19.23 | 20.27 | −0.34 | −0.75 |
| Mobility | M | 25.13 | 6.91 | 24.01 | 24.82 | −0.35 | −0.68 |
| (3) | F | 21.38 | 7.17 | 20.93 | 21.23 | −0.12 | −0.61 |
|  | M+F | 23.26 | 7.27 | 22.43 | 23.01 | −0.24 | −0.62 |
| Regularity | M | 12.07 | 5.89 | 14.11 | 12.75 | 0.69 | 0.36 |
| (4) | F | 13.14 | 6.57 | 13.88 | 13.46 | 0.19 | −0.63 |
|  | M+F | 12.61 | 6.24 | 14.01 | 13.11 | 0.44 | −0.22 |
| Speed | M | 25.66 | 5.31 | 25.29 | 25.53 | −0.14 | −0.63 |
| (5) | F | 23.91 | 5.33 | 24.32 | 24.04 | 0.16 | −0.14 |
|  | M+F | 24.79 | 5.38 | 24.80 | 24.79 | 0.01 | −0.44 |
| Tempo | M | 25.48 | 5.70 | 24.45 | 25.13 | −0.35 | −0.26 |
| (6) | F | 20.56 | 6.69 | 21.07 | 20.71 | 0.71 | −0.61 |
|  | M+F | 23.02 | 6.67 | 22.35 | 22.78 | −0.20 | −0.60 |

TABLE XXXV. Internal consistency for the temporal traits of behaviour

| Trait | Male | Sex Female | M + F |
|---|---|---|---|
| Persistence | 0.70 | 0.71 | 0.74 |
| Recurrence | 0.82 | 0.77 | 0.82 |
| Mobility | 0.76 | 0.75 | 0.77 |
| Regularity | 0.76 | 0.76 | 0.74 |
| Speed | 0.55 | 0.58 | 0.55 |
| Tempo | 0.61 | 0.71 | 0.71 |

split-half reliability. The data in Table XXXV, obtained by using the Spearman–Brown reliability coefficient, reveal satisfactory estimations except for reaction speed, where the coefficient for both sexes are fairly low.

Stability of the temporal traits of behaviour was measured by repeating the investigation after an interval of one month and by calculating Pearson's stability coefficient ($r$) and the Scott–Wertheimer coefficient of absolute stability ($r_{sb}$). The results are displayed in Table XXXVI.

For each of the six scales, the two stability coefficients assume high values thus suggesting high stability for the results of the Temporal Traits Inventory. Fairly high consistency of response (ranging from 73 to 81%) has been obtained within each of the scales. Fractional differences between the two investigations separated by a one-month interval were insignificant for practically all items (except item 4) suggesting high consistency of responses.

To see whether the two male and female samples differed significantly in the structure of the tested temperament traits, Pearson's correlation coefficients for each of the six scales were calculated separately for males

TABLE XXXVI. Pearson's ($r$) and Scott-Wertheimer's ($r_{sb}$) stability coefficients for TTI

| Trait | $r$ | $r_{sb}$ |
|---|---|---|
| Persistence | 0.88 | 0.93 |
| Recurrence | 0.86 | 0.93 |
| Mobility | 0.90 | 0.94 |
| Regularity | 0.82 | 0.91 |
| Speed | 0.90 | 0.94 |
| Tempo | 0.85 | 0.92 |

TABLE XXXVII. The structure of six temperament traits in males and females

| Trait | 1 | 2 | 3 | Female 4 | 5 | 6 |
|---|---|---|---|---|---|---|
| Persistence (1) | | 0.630$^c$ | 0.512$^c$ | 0.284$^b$ | −0.278$^b$ | −0.264$^a$ |
| Recurrence (2) | 0.613$^c$ | | −0.430$^c$ | 0.064 | −0.287$^b$ | −0.061 |
| Mobility (3) | −0.628$^c$ | −0.361$^c$ | | −0.308$^b$ | 0.430$^c$ | 0.323$^b$ |
| Regularity (4) | 0.226$^a$ | 0.065 | −0.291$^b$ | | 0.291$^b$ | −0.273$^b$ |
| Speed (5) | −0.218$^a$ | −0.103 | 0.172 | 0.079 | | 0.401$^c$ |
| Tempo (6) | −0.194 | −0.044 | 0.351$^b$ | −0.143 | 0.443$^c$ | |

(Male rows)

$a = p < 0.05$
$b = p < 0.01$
$c = p < 0.001$

and females. The results presented in Table XXXVII show that the two samples do not differ significantly in their temperament structure, although differences in the mean values of the given traits have been stated (see above). This entitled the author to apply factor analysis to the combined matrix of correlations as discussed earlier (Table XXX).

The two factors that we were able to separate, perseverance (Factor I) and liveliness of behaviour (Factor II), as well as the separate temporal characteristic traits, were further tested by comparing their scores with the Mobility scale of the STI. So, to a certain degree, the construct and diagnostic validity of the TTI could be estimated. The results are displayed in Table XXXVIII.

As might be expected, the highest correlation occurs between mobility of behaviour as measured by both inventories, which stems from the fact that both techniques were based on a similar operational definition of mobility. In Table XXX (p. 196), which shows that mobility shares

TABLE XXXVIII. Traits and factors of the temporal characteristic of behaviour estimated by TTI and mobility measured by STI

| Temporal Characteristic of behaviour | r |
|---|---|
| (1) Persistence | −0.54 |
| (2) Recurrence | −0.35 |
| (3) Mobility | 0·78 |
| (4) Regularity | −0.55 |
| (5) Speed | 0.63 |
| (6) Tempo | 0.59 |
| Factor I | −0.59 |
| Factor II | 0.81 |

All coefficients significant at the 0.01 level.

its factor loadings between both factors (in Factor I with negative, in Factor II with positive signs), the correlations between mobility measured by STI and both separated factors are consistent. However, the question remains open as to why Factor II has the highest correlation coefficient with mobility. Generally, it should be concluded that the comparison of the two tools used for measuring mobility gives evidence for satisfactory validity of the TTI.

## Final Remarks

Our laboratory has developed several other inventories and rating scales, primarily aimed at measuring reactivity (see Strelau, 1978; Grodner, 1973). However, they do not fulfil the expected psychometric criteria.

As regards laboratory methods, the Nebylitsyn method for diagnosing strength of the nervous system referred to as "Slope of RT curve" (see p. 86) is sometimes used. There is a fixed relationship between RT and intensity of stimuli, as is the case between the latter and reaction magnitude (see Boiko, 1961; see also pp. 86 and 90). Because of this, the method in question is, by the definition of reactivity, an exact measure of this phenomenon. If reactivity is revealed in individual differences in the intensity (magnitude) of reactions, the most convenient laboratory method is to use stimuli of different intensities which are neutral or which have approximately the same signal value for each subject. The Nebylitsyn method seems to meet this requirement. Taking into account the sensitivity/endurance ratio on which this method is based it is assumed that in low-reactive individuals, as in subjects with strong NS, the slope of reaction time is more declined as compared with high-reactive individuals (weak NS); i.e. the higher the coefficient $b$ the lower the level of reactivity (see p. 88).

The temporal characteristic of behaviour has rarely been subject to experimental studies in our laboratory, except for an investigation conducted by Strelau *et al.* (1974) and described in Chapter 2.

As previously mentioned, the experimental method used by the Ukrainian psychologists Khilchenko and Troshikhin and described in detail on p. 105 exactly fits the operational definition of mobility of behaviour. In this method the "speed of reaction change to rapidly changing stimuli" is measured with stimuli familiar to the subject and on the ability to perform without learning the reactions during the experiment. This requirement follows from our understanding of temperament which has been stressed several times before. When the diagnosis of nervous system properties, particularly NS strength and mobility of nervous processes, is based on methods where psychological or psychophysiological phenomena are used as dependent variables, we are usually able to reinterpret this data within our concept of temperament. This has allowed us to refer to many experiments conducted within the framework of NSP investigation and to make use of facts established by Pavlovian typologists.

# 6
# Temperament and Activity

It has been argued in Chapter 5 that activity, described as a feature which determines the amount and range of undertaken actions of a given stimulative value, should be conceived as a temperament trait, and that activity thus understood has important functions in providing or maintaining an optimal level of activation. The aim of this chapter is to provide evidence showing activity to be a regulator of stimulation need. The data has been mainly collected in our own laboratory and may be divided into three groups illustrating different functions of activity as a regulator of stimulation. First, a discussion of the style of action co-determined by the individual's reactivity will show that, depending on need for stimulation, the style of action may develop to ensure the optimal level of stimulation. In Chapter 5 activity was acknowledged as a direct source of stimulation (particularly because of its emotional connotations). On the other hand, to the extent that it can "organize" situations of given stimulative value, it regulates stimulation. This will be discussed in the next section. Finally, evidence will be shown to illustrate that where there is no possibility of regulating the amount of stimulation by a given kind of activity or by changing the situation appropriate to the stimulation need, the efficiency of behaviour varies depending on the individual's temperament traits.

## STYLE OF ACTION RELATED TO TEMPERAMENT AND AS A REGULATOR OF STIMULATIVE VALUE OF SITUATIONS

Behavioural style has long been considered one of the main characteristics of temperament. Teplov (1956, 1964a) hypothesized that what really enables us to characterize the type of nervous system in everyday behaviour is not efficacy of performance but the way a given activity is performed. As shown in Chapter 1, the style of action (described as stable modes and forms of reaction determined by the TNS) was thoroughly studied by Soviet psychologists, particularly by the Merlin school. They demonstrated several relationships between style of action and temperament (especially strength of the NS). Behavioural style became the central notion in Thomas and Chess's (1977; Thomas *et al.*, 1968) concept of temperament. According to them, the main difference between abilities and temperament is that in the case of abilities the question in behaviour concerns *what* and *how well*, whereas in temperament the *way* in which an individual behaves is the crucial question. Thomas and Chess assume (1977) that temperament can be equated with the term behavioural style or with so-called stylistic characteristics. A similar position has been taken by Buss and Plomin (1975, p. 5) who refer to Thomas and Chess's concept of temperament. They differentiate between the content and style of behaviour.

> Content refers to *what* the response is: affection, aggression, problem solving, etc. Style refers to *how* the response is made: fast or slow, mild or intense, sparse and unelaborated or adorned and elaborated, etc. Temperament generally deals more with the stylistic aspects of behaviour.

Burks and Rubenstein (1979), adapted Thomas and Chess's theory of temperament to psychotherapy and took as point of departure their nine dimensions of temperament and distinguished six styles (clusters) of behaviour: withdrawal, persistence, intensity, approachability, adaptability, and activity. However, Burks and Rubenstein's position, according to which the styles of behaviour regarded as temperament are treated as inherent patterns, can hardly be accepted.

## Theoretical Approach

In our concept of temperament the style of action, i.e. the typical manner in which an action is performed by the individual, should be regarded differently from the above. It refers to the structure of goal-directed activity and cannot be equated with temperament. Temperament, which refers above all to the question of *how* the response is made, is regarded as one of the co-determiners of the style of action. Within the framework of my theory, the style of action, which develops under environmental influences on the basis of the temperamental endowment (especially reactivity and mobility of behaviour) is considered to be one of the regulators of stimulation need. This paradigm needs explanation.

Let us take as a point of departure the concept of activity taken from Rubinstein (1946) and developed in Poland by Tomaszewski (1963, 1978). According to the latter author, to whom we refer when speaking of the style of action, activity as a goal-directed behaviour has a given structure (see also Miller *et al.*, 1960) which might be considered from different angles. As regards the temperament approach, the functional aspect of activity is especially interesting. According to Tomaszewski (1967), taking into consideration the role which the separate components of activity play in approaching any result, all activities may be divided into basic or executive activities and auxiliary ones.[1]

Those activities which lead directly to the attainment of a certain goal should be regarded as basic. The function of auxiliary activities consists of organizing conditions for the performance of primary activities. They are more differentiated and, according to Tomaszewski (1967), they may be divided into preparatory, corrective, controlling, and protective activities. While basic activities directly modify the result of action, the modifying role of auxiliary activities is indirect (Tomaszewski, 1967; Materska, 1972). Preparatory and protective activities are aimed at modifying the conditions under which the activity takes place. Control activity consists in establishing the degree of convergence between the obtained results of performance as compared with the expected ones. In the case of corrective activities, the major concern is with a modification of conditions during the performance of executive actions or with the modification of the latter activity itself.

Without going into details of the functional structure of activity,[2] the main function of auxiliary actions can be said to ensure the performance of basic actions and to raise the probability of attaining the goal of the performed action. In other words, a given number of auxiliary actions lowers the risk of failure in task performance, especially in difficult situations. Considering the relation between auxiliary and basic actions from the point of view of intensity of stimulation this means that auxiliary actions, by safeguarding, facilitating or simplifying the basic ones, lower the stimulative value of activity or of the situation in which the activity is performed. From this it follows that high-reactive individuals, whose physiological mechanism enhances stimulation (see p. 180), will undertake more auxiliary actions to decrease the stimulative value of the performed activity (or situation in which activity is performed) as compared with low-reactive individuals, characterized by a low stimulus processing coefficient. One may assume that in high-reactive individuals auxiliary actions (AA) will dominate over basic ones (BA), whereas in low-reactive individuals there will be more of an equilibrium between both types of action or even a predominance of executive actions. This hypothesis, set forward at the beginning of the 1970s (Strelau, 1970b, 1975c), and which was used as the starting-point of several of our experiments, may be presented as follows:

*(1) high-reactive individuals: $BA < AA$*
*low-reactive individuals: $BA \geq AA$*

Taking recourse to auxiliary actions high-reactive persons may avoid tension or stressful situations that might considerably lower their efficiency or productivity. Thus high-reactive persons may attain the same level of effect in their activity as do low-reactive persons. This seems to be of considerable importance in real-life situations, as will be seen, especially in professional activity and school performance.

A similar distinction between low- and high-reactive individuals can be made in terms of the temporal structure of actions. If one differentiates actions as being either continuous or interrupted, it is easy to assume that a continuous action, which leads mostly to fatigue, should be regarded as a source of higher stimulation compared with interrupted action. The latter, which involves taking breaks during performance, is of lower stimulative value. By taking breaks, the individual avoids overstimulation. Due to their high sensitivity and low endurance, high-reactive persons tend to organize their activity in such a way as to ensure themselves more rest periods. The high endurance and low sensitivity of low-reactive persons enables them to engage in an activity at considerable length without any urgent need for rest or breaks. When obliged to perform an activity over a long period high-reactive persons tend to organize this in such a way as to ensure the predominance of interrupted actions (IA) over continuous actions (CA). In low-reactive individuals there is an equilibrium between both kinds of action or, because of their high endurance, continuous actions may even dominate over interrupted ones. This hypothesis may be expressed in the following way:

*(2) high-reactive individuals: $CA < IA$*
*low-reactive individuals: $CA \geq IA$*

However, there are some limitations, We assume that continuous activity, although homogeneous, is performed in an intensive manner with adequate motivation. In a monotonous situation, where the activity is of low intensity and the separate components of activity as well as all operations are almost identical and performed in surroundings of low stimulative value, the opposite may occur.

This temporal organization of activities applies as a rule to homogeneous actions. In real life we are usually compelled to pursue a number of heterogeneous actions concurrently. Homogeneous versus heterogeneous actions may also be considered with respect to their stimulative value. At first glance, taking into account the fact that novelty and variety are regarded as sources of stimulation (see Fiske and Maddi, 1961; Zuckerman, 1979), it might be suggested that high-reactive individuals, having lower stimulation need, should prefer homogeneous actions to heterogeneous ones. However, I propose an opposite hypothesis. High-reactive persons tend to alternate their actions; not infrequently, a new action is started before the ongoing one has terminated. Low-reactive individuals do not exhibit this tendency. As is the case for the temporal structure of actions, the reason for these frequent shifts from one action to another in high-reactive persons is presumably their tendency to tire easily and their low endurance. Since prolonged action[3] of one type or another tends to evoke transmarginal inhibition in the nervous system of the high-reactive person, he attempts to alternate his actions, thus engaging different nervous centres in succession in order to give the overburdened centres a chance to recover (see also Rozhdestvenskaya, 1980). Shifting activation from one centre to another, the high-reactive individual is able to work continuously, but only by dint of alternating the type of action in rapid succession.

In conclusion, the high-reactive type reveals a domination of heterogeneous (HeA) over homogeneous actions (HoA) while the low-reactive type exhibits predominantly homogeneous actions or an absence of a clear-cut preference for one or other of the two types of action. Schematically this hypothesis may be introduced as below:

*(3) high-reactive individuals: $HoA < HeA$*
  *low-reactive individuals: $HoA \geq HeA$*

All three hypotheses, particularly that which refers to the type of action based on the functional structure of activity, have been subjected to investigation in our laboratory. We were interested in verifying the hypotheses in natural settings, e.g. professional activity (Uszyńska, 1971; Strelau and Krajewski, 1974; Strelau, 1975c) or situations analogous to school performance (Cymes, 1974; Friedensberg, 1974), as well as under laboratory conditions (Klonowicz, 1974a, in press, a and b; Czyżkowska, 1974; Nosarzewski, 1974). A special study was conducted to show the developmental specificity as regards the moulding of the style of action depending on reactivity level (Friedensberg, in press). It is impossible to present in detail the data collected to verify our hypotheses[4] but some examples will illustrate the main direction of our research in this area.

## The Style of Action in Natural Settings

In order to exemplify our research as regards the relation between reactivity and style of action let me describe the first of our studies (Uszyńska, 1971; Strelau, 1975c) designed to determine the relation between level of reactivity and style of action in the foundryman. His type of job conditions cannot be freely manipulated because of technological limitations. Unable to modify the conditions of work, the labourer who strives to achieve high productivity is bound to organize the structure of actions in an optimal manner in terms of his organic capacities. In our study we concentrated on the functional structure of actions, i.e. the (quantitative and temporal) ratio between basic and auxiliary actions.

Reactivity in subjects was estimated by the slope of RT curve (see p. 86) which, as argued earlier, enables the property in question to be measured. The ratio between RT to weakest (30 dB) and strongest (105 dB) stimuli was adopted as the measure of reactivity. The greater the nominal value of this ratio the less reactive the given person.

The style of action of foundrymen working with permanent moulds was monitored using specially designed observation charts. These were based on a technological chart which specifies with considerable precision the sequence and duration of operations.

The sample studied was composed of 20 foundrymen working at the Warsaw Motor Car Factory. The age of subjects varied from 23 to 47 years, and they had been on the job from 3 to 5 years. Subjects were studied on the job between the working hours of 6 a.m. and 2 p.m. Two principal stages were distinguished in the work of foundrymen: preparation for work and production work proper.

(1) The preparatory stage comprises preparatory actions which precede the production process. These are: clearing the moulds, coating them, heating them, preparing the shank ladle, and renewed heating of the moulds. These preparatory actions may assume different temporal structures and can be engaged in either continuously or alternately with other forms of behaviour; the latter have been subdivided into auxiliary and incidental actions. The auxiliary actions are: checking operations of all kinds, measures designed to facilitate or accelerate various operations; operations aimed at safeguarding a normal course of work when new, unexpected tasks are offered; preparation of the work-stand; arranging the necessary objects; securing spare parts for the production process; checking the state of the solution; checking the flow of air, etc. Incidental actions have no connection with the production process and they comprise: actions serving to meet the need for contacting other

people (e.g. conversation), or actions serving to satisfy personal needs, such as smoking a cigarette, leaving the stand to drink some water, etc.

(2) The production stage proper comprises: filling the moulds, solidifying their contents, and emptying the moulds. This entire process takes six minutes, of which only the first and the last stage are productive, whereas the intermediate one (awaiting solidification) remains at the disposal of the labourer. This free interval lasts from 2.5 to 3 minutes. These operations recur in cycles, each yielding a number of finished casts, with the day's productivity expressed in the number of casts produced. Due to the 3-min intervals the labourer is in a position to organize his actions so as to achieve an optimum on several counts (variables), including the need for stimulation determined by the level of reactivity. Hence the behaviour of subjects during this interval was considered to be of particular diagnostic value.

Having adopted the mean number and duration of auxiliary actions, as well as the mean number of incidental actions as the basis, the results obtained in the group of high-reactive subjects were compared with those of the low-reactive ones during the preparatory stage and the stage of production proper separately. The two groups (10 subjects in each) were separated by means of the median of results in the RT experiment. The predicted interrelations are clearly reflected in these data. As shown in Table XXXIX, in each case high-reactive individuals performed approximately twice as many auxiliary actions as did the low-reactive individuals.

The same relationship is revealed in the duration of auxiliary actions, which is likewise approximately twice as long in high-reactive subjects as in low-reactive ones. A converse relationship was obtained for the incidental actions (cigarette smoking, conversation with co-workers, leaving the workstand for a drink of water, etc.). In each case low-reac-

TABLE XXXIX. Auxiliary (A) and incidental (I) actions in high-reactive and low-reactive groups (taken from Uszyńska, 1971)

| Stage of Work | Index | Reactive High (H) | Low (L) | H–L | $p$ |
|---|---|---|---|---|---|
| Preparatory | Number of A | 8.2 | 3.7 | 4.5 | 0.05 |
| | Duration of A | 19.3 | 8.4 | 10.9 | 0.01 |
| | Number of I | 3.0 | 4.6 | 1.6 | 0.10 |
| Production | Number of A | 8.4 | 3.9 | 4.5 | 0.01 |
| | Duration of A | 11.6 | 6.5 | 5.1 | 0.05 |
| | Number of I | 0.5 | 1.9 | 1.4 | 0.01 |

tive subjects are in the lead, which is understandable in view of the fact that, by performing fewer auxiliary actions and devoting less time to them than do the high-reactive subjects, the low-reactive ones can spend more time on incidental actions.

In search of a relationship between the level of reactivity and the expressiveness of auxiliary actions we calculated the rank correlation coefficients for these two variables. All these coefficients were found to be very high and statistically significant; this means that both the number and duration of auxiliary actions increase with the rise in reactivity level (Strelau, 1975c). Thus the results obtained in this study fully confirmed our hypothesis on the relation between level of reactivity and the functional structure of actions as discernible in the subjects' activities.

It is worth noting that the two groups studied did not differ in the ultimate efficacy of activities. Their productivity, expressed in percentage of normal monthly performance, did not depend on the level of reactivity. The pertinent figures are: 103.5% for the low-reactive group and 102% for the high-reactive group. The difference, 1.5%, is statistically insignificant. Neither was there any difference in the quality of the casts produced by either group.

Another experiment (Strelau and Krajewski, 1974), devoted to the relationship between reactivity level and style of action in taxi-drivers, produced similar results, though quite different techniques were used: reactivity was measured by the STI and style of action by a questionnaire constructed especially for this study. For example, high-reactive persons were found to devote more time than low-reactive ones to technical check-ups of their car without being obliged to do so ($p < 0.05$). The duration of the nocturnal breaks is twice as long for the high-reactive drivers as that of their diurnal breaks; in the case of low-reactive drivers the difference averages only 11% in the same direction ($p < 0.05$). This finding relates to our hypothesis that the temporal structure of activities is affected by reactivity. High-reactive drivers prefer to work in the morning while low-reactive ones show a preference for work in the evening or at night ($p < 0.05$). The preference of the high-reactive drivers may well be due to their greater tendency to tire.

The differences between high-reactive and low-reactive drivers, established in this study, support our hypotheses in principle, and yet these two types of persons do not differ in their work efficiency. The two groups did not differ significantly in such objective criteria of driver performance as earnings, number of fares paid, and number of accidents caused. The data are not in line with the research conducted by

Gurevich *et al.* (1975) and by Klyagin *et al.* (1977). In the former study the authors stated that truck-drivers with a strong NS reveal higher infallibility in truck-driving than individuals with a weak NS. However, the authors of the latter study, where truck-drivers were also investigated, obtained quite contradictory results, i.e. weak TNS individuals displayed higher infallibility in driving.

From the functional point of view, a study conducted outside our laboratory by Mündelein (1981), in which the reactivity of 72 subjects was measured by the STI and compared with style of performance, supports our first hypothesis. The author arranged laboratory conditions similar to the natural settings of an insurance agent working within the computer system. The task of the subject, playing the role of the agent, was to calculate the amount of compensation for clients suffering loss. The subject used the computer system (with which he had been acquainted in the preliminary stage), where all information needed to make the final decision was stored. The experiment lasted 3 hours, for which the individual was well paid. A subject's behaviour was estimated, among other things, according to the amount and duration of basic and auxiliary actions. The basic actions included collecting and processing information and decision making. Such activities as: preparing paper for making notes, preparing pens, closing the window etc., were regarded as auxiliary actions. The latter were performed more frequently by high-reactive individuals. The subjects were additionally informed that the computer system, also used by people working in other "offices", may become overloaded and that this could be checked by pressing the button "system". If the button "system" informed that the computer was overloaded, the subject, to avoid unexpected disturbances, could press the button "priority", to insure undisturbed computer operation for a given period. As shown by the author, the high-reactive subjects pressed both "system" and "priority" buttons significantly more frequently than did low-reactive subjects. As well demonstrated in Mündelein's experiment conducted in natural settings such auxiliary activities as preparatory and protective ones occur in high-reactive individuals significantly more often than in low-reactive ones.

All three studies described above deal with professional activity, although of different kinds (foundrymen, taxi-drivers, and activity imitating the work of an insurance agent). Despite differences among them it has been shown that the individual's level of reactivity plays an important role in determining the functional structure of professional activity. Moreover, the experiments conducted in foundrymen and taxi-drivers gave evidence that the efficiency of work does not differ despite levels of reactivity. This can be accounted for by the fact that the settings in which the subjects worked allow them to organize the structure of activity in such a way as to ensure the stimulative value of the situation on a level which corresponds with their stimulation need.

In order to check whether there is any similarity between the level of reactivity and the functional structure of activity in situations dealing with school performance two studies were conducted (Cymes, 1974; Friedensberg, 1974) in which the subjects were asked to learn given texts in any manner they preferred, i.e. they were allowed to organize the structure of their activity by themselves. Let me describe in some detail the experiment conducted by Cymes (1974), in which the dependency between the level of reactivity and style of action in task performance is unequivocally expressed.

From a total of 616 high-school students of both sexes (ranging in age from 15 to 18 years) 194 were selected as having similar scores in speed of learning which was measured by a special test in a preliminary experiment. Taking the quartile deviation as the criterion, 2 groups differing in reactivity were selected from this sample: high-reactive (38 Ss) and low-reactive (39 Ss) individuals. To each subject a one-and-a-half page text dealing with the anatomy of man's liver was given and Ss were instructed to learn it in an optional manner without any time limit. The subjects were allowed to make notes, to use pencils or pens of different colours, and to use two diagrams illustrating the position and surface of the liver. After the text had been mastered 80 questions were given to the subjects in a form of a questionnaire, the answers to which were used as indicators of learning efficiency.

The data show no difference between the high- and low-reactive groups in the learning efficiency as measured by the number of details recalled and the duration of learning. However, both groups differ when the functional structure of activity during learning is taken into account. While there are no differences in the number of basic actions between the high- and low-reactive individuals, there is a statistically significant difference ($p < 0.01$) between both groups in the ratio of the mean number of auxiliary actions to the basic ones; this ratio being higher in high-reactive subjects (1.06) than in the low-reactive ones (0.53). The difference between both groups is also evident when the separate kinds of auxiliary actions extracted in this study are considered (see Table XL). Taking into account the ten auxiliary actions, in eight of these the number of high-reactive subjects dominates significantly, or by an expressed tendency, over the number of low-reactive subjects. In one case (drawing diagrams) there is no difference between groups and the only auxiliary action which was performed to a greater extent by

TABLE XL. Proportions of high- (HR) and low-reactive (LR) individuals in performing auxiliary actions (adapted from Cymes, 1974)

| Auxiliary Activity | HR | LR | p |
|---|---|---|---|
| (1) Underlining | + | | 0.1 |
| (2) Writing up more difficult parts | | + | 0.01 |
| (3) Drawing schemata | no difference | | |
| (4) Making summaries | + | | 0.1 |
| (5) Inspection of schemata | + | | 0.06 |
| (6) Checking notes | + | | 0.1 |
| (7) Correcting notes | + | | 0.1 |
| (8) Making notes from memory | + | | 0.05 |
| (9) Dividing the text into fractions | + | | 0.01 |
| (10) Reviewing the text | + | | 0.01 |

low-reactive individuals was the noting down of difficult parts of the text. The latter fact, which is contrary to our expectation, is not easy to explain within the concept of the regulatory role of the style of action in maintaining a given stimulative value in accordance with the subject's level of reactivity. However, it has to be acknowledged that the style of action is regarded in our concept as a result of the interaction between the individual's temperament traits and environmental influences, among which education and upbringing play a special role. Thus it should not matter that the style of action assimilated by the individual may be contrary to his need for stimulation as determined by temperament.

Similar results, but with essential discrepancies, were obtained by Friedensberg (1974), the main difference lying in the kind of text used (geographical descriptions). As in the formative study, there were no differences between low- and high-reactive subjects in the efficiency of learning when measured by the number of details recalled; however, the high-reactive group needed significantly more time to solve the task. In this study the auxiliary activities were emphasized much less compared with Cymes' experiment, thus making it frequently impossible to analyse the data for statistical significance. Nevertheless, the tendency for predominance of auxiliary actions rather than basic ones was confirmed. Concerning preferences for work on smaller sections of the text and repeating the information selected when reading, statistically significant differences were found in favour of high-reactive subjects. Taking into consideration the fact that both groups were matched for speed of learning, the significantly longer time needed to learn the text in high-reactive subjects is more easily understood if we assume that the difference derives mainly from the larger number of auxiliary actions in high-reactive individuals.

## Style of Action Subject to Manipulation

In several of our experiments (Klonowicz, 1974a; in press, a and b; Czyżkowska, 1974) conducted under laboratory conditions functional structure was manipulated by giving different instructions describing how a given simple construction-type task should be performed. Two instructions were used to regulate the ratio of auxiliary and basic actions. (1) The so-called heuristic instruction in which only the final goal was described and the subject was allowed to organize the activity in his own way, by using optional methods of work. (2) The algorithmic instruction which consisted of describing, not only the goal of the task, but also the operations in the order in which they had to be performed. The algorithmic instruction forces the subject to perform many auxiliary actions whereas the heuristic instruction gives the subject greater freedom to organize the functional structure of activity. Taking as the point of departure our first hypothesis (see p. 210) we assumed that the algorithmic instruction would be preferred by high-reactive subjects. Low-reactive subjects would prefer the heuristic instruction where they could avoid performing dispensable auxiliary actions, and the organization of the structure of activity by the subject seemed to have a high stimulative value.

This hypothesis was verified in an experiment conducted by Czyżkowska (1974). The author selected from a group of 400 female high-school students 97 high-reactive and 98 low-reactive subjects, using the STI for diagnosis. Next, all the selected subjects were presented with two similar tasks: to build a model axe and a model compass by using the "Little Mechano". Each subject performed both tasks, one with the heuristic and the other with the algorithmic instruction. The sequence of tasks and instructions were randomized. The next, and most interesting, part of the experiment consisted of giving the subjects a choice of instruction (heuristic vs. algorithmic) before performing the next task, the aim of which was to form an eyelet in a 2.5 × 2.5 cm square of self-adhesive plaster. As seen from Table XLI the preference for the type of instruction to which the subjects like to work accords with our expectations. In the high-reactive group more individuals prefer the algorithmic instruction whereas among low-reactive individuals a preference for the heuristic instruction prevails.

TABLE XLI. The preference of the type of instruction in high- (HR) and low-reactive (LR) individuals (taken from Czyżkowska, 1974)

| Instruction | HR | LR | Total Number of Subjects |
|---|---|---|---|
| Algorithmic | 63 | 42 | 105 |
| Heuristic | 34 | 56 | 90 |
| Total number of subjects | 97 | 98 | 195 |

$Chi^2 = 9.99; p < 0.01$

The fact that high-reactive individuals tend to perform many auxiliary actions is also evident when they are forced to perform the construction task using only heuristic instruction. Materska (1978) reanalysed Czyżkowska's data and was able to demonstrate (see Table XLII) the above-mentioned consistency in the eyelet task. Whereas the proportion of subjects with low and high ratio of auxiliary to basic actions is almost equal in the low-reactive group this picture changes completely when high-reactive individuals are taken into account. As the Table shows there is an evident predominance in this group of subjects with a high ratio of auxiliary actions to basic ones.

Klonowicz (in press, a) who also reanalysed Czyżkowska's results, put forward the hypothesis that high- and low-reactive subjects should differ in effort[5] in task performance depending on the kind of instruction. The effort would be expressed more in high-reactive subjects under heuristic instructions compared with effort during performance under algorithmic ones. As displayed in Table XLIII, Klonowicz's hypothesis seems to be supported. The expected effect, i.e. the increase in effort, is especially evident in the high-reactive subjects. They certainly invest more effort when solving the task with the heuristic instruction compared to when an algorithmic instruction is used. Also

TABLE XLII. Proportion of subjects as regards the ratio of auxiliary actions (AA) to basic actions (BA) and level of reactivity (taken from Materska, 1978)

| Ratio of AA to BA | HR | LR | Total Number of Subjects |
|---|---|---|---|
| 0–1.00 | 7 | 23 | 30 |
| 1.01–4.67 | 36 | 22 | 58 |
| Total number of subjects | 43 | 45 | 88 |

$Chi^2 = 11.90; p < 0.01$

TABLE XLIII. Effort (operational costs) according to type of instruction and reactivity (taken from Klonowicz, in press, a)

| Instruction | HR Subjects | LR Subjects | Chi$^2$ |
|---|---|---|---|
| Algorithmic | 71 | 56 | 1.772 |
| Heuristic | 124 | 74 | 12.626 ($p < 0.01$) |
| Chi$^2$ | 14.405 [$p < 0.01$] | 2.492 | |

when the efforts of both high- and low-reactive groups are compared under the heuristic instruction, it is evident that high-reactive persons invest more effort than low-reactive ones.

The result presented above conforms with the data of Klonowicz (1974a) in a study with smaller numbers of subjects (30 high-reactive vs. 30 low-reactive individuals) where the task involved the constructing of a model windmill from supplied components. Measuring, among other things, time, performance, and number of errors, the author showed that high-reactive individuals commit more errors and need more time to solve the task under the heuristic than under algorithmic instruction. This was not the case with low-reactive individuals who did not differ in either respect.

In conclusion, all experiments aimed at manipulating the functional structure of action by using different kinds of instruction, show that high-reactive persons prefer situations which ensure task performance through the use of a large number of auxiliary actions. When forced to perform tasks which contradict their preferences, the high-reactive persons invest more effort or display a lowering of performance level.

An experiment conducted by Nosarzewski (1974) was particularly concerned to verify our hypothesis that the level of performance deteriorates if the subject is forced to solve tasks in a manner which does not correspond with his temperamentally determined style of action regarding NS strength (Akimova, 1975; Akimova and Gurevich, 1978). With respect to reactivity, this deterioration will be more conspicuously expressed in high-reactive individuals. This is because these individuals are deprived of the possibility of regulating the stimulative value of their activity and this deprivation, by itself of highly stimulating value, influences the more sensitive, high-reactive people to a greater degree. In order to test this prediction Nosarzewski (1974) studied subjects of different levels of reactivity, varying the structure of their actions so as to include continuous, interrupted, and heterogeneous ones.

Two hundred and twenty college students took the STI and part of them were assigned by quartile section to two extreme groups: low-reactive (36 Ss) and high-reactive (27 Ss). These subjects were then tested under three sets of conditions, each demanding a different manner of performance:

(1) running up columns of figures in a modified Kraepelin test non-stop for three hours (continuous action);
(2) running up figures for three hours with 15 min intervals after each hour (interrupted action);
(3) performing six different activities (thirty min each) for three hours without a break (heterogeneous actions).

The third situation comprised the following tasks: the Kraepelin test, writing down words starting with successive letters of the alphabet, memorizing a poem, copying geometric figures, solving the extended Raven test, and again the Kraepelin test. The order of these tasks was constant; however, all three conditions varied at random. According to the aforementioned hypothesis, as well as taking into account hypotheses (2) and (3) formulated at the beginning of this chapter, our predictions were:

(a) that low-reactive subjects would score higher than high-reactive ones when forced to perform in a continuous manner;
(b) that high-reactive subjects would not differ in performance from low reactive ones when forced to perform in an interrupted manner and when performing heterogeneous actions.

Efficiency of performance was measured by the difference between the scores obtained during the first half-hour and the last half-hour on each test (the Kraepelin test in all three conditions). Table XLIV contains the results of this study.

TABLE XLIV. Efficiency of performance on tasks of different structure in low- and high-reactive groups (taken from Nosarzewski, 1974)

| Type of Action | Group | Mean Number of Correctly Run-up Columns | | $D^M$ | $p$ |
|---|---|---|---|---|---|
| | | 1st interval | 6th | | |
| Continuous | LR | 90.3 | 83.3 | 7.0 | 0.05 |
| | HR | 90.7 | 79.7 | 11.0 | 0.01 |
| Intermittent | LR | 90.4 | 78.0 | 12.4 | 0.01 |
| | HR | 91.1 | 82.2 | 8.9 | 0.05 |
| Heterogeneous | LR | 90.9 | 86.4 | 4.5 | n.s. |
| | HR | 90.7 | 87.4 | 3.3 | n.s. |

The data partly support the hypotheses. Though unconnected with reactivity as such, the first obvious finding is that, irrespective of condition or group, all scores are lower for the final work span than for the first one. This is understandable since the subjects were busy with the tests for three hours. From our point of view what is more interesting is that in the case of continuous action the decline in performance was more marked in high-reactive subjects than in low-reactive ones. The converse holds true for the interrupted action: though a marked decline occurred in both groups; high-reactive subjects scored somewhat better during the final work span than low-reactive ones. Vyatkin (1978), investigating the relation between style of action and strength of NS in high-school children, was able to show that when physical exercises are performed in a continuous manner the behaviour of individuals with a strong NS is more efficient. The intermittent performance of physical exercises is more favourable for individuals with a weak NS. The heterogeneous condition proved to be optimal for both groups: no significant decline in performance was recorded for either the high-reactive or low-reactive subjects.

In conclusion, the results of this study have to some extent confirmed our hypotheses; even those results which have failed to confirm them have at least in no way contradicted them.

## Some Developmental Aspects of the Relation between Level of Reactivity and Style of Action

When considering the relation between temperament traits and style of action, one has to take into account that this interdependency may change with age since style of action undergoes developmental changes and its shaping depends, among other things, upon the individual's experience and knowledge. Evidence for this has been collected by Merlin's students (Prusakova, 1974; Shtimmer, 1974; Mastvilisker and Dikopolskaya, 1976) who investigated style of action in relation to strength of the NS and IQ level in preschool and school-age children (see p. 66). A developmental study conducted in our laboratory by Friedensberg (in press) supports the Soviet psychologists' statement; however it also considers the specificity of our approach, i.e. that reactivity and not strength of NS is measured. Within our conceptual framework, style of action considered from the functional point of view refers to basic and auxiliary actions, whereas the Soviet approach subjected the ratio of orienting versus executive actions to investigation.

Friedensberg controlled such variables as age, style of action, performance level, and level of IQ. After selecting for reactivity by means of the quartile section, 184 boys were finally studied—92 of them high-reactive and 92 low-reactive. These were divided into five groups differing in age (6, 8, 10, 13, and 16 years old) and each group was subdivided into low- and high-reactive individuals. In each of the ten subgroups the number of subjects varied from 14 to 20. Reactivity was assessed by means of the Reactivity Rating Scales described in detail in Chapter 5 (see p. 198). IQ level was measured with Raven's Progressive Matrices (for either children or adults). The individual style of action regarding functional structure was studied in an experiment in which a constructional task had to be performed. The subjects had to solve either the Link Cube test (subjects aged 10 to 16) or the Red Block test which may be considered a variation of the Link Cube for younger children (6–8 years).

Without going into details of Friedensberg's results I would like to draw attention to some regularities established by this author. It was found that, irrespective of age level the total number of auxiliary actions is larger in the high-reactive groups than in the low-reactive ones (see Table XLV), convincing us that the dominance of auxiliary actions over basic ones in high reactive individuals is generally common.

Friedensberg was able to show that, irrespective of reactivity level, there is a specificity in kind of auxiliary actions depending on the age of the subject. In 6 and 8-year-old children there is a predominance of corrective actions; however, in the youngest group, the corrective actions are of a specific nature. These children manifest many faulty corrections resembling the "trial and error" method also studied by Mastvilisker and Dikopolskaya (1976) and related by them, not to strength of the NS, but to the individual's IQ level. According to Mastvilisker (1967) the modes of reaction which are typical for 6 to

TABLE XLV. Number of auxiliary actions and level of performance in high- and low-reactive individuals differing in age (based on Friedensberg, in press)

| Age | Number of Auxiliary Actions | | Level of Performance | | | |
|---|---|---|---|---|---|---|
| | | | Duration | | Errors | |
| | HR | LR | HR | LR | HR | LR |
| 6 | 155 | 123 | 1539 | 1303 | 44 | 37 |
| 8 | 136 ·······→ | 79 | 1194 ←——→ | 654 | 39 ·······→ | 20 |
| 10 | 124 | 121 | 1034 | 996 | 23 | 20 |
| 13 | 180 ·······→ | 95 | 1352 ←——→ | 682 | 34 ←——→ | 15 |
| 16 | 67 ·······→ | 40 | 497 ·······→ | 347 | 8 | 5 |

·······→ $p < 0.01$    ←——→ $p < 0.001$

7-year-old children (probably this is what Thomas and Chess (1977) would regard as the "how" of behaviour) cannot be considered as style of action which develops later as the result of experience and education. In older children, from 8 years on, control activity develops and coexists with corrective activity, which becomes more and more accurate. The older the child the more differentiated are the auxiliary actions which may be attributed to the accumulation of experience and knowledge positively correlated with age.

Turning back to Table XLV, it can be seen that in some groups there is also a significant difference in the level of performance if one considers the time needed to solve the test (8-, 13-, and 16-year-old children) and the total number of errors (subjects aged 8 and 13 years). The difference in task performance duration to the disadvantage of high-reactive subjects is consistent with the fact that they perform more auxiliary actions than do low-reactive individuals. However, it is not easy to explain why high-reactive individuals, irrespective of their age, make more mistakes than low-reactive ones (this tendency was statistically significant twice). This could be more understandable if the situation had forced the subjects to solve the construction task in a given manner, as was the case in Klonowicz's (1974a) experiment (see p. 220). Task performance errors are one of the main indices of efficiency level and as our studies have shown (Uszyńska, 1971; Strelau and Krajewski, 1974; Strelau, 1975c; Cymes, 1974), the latter does not differentiate high- and low-reactive subjects if they are allowed to develop their own style of action.

The fact that high-reactive subjects make more mistakes is probably due to the type of the task performed by these individuals. Efficient solution of the Link Cube test requires a given level of ability. Nevertheless, the correlational analysis between the level of reactivity and IQ conducted separately for each age group did not show any statistical significance, this result being consistent with other studies (see Prusakova, 1974). Friedensberg (in press) was able to demonstrate that the efficacy of performance (duration and errors) depends on the individual's IQ. Taking the median as a criterion which allowed each age group to be divided into two subgroups, below and above the median of IQ, the author showed that in all groups, except the 10-year-olds, the duration of performance and the number of errors was higher in individuals with an IQ below this median. She has also shown that in the two youngest groups (6 and 8-year-olds) and in the oldest one (16-year-olds) there is a predominance of auxiliary actions in individuals with below median IQ. Unfortunately, the author did not use the ANOVA to show the interaction between level of reactivity and IQ;

however, the data presented by Friedensberg allow us to conjecture that, in shaping the style of action, both reactivity and IQ probably play an important part. This has also been suggested by Merlin's associates.

The individual's own experience, and the education system in particular are not without influence on the moulding of the style of action. As stated by Mastvilisker and Dikopolskaya (1976), prolonged training may change the individual's style of action to some extent. Many other studies have also supported this assumption (see Sukhareva, 1967; Shchukin, 1977; Vyatkin, 1978; Akimova, 1980). Bearing in mind our experiments, where the style of action was provoked by the kind of instruction given to the individuals, one may hypothesize that the educational system in which the more stimulating (in the specific and unspecific sense) heuristic method of teaching predominates, favours the style of action typical for low-reactive individuals in whom the basic and auxiliary activities are well balanced or where basic actions predominate. The educational system based on the algorithmic method of teaching, though less stimulating in itself, favours the high-reactive individuals due to the many auxiliary actions this method of teaching offers.

## THE INFLUENCE OF TEMPERAMENT ON THE CHOICE OF ACTIVITY AND SITUATION OF A GIVEN STIMULATIVE VALUE

Style of action is one of the possible ways in which activity regulates the amount of stimulation according to the individual's stimulation need as determined by the level of reactivity. As shown before, if one has the chance to develop and to use the style of action according to one's reactivity level, one can then perform many kinds of activity efficiently, because the style of action allows the stimulative value of performed activity or of the situation in which it is performed to decrease or increase in accordance with one's needs.

However, in many cases the individual regulates his need for stimulation by choosing activities that are more or less stimulating in themselves, mostly because of different degrees of risk, threat, difficulty, etc. involved. The stimulative value of different kinds of activity has been discussed in Chapter 5, where the author also acknowledged the fact that the content of activity (e.g. mountain climbing vs. bank robbing) does not depend on the individual's temperament traits, although they do influence the preference for activity of a given stimulative load. It has been also argued in Chapter 5 that high-reactive individuals tend to prefer activity or situations of low stimulative value, whereas low-reactive individuals reveal an opposite tendency: they are known to seek activities or situations which are rich in stimulation. This hypothesis can be shown schematically as follows:

$$\text{high-reactive individuals: } LS_{(a,e)} > HS_{(a,e)}$$
$$\text{low-reactive individuals: } LS_{(a,e)} < HS_{(a,e)}$$

where: LS = low stimulation; HS = high stimulation; a = activity; e = situation, surroundings.

Over the last ten years or so we have collected data which enable us to show the degree to which our hypothesis is correct. Two lines of research may be distinguished. In some studies we were interested in whether the way individuals perform activity of different stimulative load is related to their level of reactivity. The second group of studies was concerned with searching for relations between preferences for strategies of actions, considered from the point of view of their stimulative value, and reactivity.

## Preferences for Activities Varying in Stimulation Load and the Level of Reactivity

If the hypothesis that the preference for situations and activities of a particular stimulation load conforms with one's reactivity level is correct, we should expect individuals enjoying certain freedom in the choice of their surroundings and activities to use this freedom to suit their temperamentally determined stimulation need.

With this assumption in mind, a study was conducted by Danielak (1972) on subjects employed in three types of jobs, each representing a different degree of social threat considered to be equivalent to three levels of stimulation.

Among the subjects whose job involved considerable social threat, and hence provided rich stimulation, we expected to find a larger number of low-reactive persons than high-reactive ones. In the occupational group engaged in activities of limited social threat, and hence of poor stimulation, the ratio was expected to be reversed. In the intermediate occupational group no clear-cut predominance of either high- or low-reactive subjects was anticipated. The study was further based on the assumption that the variables which are responsible for the adoption of a particular job (abilities, interests, etc.) are distributed at random in all three samples.

The group engaged in activities supplying rich stimulation was composed of lawyers (33 Ss), the intermediate group consisted of office workers (35 Ss) with a lawyer's diploma, and the poor-stimulation group (with minimal social threat) was composed of librarians (46 Ss). This kind of group qualification (referred to the degree of social threat inherent in the profession) was obtained from evaluations contributed by competent judges who had a good knowledge of each profession. Reactivity was measured by STI. Those subjects who had scored either below the first or above the third quartiles (the latter being derived from tests conducted on a normative group) were assigned to the two extreme groups of reactivity level. Those subjects whose scores fell in the two intermediate quartiles were excluded.

The results, as shown in Table XLVI, have borne out our hypothesis concerning the ratio of reactive and non-reactive persons in the occupational group of considerable social threat (lawyers). The pattern of results in the other two groups likewise meets our expectations. In the occupational group with little load (librarians) we found a majority of high-reactive subjects.

TABLE XLVI. Distribution of high- and low-reactive individuals in occupational groups differing in stimulation value (based on Danielak, 1972)

| Group | LR | HR | Total Number of Subjects |
|---|---|---|---|
| Lawyers | 14 | 5 | 19 |
| Office workers | 8 | 4 | 12 |
| Librarians | 8 | 15 | 23 |
| Total number of subjects | 30 | 24 | 54 |

$Chi^2 = 5.991; p < 0.05$

Parallel to the study reported above, an investigation was launched in order to find out whether high-reactive vs. low-reactive subjects would be similarly distributed when stimulation was derived from another type of activity. Based on the same methodology, the study by Popielarska (1972) differed from the one described earlier in that the occupation of varying degree of social threat was replaced by sports activities of varying degree of physical danger.

The group engaged in highly stimulating activities was composed of glider pilots and mountain climbers (105 Ss), the intermediate group of basket-ball and volley-ball players (29 Ss), and the low-stimulation group of people not engaged in any sport and not compensating for this by any other activity (46 Ss). Otherwise the procedure and analysis of data were the same.

Table XLVII. Distribution of high- and low-reactive individuals in groups differing in sports activity (based on Popielarska, 1972)

| Group | LR | HR | Total number of Subjects |
|---|---|---|---|
| Mountain climbers and glider pilots | 48 | 17 | 65 |
| Basket-ball and volley-ball players | 11 | 4 | 15 |
| Non-sportsmen | 8 | 15 | 23 |
| Total number of subjects | 67 | 36 | 103 |

$Chi^2 = 12.086$; $p < 0.01$

The results shown in Table XLVII are striking by their far-reaching coincidence with those reported above. Their evidence is that in the group of subjects engaged in strongly stimulating sports activities, there is a statistically significant predominance of low-reactive persons, whereas in the group comprising persons not exposed to any physical danger there were many more high-reactive than low-reactive subjects.

This agreement, in spite of quite different indices of stimulation load applied in those two studies, confirms the belief that our explorations were aimed in the right direction. But we are also aware of their methodological shortcomings, the major ones being: the ambiguity of criteria applied, and hence of the measurement of stimulation load, inadequate homogeneity of the isolated groups, and the small number of subjects, too small for this kind of investigation.

The dependency between stimulatory value of professional activity which the individual would like to perform or, on the contrary, would like to avoid, and reactivity level was studied by Oleszkiewicz (1982). A list of 44 professions was presented to 171 college students (16 to 20-year-old men) and they were asked to make three positive choices (professions which they would like to perform) and three negative ones (professions which they would like to avoid). The stimulatory value of professions was judged by 50 independent judges separately for four dimensions: social stimulation, new experiences and sensations, cognitive-intellectual stimulation, and physical threat. Reactivity level was measured by STI.

The results are interesting. As regards the professions which the persons would like to perform, there was no correlation between the stimulatory value of the chosen professions and level of reactivity (see Table XLVIII). This regularity changed, however, when the professions to be avoided were taken into account. In all four dimensions the correlations with reactivity (Strength of Excitation) scale of the STI was negative, although not high, and in one case not significant. These

TABLE XLVIII. Reactivity and stimulative value of chosen and rejected professions (taken from Oleszkiewicz, 1982)

| Categories of Profession | Social Stimulation | New experiences and Sensations | Cognitive-Intellectual Stimulation | Physical Threat |
|---|---|---|---|---|
| Chosen professions | 0.04 | 0.14 | 0.01 | 0.14 |
| Rejected professions | −0.30* | −0.34* | −0.16 | −0.26* |

* $p < 0.001$

data allow us, with some caution, to conclude that the higher the reactivity the higher the probability that the subject wishes to avoid a profession of high stimulatory value, which is in line with our expectations. The low coefficients of correlation should not bother us because reactivity is not the only variable which determines the avoidance of given professions. Nevertheless, reactivity seems to be an important dimension co-determining the negative selection of professions characterized by high stimulative value. The lack of relation between level of reactivity and stimulatory value of the chosen professions may be due to the fact that in this case the interests, motivation, or attraction of the proposed professions play the crucial role in making the choice.

If our hypothesis about the dependence between level of reactivity and preferences of activity differing in stimulative value is justified, the relation between level of reactivity and stimulation load of professional activity should be particularly pronounced when considering activity which supplies extremely rich stimulation. In order to cope efficiently with activity of a very high stimulative value and performed over a longer period, the individual must have a given level of endurance which might be met in low-reactive persons. If the stimulative value of the professional activity cannot be lowered by a given style of action (as may be the case in several professions) we may expect high-reactive persons to avoid performing such activity or, having performed it for a given period, to abandon it as leading to overstimulation.

The dependence between reactivity and stimulative value of a given professional activity under investigation may not occur when professional activity of low stimulative value is taken into account. This happens because low-reactive individuals are able to compensate for lack of stimulation by performing highly stimulating activity outside their professional work or they may use different kinds of self-stimulation to compensate for the lack of stimulation in their professional activity.

TABLE XLIX. Reactivity level in men performing in highly stimulating professions

| Study | Group | Mean Value of Reactivity | Standard Scores (C scale) |
|---|---|---|---|
| (1) Stawowska, 1973, 1977 | Standardization sample (N = 1265) | 56.0 | 5 |
| (2) Ciosek and Oszmiańczuk, 1974 | Fishermen on long-term voyages (N = 70) | 70.1 | 8 |
| (3) Terelak, 1974 | Pilots (N = 115) | 64.4 | 7 |
|  | Pilots (N = 95) | 62.2 | 6 |
| (4) Zarzycka, 1980 | Train-drivers (N = 59) | 66.1 | 7 |
| (5) Eliasz, 1981 | Steel-workers (N = 192) | 61.8 | 6 |
| (6) Terelak, 1982 | Participants of an Arctic expedition (N = 21) | 65.7 | 7 |

There are no studies specifically devoted to checking the validity of our assumption; nevertheless, we do have some data scattered over several experiments on men only which throw some light on the relation between level of reactivity and highly stimulating professional activity. They are shown in Table XLIX.

Taking as the starting-point the mean value of reactivity calculated on a standardized sample of 1265 men (ranging in age from 17 to 60 years) with which the other measures of reactivity are compared, in all professional groups characterized as having high stimulation load the level of reactivity is shown to be lower, in accordance with our hypothesis. No study conducted in our laboratory contradicts the regularity portrayed in Table XLIX.

Data from research aimed at relating the strength of excitation measured by the RT methods to a professional activity also support our position. Klyagin (1975) diagnosed the strength of excitation in a group of 78 bus drivers, driving on very difficult and long-distance routes, and found that 54 of the 78 drivers had a strong TNS, only four were recognized as having a weak TNS, and the remaining 20 subjects had an average NS strength. Similar results were obtained by Troshikhin et al. (1978) who stated that, among 65 truck drivers, not one could be characterized as having a pronounced weak NS.

Eliasz's (1981) study of steel-workers, who are generally low-reactive (see Table XLIX), shows that there is a dependency between reactivity level and professional activity conducted in conditions differing in stimulative load. Several conditions of work were taken into account as criteria of stimulation intensity, i.e. noise, physical threat (number and kind of accidents), and high temperature in the foundry. Competent judges distinguished two conditions differing in stimulation load: relatively high and very high stimulation. The author was able to show that the whole sample of steel-workers (192 men ranging in age from 25 to 50 years, which scored $M = 61.8$ in reactivity), differed in reactivity level when divided into two groups, working under relatively high and very high stimulation. The group working in very high stimulative conditions had a lower level of reactivity ($M = 63.7$; 84 subjects) than the one working in conditions of relatively high stimulative value ($M = 60.4$, 108 subjects), these differences being statistically significant ($p < 0.025$).

The experiment conducted by Eliasz (1981) enables one to conclude that, even within one professional activity, differences in reactivity level may be found if this activity is performed in conditions constantly differing in stimulation load. The fact that the reactivity level of subjects working in highly stimulating conditions is significantly lower compared with individuals working under lower stimulation, is consistent with our expectation.

Activity, being the main regulator of stimulation need, may be considered to be a function of the interaction between reactivity level and the stimulation load of the situation. If the situation is highly stimulating we may expect high-reactive individuals to reveal lower stimulation-seeking activity in order to attain their optimal level of activation (see p. 188), than individuals scoring low in the reactivity dimension. Taking this assumption as a starting point Sosnowski (1978) conducted an experiment to discover whether activity expressed in verbal behaviour of members of a small group depends on their reactivity level and on the stimulation load of the situation in which this activity is performed.

The small groups were composed of three subjects: low, medium, and high-reactive individuals. Reactivity level was measured by the STI. Two kinds of experimental situation were arranged: a social threat situation (resulting from others' evaluation of an individual and from the individual's belief in the importance of such evaluation) and a non-threat situation. The task of the subjects was to rank 11 values (e.g. independence, love, knowledge) for personal importance. Each value had a short description and, before the experiment proper, the individual was asked to rank the list of values. The task of the small group was to discuss the values, to adjust their position as regards their importance, and to prepare the final ordering of the 11 values. The behaviour of subjects during task performance was analysed by the Bales' (1951) Interaction Process Analysis category system. Altogether

30 groups (15 in each threat and non-threat situation) were investigated and the selection of subjects differing in reactivity was made from a group of 453 schoolboys (15–17 years old). The subjects did not know each other within the small groups. The quantitative indices of social behaviour based on the Bales' category system enabled the total number and percentage of behaviour units to be estimated, as well as the number and percentage of behavioural units in each of the 12 categories separated by Bales. All these scores were computed separately for high, medium, and low-reactive individuals. The raw scores of the total number of behavioural acts were transformed into standard T-scores. Their distribution for all three groups differing in reactivity as regards both situations (threat vs. non-threat) is presented in Table L.

TABLE L. Total number of behavioural units (T-scores) in subjects differing in reactivity in threat and non-threat situations (taken from Sosnowski, 1978)

| Situation | Subjects | | | | | |
|---|---|---|---|---|---|---|
| | High-reactive | | Moderate-reactive | | Low-reactive | |
| | M | SD | M | SD | M | SD |
| Non-threat | 50.1 | 11.3 | 50.7 | 10.1 | 49.0 | 11.7 |
| Threat | 48.5 | 10.2 | 48.9 | 8.4 | 52.9 | 8.4 |

The analysis of variance did not allow the author to make any statistically justified conclusions as to the significance of any of the variables under investigation nor of their interaction. However, there is a tendency towards our expectation. With high-reactive subjects it seems that the number of behavioural units decreases under stress conditions compared with the normal ones, whereas in low-reactive individuals there is a reverse tendency—a growing number of behavioural units occurring under threat. Also a tendency in all three groups for the variance of scores to decrease under threat condition shows, according to Sosnowski (1978), that the higher the stimulative value of the situation the lower the influence of uncontrolled variables and the higher the influence of reactivity.

Taking the total number of behavioural units as an index of activity level it should be stated that Sosnowski's experiment does not allow for any uniequivocal conclusion concerning the relation between level of reactivity, stimulative value of situation, and the individual's activity, although the whole configuration of results is in line with our hypothesis. This low-expressed dependency between reactivity level, stimulative value of situation and activity manifested in social behaviour agrees with some studies in social psychology which suggest that the prediction of social behaviour on the basis of individual differences is rather low (Mann, 1959; Argyle, 1975; both authors cited by Sosnowski, 1978).

The results analysed from the point of view of 12 separate, qualitatively differentiated categories of social behaviour showed that there is no difference in the percentage of behaviour units between low, medium, and high-reactive individuals. If one assumes that Bales' separate categories are concerned more with the content of behaviour than with its formal characteristics, then Sosnowski's findings are in accordance with our expectations (see p. 189).

However, they are not consistent with the results of Likhachev (1976) who proved that high-reactive individuals differed from the low-reactive ones (as measured by STI) in specific kinds of social activity such as that observed during routine training (lower stimulation) and contests (higher stimulation) of basket-ball teams. Twenty females ranging in age from 18 to 25 were studied. The author distinguished seven kinds of interpersonal contacts and found that the low-reactive individuals generally manage the game better than high-reactives, under both training and contest conditions. During competitions, the intensity of interpersonal contacts in high-reactive subjects dropped and the players were more prone to negative emotional reactions against their partners.

Perczyńska and Żuchowska (1976) were also interested in the relation of social activity to individual temperament traits. These authors selected from among 643 female and male pupils (aged 14–15 years) two groups differing in social activity: so-called socially active (91 Ss) and socially passive (74 Ss) individuals. The diagnosis of social activity was based on a rating scale given to the teacher and on the sociometric method. However, no information is given about the criteria used for diagnosing pupils as socially active or passive. Reactivity and mobility of behaviour were computed on the basis of the STI.

The socially active and socially passive groups were shown not to differ in the proportion of high- and low-reactive subjects. Mobility of behaviour, on the other hand, was positively correlated with social activity. There was a statistically significant predominance of "mobile" individuals over "slow" ones in the socially active group, whereas in the socially passive one "slow" individuals predominated over the "mobile" ones.

Fifteen years earlier Ilina (1961), in an investigation based on case-studies in high-school students, found mobility of the NS to be positively related to social activity. Temperament traits and social activity were estimated qualitatively by observation.

Taking into account all data reported in this section we are able to conclude that the dependency between reactivity and activity, theoretically justified in Chapter 5, has usually found empirical support. In order to attain their optimal level of activation, people perform activities of different stimulative value, the latter being dependent on their reactivity level. High-reactive individuals prefer less stimulating activities whereas low-reactive individuals prefer more stimulating activities. The level of reactivity is clearly lower in subjects who perform professional activity of a very high stimulatory value, probably due to the fact that high-reactive subjects avoid highly stimulating professional activities, particularly when the activity has no leeway for modifying the style of action in accordance with reactivity level. In further studies, mobility should also be acknowledged when studying the relation between the primary temperament traits and activity. As revealed by our own data based on the STI, reactivity (strength of excitation) is positively correlated with mobility of behaviour (mobility of NP) thus allowing us to assume that mobility may also be positively correlated with activity. Both Ilina's (1961) and Perczyńska and Żuckowska's (1976) results support this assumption.

## Stimulative Value of Action Strategy in Individuals Differing in Reactivity

The way an individual copes with tasks and everyday situations causes the development of given strategies of behaviour. These differ in their stimulatory value. As may be hypothesized from our theoretical considerations, high-reactive individuals, who only need rather low stimulation to attain their optimal level of activation, should be inclined to develop relatively unstimulating action strategies. In turn, low-reactive individuals who need higher stimulation to attain their optimal level of activity will develop such strategies of action in order to ensure stimulation of high intensity.

Two studies were conducted in our laboratory to verify this hypothesis. The first, by Eliasz (1973), studied the relation between the strategy of action and level of reactivity, also borrowing from Nuttin (1965) the concept of the style of self-regulation, within which active and passive styles of self-regulation may be differentiated. Active self-regulation refers to a strong engagement of behaviour which removes any organism-environment mismatch, i.e. behaviour demanding an active improvement in one's functioning, or else a change of environment. Conversely, behaviour which supplies the person with limited stimulation is described as passive self-regulation. Both these styles differ conspicuously in the amount of stimulation offered to the individual. The active style of self-regulation is highly stimulating, whereas the passive style of self-regulation supplies less stimulation. Eliasz (1973) hypothesized that low-reactive individuals tend toward an active style of self-regulation in contrast to high-reactive individuals, who show a tendency toward a passive style of self-regulation.

Self-regulation style was tested in the following three experimental situations:

(a) adjustment of one's goals to actual achievements (ratio of aspiration level to achievement level);
(b) adjustment of one's activity so as to ensure goal attainment in a new situation (effectiveness of action);
(c) engagement in tasks when the situation is not conducive to goal attainment (persistence).

The adoption of realistic goals and their effective and persistent pursuit were interpreted as indicating an active style of self-regulation, while the opposite behaviour was interpreted as evidence of the passive style of self-regulation. Reactivity was estimated by the STI. In this experiment other variables were also investigated (neuroticism and level of frustration); however, it is not necessary to discuss them here (see Eliasz, 1973). Altogether 130 male subjects ranging in age from 15 to 17 years were investigated.

Subjects were divided by quartile section into two groups: high and low-reactive. To measure persistence and effectiveness a standard tracking task, used to assess visual and motor co-ordination, was used. The task was performed in two situations. In the first one the subject, highly motivated by the experimenter, was asked to repeat the task until he reached the upper limit of his capacity. In the second situation the task was made more difficult. It consisted of providing visual control of the performed task (the movement of the needle) by way of a mirror instead of direct control as in the first situation. Persistence was measured by the ratio of the number of trials in the second situation to the number of trials in the first one. The higher the ratio, the more persistent the subject; consequently, the more active is his style of self-regulation. Effectiveness was measured by the ratio of best performance in the first situation to the best performance in the second one. Since the time needed for completing the task was used as indicator, the higher the ratio, the greater the improvement. Hence, the high ratio was an indicator of the active style of self-regulation. As regards the third indicator of the style of self-regulation, underestimation of aspiration as well as overestimation (unrealistic goals) were assumed to be indicators

TABLE LI. Active (AS) and passive (PS) style of self-regulation as measured by persistence in high- and low-reactive subjects (taken from Eliasz, 1973)

| Reactivity | AS | PS | Total Number of Subjects |
|---|---|---|---|
| LR | 16 | 25 | 41 |
| HR | 8 | 35 | 43 |
| Total number of subjects | 24 | 60 | 84 |

$Chi^2 = 7.363; p < 0.01$

of passive self-regulation, whereas realistic aspiration (concordance between aspiration and achievement) should be considered as an indicator of active self-regulation. This assumption is consistent within Atkinson's (1965) theory of motivation in which he argues that when probability of achievement approaches 50% the individual becomes most emotionally involved. The ratio of aspiration to achievement was measured in a task which consisted of fitting rings on a rod (dexterimenter).

The results obtained by Eliasz support to a considerable extent the hypothesis concerning the relation between reactivity and style of self-regulation. As Table LI shows, when persistence is used as indicator of the style of self-regulation the number of high-reactive subjects who manifest the passive style of self-regulation is extremely high. Although the passive style of self-regulation predominates over the active one in low-reactive subjects, the ratio is far from the one attained by the high-reactive individuals.

When effectiveness of action is taken into account (see Table LII) the number of low-reactive individuals who express the active style of self-regulation is evidently higher than those who express the passive style of self-regulation. The opposite ratio of number of persons is met in high-reactive subjects in whom there is a predominance of the passive style of self-regulation over the active one.

TABLE LII. Active (AS) and passive (PS) style of self-regulation as measured by effectiveness in high- and low-reactive subjects (taken from Eliasz, 1973)

| Reactivity | AS | PS | Total Number of Subjects |
|---|---|---|---|
| LR | 25 | 16 | 41 |
| HR | 15 | 28 | 43 |
| Total number of subjects | 40 | 44 | 84 |

$Chi^2 = 5.735; p < 0.02$

As regards the third indicator of the style of self-regulation the results did not bear out Eliasz's hypothesis. However, the distribution of subjects with passive and active styles of self-regulation related to level of reactivity is, in the case of the high-reactive group, in accordance with expectations.

Generally speaking, Eliasz's data support the hypothesis that the strategy of action (active vs. passive style of self-regulation) depends on the individual's level of reactivity, the direction of interdependency according with our theoretical considerations.

A second study by Kozłowski (1977) aimed to test whether high-reactive subjects differed from low-reactive ones in the stimulative value of strategies of action, i.e. whether the latter was lower in high-reactive individuals. The experiment aimed at answering the question of whether individual differences in preference for given levels of probability taken as a measure of risk are due to individual differences in stimulation need.

The literature supports the assumption that there is a rather stable tendency to prefer risk or probability in decision-making in gambling situations (e.g. Edwards, 1953; Cameron and Myers, 1966; cited by Kozłowski, 1977). Kozłowski hypothesized that individuals characterized by a high demand for stimulation preferred the value of the goal over the probability of its achievement (risky strategy). The opposite occurs in individuals with low demand for stimulation. They manifest a risk-avoidance strategy which results from a preference for probability to attain the goal over its value. This hypothesis is based on the following consideration: a risky situation causes emotional tension which has its physiological correlates in a high level of arousal, thus heightening the stimulative value of the situation. High-reactive individuals known as having low stimulation need will avoid situations which evoke strong emotional tension, i.e. they avoid risk. This in turn provides for the development of a risk-avoidance strategy of action. The opposite occurs in individuals with a low level of reactivity, characterized by a high demand for stimulation. For these individuals the situation of risk is a desirable one because of its high stimulative value. This results in the development of a risky strategy of action.

In Kozłowski's experiment 144 male high-school students (aged 18–21) were investigated. The STI was used to estimate the level of reactivity. Two extreme groups differing in reactivity were separated on the basis of the quartile deviation: high- and low-reactive, 36 subjects each. Moreover, both groups were divided (at the median) into two subgroups differing in the level of neuroticism measured by the MPI. As a result the following four groups were separated: high reactivity and high neuroticism (RN), high reactivity and low neuroticism (Rn), low reactivity and high neuroticism (rN), and low reactivity and low neuroticism (rn). It was assumed that the group with low reactivity and low neuroticism might be characterized as having high stimulation need and the group with high reactivity and high neuroticism as having low demand for stimulation.[6] The two remaining groups were intermediate regarding stimulation need.

The preference for risk or probability was measured by summing up the results of five different games. In each game the subject had to choose from five alternatives with the probability of winning ranging from 1/6 to 5/6. The number of points to be won varied from 12 to 60. To eliminate the influence of success or failure the subjects were asked to make the five choices one after the other. Information about the result obtained by the individual was given after the experiment had finished. Two subjects took part in each game. No information was given to the subject about the partner's choice. The subject who won more points in the five games taken together was the winner. The experiment consisted of two series which differed in the monetary pay-out; in the second series the pay-out was doubled from that of the first one.

The following five games were used:

(1) cards—the subject was asked to guess in which of six rows (4 cards in each row) the ace of spades lay;

(2) dice—the subject could bet on one to five at any one toss;

(3) balls—three urns contained 60 balls in two colours of varying proportion for each colour; the subject was asked to bet on one colour and then to draw a ball from one of the urns;

(4) roulette—the player could bet on any one of five sections varying in width;

(5) urns—a black ball was hidden in one of six urns and the subject was asked to guess which by pointing to 1, 2, 3, 4, or 5 urns.

The skew coefficient,[7] which represents preference with respect to probabilities was used as the measure of the subject's preferences. Subjects who scored above or equal to the median value of SK = 0.424 were considered to prefer low probabilities and were henceforth regarded as manifesting the risk-taking strategy. Subjects whose SK was below the median preferred high probabilities and therefore represented the risk-avoidance strategy.

Kozłowski's results generally support the hypothesis concerning the relation between stimulation need and the preference for strategy (risk-taking vs. risk-avoidance). As seen in Table LIII, which displays the results of the first series of the experiment, the amount of subjects

Table LIII. Strategy of action in groups differing in stimulation demand: series I (taken from Kozłowski, 1977)

| Stimulation Demand | Strategy of Action | | Total Number of Subjects |
|---|---|---|---|
| | Risk-taking | Risk-avoiding | |
| rn | 10 | 8 | 18 |
| rN | 11 | 7 | 18 |
| Rn | 10 | 8 | 18 |
| RN | 4 | 14 | 18 |

$Chi^2 = 8.217; p < 0.05$

representing risk-avoidance strategies clearly predominates over those who represent risk-taking strategies in the group with lowest stimulation need. As regards remaining groups, the proportion of "risk-takers" and "risk-avoiders" does not differentiate between the group with high demand for stimulation and either of the intermediary groups, and a slight predominance of "risk-takers" in all three groups may be found.

The interdependency of stimulation need and the strategy of decision-making in gambling situations became more clear in the second case, when the stimulative value of the situation was increased by doubling the monetary pay-out (see Table LIV). The distribution of subjects manifesting risk-taking and risk-avoidance strategies is clearcut in both extreme groups differing in stimulation need. In the group with high stimulation demand the predominance of "risk-takers" may be observed, whereas in the group with low demand for stimulation, the preponderance of "risk-avoiders" is evident.

The dependency between reactivity and strategy of action regarding the degree of risk in behaviour has also been found in other investigations. Zarzycka (1980) studying the causes of accidents in train-drivers

TABLE LIV. Strategy of action in groups differing in stimulation demand: series II (taken from Kozłowski, 1977)

| Stimulation Demand | Strategy of Action | | Total Number of Subjects |
|---|---|---|---|
| | Risk-taking | Risk-avoiding | |
| rn | 12 | 6 | 18 |
| rN | 10 | 8 | 18 |
| Rn | 11 | 7 | 18 |
| RN | 3 | 15 | 18 |

$Chi^2 = 11.1; p < 0.02$

was able to show that in high- and low-reactive individuals the probability of causing accidents is approximately the same. However, what distinguishes both these groups is the way in which an accident is committed. In the low-reactive group there was a preponderance of individuals who caused accidents through risky behaviour. In high-reactive individuals the accident resulted mostly because of ineffective behaviour (low efficiency, high distractability).

A study conducted outside our laboratory by Strykowska (1978) strongly supports the data presented by Kozłowski. Strykowska's experiment consisted of solving problems typical for computer-controlled traffic manager tasks. The author was able to show that, depending on their reactivity level (measured among other things by STI), individuals differed in their task solution strategy. Taking as a criterion the volume of information received before construction of the hypothesis, Strykowska distinguished between risky and cautious strategies on the basis of information received before constructing this hypothesis. This division has been accepted by Bruner (1961, cited by Strykowska, 1978). The dependency between problem-solving strategy and level of reactivity was tested in two situations differing in motivation level evoked in the subjects (personal vs. task-oriented motivation). The results obtained enabled the author to conclude that high-reactive individuals differ from low-reactive ones in their choice of task-solving strategy in both situations. High-reactive individuals prefer a cautious strategy whereas individuals with low reactivity prefer risky strategies when solving problems.

Taking into account the results of experiments presented in this section, it may be said that, depending on the level of reactivity, people prefer strategies of action differing in stimulatory value. Risky behaviour and strong engagement in behaviour that leads to change of the environment or to improvement of the individual's functioning, and regarded as strategies of high stimulative value, are mostly to be found in low-reactive subjects. Individuals with high levels of reactivity, on the other hand, manifest cautious behaviour and passive style of self-regulation which should be considered as strategies of action of lower stimulative value.

## EFFICIENCY OF ACTION AND PSYCHOPHYSIOLOGICAL CHANGES UNDER SITUATIONS IMPOSED UPON STIMULATIVE VALUE AND TEMPERAMENTAL TRAITS

High levels of stress may result from a discrepancy between the need for stimulation and the stimulative value of situations, which occurs during a disturbance of equilibrium between task demand and conditions (external and internal) under which the task is performed (e.g. Lazarus, 1966; Tomaszewski, 1967; Schulz and Schönpflug, 1982). When the stimulative value of the situation is highly unfavourable to the individual, it is hypothesized that reactivity, as one of the internal conditions determining equilibrium, should be regarded as an important variable. It determines whether a given stimulation load of the situation is appraised as difficult or not.

The point of departure for our considerations is the well-known assumption that individuals, depending on their reactivity level, demand different levels of stimulation to maintain the optimal level of activation. When the stimulative value of a given situation is discordant with the individual's stimulation need, it may result in a decrease of performance or in psychophysiological changes, both of which are different in high- and low-reactive individuals. As stated by Reykowski, "people may differ in a stable manner as to the stage of functioning (loading or overloading) which may be evoked in them by stress of a given strength and intensity" [1966, p. 249). Reactivity is one of the major determinants of whether stress of high stimulative value will evoke symptoms of overloading or not. It follows that high-reactive people can be pushed to the point of overload by much less stress than for low-reactive individuals. Thus, the intensification of stress, which evokes optimal responding in low-reactive people, may evoke overloading in high-reactive persons. Overloading is generally manifested in a decline in effectiveness of actions or in physiological changes which may be regarded as having high psychophysiological cost of performance. If lack of stimulation (deprivation, monotony) is considered a stressful situation, a reverse interrelation may be expected with regard to the level of reactivity and to efficiency of performance; i.e. in deprivation we may expect more efficiency in high-reactive subjects, and their physiological changes during this situation should be regarded as symptoms of lower psychophysiological cost of performance as compared with low-reactive persons. Studies conducted by Rozhdestvenskaya and associates and by the Merlin group (see Chapter 1) are consistent with our considerations of the similarities between strength of excitation and the reactivity dimension.

## Level of Performance and Temperamental Traits

The relation between level of performance, stimulative value of a situation, and reactivity has been investigated in our laboratory, especially with respect to situations of high stimulative value. As mentioned before, it was expected that under high levels of stimulation, the level of performance in high- and low-reactive subjects would differ in favour of the latter group. In two of our field studies (Grodner, 1973; Kłodecka-Rożalska, 1982) it was assumed that competitive sport activities would be regarded as highly stimulating. If people have no opportunity to develop their own style of action in such situations we may expect a decrease of performance under competition in high-reactive subjects compared with performance in training situations. Low-reactive subjects, known as stimulation seekers, are expected to increase their sports performance under competitive conditions.

In a simple study conducted by Grodner (1973; Strelau, 1978) this hypothesis was verified through a sample of 12 to 15-year-old boys. These boys performed the task of pushing a 2 kg ball as far as possible with both hands. The task had to be performed twice: in a normal training setting and in competition—five trials in each situation. The former was a routine gym lesson and the subjects were asked to push the ball in order to check whether it was appropriate for gym lessons with such boys. In the competitive situation the boys had to perform the task with the aim of selecting the best class in the school and, thereafter, in the city. Attractive prizes were offered for the winners. The level of reactivity was estimated, by pre-trained teachers, on a 5-point rating scale (see Strelau, 1978) similar to that described on p. 198. Two extreme groups were selected from a sample of 103 pupils: high-reactive (15 Ss) and low-reactive (14 Ss).

Comparing the change of results under stress (competition) with those in a normal situation (training) it was found that the average achievements under stress increased significantly in the low-reactive group and decreased more frequently in high-reactive group (see Table LV).

The data shows that competition increased the level of activation in most of the low-reactive subjects so as to improve task performance.

TABLE LV. Changes in motor task performance level under stress in high- and low-reactive pupils (taken from Grodner, 1973)

| Subjects | Change of Performance under Stress | | Total Number of Subjects |
|---|---|---|---|
| | Increase | Decrease | |
| LR | 11 | 3 | 14 |
| HR | 5 | 10 | 15 |
| Total number of subjects | 16 | 13 | 29 |

$Chi^2 = 5.991; p < 0.02$

The increase in stimulation under competition in the high-reactive individuals was excessive, thus leading to a decrease in performance. This regularity is consistent with our theoretical considerations as well as with the results of Vyatkin (1964b, 1974b). Taking into account five different sports activities performed by 15 to 16-year-old pupils, Vyatkin could state that individuals with high NS strength performed better under competitive conditions, whereas individuals with a weak NS achieved more in routine training (Vyatkin, 1974b). NS strength was assessed by the method of repeatedly exposed stimuli (see Chapter 2).

A study conducted in our laboratory by Kłodecka-Rożalska (1982), also using physical exercises as the observation task, does not support any assumptions concerning the interrelations of level of performance, stimulative value of situation, and reactivity. The methodology used in this investigation differs essentially from that used by Grodner. The aim of Kłodecka-Rożalska's experiment was to see if the individuals who improved their results under competition rather than under training conditions also differed in their temperament structure from individuals who did not improve or whose results decreased under competition. Two hundred and one high-school pupils (males, aged from 16 to 18) were studied. A standardized test developed by Denisiuk (see Kłodecka-Rożalska, 1982) to diagnose motor efficiency level was used in two situations: competition and training. Tasks for measuring speed, agility, and endurance (the most differentiated among the five included in the Denisiuk test) were used in the data analysis. For the training situation, tasks were performed during normal gym lessons. The pupils were informed by the teacher that these tasks were being conducted all over the country for normalization purposes and had to be performed well in order not to disrupt the averages to be established for Polish students. Under competitive conditions an atmosphere of great rivalry was arranged. The pupils were informed that their final grades would depend upon the level of task performance and that their results would serve to select the best athletes. The tasks were performed in the presence of school authorities and pupils from other classes. Each pupil's results were to be published in the school newsletter.

The ratio of the total number of standardized points derived from all three tasks performed under competition, including the points obtained under the training conditions, served as the measure of changes in performance under stress. From the total number (201) of subjects two extreme groups were selected by means of the quartile deviation: individuals resistant to stress (51 Ss) and individuals non-resistant to stress (46 Ss). The stress-resistant group included subjects who performed better under competition rather than training conditions ($>1$

ratio), whereas the non-resistant group consisted of subjects who did not change their results or who manifested a decrease in performance under stress (≤1 ratio).

As mentioned before, the crucial question was whether both groups differed in temperament traits. The latter were diagnosed using the following inventories: Guilford Zimmerman's GZTS, Thurstone's TTS, Eysenck's MPI, Taylor's MAS, and Strelau's STI. Altogether 24 dimensions were separated among which only five significantly distinguished the stress-resistant group from the non-resistant one. In five other dimensions only a tendency relating to both groups was found. The results are given in Table LVI.

TABLE LVI. Temperament dimensions which distinguish the stress resistant from the non-stress-resistant group (adapted from Kłodecka-Rożalska, 1982)

| Inventory | Dimensions | Stress Resistant Group M | SD | Non-stress Resistant Group M | SD | $t$ | $p$ |
|---|---|---|---|---|---|---|---|
| MPI | Extraversion | 27.43 | 7.18 | 30.08 | 8.33 | 1.71 | 0.1 |
| STI | Strength of E | 55.34 | 12.80 | 59.56 | 11.12 | 1.74 | 0.1 |
| | Equilibrium | 0.89 | 0.22 | 0.97 | 0.19 | 1.77 | 0.1 |
| GZTS | General activity | 32.78 | 8.16 | 36.69 | 7.20 | 2.54 | 0.05 |
| | Masculinity | 30.84 | 7.72 | 27.96 | 6.29 | 2.03 | 0.05 |
| TTS | Vigorous | 28.82 | 5.77 | 30.82 | 5.51 | 1.77 | 0.1 |
| | Impulsive | 25.76 | 5.23 | 28.00 | 6.04 | 1.98 | 0.05 |
| | Dominant | 13.46 | 7.32 | 17.06 | 9.29 | 2.17 | 0.05 |
| | Emotionally stable | 22.47 | 7.49 | 19.29 | 9.23 | 1.92 | 0.1 |
| | Reflective | 18.94 | 7.91 | 22.04 | 5.82 | 2.23 | 0.05 |

The group which improved performance under high stimulation differs from the one which did not improve. The former might be characterized as having lower general activity, impulsivity, dominance, reflectivity, extraversion, strength of excitation (higher reactivity), equilibrium and vigorousness. The stress-resistant subjects also display higher masculinity and emotional stability compared with the non-resistant group. It should also be mentioned that there were no differences between both groups in other dimensions known as codeterminants of behaviour in stress situations, e.g. neuroticism, anxiety or mobility. As regards extraversion, strength of NS (reactivity), general activity, vigourousness, and dominance, we would be inclined to expect a converse interrelation regarding resistance to stress, assuming that these temperament traits have many elements in common with the so-called energetic characteristic of behaviour.

Using the method of principal components and Kaiser's Varimax, Kłodecka-Rożalska factor-analysed the temperament trait data measured in all 201 subjects. The results do not differ essentially from the data presented by Terelak (1974; Strelau and Terelak, 1974) and decribed on p. 165. Taking into account the specificity of the temperament structure in groups differing in resistance to stress, the former author factor-analysed the data separately for the resistant and non-resistant groups. In the stress-resistant group, six factors were isolated, whereas in the non-resistant group the number of factors increased to eight. Taking into consideration the first four factors, which account for most of the variance the temperament characteristic of the two groups are presented in Table LVII.

TABLE LVII. Temperament structure in stress-resistant and non-stress-resistant groups (adapted from Kłodecka-Rożalska, 1982)

| Stress-resistant subjects | | Non-stress-resistant subjects | |
|---|---|---|---|
| *Factor I* | | *Factor I* | |
| Sociable (TTS) | −0.823 | Neuroticism (MPI) | 0.868 |
| Sociability (GZTS) | −0.811 | Emotional stability (GZTS) | −0.804 |
| Ascendance (GZTS) | −0.765 | Emotionally stable (TTS) | −0.724 |
| Extraversion (MPI) | −0.757 | Manifest anxiety (MAS) | 0.705 |
| Dominant (TTS) | −0.754 | Objectivity (GZTS) | −0.657 |
| Impulsive (TTS) | −0.565 | Masculinity (GZTS) | −0.601 |
| | | Friendliness (GZTS) | −0.531 |
| *Factor II* | | *Factor II* | |
| Objectivity (GZTS) | −0.788 | Restraint (GZTS) | −0.824 |
| Emotional stability (GZTS) | −0.753 | Reflective (TTS) | −0.732 |
| Emotionally stable (TTS) | −0.718 | Thoughtfulness (GZTS) | −0.722 |
| Neuroticism (MPI) | 0.699 | | |
| Manifest anxiety (MAS) | 0.653 | | |
| Friendliness (GZTS) | −0.572 | | |
| *Factor III* | | *Factor III* | |
| Reflective (TTS) | 0.773 | Mobility of NP (STI) | 0.877 |
| Strength of E (STI) | 0.706 | General activity (GZTS) | 0.721 |
| Mobility of NP (STI) | 0.644 | Strength of E (STI) | 0.655 |
| *Factor IV* | | *Factor IV* | |
| Restraint (GZTS) | 0.820 | Sociable (TTS) | −0.875 |
| Thoughtfulness (GZTS) | 0.617 | Dominant (TTS) | −0.667 |
| | | Sociability (GZTS) | −0.648 |

The most obvious difference in the temperament structure consists of the configuration of isolated factors. But if one observes the separate dimensions, then it is seen that despite the fact that these are often included in different factors, they usually occur with the same sign in both groups (see, e.g. neuroticism, anxiety, strength of excitation, mobility, or sociability). The factor analytic study does not seem to dispel the doubts about efficiency of performance under stress in relation to the individual's temperament traits. Stress-resistant individuals would be expected to manifest a temperament-structure factor suggestive of stimulation seeking—high on endurance and low on sensitivity—a conclusion not supported by Kłodecka-Rożalska's data. It is not easy to explain these results within our conceptual framework nor within other arousal theories and they need further investigation.

A similar experiment was conducted by Vyatkin (1974b, 1978). He was able to show that subjects who performed better in a sports contest than in routine training did not differ in isolated temperament traits from individuals in whom a decrement under competition was observed. What *did* differentiate both groups was the specific composition of temperament traits. However, the statistics adopted by Vyatkin (discriminant analysis) did not lead to any conclusion about the specificity of these configurations. Such temperament traits as anxiety, emotional excitability, rigidity, general activity, and extraversion were investigated.[8]

Maciejczyk (1974), studying decision-making ability in pilots under stressful conditions found their level of performance to depend on the reactivity level measured by the alpha index.[9] Subjects with a high alpha index (regarded in this study as low-reactive individuals) performed better under stress than with no stress, whereas with individuals with a low alpha index (classified here as high-reactive subjects) the reverse was found, i.e. they performed better in a normal, stressless situation. The speed and quality of pilots' decision-making were recorded during laboratory-simulated flight conditions. The stressful situation was arranged by setting a time limit on decision-making and by introducing social threat. Thirty-five high-reactive (low alpha index) and 35 low-reactive (high alpha index) individuals were selected from a group of 173 pilots aged from 20 to 40. The detailed description of this study may be found elsewhere (Strelau and Maciejczyk, 1977).

Klonowicz (in press, b) arranged a situation which consisted of reading and correcting proofs during one hour, in three conditions differing in stimulation load: quiet conditions, white noise and free-field noise. Two measures of performance level were applied: proficiency (number of proofs corrected) and quality of work (number of errors).

Klonowicz found that the subjects differed in performance level according to their temperament traits. Although in general all subjects displayed higher proficiency under noise, the analysis of variance conducted by the author revealed that additional stimulation had a significantly negative effect on the quality of work in high-reactive individuals and the same was true as regards mobility. The low-mobile group performed significantly worse under noise as compared with normal conditions. In this study reactivity and mobility were assessed by means of the STI.

In summary it must be stated that the studies reported in this section are not unequivocal in their conclusion on the relation between level of performance and stimulative value of a situation with respect to temperament and, particularly, reactivity. Most surprising are the results obtained by Kłodecka-Rożalska (1982) which are quite at odds with our expectations. However, taking into account Grodner's (1973) study, as well as Klonowicz's (in press, b) data and to some extent those collected by Maciejczyk (1974), it may be cautiously concluded that there is a decrease in efficiency under high stimulation with high-reactive individuals. This conclusion accords with Vyatkin's (1974b) data presented above as well as with Gurevich's (1970) field study described in Chapter 1. Both authors showed a decrement of performance in individuals with a weak NS in situations characterized as being highly stimulating.

## Psychophysiological Cost and Level of Reactivity

In the stress literature, it is acknowledged that the maintenance of high and constant performance under stress-inducing stimulation (overload or underload) may lead to several psychophysiological changes or side-effects which may be classified as psychophysiological cost (e.g. Glass and Singer, 1972; Lundberg and Frankenhaeuser, 1978). The coronary-prone Type A (Friedman and Roseman, 1974) is an extreme example of the price an individual pays to maintain a given performance level. Psychophysiological changes, as a result of which performance may be efficiently maintained under stress-inducing stimulation, may be regarded as a strategy for coping with stress (Lundberg, 1982). These psychophysiological changes will be less expressed in individuals resistant to stress than in non-resistant individuals.

High discrepancy between stimulation need and the stimulation actually delivered should be regarded as stress-inducing. When overload occurs we may expect the discrepancy between stimulation need and the actual stimulation to be higher in high-reactive persons, who consequently perceive such situations as more stressful than do low-reactive individuals. The opposite is expected, however, if deprivation or monotony is taken into account. In this case the discrepancy between stimulation need and the actual stimulative value of the situation is higher in low-reactive individuals, so this situation is more stress-inducing to them than to the high-reactive individuals. With respect to stress, the differences between high-reactive and low-reactive persons may be manifested not only in level of performance (as discussed in the previous section), but also in their psychophysiological changes developed in the situation. As mentioned above, these changes would probably be more pronounced when the individual tried, in spite of stress, to maintain a high level of performance.

In line with these considerations it was expected that in highly stimulative situations the psychophysiological costs should be more pronounced in high-reactive subjects, whereas the reverse should occur when low stimulation (deprivation or monotony) is experienced. In this case the psychophysiological changes should be higher in low-reactive subjects. These hypotheses are also in accordance with Rozhdestvenskaya's data on the relation between strength of the NS and psychophysiological changes under situations inducing fatigue and monotony (discussed in detail in Chapter 1). In our laboratory Klonowicz (1974b, in press, a and b) has conducted several studies to investigate the relation between level of reactivity, stimulative value of a situation, and the psychophysiological costs paid by the individual during task performance. To illustrate our research in this area, which is still in the preliminary stage, let me describe two experiments, one of which was carried out by Klonowicz.

In Klonowicz's (1974b) experiment, two groups of subjects radically differing in reactivity and exposed to situations differing in stimulation load, were studied. The less stimulating condition involved the application of Mackworth's vigilance test (auditory version), in which subjects are asked to respond by pressing a key to stimuli of double duration as opposed to neutral ones. All in all, 24 such stimuli were presented at irregular intervals (ranging from 30 s to 10 min). The neutral stimuli were presented at regular intervals for one hour. The more stimulating condition required subjects to work on a modified version of Kraepelin's arithmetic test for one hour without break. The stimulation consisted primarily of the subject's own uninterrupted activity. In both conditions[10] recordings of performance level and psychophysiological changes were made prior to and after the task. With regard to the psychophysiological changes evoked by both conditions the following measurements were taken: choice RT (to visual and auditory stimuli) and changes in electrodermal activity (EDA). RT was measured only immediately before and after the experiment proper, whereas the changes in EDA, expressed in skin resistance units, were recorded continuously (at 1-min intervals) throughout the experiment.

For diagnosing reactivity the method known as the slope of RT curve (see pp. 86 and 205) was used. Altogether, 163 17–19- year-old high-school students (males) were investigated. From this group 18 high- and 17 low-reactive persons were isolated.

The results obtained by Klonowicz suggest that under the poor-stimulation conditions, high-reactive subjects perform better than low-reactive ones, as chiefly reflected in the smaller number of errors (i.e. missing the signals). Under the more stimulating situation (Kraepelin's arithmetic test) both groups showed the same level of performance. The data concerning the psychophysiological cost indicate that under the vigilance condition (poor stimulation), less pronounced changes in RT were recorded in the high-reactive subjects, whereas under the stimulating conditions (Kraepelin's test) smaller changes occurred in the low-reactive subjects.

Very distinct differences were recorded in the subjects' psychophysiological functioning under the two experimental conditions, with regard to EDA. Under the vigilance conditions (poor stimulation) high-reactive subjects were relaxed, as indicated by their increased skin resistance; while low-reactive subjects exhibited symptoms of increased activation, as reflected in their reduced skin resistance (see Fig. 13). As the experiment progressed, the differences between high- and low-reactive subjects gradually increased finally to reach the level of statistical significance.

As shown in Fig. 14 the situation is exactly reversed under highly-stimulating conditions. The curve representing the EDA of high-reactive subjects indicates their increased activation, while the graph of the low-reactive subjects fails to reveal any psychophysiological changes in this condition. Here again the differences between both groups are very distinct and their statistical significance tends to increase with the progress of the experiment.

In conclusion, it may be stated that the data obtained by Klonowicz support our expectations that the psychophysiological changes under highly stimulating conditions should be more pronounced in high-reactive individuals, whereas low-reactive subjects should express more evident changes in situations characterized by low stimulation.

In another study (Strelau *et al.*, in press), two widely differing situations were arranged: deprivation and physical threat resulting from the state of hypoxia. It was predicted that high-reactive subjects would show greater psychophysiological changes under threat, this

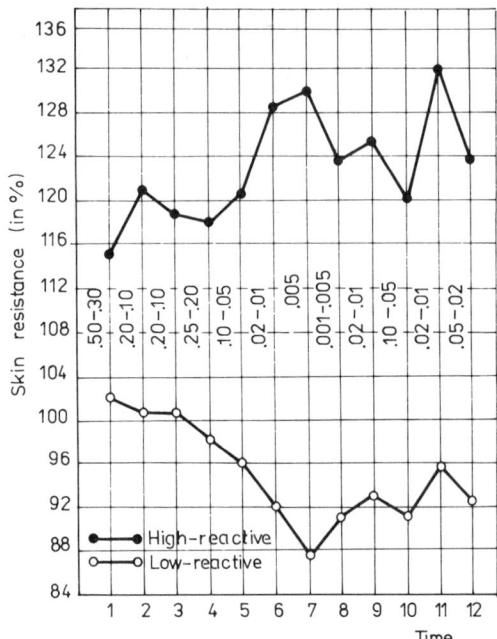

FIG. 13. Changes in skin resistance recorded under poor stimulation conditions in high- and low-reactive subjects (adapted from Klonowicz, 1974b). The numbers illustrate the significance of the differences between the harmonic means of the skin resistance value, characteristic of high- and low-reactive subjects, at 5-min intervals respectively. Resistance values are related to the basic score which was taken as 100%.

being a highly stimulating condition. In low-reactive subjects these changes would be more pronounced in the sensory deprivation condition which does not meet the subjects' stimulation need.

Level of reactivity was measured by the STI[11] and the subjects were divided across the median into high- and low-reactive groups. Skin resistance, heart rate and state anxiety (measured by the X-1 scale of STAI) were used as indicators of psychophysiological changes. With regard to the highly stimulating condition, subjects (two at a time) were placed for 50 min in a low-pressure chamber (LPC). By lowering the pressure (state of hypoxia) a physical atmosphere was created resembling that at an altitude of 5000 m. During the experiment in the LPC, all three psychophysiological variables were recorded. State anxiety was measured twice: just before lowering the pressure ("eleva-

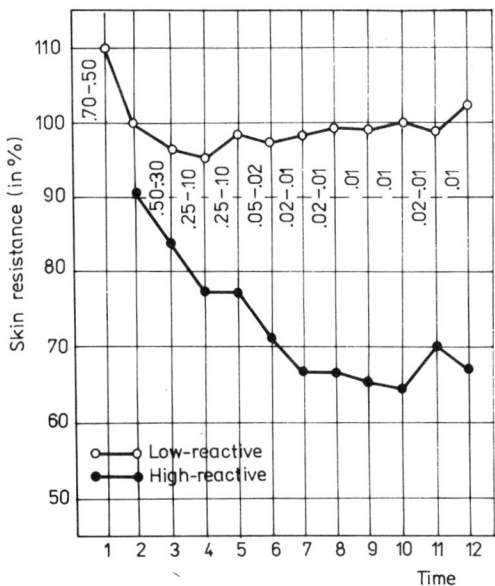

FIG. 14. Changes in skin resistance in situations of higher stimulative value in high- and low-reactive subjects (adapted from Klonowicz, 1974b). For explanation see legend to Fig. 13.

tion") and just after raising it to the starting-point ("ground level"). At the same moment, heart rate was measured. Skin resistance was recorded nine times at various stages of the experiment: during "elevation" (records I–III), at 5000 m altitude (IV–VI), and at "ground level" (VII–IX).

The deprivation experiment, conducted individually, lasted 6 hours. The deprivation chamber (DC) was dark and white noise of low intensity was emitted continuously. The subject sat in an airliner type seat and his freedom of hand and body movements was restricted by belts. The same measurements were made in the DC as in the LPC. State anxiety was measured immediately before and after the experiment. Heart rate and skin resistance were measured 14 times in the following way: every 15 min during the first (I–V) and sixth hour (X–XIII) of deprivation, every 60 min during the remaining period (VI–IX), and once (XIV) when the subjects had been told that the experiment was over. Both experiments took place alternately, on consecutive days. Complete results were obtained from 37 subjects (soldiers in military training) aged from 18 to 24 years.

Without going into details, it should be said that both experimental conditions vary greatly in terms of the psychophysiological indices being recorded. The lowest mean value of skin resistance during DC was 183 kilo-ohms while the highest value of skin resistance during LPC was 89 kilo-ohms. This difference is statistically significant ($p < 0.02$). Similar differences were noted with regard to heart rate. The mean value of the two records from the LPC are 78 and 76 bpm, suggesting that the relatively high level of arousal does not change throughout the experiment. The mean values obtained during DC vary from 79 (record I) to 63 bpm (record XIII), this significant difference suggesting a decrease of arousal level as deprivation proceeds. Also the statistically significant ($p < 0.05$) increase of state anxiety measured immediately before the onset of the LPC experiment, compared with the initial level as well as with state anxiety level after the experiment was finished, show that the LPC condition was of higher stimulative value than the DC one.

No differences in heart rate were recorded between the groups differing in reactivity. However, the picture changed when EDA was taken into account. The dynamics of EDA changes, in respect to reactivity, which is of major interest to us, is shown in Figs 15 and 16, separately for LPC and DS conditions.

As may be seen from Fig. 15, eight out of nine measures of EDA indicate higher arousal level in low-reactive subjects for the LPC situation. However the differences in skin resistance between high- and low-reactive individuals are insignificant, this being due to their high variability. The dynamics of change during the 50-min period of the experiment is similar in both groups. Surprising enough is the systematically higher arousal level in low-reactive subjects, which is contrary to our expectations as well as to the data obtained by Klonowicz (1974b). It is possible that some adaptive processes occurred, consisting of lowering the arousal level of high-reactive subjects in order to cope efficiently with the threat-inducing situation.

As Fig. 16 shows, an opposite relationship occurs in the DC situation as regards changes in EDA. In all but one of the 14 tests (test IX), higher arousal level, measured by skin resistance, occurs in the high-reactive subjects, although only in one case (test VIII) was statistical significance obtained. This result also contradicts our hypothesis and Klonowicz's (1974b) data on the monotonous situation; however, the lower arousal level manifested by low-reactive subjects may be explained by the fact that this situation was of a lower stimulative value for these subjects than for high-reactive individuals. The dynamics of the curve, which displays the changes in arousal level as the experiment

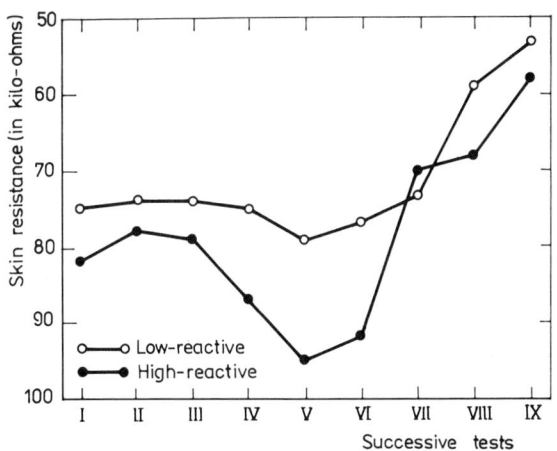

FIG. 15. Changes in EDA under LPC conditions in low- and high-reactive subjects (taken from Strelau et al., in press).

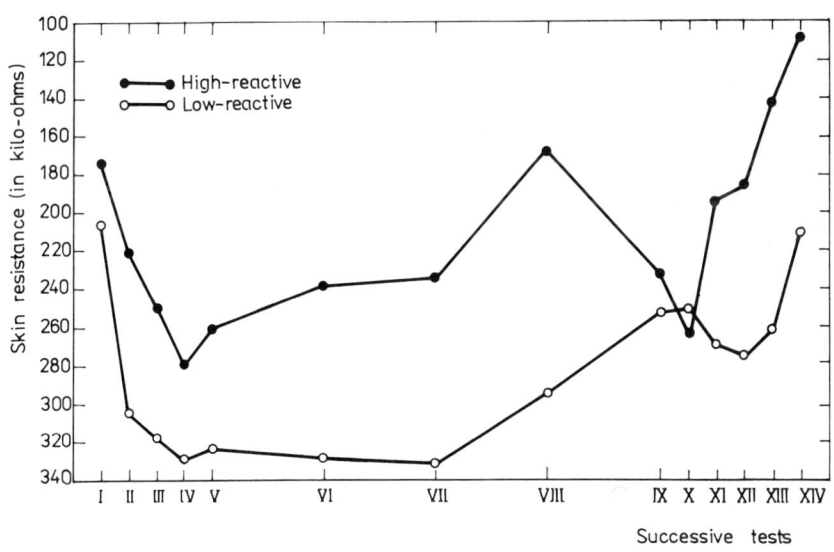

FIG. 16. Changes in EDA under DC conditions in low- and high-reactive subjects (taken from Strelau et al., in press).

progresses, does not generally vary from the findings in the literature and so will not be discussed here.

In summary, it should be stated that the psychophysiological changes under conditions varying in stimulation load have a different nature depending on the individuals' reactivity level; however, it is not yet possible to offer an unequivocal interpretation of this interdependency. The experiments conducted by Klonowicz (1974b), as compared with our own (Strelau et al., in press), differ in more than stimulation load and duration. One of the main differences is that in both situations arranged by Klonowicz the subjects had to perform tasks, whereas in our study no tasks were performed at all. The discrepancies in experimental settings are not irrelevant to the inconsistency between psychophysiological changes and level of reactivity.

# 7

# Temperament and Personality

## THEORETICAL CONSIDERATIONS

### Biological vs. Social Determinants of Individual Differences

As in most cases of psychological inquiry, it seems worthwhile recalling the ancient philosophers when considering the relation between temperament and personality. Galen, the most outstanding physician of post-Hippocratic times, framed the first typology of temperament in his well-known dissertation *De Temperamentis*, inspired by the concepts of his predecessor. This earliest typology is still popular today.

Galen's main concept, stating the proportion of four "cardinal humours" which form the nature of the body, and hence the physiological basis of behavioural traits, has been partially confirmed in contemporary endocrinological and psychopharmacological research. Hippocrates and Galen were persistent in their search for the clue to individual differences in the human psyche within the internal factors of the human body or, more precisely, in its hormonal system. Thus, their theory of temperament is a classic example of endogenic conceptions of human nature.

Antiquity also provides another idea, i.e. that human nature depends upon extra-organismic factors. As an example of such an exogenic conception, let us recall the theory of Theophrastus, a colourful description of types of human behaviour (types of personality as we would say today) presented under the distinctive title of *Characters*.

Although undoubtedly over-simplified, the opinion that individual differences in behaviour determined by physiological factors of the organism belong to the sphere of temperament, while the typical behaviour exhibited by an individual and determined by external conditions is denoted by the concept of personality, has lost little of its popularity.

Of course, there are personality theories (the psychoanalytic approach being the best example) which acknowledge the role of endogenic factors in shaping personality; however, even here external conditions seem to be the decisive determinants in personality development. The opposite should be stated about temperament, where the classical concepts of this phenomenon are strongly concentrated on determinants within the organism, although in some theories the environment plays a significant role in moulding temperament; the concept of the so-called situational temperament proposed by Wundt as early as 1911 may serve as an example here.

The constitutional approach to temperament, which predominated from antiquity until the 1940s, has focused much attention not only on the endogenic determination of temperament (the latter regarded as inherited or inborn) but also on temperament as directly related to the content, i.e. the goal-directed features of behaviour. An outstanding example is Kretschmer's (1944) typology of temperament and the even more extreme constitutional typology of Conrad (1963). Conrad's concept is less known in the psychological literature, but it illustrates better than any other the essence of the constitutional way of thinking. According to Conrad, the variety of body structure and the relation between body structure and temperament in humans can only be explained by referring to specific dominant genes determining the type of body structure and related temperamental traits. Conrad, describing one of his types, the so-called hypoplastic body type (Kretschmer's astenic type) that corresponds to the "spiritualistic" temperament, characterizes the type disposed to cosmopolitanism, internationalism and intellectualism (1963, p. 172).

According to his position, like other constitutional typologies, including Sheldon and Stevens' (1942) well-known temperament typology, the content and direction of behaviour is determined by biological mechanisms (genes, endocrine system) or by the individual's body structure. This kind of "scientific" justification of racist ideology was, irrespective of the investigators' intention, unacceptable to psychologists, especially to those involved in personality research. One of the reactions was to remove almost completely the term "temperament", discredited by constitutional psychologists, from psychological textbooks and personality monographs.

Among personality theorists, an opinion which views personality as a product of external conditions of specific character, i.e. social conditions, is becoming more and more popular. The specific human rela-

## 7. Temperament and Personality

tions into which the individual enters during his activity determine the essence of personality. There is a strong conviction that no endogenic structures of personality exist other than those whose substance or content is determined by the external world into which the human enters. The personality theorists bound up with the materialistic current in psychology, independent of concrete solutions regarding the structure and development of personality, fully agree that the shaping of personality may occur only through human activity. Personality should be considered as a result of human activity and a product of socio-historical conditions (e.g. Tomaszewski, 1968; Shorokhova, 1974; Leontev, 1978; Reykowski, 1977).

However, personality psychologists cannot ignore the fact that people do differ when it comes to various behavioural traits that can no longer be considered a matter of physiology and yet can hardly be treated as phenomena belonging to personality. Thus new concepts have emerged, e.g. the dynamic aspect of personality (Rubinstein, 1946; Merlin, 1973), the intensity dimension of behaviour (Duffy, 1962; Petrie, 1967) sensation and stimulus-seeking dimensions (Zuckerman, 1979; Sales *et al.*, 1974), or the concept of NS strength (Pavlov, 1951–52; Teplov, 1964a; Nebylitsyn, 1972a). These traits (dimensions), like our own concept of reactivity, have their roots in the Wundt (1911) tradition of temperament where the formal aspect but not the content of behaviour is exposed.

If we assume, in accordance with the common tradition in psychology, that personality is a typically human phenomenon (L. *persona*— actor's face, mask, character, person) and is a product of conditions that are specific for human development (i.e. socio-historical conditions) (Leontev, 1978; Hjelle and Ziegler, 1981), then such dimensions as stimulation or sensation seeking, intensity of behaviour, reactivity, dynamics of behaviour etc. can hardly be treated as personality, for they exist in animals too. They are, in a way, a product of biological evolution, which does not by any means imply that they cannot acquire a different aspect in humans. If the afore-mentioned dimensions of behaviour, which have a large physiological component and are a result of biological evolution, were to be considered an aspect of temperament, and all the traits (mechanisms) that are mostly a product of socio-historical conditions were to be included in personality, then a lot of misunderstanding would be avoided.

The present author is aware that humans are biosocial beings, i.e. that human development is a result of the interaction of biological and social factors. It follows from this that temperament and personality can hardly be separated from each other. It also means that the development of personality cannot be considered in isolation from biological factors. As regards humans, the treatment of temperament with the exclusion of the social factor should also be considered a kind of reductionism. Nevertheless, in order to study these phenomena it is convenient to separate temperament and personality.

The aim of this chapter is not to discuss in detail either the understanding of temperament (this was partially done in Chapter 5) or personality (this would require a separate monograph). We are interested rather in the interrelations and dependencies of both phenomena, assuming that the main differences between temperament and personality have been shown above. In summary these are as follows:

(1) Temperament is a result of biological evolution whereas personality should be regarded as a product of socio-historical conditions.
(2) Temperament is peculiar to both humans and animals, which cannot be said of personality. The latter is an attribute of humans only.
(3) The individual has a temperament from the moment of birth, since it is determined by inborn physiological mechanisms which, in turn, may be modified under environmental influences. Personality does not exist from the very beginning of the individual's life. It is moulded through human activity and interaction with the social environment.
(4) As has been argued in detail in Chapter 5, temperament is composed of formal traits (dimensions) of behaviour, independent of its content. Personality primarily comprises the content of behaviour in which the individual's relationship toward the world and to himself is expressed.

## Interrelations and Dependencies of Temperament and Personality

If we take as point of departure the understanding of temperament and personality introduced in the above section, the question arises as to the main relations between both phenomena. With a few exceptions (e.g. Thomas *et al.*, 1968; Thomas and Chess, 1977) the psychological literature does not provide systematic evidence of the dependencies between temperament resulting from biological evolution and personality conceived as a result of socio-historical conditions. This problem attracted our interest many years ago. The data we have collected do not illustrate all possible alterations which may occur within the temperament and personality relationships; however, they convince us that close bonds exist between the phenomena in question, Generally, these fall into at least four categories which we shall now discuss.

*The influence of temperament on the interaction between the individual and his surroundings*

Personality develops from the very beginning on the basis of the primary drives and emotions which include thirst, hunger, fear, and pleasure vs. displeasure derived from sensations caused by external and internal stimuli etc. (Reykowski, 1977). All these, independent of their specificity as determined by the individual's needs, quality of stimuli, or more generally, by the situation which evokes given states of emotion and drives, can be characterized by intensity, magnitude, speed, duration, or other temporal traits of behaviour. These characteristics, being temperamentally co-determined, differ from individual to individual. These differences are expressed, for example, in the fact that, from birth, some children cry or laugh more than others in similar situations; they differ in the intensity with which they express these reactions—some children lie quietly in bed while others are constantly on the move. In some children very weak environmental stimuli are sufficient to evoke some response whereas the same stimuli do not cause any changes in the behaviour of others. In the course of development, temperament traits begin to reveal themselves not only in the primary drives and emotions but also in more complex and diverse reactions, in all kinds of acquired behaviour and activities.

All these modes of behaviour, in which temperament is manifested and which are expressed from early ontogenesis on, cannot be indifferent to the behaviour of those who constitute the baby's immediate social environment. Temperamental traits affect the family environment, mainly the mother, father, or other caretakers, thus modifying their behaviour. So, for example, the infant who cries louder and longer evokes different treatment from the infant who lies calmly in bed. The parents will react differently when the child frequently displays avoidance reactions (which may be caused by his high reactivity) than they would if their child were curious and approachable in similar situations.

The temperament which co-determines the behaviour of the surroundings influences, by means of induced changes in those surroundings, the development of the individual's cognitive structures, activity patterns, and motivational mechanisms. This is an indirect influence, because the personality structure depends directly on the quality and methods of education and social interaction. Temperament should be regarded here as one of the variables which provoke certain treatment or behaviour in the environment. This regularity can be presented as follows:

(1) $T \rightarrow E \rightarrow P$

which means that the individual's temperament (T) induces changes in the environment (E), which in turn have certain consequences for the development of the individual's personality (P).

The research carried out by Thomas et al. (1968) clearly illustrates the way in which the child's temperament traits may influence the behaviour of parents toward him.

*Temperament as modifier of environmental influences*

Temperament may also affect personality development because any environment, irrespective of its objective features, gains a specific, subjective value for an individual possessing certain temperamental traits. For instance, someone of high sensitivity and low efficiency will react to the same difficulties, obstacles, or other people's behaviour differently from one who is highly efficient and not overly sensitive. The fact that temperamental traits have a modifying effect upon environmental influences cannot be irrelevant to personality development. This influence, modified by temperamental traits, becomes more comprehensible if one considers the concept of situation. "Each situation", says Tomaszewski (1975, p. 18), "is delineated by its component elements, their features, the state of particular elements at a given moment, and by mutual relations that existed between the elements at a given moment in the first place". Man himself, i.e. his state (mental and physical) and all those traits that at a given moment determine the variability of an individual's behaviour, constitutes elements of the situation. The individual's temperament is also an element. It modifies the environment (which is objectively the same) according to individual differences in this respect. This conceptualization conforms to the interactional approach in psychology (Magnusson and Endler, 1977).

As follows from these considerations, in a situation where the same objective educational measures are undertaken there exist only manifestations of identity. Limiting myself to reactivity it is easy to conclude that the same educational treatment, e.g. a given form of punishment, will be perceived differently by individuals differing in reactivity level. In high-reactive children the punishment may be taken as a strong stimulus causing deep changes in their behaviour, whereas in low-reactive individuals the same punishment, perceived as a weaker stimulus, may evoke much smaller changes in behaviour. Assuming that persons do not differ in other variables which could determine the behaviour in the situation of punishment, it may be concluded that, depending on the level of reactivity, the same objective punishment has a different subjective effect.

This relationship is illustrated by studies conducted in Merlin's laboratory on the effect of negative grades on the behaviour of pupils with different NS strength. As mentioned in Chapter 1, Merlin (1955) found that pupils with a strong NS (equivalent to low reactivity) reacted to negative grades with high arousal and behaviour, leading to improvement in school work. Pupils with a weak NS (equivalent to high reactivity), in the same situation, i.e. in response to low grades, withdrew and tended to give up further activity. This difference in response to low grades in pupils with differing TNS (reactivity) was borne out in later studies (Utkina, 1964).

In conclusion, it may be said that the value of situation depends, among other things, on an individual's temperament. The role of temperament in shaping personality consists of modifying the environment, including educational treatment. Depending on the value of temperament traits, the influence of the surroundings may be stronger or weaker, of longer or shorter duration, more or less constant, etc., so shaping the personality structure. The relationship between temperament and personality discussed above can be presented as follows:

(2) $E \to T \to P$

The environment (E) may differ in its effect upon individuals, depending on their temperamental traits (T), and this in turn indirectly affects the formation of personality (P).

*Temperamentally determined stimulation need as a factor influencing the shaping of personality*

As has been argued in Chapter 5, the need for stimulation is determined by the physiological mechanism which underlies the reactivity dimension. It has also been stressed that any situations and behaviour, independent of their content, have a given stimulative value and may become sources of stimulation.

The individual, however, being reared in a given family or other social situations, can be punished or rewarded for choosing certain situations or for avoiding others. The same is true with regard to the individual's activity. Some kinds of activity may be positively reinforced whereas others may be punished. Consequently, the individual, to satisfy his temperamentally determined stimulation need, chooses such situations or undertakes such actions that allow on the one hand, the optimal level of activation to be maintained and, on the other, are in accordance with the individual's specific needs or with the expectations of the environment. The person who constantly chooses given activities or permanently prefers certain situations, both as a result of the process of socialization and need for stimulation, develops over time certain habits, stereotypes or patterns of activity which, when generalized to given situations and behaviours, may become components of the personality structure. Experiments in which risk-taking behaviour was studied in relation to reactivity (see p. 237) may serve as an example, if it is assumed that the risk-taking or risk-avoiding strategy of action develops into a more or less stable attitude. This dependency between temperament and personality may be presented in the following way:

(3) $T \rightarrow A_{B,E} \rightarrow P$

which means that temperament traits (T) determine activity (A) aimed at modulating stimulation by choice of adequate activity, this being a direct source of stimulation (B), or by activity the aim of which is to organize the environment (E) of given stimulative value (see p. 188). These preferences for activities and environments, by acquiring some stability in the course of ontogenesis, affect personality development (P).

Most studies conducted in our laboratory investigating the relations between temperament and personality deal with this kind of dependency between both phenomena in question. Some of these experiments will be described in a separate section.

*The influence of personality dimensions on temperament*

All three kinds of relations between temperament and personality discussed above are based on the assumption that temperament, being a primary phenomenon, compared with personality, influences or co-determines the shaping of the latter. The question arises of whether an opposite direction of this interdependency is possible, i.e. does personality influence the shaping of temperament traits? This question is not easy to answer. First, longitudinal studies are needed to grasp the moment when and in which way a given personality dimension, when developed, causes changes in the temperament characteristics. Secondly, as shown above, the development of personality dimensions is determined by temperament traits, and this kind of interaction may cause difficulties in separating personality in its pure form, as uncontaminated by temperament. Thirdly, the changes in temperament, as argued in Chapter 5 (see p. 171), are naturally slow and in the early stage of ontogenesis, when the organism reveals maximal plasticity, most personality dimensions are not yet formed.

Nevertheless, taking the interactional approach in psychology as the point of departure, which has strong empirical justification (Magnusson and Endler, 1977), it is worth assuming that personality dimensions may influence temperament. Traits or mechanisms of personality, independent of their content and the specificity in which the relationship of the individual to himself or toward the external world is expressed, may generate given stimulation. The discrepancy of real and ideal self may serve as an example. As will be argued in the next section, a large discrepancy between both selves is highly stimulating. The personality dimension, being by itself a source of stimulation, may affect the individual's behaviour in such a way as to evoke approach or avoidance activities of a given stimulus load because of stimulation governed by personality patterns developed in ontogenesis. One may say with some caution that personality dimensions (P), when acquiring a given stimulative value (S), may indirectly affect temperament traits (T). This may be expressed as follows:

(4) $P \rightarrow S \rightarrow T$

Grzegołowska-Klarkowska (1980), in a study investigating the relation between defence mechanisms, reactivity level, and level of activation, has argued that defence mechanisms, which should be regarded as a personality phenomenon, do regulate the level of activation. With regard to stimulative value, the primary function of defence mechanisms is to reduce stimulation. Taking into account the fact that high-reactive individuals need lower stimulation to maintain their optimal level of activation, Grzegołowska-Klarkowska hypothesized that this type of individual, when placed in a highly stimulating and ego-threatening situation, would employ more defence mechanisms. However, the results of this study did not support that hypothesis. Nevertheless, Grzegołowska-Klarkowska's theoretical considerations concerning the significance of defence mechanisms as the regulator of the stimulative value of the perceived reality seem to be highly original and merit further investigation.

## EMPIRICAL EVIDENCE AS REGARDS THE RELATION BETWEEN TEMPERAMENT AND PERSONALITY

Our studies investigating the relations between temperament and personality are still far from fully realizing the paradigms presented in the above section. As mentioned above, we have concentrated our research on that aspect of the interdependency of both phenomena in question which concerns the stimulative value of activities and situations, the preference for which, (determined by reactivity level), may influence the development of given personality dimensions. Because reactivity has been regarded as that dimension of temperament which determines individual differences in stimulation need, it seems to be pertinent to concentrate upon this trait when searching for temperament-personality links. The Strength of Excitation scale of the STI was the main tool used for diagnosing reactivity (Chapter 4), where the correspondence between NS properties as measured by our inventory and such dimensions as extraversion-introversion, neuroticism, and anxiety, may be used as corroborative evidence concerning the relations under discussion.

As argued elsewhere (Strelau, 1982, in press), the above dimensions still have much in common with our understanding of temperament, especially as regards their biological determination. Additionally at the level of laboratory indices, especially as measured by the CR procedure—as is the case with Eysenck's (1970) extraversion and Spence's (1960) anxiety dimension—they may be found not only in humans but also in animals. I have used this as one of the criteria for considering given dimensions as temperamental. For this reason I have concentrated, in this section, on personality phenomena which fulfil the criteria presented on p. 258, to make the distinction between temperament and personality clear and unequivocal.

The experiments conducted in our laboratory, within the framework of our interpretation of the temperament–personality relationship, are rather simple in their construction and without sophisticated methodology. However, they seem to enable preliminary conclusions to be reached on the dependencies between temperament and personality; what is more important, they may be used to generate new hypotheses as regards the relationships in question.

## Level of Reactivity and Resistance to Group Pressure

There is evidence to show that emotional tension may arise when information input is inconsistent with expectancy (Festinger, 1957; Reykowski, 1974). Therefore, it can be inferred that high-reactive individuals organize their activities so as to avoid larger inconsistency of this kind or they at least try to reduce it as much as possible. The opposite tendency should be expected in low-reactive individuals who, because of their high stimulation demand, have no reason to avoid situations of inconsistency between their own expectancies and information input.

The dependency between tolerance of inconsistency between information input and cognitive expectancies on the one hand and temperamental traits on the other has been investigated in an experiment by Białowąs (1976). A group-conformity paradigm was arranged. Yielding to group pressure was adopted as a measure of conformist attitude, while resistance to such pressure was adopted as an index of independence. Proceeding from the assumption of the stimulating capacity of dissonance, we hypothesized that high-reactive individuals would tend to submit to group pressure (conformists), while low-reactive individuals would be more likely to resist group opinions, such resistance favouring the development of an independent attitude.

Using the STI, Białowąs (1976) selected 24 high- and 25 low-reactive subjects from a group of 148 females (aged 18–21). Resistance to group pressure was measured for both groups. The subjects were shown eight pictures of a child's face. Their task was to ascribe to each picture one of three nouns (each group of nouns differing from presentation to presentation, e.g., earnestness, sorrow, curiosity). The experiment was conducted in groups of four, in which the subject who evaluated the child's face last was a true subject. The three others were experimenter's confederates. This situation resembles Asch's classical paradigm. Yielding to group pressure was defined as submitting to group opinion in six out of eight presentations. This criterion was arbitrary, and based mainly on the distribution of results. Twenty-eight resistant and 21 submissive subjects were selected. In order to obtain a more complete characterization of the individuals who submit or resist to group pressure, additionally controlled variables were introduced such as state and trait anxiety assessed by the STAI and self-esteem measured by the discrepancy between ideal and real self, both evaluated on a 7-point rating scale adapted by Smoleńska (1971). State anxiety was measured directly after the experiment; self-esteem and trait anxiety were estimated in a separate session preceding the experiment.

We were interested in the distribution of individuals differing in reactivity, trait anxiety, and self-esteem over submissive and resistant subgroups. Self-esteem was identical in the submissive and resistant groups, so data for this variable will be omitted here.

Regarding reactivity and the group pressure estimation results, Białowąs was able to show that there are (statistically) significantly more high-reactive individuals among the submissive subjects, whereas the low-reactive individuals are in a majority within the group of resistant subjects. This is shown in Table LVIII.

TABLE LVIII. Reactivity and resistance to group pressure (taken from Białowąs, 1976)

| Reactivity | Attitude | | Total Number of Subjects |
| --- | --- | --- | --- |
| | Submissive | Resistant | |
| HR | 16 | 8 | 24 |
| LR | 5 | 20 | 25 |
| Total number of subjects | 21 | 28 | 49 |

$Chi^2 = 10.89; p < 0.01$

The same stability may be found if we take into account the conformist attitude and the distribution of subjects with different trait anxiety level, where the median was used to distinguish between high- and low-anxiety individuals. The results are presented in Table LIX. As may be seen, high-anxiety subjects predominate in the group with the conformist attitude whereas low-anxiety subjects are the majority in the independent group.

As mentioned before, the literature provides evidence that the dissonance between information input and the individual's expectancies is a source of emotional tension. If this is the case we may expect individuals who do not reduce the inconsistency (as expressed in resistance to group pressure) to reveal higher emotional tension than those subjects who reduce the dissonance by submitting to group pressure.

To verify this hypothesis, state anxiety measured by scale X-1 of the STAI was taken into account. On the basis of the median ($Me = 34$) the whole group was divided into two subgroups with high- and low-emotional tension. The results show that the number of subjects with low

TABLE LIX. Trait anxiety and resistance to group pressure (taken from Białowąs, 1976)

| Anxiety | Attitude | | Total Number of Subjects |
| --- | --- | --- | --- |
| | Submissive | Resistant | |
| High | 15 | 9 | 24 |
| Low | 6 | 19 | 25 |
| Total number of subjects | 21 | 28 | 49 |

$Chi^2 = 7.41; p < 0.01$

and high emotional tension does not differ significantly in both submissive and resistant groups. However, a tendency appeared ($p < 0.2$) which suggested a predominance of subjects with high emotional tension in the submissive group; the opposite occurred in the resistant group.

As follows from our considerations regarding the relation between the resistance to group pressure and emotional tension, the tendency displayed in the results runs contrary to expectations. The data in this experiment suggest that emotional tension, measured by state anxiety, correlates positively with the level of reactivity and trait anxiety, which is consistent with Spielberger's (1976) theory as well as with our data on the relation between anxiety and reactivity (see Chapter 4). This interrelation probably masks the real relations between resistance to group pressure and the emotional tension evoked during this process. To verify our hypothesis we considered the results as regards the interrelation between resistance against group pressure and emotional tension separately for high- and low-reactive individuals. We expected the dependency to be expressed more in high-reactive subjects because of their lower resistance to situations of high stimulation load.

As seen from Table LX our hypothesis was supported when high-reactive subjects were taken into account. Here it is evident that in all subjects who revealed resistance against group pressure, high emotional tension (measured by state anxiety) was present. As regards subjects who were submissive to group pressure (double the number in the high-reactive group compared with individuals resistant to group pressure), there is a predominance of individuals with low emotional tension. This relationship does not occur in the low-reactive group

TABLE LX. Resistance to group pressure and emotional tension (state anxiety) in high- and low-reactive individuals (adapted from Białowąs, 1976)

| | HR | | | LR | | |
|---|---|---|---|---|---|---|
| | Emotional Tension | | Total No. | Emotional Tension | | Total No. |
| Attitude | High | Low | of Ss | High | Low | of Ss |
| Submissive | 5 | 11 | 16 | 4 | 1 | 5 |
| Independent | 8 | 0 | 8 | 10 | 10 | 20 |
| Total number of subjects | 13 | 11 | 24 | 14 | 11 | 25 |

$Chi^2 = 7.57; p < 0.01$ $\qquad$ $Chi^2 = 1.10$; n.s.

where the distribution of resistant and submissive individuals is more or less accidental. This may suggest that, for low-reactive subjects, group pressure does not have such high stimulative value as it does for high-reactive individuals. It should be mentioned here that the division of subjects into those with high and low emotional tension (state anxiety) was carried out separately for high- and low-reactive individuals. In the former group the median of state anxiety was $Me = 43$ whereas in the latter group its value dropped to $Me = 28$. This highly significant difference also illustrates that group pressure was particularly stimulating for high-reactive individuals.

In order to see whether emotional tension differentiates subjects with high and low reactivity during group pressure, irrespective of their attitude (conformist vs. independence) expressed during the experiment, Białowąs divided all subjects, by means of the median, into two groups: with high and low emotional tension. The distributions of high- and low-reactive subjects in each group separately, was then counted (see Table LXI).

TABLE LXI. Emotional tension under group pressure in high- and low-reactive individuals (taken from Białowąs, 1976)

| Reactivity | Emotional Tension | | Total Number of Subjects |
|---|---|---|---|
| | High | Low | |
| HR | 20 | 4 | 24 |
| LR | 4 | 21 | 25 |
| Total number of subjects | 24 | 25 | 49 |

$Chi^2 = 22.21; p < 0.001$

The results unequivocally support the expectation that strong emotional tension arises in most high-reactive subjects under group pressure. Among the low-reactive persons there is a predominance of individuals who display below average emotional tension.

If emotional tension (measured in this experiment by state anxiety) can be regarded, with some caution, as an index of psychophysiological cost paid during group pressure we may conclude that high-reactive subjects suffer greater psychophysiological cost compared with low-reactive individuals in this situation and this is in accordance with our expectations (see Klonowicz, 1974b and p. 247).

## Ideal and Real Self and the Need for Stimulation

As follows from the data presented in the literature (e.g. Reykowski, 1970, 1977; Łukaszewski, 1974) the discrepancy between real and ideal self should be regarded as a source of emotional tension, the latter being a function of the degree of discrepancy between both selves. A large discrepancy between real and ideal self evokes strong emotional tension and may consequently be regarded as a source of high stimulation. In turn, small discrepancy between both aspects of self has a low stimulative value since it does not generate emotional tension or the tension is of low intensity.

In accordance with these considerations one may expect, in high-reactive individuals, a tendency to organize the structure of real and ideal self in such a way as to ensure minimal discrepancy between them. The opposite should be found in low-reactive individuals in whom, due to their high stimulation need, the discrepancy between the real and ideal self will be rather high. Although no research was, until now, conducted on the dependency between level of reactivity and the consistency between real and ideal self, there are some data in the literature which seem to be discordant with our consideration. For example, Butler and Haigh (1954) found that in normals the correlation between real and ideal self is about 0.50, whereas in neurotics there is no correlation at all. Friedman (1955) showed that in healthy individuals the coefficient of correlation between real and ideal self is fairly high (0.63) but drops when measured in neurotics (0.30). Similar results are given by Reykowski (1970). As follows from several of our studies, a positive correlation exists between reactivity and neuroticism (see Table XXVII) which may suggest that the discrepancy between real and ideal self should be higher in high-reactive subjects compared with low-reactive ones. The inconsistency between our theoretical considerations and the data from studies related to neuroticism has provoked us to investigate the relation between reactivity and degree of discrepancy in the real and ideal self-ratio.

Diagnosing reactivity by means of the STI, Strzałkowska (1977) selected two groups of 40 subjects each differing in reactivity from a sample of 160 females (aged 19–23) (high- vs. low-reactive). Both groups were further sub-divided into two subgroups—neurotics and emotionally stable. Neuroticism was estimated by the Neuroticism Scale from the MPI and the median, calculated separately for high ($Me = 35.5$) and low-reactive subjects ($Me = 25.5$), was used as the criterion for dividing the individuals. Thus four groups were separated, containing 20 subjects each and differing in reactivity level and neuroticism. As explained earlier, it was assumed that the high-reactive (R) and high-neurotic (N) group would have low stimulation need, whereas the high stimulation need could characterize the low-reactive (r) and emotionally stable (n) group, with both the remaining groups (Rn and rN) expressing an intermediate stimulation need.

The discrepancy between real and ideal self was measured by the Q-sort which, in Strzałkowska's experiment, consisted of 60 items related to different aspects (physical, psychic, and social) of the self. Most of the statements included in the list were derived from Rogers' (1961) theory of self. Real-self items were sorted first. As an index of discrepancy between the real and ideal self the ratio of the results of ideal self-estimation to real self-estimation ($\times 100$) was calculated. The higher the index the higher the discrepancy between both selves.

In the first stage of analysis the discrepancy between real and ideal self referred to the reactivity dimension only. The discrepancy in both groups differing in reactivity is as follows:

high-reactive individuals: $M = 146.3$
low-reactive individuals: $M = 117.8$

The difference between the degree of discrepancy in both groups is highly significant ($p < 0.001$) and, as can be seen, the discrepancy is much higher in high-reactive individuals compared with the low-reactive ones.

The discrepancy between real and ideal self in relation to the individual's stimulation need, which was measured here by both reactivity and neuroticism, is illustrated in Table LXII.

As we can see, the highest discrepancy occurs in the RN group. The most evident difference in the degree of discrepancy may be found

TABLE LXII. Discrepancy between real and ideal self in groups with different stimulation needs (taken from Strzałkowska, 1977)

| Groups differing in Stimulation Need | Discrepancy Scores $M_1$ | $M_2$ | $M_1-M_2$ | $p$ |
|---|---|---|---|---|
| rn–rN | 104.5 | 131.2 | 26.7 | 0.001 |
| rn–Rn | 104.5 | 145.5 | 41.0 | 0.001 |
| rn–RN | 104.5 | 147.1 | 42.6 | 0.001 |
| RN–Rn | 147.1 | 145.5 | 1.6 | n.s. |
| RN–rN | 147.1 | 131.2 | 15.9 | 0.05 |
| Rn–rN | 145.5 | 131.2 | 14.3 | n.s. |

between that group and the rn group. In the latter group the discrepancy is lowest. The results in the Table show at the same time that both reactivity and neuroticism maintain the same degree of discrepancy between real and ideal self. Analysis of variance (not used by Strzałkowska (1977)), would be a better method for establishing the interaction of the dimensions under discussion.

It should be stated that Strzałkowska's results contradict our expectations, when reactivity is taken into account; however, they correspond with the data on the relation between neuroticism and degree of discrepancy between real and ideal self. It might be supposed that the dependency between both variables (reactivity and discrepancy in self-esteem) is not as simple and direct as has been previously suggested.

The self-image develops under confrontation with the external world, especially with the social environment. Such situations and behaviours in which the individual has the chance to prove his capacities probably have considerable effect on the shaping of real self-esteem. These are mostly highly stimulating and saturated by social threat. It is when perceiving ourselves in relation to others that our self-image develops. The evaluation which takes place in such situations is often negative (I am not as beautiful as my friend; others are more clever than I, etc.) as a result, a stressful situation occurs, in which high-reactive individuals, being highly sensitive, display lower resistance than the low-reactive ones. A strong reaction to negative evaluation may result in a decrease in performance level, disorganization of behaviour, or in an increased feeling of failure. All these states may lead to a decrease of emotional resistance especially in the high-reactive individuals where this resistance is, as a rule, lower than in the low-reactive individuals. This might be expressed in an increased sensitivity to emotional stimuli as well as in an increased tendency for the psychological mechanisms of regulation to become disordered under emotional excitation (Reykowski, 1974). The loss of faith in one's own possibilities, fear of failure etc., may cause a decrease in the real self estimation and this, in turn, leads to discrepancy between real and ideal self.[1]

As follows from the latter considerations, it is highly probable that the discrepancy should be larger in high-reactive individuals than in the low-reactive ones, the latter being more resistant to emotional tension. The discrepancy between real and ideal self which develops in ontogenesis may be regarded, by itself, as a source of high stimulation due to the emotional tension it evokes. Being a non-desired state in high-reactive individuals, it should be considered as more the result of the interaction between unfavourable circumstances and high reactivity. When the discrepancy between real and ideal self is of long duration, the high-reactive individuals, in order to avoid overstimulation, should reduce their activity by decreasing the amount and range of undertaken actions. Thus the personality dimension, determined indirectly by the level of reactivity, may influence the individual's temperament characteristic to a certain degree. This resembles the paradigm formulated on p. 263, in which it was assumed that some personality phenomena, because of their stimulative value, may influence temperament.

## Machiavellianism and Reactivity

In the experiment conducted by Mirkowska (1976) we were interested in the relation between reactivity and the Machiavellian attitude, revealed in the tendency to deliberately manipulate others, and the facility of reducing such attitudes in others. According to Christie (Christie and Geis, 1970) the two extremes of the Machiavellian attitude can be described as follows:

(1) The cool syndrome—typical of strong Machiavellian tendencies. It comprises such traits as: resistance to social influence and external pressure, lack of respect for others' goals and desires, great ability to function efficiently in situations evoking emotional tension, tendency to initiate and control situations etc.

(2) The soft-touch syndrome—typical of weak Machiavellian tendencies. It comprises: susceptibility to social influences, submission to the pressure of others, concentration on the partner of interaction, tendency to submit to the demand of a situation, activity that does not go beyond certain accepted rules, etc.

In this study, aimed mainly at investigating the influence of sensitivity training in reducing the Machiavellian attitude, the hypothesis was formulated that the cool syndrome would be more frequently found in low-reactive individuals, while the soft-touch syndrome would be more frequent in high-reactive individuals. In the light of our former arguments on suggestions about reactivity, this hypothesis seemed quite justified.

Mirkowska (1976) studied a group of 47 executives with at least high-school education (aged 22–45). With respect to reactivity, which was measured by the STI, the three groups were separated. The high-reactive group contained 11 subjects whereas the low-reactive one contained 12 subjects. The third group comprised all remaining individuals (24 Ss). The Machiavellian tendency was measured by the Mach IV and Mach V scales developed by Christie.[2] Because the subjects were submitted for training sessions, only the first assessments of the Machiavellian attitude, which took place prior to training, were considered. Three subgroups were again separated using the same criterion as for the reactivity dimension. The two extreme groups (high vs. low Machiavellian tendency) contained 12 subjects each. The remaining individuals (23 Ss) constituted the intermediate group regarding the Machiavellian attitude.

The results obtained in this study are displayed in Table LXIII which shows that the distribution of the number of subjects differing in both dimensions, reactivity and Machiavellian attitude, is in accordance with our expectations. No high-reactive subject revealed a high Machiavellian tendency. Exactly the opposite occurs when low-reactive individuals are considered. Nobody in this group is found with low Machiavellian tendencies. In the group with intermediate levels of reactivity, most of the subjects may be characterized as having a moderate Machiavellian tendency.

The correlation between the Machiavellian tendency and level of reactivity is consistent with the results presented in Table LXIII and shows that high Machiavellianism corresponds with low-reactivity ($r = 0.56; p < 0.01$).

The interdependency of both dimensions in question may be explained not by the specificity (quality) of high or low Machiavellianism but by the fact that the activities which may be regarded as indicators of this tendency differ significantly in their stimulative value. Entering into many social relations, resistance to external pressure, efficient functioning under social threat, manipulating others, etc., are all activities which generate emotions of high stimulative value. According to our theory (see Chapter 5) these types of activities should be preferred by low-reactive subjects. The soft-touch syndrome, typical of low

TABLE LXIII. Machiavellian tendency and reactivity
(taken from Mirkowska, 1976)

| Machiavellian Tendency | Reactivity | | | Total Number of Subjects |
|---|---|---|---|---|
| | High | Moderate | Low | |
| Strong | 0 | 3 | 9 | 12 |
| Moderate | 5 | 15 | 3 | 23 |
| Weak | 6 | 6 | 0 | 12 |
| Total number of subjects | 11 | 24 | 12 | 47 |

$Chi^2 = 24.95; p < 0.001$

Machiavellianism, includes activities of lower stimulative value than does the cool syndrome, and this is the reason why it should be met more often in the high-reactive individuals, who are stimulation avoiders.

## Level of Aspiration and Reactivity

In a study conducted by Eliasz (1973, 1974) a specific dependency between level of aspiration and reactivity was hypothesized. A level of aspiration adequate to the individual's achievements was regarded as an indicator of the so-called active style of self-regulation (see p. 235) and thus typical for low-reactive individuals. A high discrepancy between level of aspiration and achievement level (both in the positive and negative direction) was regarded by the author as an indicator of the passive style of self-regulation and, hence, as being typical for high-reactive individuals. Eliasz's consideration is based on Atkinson's achievement motivation theory, according to which the individual becomes strongly emotionally involved when probability of achievement is close to 50% (Atkinson and Feather, 1966). Thus, realistic aspirations (concordance of aspiration and achievement) should be considered as being highly stimulating, whereas unrealistic aspiration (underestimation as well as overestimation) should be regarded as having lower stimulative value. The results obtained by Eliasz (1973) do not enable any unequivocal conclusion to be made concerning the relation between reactivity and aspiration level.

This problem was again submitted to investigation by Król (1977). His experiment was aimed to relate the level of aspiration to several aspects of behaviour and personality, among which NS strength with respect to excitation was one of the main variables under control.

Strength of the NS was measured by a method adapted by the present author (Strelau, 1969) for assessing this NS property and which might be regarded as a variant of the method known as "Change of simple RT under repeatedly exposed stimuli" (see Chapter 2), primarily aimed at estimating the individual's endurance threshold. Instead of the simple motor reaction a modified Kraepelin test with 312 columns of one-digit figures was used. The subjects were required to add up as quickly and accurately as possible six randomly arranged digits after squaring each figure of 6 and below. The task lasted 60 min. Strength was assessed by the ratio of the number of columns completed during the last 5 min of work to the number of columns completed during a 5-min period of work at the beginning of the task. The higher the ratio the higher the endurance of the individual. A decrease in performance higher than 15% was taken arbitrarily by Król as an indicator of the weak NS, whereas all other scores were assumed to be indicators of a strong NS. Endurance in task performance is, according to our interpretation of reactivity, one of its main indicators. Thus the method used by Król for estimating the strength of the NS may also be considered as a measure of reactivity.

The level of aspiration, described by Król as the ratio of declared results to the results really obtained, was measured in a rather classical experimental setting. A game of darts was arranged and the subjects' task was to throw darts as accurately as possible onto the target. The game comprised 11 series of five attempts each. Before each series the subject had to declare the score he expected to gain. The subjects were informed that the experiment was to test their manual dexterity.

One-hundred-and-twenty-one college students of both sexes were studied. On the basis of the criterion used by the author, 95 subjects were selected as having strong NS and 26 as representing the weak NS.[3] Taking into account the scores of aspiration level the subjects were divided into three groups: realistic level of aspiration (75 Ss), high (34 Ss), and low level of aspiration (12 Ss). Król found, when relating these groups to the strength of NS, that most individuals with weak NS had high or low levels, whereas the majority of individuals with strong NS expressed a realistic level of aspiration, this distribution being statistically significant. Taking as a point of departure the so-called goal discrepancy index, i.e. the difference between level of aspiration and level of task performance which directly preceded the declared aspiration level, the author obtained results which are also consistent with Eliasz's hypothesis. As seen from Fig. 17, the highest percentage of low-reactive subjects has a low discrepancy index whereas most high-reactive subjects score high in both directions (positive and negative) of goal discrepancy.

Thus the results obtained in Król's experiment give unequivocal support to Eliasz's hypothesis on the interdependency of aspiration level and reactivity.

Gantman (1977) also described a similar relationship between level of aspiration and strength of NS, measured by the slope of RT curve. Level of aspiration was measured while solving mathematical tasks of different degrees of difficulty. The results obtained from 27 high-school students (12 diagnosed as "strong" and 15 as "weak") are fully consistent with Król's (1977) data. There were statistically significantly more subjects with an adequate aspiration level among those with a strong NS, whereas the group with the weak NS consisted mainly of subjects whose aspiration level was inadequate to their level of performance.

The data presented by Król (1977) and Gantman (1977) to a certain

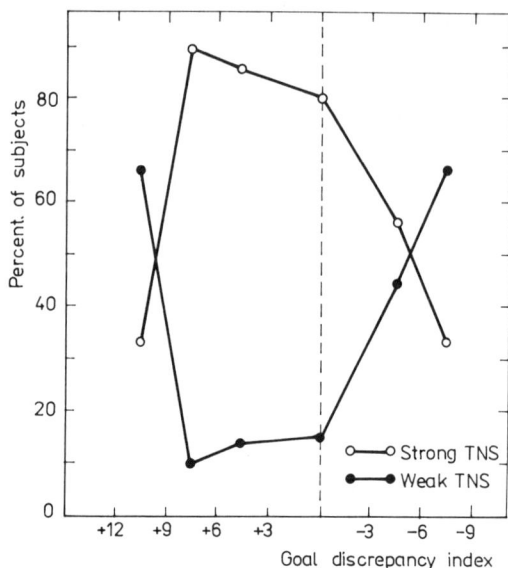

FIG. 17. Aspiration level expressed by goal discrepancy index in individuals with strong and weak NS (taken from Król, 1977).

extent contradict those of Melnichenko (1975), who also studied the interdependency of level of aspiration and strength of the NS (33 subjects aged 20–28). Using 11 different indices of aspiration level the author determined the so-called reactivity of aspiration level expressed in the adequacy of increment or decrement of aspiration level in accordance with the requirement of tasks solved by the subjects. Measuring the strength of NS by the slope of RT curve and by the sensory threshold, Melnichenko argued that individuals with a weak NS display higher adequacy of aspiration level. If high adequacy of aspiration level could be regarded as an analogy to realistic aspiration we would be inclined to expect the opposite relationship.

A series of studies conducted by Kapustin (1972, 1976), on groups performing different sports activities, partially supports the regularity stated by Król and Gantman. Kapustin found that in individuals with strong NS the level of aspiration prevailed over the level of performance, whereas in individuals with weak NS the converse occurs—level of aspiration is lower than level of performance. This relationship, not so strongly expressed during training, is particularly evident in competitive situations which might be characterized as highly stimulating. In both studies conducted by Kapustin the strength of the NS was diagnosed by the GSR variant of the extinction with reinforcement method (see Chapter 2). Level of aspiration was assessed experimentally as well as by an especially formulated questionnaire applied at different time-intervals before competition (directly prior to the competition, and 1, 2, and 3 days before).

In line with Król, Gantman, and Kapustin's studies is the decrease of aspiration level in individuals with a weak NS (high reactivity). Low level of aspiration should be regarded as a protective mechanism which enables failure to be avoided and which lowers the risk of not attaining the goal, thus causing a decrease of stimulation load in the task performance. In accordance with the theoretical assumption discussed in Chapter 5 we would expect high-reactive (weak TNS) subjects to behave in such a way as to avoid strong stimulation load (seen here in the decrease of aspiration level). In accordance with Atkinson and Feather's (1966) theory, the motive of failure avoidance, as mentioned before, is expressed not only in choosing goals which are easy to attain but also in high aspiration level. Setting of goals which are very difficult to achieve helps excuse the failure. Thus the results obtained by Król and Gantman, which show that individuals with weak nervous systems (high-reactive) also tend to have a high level of aspiration, are consistent with Atkinson's theory. In this case failure avoidance by overestimation of one's capabilities may be treated as a protective mechanism against overstimulation.

## Cognitive Style Exemplified by the Abstraction–Concreteness Dimension and Reactivity

As many studies have shown, preferences in cognitive functioning are expressed in several cognitive styles, field-dependency and field-independency (Witkin, 1978; Witkin *et al.*, 1962) and reflection-impulsivity (Kagan, 1966; Kagan *et al.*, 1973) being the most popular. These are regarded by their authors as personality dimensions. Matczak (1982a,b, in press) has conducted several experiments to study the developmental characteristics of several cognitive styles with special emphasis on the reflection-impulsivity and the abstraction–concreteness dimensions (see Gardner, 1964; Gardner and Schoen, 1962; cited by Matczak, 1982b). Being interested in temperament research, Matczak has undertaken studies to search for relations between different cognitive styles and reactivity, regarding the former as differing in stimulative value and thus influenced by the individual's reactivity level.

Let me concentrate on one study in which the interdependency of cognitive preferences, expressed in the abstraction–concreteness dimension and reactivity level was investigated, and which illustrates the type of theoretical considerations as well as the empirical data presented by Matczak (1982b, in press).

As Matczak argues, the stimulative value of cognitive activity which consists of assimilating given objects into the individual's internal cognitive patterns, depends on the degree of accommodation which should take place in order to assimilate the perceived objects. The magnitude of accommodation should be regarded as a function of discrepancy between the objects being assimilated and the cognitive patterns, this discrepancy resulting from the effect of novelty and complexity of the perceived objects (Berlyne, 1960).

Matczak (in press) has formulated a hypothesis according to which cognitive preferences, expressed in given cognitive styles, determine the stimulative value of perceived objects, thus playing a role in the regulation of activation level. One may expect that the development of cognitive preferences is influenced by these temperament traits which determine stimulation need; therefore, there should be an interdependency of cognitive style and reactivity. Low-reactive subjects, because of their high stimulation need, should prefer cognitive styles that might be characterized as educing maximum novelty and complexity from the perceived environment. High-reactive individuals, having a low stimulation need, should prefer cognitive styles in which a tendency to ignore or to reduce novelty and complexity is revealed.

The hypothesis regarding the dependency between reactivity level and cognitive style were verified for the abstraction–concreteness dimension which is expressed primarily in the process of categorization. This dimension should be regarded as a property of cognitive functioning which determines the degree of generality of the categories into which the perceived objects are included. As Piaget shows (1964, cited by Matczak, in press), perception of the surroundings changes in the process of development from concrete to abstract cognitive functioning. Besides the developmental changes, clearly expressed individual differences within the dimension in question may be found (Gardner and Schoen, 1962, cited by Matczak, in press).

Matczak makes the assumption that the abstraction–concreteness dimension, like other cognitive styles, takes part in the regulation of activation, and is thus linked to reactivity. However, the direction of interdependency between reactivity and the abstraction–concreteness dimension is not obvious since the stimulative value of the cognitive style under discussion is equivocal. There are some data which suggest that abstract cognitive functioning has a higher stimulative value than concrete functioning. Abstraction implies a high degree of complexity in perception, and indicates developmental superiority (being a more difficult cognitive process). As shown by Obuchowski (1970) abstract cognitive functioning may change into concrete functioning under high activation. If abstract functioning is thus conceptualized it should be burdened with greater "costs" and so we should expect it to be preferred by low-reactive individuals. According to Berlyne (1965) abstraction leads to the reduction of novelty and variety, thus being one of the main mechanisms causing rejection of information. The concentration on similarities, which results from the abstract style of cognitive functioning, leads to a reduction of the stimulative value of the perceived environment. As has been shown, the stimulative value of abstract functioning depends on whether it is regarded from the point of view of costs paid during cognition or of effects of cognitive activity.

On the basis of these considerations Matczak (1982b, in press) hypothesized that the dependency between reactivity level and the abstract–concrete cognitive style changes with age. As development proceeds, the cost of abstract functioning decreases due to the decrease in difficulty of abstraction processes. At the same time, as a result of experience, the recognition of the stimulative value of abstract functioning occurs, with the latter being used to lower the stimulative value of perceived objects.

In an experiment aimed at verifying Matczak's hypotheses 450 subjects of both sexes and different age (7–22 years) took part. All were either pupils from elementary (grades: 1, 2, 4, 6 and 7) and high schools (grades: 10 and 11) or college students. To estimate the position on the abstraction–concreteness dimension the modified Conceptual Style Test (CST) developed by Kagan (Kagan *et al.*, 1973) was used. The subject was shown three different pictures of well-known objects, one of which was used as a standard picture. The task was to choose from the two remaining pictures the one which fitted the standard picture best. Thirty different triads of pictures were presented in all. The subject was asked to justify his choice after each presentation. It was stressed that any solution was correct and that the pairs of pictures should be chosen in such a way as to satisfy the subject. This arrangement allowed the subject to manifest his cognitive preferences but not his cognitive capacities, which is an important factor in the diagnosis of cognitive styles regarded as personality dimensions.

Each of the 30 answers (30 presentations of 3 pictures) was classified into one of the following four categories: (1) nominal answers; (2) functional answers; (3) analytic answers; and (4) relational answers. These categories have been distinguished by several authors (Bruner,

1966, Kagan *et al.*, 1973; Gardner and Schoen, 1962, cited by Matczak, in press) who agree that the categories represent different positions on the abstraction–concreteness dimension. Nominal answers (allocation of selected pictures to a superordinate concept) are taken as a sign of extreme abstract functioning, whereas relational answers (temporal–spatial–functional connections between selected objects) are regarded as an index of concrete functioning. The two remaining cognitive categories fall into intermediate position on the dimension, the functional answers being closer to the abstraction pole and the analytic answers closer to the concreteness pole.

The subjects' answers were classified by two independent judges; judge reliability fluctuated from 84 to 89%. Weights were ascribed arbitrarily to the separate categories of answers (from 0 to 3). Weight 0 was given for relational answers and weight 3 for nominal ones. Thus an abstraction index (AI) was obtained oscillating between 0 to 90 points.

Reactivity was measured by the STI (all subjects post-elementary school) whereas elementary school children were diagnosed by an especially elaborated 5-point rating scale. The scale consists of 32 items concerned with behaviours in different school situations accepted as diagnostic for reactivity. Sixteen pairs of parallel items are included enabling the split-half reliability (0.80) to be estimated.

Matczak's results were analysed in two different ways. The rank correlation coefficients between level of reactivity and AI as well as the number of separate categories of answers were calculated.[4] Thereafter, taking as a point of departure the AI and the number of nominal answers, four different groups (each counting 25% of Ss) were separated on the basis of the quartile deviation (separately for elementary school, high school and college subjects) and compared with reactivity level.

The correlation between the abstraction index and number of answers in the separate categories on the one hand and level of reactivity on the other was calculated separately for groups representing different school grades and sexes. Among the 64 coefficients only six obtained the required level of statistical significance—five of these were for females. As regards the AI and nominal categories, all coefficients above 0.20, even if insignificant, were negative, suggesting that low-reactivity tends to correspond with high abstraction. No significant correlations were found for older subjects (high-school and college students).

The relation between AI and reactivity met in elementary school children is displayed in Table LXIV, which shows that the number of high-reactive subjects (selected by means of quartile deviation) is greatest within the group which is most concrete in its cognitive

TABLE LXIV. The number of high- and low-reactive children in groups differing in the abstraction index (AI) (adapted from Matczak, in press)

| Reactivity | Groups Differing in AI | | | | Total Number of subjects |
|---|---|---|---|---|---|
| | A--[a] | A- | A+ | A++ | |
| HR | 41 | 27 | 34 | 24 | 126 |
| LR | 19 | 34 | 27 | 40 | 120 |
| Total number of subjects | 60 | 61 | 61 | 64 | 246 |

$\text{Chi}^2 = 14.22; p < 0.01$

[a] A-- is the lowest AI (high concreteness), A++ the highest AI (high abstraction). The groups were selected by means of quartile deviation.

functioning. The opposite occurs when the most abstract group is taken into account; there low-reactive subjects are in the majority. A similar and statistically significant distribution of high- and low-reactive individuals was found when the number of nominal answers was considered. This gives support to the contention that the tendency to prefer abstract functioning, more pronounced in low-reactive individuals, and the preference for a concrete cognitive style, typical for high-reactive children (elementary school pupils aged from 7 to 14), is not accidental. These data are consistent with the correlational analysis where an interdependency between low-reactivity and abstraction was found.

The relation between reactivity and cognitive style as regards abstraction–concreteness in high-school and college students is different from the relationship described above. Since reactivity was measured by the STI it was possible to use mean reactivity scores to compare subjects differing in level of abstraction. As seen from Table LXV the differences in reactivity between the four groups differently placed on the dimension of abstraction are almost insignificant, except for the high-school sample. In the latter the two intermediate groups differ significantly in reactivity, the group being closer to the abstraction pole displaying lower reactivity. When the high-school students are divided at the median into two groups differing in cognitive style, the group below the median (concrete functioning) shows significantly higher reactivity than the above-median group (abstract functioning).

Interestingly, in both extreme groups of college students (high abstraction and high concreteness) reactivity is higher than in both intermediate groups with respect to cognitive style. However, these insignificant differences did reach statistical significance when the number of nominal answers was considered as indicator of cognitive

TABLE LXV. Mean level of reactivity measured by STI in high-school and college students with different AI (adapted from Matczak, in press)

| Students | Groups Differing in AI | | | |
|---|---|---|---|---|
| | A--[a] | A- | A+ | A++ |
| High-school | 51.1 | 47.3 ⟵⟶ 55.9 | | 54.8 |
| | | 49.2 ⟵————⟶ 55.4 | | |
| College | 49.3 | 55.4 | 55.1 | 48.3 |

⟵⟶ $p < 0.05$

[a] For explanation see note to Table LXIV.

style. In this case the two extreme subgroups, which gave the highest and the lowest number of nominal answers, did not differ from each other but they differed significantly from both intermediate groups. In the latter the level of reactivity was significantly lower than in the extreme groups.

Concluding, it may be stated that high-reactive children (7–14 years old) reveal a tendency to prefer a concrete style whereas low-reactive individuals display an abstraction tendency. In this case concrete functioning, being regarded as an easier form of cognitive activity, and at the same time developmentally prior to the abstract style, may be used as a means of lowering the stimulative value of perceived stimuli and thus is met more frequently in high-reactive individuals.

With adults (college students aged 19–22) the data suggest that high concreteness as well as high abstraction may occur in high-reactive individuals. Considering the cognitive style from the point of view of stimulative value one may assume that, where abstract functioning does not cause the difficulties met in younger individuals, this type of cognitive preference is used to reduce the variety and novelty of perceived stimuli, so causing a decrease in the stimulative value of the perceived objects. This assumption allows us to explain why reactivity was higher among subjects with abstract functioning.

The development of preferences in cognitive functioning expressed in the abstract–concrete cognitive style and their different role in the regulation of the stimulative value of the perceived environment as related to reactivity level has been discussed in detail by Matczak (1982b, in press).

## FINAL REMARKS

The empirical evidence discussed in the former section illustrates that temperament influences the shaping of personality mainly by means of modifying the stimulative value of the surroundings or by a given activity aimed at regulating the amount of stimulation load to suit the individual's need for stimulation. Several types of behaviour generally accepted as manifestations of personality may also be regarded as playing a role in the regulation of stimulation need, and thus are related to temperament. However, the interrelation is mostly complex and not unequivocal as exemplified in Strzałkowska's (1977) study on the relationship between reactivity and discrepancy between ideal and real self (see p. 269). The complexity of the relations between temperament and personality, illustrated by aggressive behaviour, has been shown by Reykowski (1979). This author, in a discussion of the problem of intrinsic motivation to aggression, has acknowledged that aggressive behaviour may be considered as a source of strong stimulation. Many variables may be mentioned here as having high stimulative value: the individual's own activity (e.g. physical attack), threat accompanying aggression, violation of norms, change in the physical state of the object being attacked (e.g. wounds, cries), etc. Thus, if aggression becomes, under given social influences, an acquired form of behaviour it might be used by low-reactive persons as a technique by which they compensate for their stimulation deficiency. But, as shown by Reykowski (1979) increased reactivity may also be considered a co-determinant of aggressive behaviour, although the bases of this behaviour are different. Aggression may be regarded here as a reaction against stimulation overload and thus aimed at reducing stimulation. This defensive aggression, which should be treated as a result of reactive behaviour, may, in a given social environment, develop as an effective way for the high-reactive individual to decrease the stimulative value of the situation. Frączek (1979) also suggests a positive correlation between reactivity and reactive forms of aggression. Thus one may conclude that, externally, the same activity (in this case diagnosed as aggression) plays different roles in regulating the stimulation need whether a result of operant or reactive behaviour. Aggressive behaviour may be aimed at delivering stimulation (operant aggression) or, on the contrary, by means of aggressive behaviour the individual may be protecting himself against overstimulation (reactive aggression).

The interdependencies to be found between reactivity, which was our main subject of investigation, and several personality dimensions can hardly be explained if one refers to the content or specificity of behaviour in which these dimensions are manifested. When interpreting the interdependency between temperament and personality, the feature common to both would appear to be the role which both phenomena play in the regulation of stimulation. Of course, if other temperament dimensions (e.g. mobility) were considered, the interdependency of temperament and personality could be different. Nevertheless, the probability that temperament traits will directly influence the shaping of personality is rather low.

To return to our initial considerations concerning interrelation of temperament and personality, we assume that temperament dimensions are determined directly by the individual's biological endowment, which, being primarily inherited, may develop and change under environmental influences. The physical factors of the environment, common for humans and animals, contribute to the variance of temperament mainly when they assume extreme value, e.g. overstimulation or deprivation. The environmental factors causing changes in temperament may be of lower (in both extremes) stimulating value if their action is prolonged or systematic. Under the latter conditions other factors of the physical environment (e.g. temperature, nutrition) may also cause changes in temperament. In these cases changes in temperament depend upon the degree to which the environmental factors cause changes in the physiological mechanism directly determining the temperamental traits. The social environment, to the extent to which it influences the moulding of temperamental traits (as is the case in human beings), acts not so much by means of its content (specificity), but through certain formal attributes of the social environment, such as: excessive tension, threat, aggression, or other situations and reactions evoking permanent over or understimulation. Consequently, it influences temperamental traits by means of its physical properties. The above discussed interdependencies are illustrated in Figure 18.

As mentioned before, the shaping of personality is attributable mainly to the social environment which acts on the individual's biological endowment. The biological factor contributes significantly to the variance of personality, mainly when disturbances in its functioning or pathology occur. It may also influence personality development indirectly, e.g. by the physiological basis of temperament. Furthermore, the physical environment may have a strong influence on personality development when extreme and prolonged changes occur (e.g. physical threat, lack of nutrition). In normal situations the influence of the physical environment is rather unspecific and does not directly cause changes in personality.

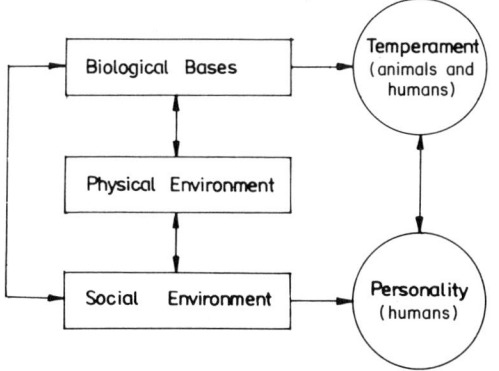

FIG. 18. Determinants of temperament and personality.

As illustrated in both preceding sections, temperament by itself, as one of the many variables taking part in the interaction of the individual and his environment, may influence personality moulding and vice versa. Personality, regarded as a generator of stimulation, may influence the development of temperament traits.

# REFERENCES

Adrian, E. D. and Matthews, B. H. (1934). The interpretation of potential waves in the cortex. *J. Physiology* **81**, 440–471.
Akimova, M. K. (1974). The acquisition of high-speed motor habits in relation to individual properties of strength and lability of nervous processes. *In* (K. M. Gurevich, ed.) "Psychophysiological problems of higher level professional experience". Vol. 1. Sovetskaya Rossiya, Moscow (in Russian).
Akimova, M. K. (1975). Manifestation of strength of the nervous system in the resultant aspect of some types of intellectual activity. *In* (K. M. Gurevich and V. I. Lubovsky, eds) "Psychological diagnosis: Problems and methods". RSFSR Academy of Pedagogical Sciences, Moscow (in Russian).
Akimova, M. K. (1980). Dynamic characteristics of the nervous system and the problem of natural roots of abilities. *Voprosy Psikhologii* **26**, 101–108 (in Russian).
Akimova, M. K. and Gurevich, K. M. (1978). Individual differences in some types of intellectual activity and strength of the nervous system. *In* (V. V. Davydov, ed.) "Problems of general, developmental, and pedagogical psychology". Pedagogika, Moscow (in Russian).
Aleksandrova, N. I. (1969). On the relationship between background alpha-activity and characteristics of the components of visual evoked potentials. *In* (V. D. Nebylitsyn, ed.) "Problems of differential psychophysiology". Vol. 6. Prosveshcheniye, Moscow (in Russian).
Aleksandrova, N. I. (1977). On the problem of morphological basis of the general properties of the nervous system (the influence of aminazine on bioelectrical activity of frontal and occipital brain areas). *In* (M. N. Borisova *et al.*, eds) "Problems of differential psychophysiology". Vol. 9. Pedagogika, Moscow (in Russian).
Alekseyeva, M. S. (1953). Determination of type of nervous system in the dog on the basis of different unconditioned reinforcements—alimentary and acid-defence. *Trudy Instituta Fiziologii im. I. P. Pavlova* **2**, 193–211 (in Russian).
Allport, G. W. (1937). "Personality: a psychological interpretation". Holt, New York.
Anastasi, A. (1961). "Psychological testing". Macmillan, New York.
Anokhin, P. K. (1958). "Electroencephalographic study of the conditioned reflex". Medgiz, Moscow (in Russian).

# References

Anokhin, P. K. (1969). Cybernetics and the integrative activity of the brain. *In* (M. Cole and I. Maltzman, eds) "A handbook of contemporary Soviet psychology". Basic Books, New York.

Anokhin, P. K. (1978). "Collected works. Philosophical aspects of the theory of the functional system". Nauka, Moscow (in Russian).

Apter, I. M. (1966). On the dependency of the development of different neuroses on the typological properties of the nervous system. *In* "Clinic problems, pathophysiology, and treatment of psychological diseases". Lugansk Medical College Press, Lugansk (in Russian).

Argyle, M. (1975). "Predictive and generative rules models of P × S interaction". Paper presented at the Symposium on Interactional Psychology. Stockholm, June 22–27.

Asratyan, E. A. (1939). The study of the physiological lability of the highest central levels. "Uchenye Zapiski LGU". Vol. 41. Leningrad University Press, Leningrad (in Russian).

Atkinson, J. (1965). "An introduction to motivation". Van Nostrand, New York.

Atkinson, J. W. and Feather, N. T. (1966). "A theory of achievement motivation". Wiley, New York.

Bakulev, A. N. and Busalov, A. A. (1957). The significance of I. P. Pavlov's theory on types of higher nervous activity for applied surgery. *In* "Problems of physiology of the central nervous system". SSSR Academy of Sciences, Leningrad (in Russian).

Bales, R. F. (1951). "Interaction process analysis". Addison-Wesley, Oxford.

Barkhudaryan, S. S. (1956). Characteristics of dogs with intermediate types of nervous system. *Trudy Instituta Fiziologii im. I. P. Pavlova* **5**, 203–216 (in Russian).

Barnes, G. E. (1976). Individual differences in perceptual reactance: A review of the stimulus intensity modulation individual differences dimension. *Canadian Psychological Review* **17**, 29–52.

Basan, L. I. (1960). Technique of investigation of higher nervous activity in children in natural settings. *Zhurnal vysshei nervnoi Deyatelnosti* **10**, 800–803 (in Russian).

Baymetov, A. K. (1967). Some factors of individual style of learning activity in high-school students determined by strength of excitation. *In* (V. S. Merlin, ed.) "Typological investigations in psychology of personality". Vol. 4. UOOP and PGPI, Perm (in Russian).

Bazylevich, T. F. (1974a). The syndrome of strength of the regulative brain system. *In* (V. D. Nebylitsyn, ed.) "Problems of differential psychophysiology. Electrophysiological studies on the fundamental properties of the nervous system". Vol. 8, Nauka, Moscow (in Russian).

Bazylevich, T. F. (1974b). The expression of strength of the regulative brain system in the dynamics of the somatosensory evoked potential. *In* (V. D. Nebylitsyn, ed.) "Problems of differential psychophysiology. Electrophysiological studies on the fundamental properties of the nervous system". Vol. 8, Nauka, Moscow (in Russian).

Becker-Carus, C. (1971). Relationships between EEG, personality and vigilance. *Electroencephalography and Clinical Neurophysiology* **30**, 519–526.
Belous, V. V. (1968). Type of temperament as complex of symptoms and as invariance. *In* (V. S. Merlin, ed.) "Problems of experimental psychology of personality". Vol. 5, UOOP and PGPI, Perm (in Russian).
Belous, V. V. (1970). Species-specific curvilinear invariances of the orthogonal traits of temperament. *In* (V. S. Merlin, ed.) "Problems of experimental psychology of personality". Vol. 6. UOOP and PGPI, Perm (in Russian).
Belous, V. V. (1972). Species-specific curvilinear invariances of the orthogonal traits of temperament. *Voprosy Psikhologii* **18**, 14–24 (in Russian).
Belous, V. V. (1976). Mathematical models of temperament from the point of view of systems theory. *In* (V. S. Merlin, ed.) "Temperament". MP RSFSR and PGPI, Perm (in Russian).
Belous, V. V. (1977). Developmental-sex differences in the adaptive role of temperament traits (as the invariance of parabola equation type). *In* (V. S. Merlin, ed.) "Theoretical bases, application, and methods of differential psychophysiology". MP RSFSR and PGPI, Perm (in Russian).
Belous, V. V. and Palkina, T. P. (1974). The problem of the quantitative criterion of the species-specific invariance of temperament. *In* (V. S. Merlin, ed.) "The problems of temperament theory". MP RSFSR and PGPI, Perm (in Russian).
Berlyne, D. E. (1960). "Conflict, arousal, and curiosity". McGraw-Hill, New York and London.
Berlyne, D. E. (1965). "Structure and direction in thinking". Wiley, New York.
Białowąs, D. (1976). "Uleganie naciskowi grupowemu a reaktywność jako przykład wpływu cech temperamentalnych na zachowania społeczne". Unpublished M.A. thesis, University of Warsaw.
Birman, B. N. (1951). An attempt to make a clinico-physiological determination of types of higher nervous activity. *Zhurnal vysshei nervnoi Deyatelnosti* **1**, 879–888 (in Russian).
Biryukova, Z. (1961). "Higher nervous activity in sportsmen. Typological investigation of nervous system properties". Fizkultura i sport, Moscow (in Russian).
Bitterman, M. E. (1965). The evolution of intelligence. *Scientific American* **212**, 92–100.
Bloom, B. S. (1964). "Stability and change in human characteristics". Wiley, New York.
Boiko, E. I. (1961). Reaction time and the physiological law of strength. *In* (E. I. Boiko, ed.) "Common problems of psychology and physiology". RSFSR Academy of Pedagogical Sciences, Moscow (in Russian).
Boiko, E. I. (1964). From the history of chronometrical investigation of the reaction. *Voprosy Psikhologii* **10**, 135–144 (in Russian).
Borisova, M. N. (1959). Determination of discrimination thresholds and elaboration of fine sensory differentiations as a means of studying the concentration of excitation. *In* (B. M. Teplov, ed.) "Typological features of

higher nervous activity in man". Vol. 2. RSFSR Academy of Pedagogical Sciences, Moscow (in Russian).

Borisova, M. N. (1965). Individual differences and typological correlates of simple reactions. *In* (B. M. Teplov, ed.) "Typological features of higher nervous activity in man". Vol. 4. Prosveshcheniye, Moscow (in Russian).

Borisova, M. N. (1969a). On the evaluation of visual sensitivity measurements. *In* (V. D. Nebylitsyn, ed.) "Problems of differential psychophysiology". Vol. 6. Prosveshcheniye, Moscow (in Russian).

Borisova, M. N. (1969b). On the typological significance of some indices of motor reactions. *In* (V. D. Nebylitsyn, ed.) "Problems of differential psychophysiology". Vol. 6. Prosveshcheniye, Moscow (in Russian).

Borisova, M. N. (1972). Concentration of nervous processes as an individual typological feature of higher nervous activity. *In* (V. D. Nebylitsyn and J. A. Gray, eds) "Biological basis of individual behavior". Academic Press, New York and London.

Borisova, M. N. (1977). Concentration of nervous processes as a feature of higher nervous activity. *In* (A. A. Smirnov, ed.) "Psychology and psychophysiology of individual differences". Pedagogika, Moscow (in Russian).

Borisova, M. N. (1978). Investigation of the hereditary determination of the discrimination threshold. *In* (B. F. Lomov and I. V. Ravich-Shcherbo, eds) "The problems of genetic psychophysiology in man". Nauka, Moscow (in Russian).

Borisova, M. N., Golubeva, E. A., Leites, N. S., Olshannikova, A. E., Ravich-Shcherbo, I. W., Rozhdestvenskaya, V. I., and Rusalov, V. M. (eds) (1977). "Problems of differential psychophysiology". Vol. 9. Pedagogika, Moscow (in Russian).

Borisova, M. N., Gurevich, K. M., Yermolayeva-Tomina, L. B., Kolodnaya, A. Ya., Ravich-Shcherbo I. V., and Shvarts. L. A. (1963). Materials for comparative studies of various indices of the mobility of the nervous system in man. *In* (B. M. Teplov, ed.) "Typological features of higher nervous activity in man". Vol. 3. RSFSR Academy of Pedagogical Sciences, Moscow (in Russian).

Borisova, M. N. and Ravich-Shcherbo, I. V. (1967). On the interrelation between some indicators of absolute and relative strength of nervous processes. *In* (B. M. Teplov, ed.) "Typological features of higher nervous activity in man". Vol. 5. Prosveshcheniye, Moscow (in Russian).

Borisova, M. N., Yermolayeva-Tomina, L. B. and Ravich-Shcherbo, I. V. (1969). On the reliability and the validity of some indices connected with measurements of visual sensitivity. *In* (V. D. Nebylitsyn, ed.) "Problems of differential psychophysiology". Vol. 6. Prosveshcheniye, Moscow (in Russian).

Brebner, J. M. T. (1980). Reaction time in personality theory. *In* (A. T. Welford, ed.) "Reaction times". Academic Press, New York and London.

Brebner, J. and Cooper, C. (1974). The effect of a low rate of regular signals upon the reaction times of introverts and extraverts. *J. Research in Personality* **8**, 263–276.

Brebner, J. and Cooper, C. (1978). Stimulus- or response-induced excitation. A comparison of the behaviour of introverts and extraverts. *J. Research in Personality* **12**, 306–311.

Bruner, J. S. (1961). The act of discovery. *Harvard Educational Review* **1**, 21–32.

Bruner, J. S. (1966). On cognitive growth. *In* (J. S. Bruner, R. R. Olver and P. M. Greenfield, eds) "Studies in cognitive growth". Wiley, New York.

Brzezicki, E. (1946). O potrzebie rozszerzenia typologii Kretschmera. *Życie Nauki* **1**, 352–369.

Buchsbaum, M. S. (1976). Self-regulation of stimulus intensity: Augmenting/reducing and the average evoked response. *In* (G. E. Schwarth and D. Shapiro, eds) "Consciousness and self-regulation". Plenum Press, New York.

Buchsbaum, M. S. (1978). Neurophysiological studies of reduction and augmentation. *In* (A. Petrie, ed.) "Individuality in pain and suffering". Chicago University Press, Chicago.

Buchsbaum, M. S. (1979) Neurophysiological reactivity, stimulus intensity modulation and the depressive disorders. *In* (R. A. Depue, ed.) "The psychobiology of the depressive disorders: implications for the effects of stress". Academic Press, New York and London.

Buchsbaum, M. S., Haier, R. and Johnson, J. (in press). Augmenting and reducing. Individual differences in evoked potentials. *In* (A. Gale and J. Edwards, eds) "Physiological correlates of human behaviour". Academic Press, New York and London.

Buchsbaum, M. S. and Silverman, J. (1968). Stimulus intensity control and the cortical evoked response. *Psychosomatic Medicine* **30**, 12–22.

Bundych, T. B. (1974). On standardization of techniques of assessment of lability of the nervous system. *In* (N. M. Peysakhov, V. M. Shadrin, and A. P. Kashin, eds) "Problems of psychology of individual differences". Kazan University Press, Kazan (in Russian).

Burdina, V. N., Krasusky, V. K., and Chebykin, D. A. (1960). On the problem of dependency of higher nervous activity development in dogs on rearing conditions in ontogenesis. *Zhurnal vysshei nervnoi Deyatelnosti* **10**, 427–434 (in Russian).

Burks, J. and Rubenstein, M. (1979). "Temperament styles in adult interaction: Applications in psychotherapy". Brunner/Mazel, New York.

Buss, A. H. and Plomin, R. (1975). "A temperament theory of personality development". Wiley, New York.

Butler, J. M. and Haigh, E. V. (1954). Changes in the relations between self-concepts and ideal concepts consequent upon client-centered counselling. *In* (C. R. Rogers and R. F. Dymond, eds) "Psychotherapy and personality change". University of Chicago Press, Chicago.

Cameron, B. and Myers, J. (1966). Some personality correlates of risk taking. *J. General Psychology* **74**, 51–60.

Carlier, M. (in press). Factor analysis of Strelau's questionnaire and an attempt to validate some of the factors. *In* (J. Strelau, F. H. Farley, and A.

Gale, eds) "The biological foundations of personality and behavior". Hemisphere Publishing Corporation, Washington and London.
Castaneda, A. (1956). Reaction time and response amplitude as a function of anxiety and stimulus intensity. *J. Abnormal and Social Psychology* **53**, 225–228.
Cattell, R. B. (1948). "A guide to mental testing". University of London Press, London.
Cattell, R. B. (1965). "The scientific analysis of personality". Penguin Books, Harmondsworth.
Cattell, R. B. (1971). "Abilities. Their structure, growth and action". Houghton Mifflin, Boston.
Cattell, R. B. (1972). The interpretation of Pavlov's typology and the arousal concept, in replicated trait and state factors. *In* (V. D. Nebylitsyn and J. A. Gray, eds) "Biological bases of individual behavior". Academic Press, New York and London.
Cazzullo, C. L., Goldwurm, G. F., and Petrella, F. (1970). Correlation between psychopathological data and higher nervous activity evaluated by four classical reflexological methods in neuropsychiatric patients. *Conditional Reflex* **5**, 207–232.
Chebykin, D. A. (1961). Comparative characteristics of the typological features of the nervous system and overall behaviour in dogs. *Zhurnal vysshei nervnoi Deyatelnosti* **11**, 119–126 (in Russian).
Choynowski, M. (1977). Podręcznik do "Inwentarza Osobowości" H. J. Eysencka. *In* (M. Choynowski, ed.) "Testy psychologiczne w poradnictwie wychowawczo-zawodowym". Państwowe Wydawnictwo Naukowe, Warsaw.
Christie, R. and Geis, F. (1970). "Studies in Machiavellianism". Academic Press, New York and London.
Chudnovsky, V. E. (1963). Concerning the age approach to typological features. *Voprosy Psikhologii* **9**, 23–34 (in Russian).
Chuprikova, N. I. (1977). The analysis of psychological structure and physiological mechanisms of activity as a condition of the diagnosis of nervous system properties. *In* (A. A. Smirnov, ed.) "Psychology and psychophysiology of individual differences". Pedagogika, Moscow (in Russian).
Ciosek, M. and Oszmiańczuk, J. (1974). Właściwości procesów nerwowych a ekstrawersja i neurotyzm. *Przegląd Psychologiczny* **17**, 235–246.
Colquhoun, W. P. (1971). Circadian variations in mental efficiency. *In* (W. P. Colquhoun, ed.) "Biological rhythms and human performance". Academic Press, New York and London.
Conrad, K. (1963). "Der Konstitutionstypus. Theoretiche Grundlegung und praktische Bestimmung" (2nd ed.). Springer Verlag, Berlin.
Cymes, I. (1974). "Reaktywność a indywidualny styl pracy umysłowej ucznia—na przykładzie uczenia się tekstu biologicznego". Unpublished M.A. Thesis, University of Warsaw.

Cytawa, J. (1959). Badanie typu układu nerwowego człowieka na podstawie wywiadu. *Annales Universitatis Mariae Curie-Skłodowska* **14**, 137–156.
Cytawa, J. and Jakubowicz, J. (1961). Ergograficzne badania zjawiska znużenia a typ układu nerwowego. *Acta Physiologica Polonica* **12**, 185–194.
Czyżkowska, A. M. (1974). "Wpływ poziomu reaktywności i rodzaju instrukcji na wykonywanie zadań". Unpublished M.A. Thesis, University of Warsaw.
Danch, I. (1974). Manifestation of individual nervous system properties in an apprentice-turner under different conditions of activity. *In* (K. M. Gurevich, ed.) "Psychophysiological problems of higher level professional experience". Vol. 1. Sovetskaya Rossiya, Moscow (in Russian).
Danielak, M. (1972). "Reaktywność a wybór zawodów związanych z różnym stopniem natężenia stymulacji". Unpublished M.A. thesis, University of Warsaw.
Danilova, N. N. (1961). Changes in electrical activity of the brain in response to a pulsing light corresponding to the alpha frequencies. *Zhurnal vysshei nervnoi Deyatelnosti* **11**, 12–21 (in Russian).
Davidenkov, S. N. (1947). "Problems of evolutionary genetics in neuropathology". Izdatelstvo GIUV im. Kirova, Leningrad (in Russian).
Davydova, A. N. (1954). Monographic study of children with features of various types of nervous system. *Izvestiya Academii Pedagogicheskikh Nauk RSFSR* **52**, 141–183 (in Russian).
Diamond, S. (1957) "Personality and temperament". Harper and Row, New York.
Dolin, A. O. (1936). New material for the physiological understanding of association in man. (The photochemical conditioned reflex in the eye). *Arkhiv biologicheskikh Nauk* **42**, 275–284 (in Russian).
Dorfman, L. Ya. (1976). The effect of music's tempo and harmony on the dynamics of efficiency restitution after physical overload depending on the strength of the nervous system. (B. A. Vyatkin, ed.) *In* "Temperament and sport". Vol. 3. MP RSFSR, PGPI and UOOP, Perm (in Russian).
Duffy, E. (1951). The concept of energy mobilization. *Psychological Review* **58**, 30–40.
Duffy, E. (1957). The psychological significance of the concept of "arousal" or "activation". *Psychological Review* **64**, 265–275.
Duffy, E. (1962). "Activation and behavior". Wiley, New York.
Edwards, W. (1953). Probability preferences in gambling. *American J. Psychology* **66**, 349–364.
Eliasz, A. (1972). Postulaty metodyczne ważne przy diagnozie temperamentu. *Psychologia Wychowawcza* **15**, 62–75.
Eliasz, A. (1973). Temperament traits and reaction preferences depending on stimulation load. *Polish Psychological Bulletin* **4**, 103–114.
Eliasz, A. (1974). "Temperament a osobowość". Ossolineum, Wroclaw–Warsaw.
Eliasz, A. (1979). Temporal stability of reactivity. *Polish Psychological Bulletin* **10**, 187–198.

Eliasz, A. (1981). "Temperament a system regulacji stymulacji". Państwowe Wydawnictwo Naukowe, Warsaw.
Elkin, D. G., Belenkaya, L. Ya., and Zimienko, V. D. (1961). The ergographic method for assessing the typological features of higher nervous activity in man. *Voprosy Psikhologii* **7**, 157–164.
Erlenmeyer-Kimling, L. and Jarvik, L. F. (1963). Genetics and intelligence: a review. *Science* **142**, 1477–1479.
Ewald, G. (1924). "Temperament und Charakter". Springer Verlag, Berlin.
Eysenck, H. J. (1947). "Dimensions of personality". Kegan Paul, Trench, Trubner and Co., London.
Eysenck, H. J. (1957). "The dynamics of anxiety and hysteria". Routledge and Kegan Paul, London.
Eysenck, H. J. (1963). Comment on the relation of neuroticism and extraversion to intelligence and educational attainment. *British J. Educational Psychology* **33**, 192.
Eysenck, H. J. (1965). Extraversion and the acquisition of eye-blink and GSR conditional responses. *Psychological Bulletin* **63**, 258–270.
Eysenck, H. J. (1966). "Conditioning, introversion-extraversion and the strength of the nervous system". Paper presented at the meeting of the International Congress of Psychology, Moscow.
Eysenck, H. J. (1967). "The biological basis of personality". Thomas, Springfield.
Eysenck, H. J. (1970). "The structure of human personality". Methuen, London.
Eysenck, H. J. (1972). Human typology, higher nervous activity, and factor analysis. *In* (V. D. Nebylitsyn and J. A. Gray, eds) "Biological bases of individual behavior". Academic Press, New York and London.
Eysenck, H. J. (ed.) (1981). "A model for personality". Springer Verlag, Berlin and New York.
Eysenck, H. J. (in press). Pavlovian concepts and personality dimensions: The nature of modern typology. *In* (G. L. Mangan and T. J. H. Paisey, eds) "Contemporary approaches to temperament and personality: An East–West dialogue". Pergamon Press, Oxford.
Eysenck, H. J. and Levey, A. (1972). Conditioning, introversion–extraversion and the strength of the nervous system. *In* (V. D. Nebylitsyn and J. A. Gray, eds) "Biological bases of individual behavior". Academic Press, New York and London.
Eysenck, S. B. G. and Zuckerman, M. (1978). The relationship between sensation seeking and Eysenck's dimensions of personality. *British J. Psychology* **69**, 483–487.
Fahrenberg, J. (1980). "A multivariate study of activation processes—operationalization and prediction of individual differences". Paper presented at the meeting of the International Congress of Psychology, Leipzig.
Fedorov, V. K. (1951). Senile changes in mobility of nervous processes. *Fiziologicheskii Zhurnal SSSR* **37**, 446–452 (in Russian).

Fedorov, V. K. (1953). The effects of training of nervous systems of parent mice on the mobility of nervous processes in offspring. *Trudy Instituta Fiziologii im. I. P. Pavlova* **2**, 276–286 (in Russian).
Fedorov, V. K. (1961). Comparison of results of different studies of basic properties of higher nervous activity in mice. *Zhurnal vysshei nervnoi Deyatelnosti* **11**, 746–752 (in Russian).
Fedorov, V. K. (1962a). Investigation of higher nervous activity of four generations of descendants of specially trained and control parents by the method of motor avoidance conditioned reflexes. *Trudy Instituta Fiziologii im. I. P. Pavlova* **10**, 143–151 (in Russian).
Fedorov, V. K. (1962b). Some results of investigation of typological features of higher nervous activity in animals. *Doklady Akademii Nauk SSSR* **142**, 1432–1435 (in Russian).
Fedorov, V. K. (1964). Validity of some indices of mobility of the nervous processes. *In* (V. N. Chernigovsky, ed.) "Methods of study of typological features of higher nervous activity in animals". Nauka, Moscow and Leningrad (in Russian).
Fedorov, V. K. (ed.) (1969). "Behaviour genetics". Nauka, Leningrad (in Russian).
Festinger, L. (1957). "A theory of cognitive dissonance". Stanford University Press, Stanford.
Fiske, D. W. and Maddi, S. R. (eds) (1961). "Functions of varied experience". Dorsey Press, Homewood.
Frankenhaeuser, M., Nordheden, B., Myrsten, A. L. and Post, B. (1971). Psychophysiological reactions to understimulation and overstimulation. *Acta Psychologica* **35**, 298–308.
Franks, C. M. (1956). Conditioning and personality: A study of normal and neurotic subjects. *J. Abnormal and Social Psychology* **52**, 143–150.
Franks, C. M. (1957). Personality factors and rate of conditioning. *British J. Psychology* **48**, 119–126.
Frączek, A. (1979). Functions of emotional and cognitive mechanisms in the regulation of aggressive behavior. *In* (S. Feshbach and A. Frączek, eds) "Aggression and behavior change. Biological and social processes". Praeger Publishers, New York.
Freeman, G. L. (1948). "The energetics of human behavior". Cornell University Press, Ithaca, New York.
Friedensberg, E. (1974). "Reaktywność a indywidualny styl pracy umysłowej ucznia—na przykładzie uczenia się tekstu geograficznego". Unpublished M.A. Thesis, University of Warsaw.
Friedensberg, E. (1982). Skala ocen jako narzędzie do pomiaru reaktywności. *In* (J. Strelau, ed.) "Regulacyjne funkcje temperamentu" Ossolineum, Wroclaw–Warsaw.
Friedensberg, E. (in press). Reactivity and individual style of work exemplified by constructional-type task performance: A developmental study. *In* (J. Strelau, F. H. Farley, and A. Gale, eds) "The biological foundations of personality and behavior". Hemisphere Publishing Corporation, Washington and London.

Friedman, I. (1955). Fenomenal, ideal and projected conceptions of self. *J. Abnormal and Social Psychology* **51**, 611–615.
Friedman, M. and Rosenman, R. H. (1974). "Type A behavior and your heart". Knopf, New York.
Frigon, J. Y. (1976). Extraversion, neuroticism and strength of the nervous system. *British J. Psychology* **67**, 467–474.
Furukawa, T. (1927). A study of temperament by means of human blood groups. *Japanese J. Psychology* **4**, 613–634.
Gagné, R. M. (ed.) (1967). "Learning and individual differences". C. E. Merrill Books, Columbus, Ohio.
Gale, A. (1973). The psychophysiology of individual differences: Studies of extraversion and the EEG". *In*(P. Kline, ed.) "New approaches in psychological measurement". Wiley, New York.
Gale, A. (1981). EEG studies of extraversion–introversion. *In* (R. Lynn, ed.) "Dimensions of personality. Papers in honour of H. J. Eysenck". Pergamon Press, Oxford and Frankfurt.
Gale, A., Coles, M., and Blaydon, J. (1969). Extraversion–introversion and the EEG. *British J. Psychology* **60**, 209–223.
Gantman, Yu. N. (1977). Self-evaluation of aptitude by students in connection with individual differences in the strength of the nervous system. *In* (K. M. Gurevich and Yu. L. Syerda, eds) "Problems of psychological diagnosis. Theory and practice". NIIP ESSR, Tallinn (in Russian).
Gardner, R. W. (1964). The development of cognitive structure. *In* (C. Sheerer, ed.) "Cognition: Theory, research, promise". Harper and Row, New York.
Gardner, R. W. and Schoen, R. A. (1962). Differentiation and abstraction in concept formation. *Psychological Monographs* **76**, 1–21.
Gastaut, H. (1954). The brain stem and cerebral electrogenesis in relation to consciousness. *In* (J. F. Delafresnaye, ed.) "Brain mechanisms and consciousness". Thomas, Springfield.
Gastaut, H., Gastaut, G., Roget, A., Corriol, J., and Naquet, R. (1951). Étude électrographique du cycle d'excitabilité cortical. *Electroencephalography and Clinical Neurophysiology* **3**, 401–428.
Gerasimov, V. P. (1976). Some peculiarities of school children's learning activity in connection with their characteristics in the mobility of nervous processes. *Voprosy Psikhologii* **22**, 108–113 (in Russian).
Gerstmann, S., Orlikowska, H. and Urbańska, J. (1961). "Cechy temperamentu i ich zmienność u dzieci". TNT, Toruń.
Gilliland, K. (in press). Comparisons between nervous system typology and extraversion. *In* (J. Strelau, F. H. Farley, and A. Gale, eds) "The biological foundations of personality and behavior". Hemisphere Publishing Corporation, Washington and London.
Glass, D. C. and Singer, J. E. (1972). "Urban stress: Experiments on noise and social stressors". Academic Press, New York and London.
Golikov, N. V. (1950). "Physiological lability and its changes in the basic nervous processes". Leningrad University Press, Leningrad (in Russian).
Golikov, N. V. (1956). Physiological bases of EEG theory. *In* (N. V. Golikov

and V. N. Myasishchev, eds) "Problems in the theory and practice of electroencephalography". Leningrad University Press, Leningrad (in Russian).
Golubeva, E. A. (1963). An attempt to investigate the re-establishment of brain biopotentials as an index of individual differences in equilibrium of nervous processes. *In* (B. M. Teplov, ed.) "Typological features of higher nervous activity in man". Vol. 3. RSFSR Academy of Pedagogical Sciences, Moscow (in Russian).
Golubeva, E. A. (1965). The re-establishment of brain biopotentials and typological properties of the nervous system. *In* (B. M. Teplov, ed.) "Typological features of higher nervous activity in man". Vol. 4. Prosveshcheniye, Moscow (in Russian).
Golubeva, E. A. (1972a). On the study of bioelectrical correlates of memory in differential psychophysiology. *Voprosy Psikhologii* **18**, 25–36 (in Russian).
Golubeva, E. A. (1972b). The driving reaction as a method of study in differential psychophysiology. *In* (V. D. Nebylitsyn and J. A. Gray, eds) "Biological bases of individual behavior". Academic Press, New York and London.
Golubeva, E. A. (1975). Unconditioned- and conditioned-reflex characteristics of individual differences and the problem of nervous system properties' splitting. *In* (B. A. Nikityuk, ed.) "Differential psychophysiology and its genetic aspects". SSSR Academy of Pedagogical Sciences, Moscow (in Russian).
Golubeva, E. A. (1980a). "Individual properties of human memory (psychophysiological study)". Pedagogika, Moscow (in Russian).
Golubeva, E. A. (1980b). Some problems of the experimental study of the inborn prerequisites of general capacities. *Voprosy Psikhologii* **26**, 23–37 (in Russian).
Golubeva, E. A. (1980c). On typological premises of some involuntary and voluntary functions. *In* (V. M. Rusalov and E. A. Golubeva, eds) "Psychophysiological investigations on intellectual self-regulation and activity". Nauka, Moscow (in Russian).
Golubeva, E. A. and Guseva, E. P. (1972). Properties of the nervous system as a factor of efficiency in involuntary and voluntary memorization. *In* (V. D. Nebylitsyn, ed.) "Problems of differential psychophysiology". Vol. 7. Pedagogika, Moscow (in Russian).
Golubeva, E. A., Guseva, E. P., and Izyumova, S. A. (1977a). The lability-inertia property, memory and trace processes. *In* (A. A. Smirnov, ed.) "Psychology and psychophysiology of individual differences". Pedagogika, Moscow (in Russian).
Golubeva, E. A., Izyumova, S. A., and Pechenkov, V. V. (1977b). Parameters of the evoked potentials and their relation to the efficiency of involuntary and voluntary memory. In (M. N. Borisova *et al.*, eds) "Problems of differential psychophysiology". Vol. 9. Pedagogika, Moscow (in Russian).
Golubeva, E. A., Izyumova, S. A., Trubnikova, R. S., and Pechenkov, V. V. (1974). Relationship between EEG rhythms and basic nervous system

properties. *In* (V. D. Nebylitsyn, ed.) "Problems of differential psychophysiology". Electrophysiological studies on the fundamental properties of the nervous system. Vol. 8. Nauka, Moscow (in Russian).
Golubeva, E. A. and Rozhdestvenskaya, V. I. (1969). Changes of brain biopotentials in the course of mental activity and typological differences in lability and dynamism of the nervous system. *In* (V. D. Nebylitsyn, ed.) "Problems of differential psychophysiology". Vol. 6. Prosveshcheniye, Moscow (in Russian).
Golubeva, E. A. and Rozhdestvenskaya, V. I. (1976). On the psychological manifestations of the properties of the nervous system. *Voprosy Psikhologii* **22**, 37–44 (in Russian).
Golubeva, E. A. and Rozhdestvenskaya, V. I. (1978). Psychological manifestation of the strength of the nervous system. *In* (V. V. Davydov, ed.) "Problems of general, developmental and pedagogical psychology". Pedagogika, Moscow (in Russian).
Golubeva, E. A. and Shvarts, L. A. (1965). The relationship of biological indices of lability with CFF and speed of restoration of light sensitivity. *In* (B. M. Teplov, ed.) "Typological features of higher nervous activity in man". Vol. 4. Prosveshcheniye, Moscow (in Russian).
Golubeva, E. A. and Trubnikova, R. S. (1971). On the correlations between efficiency of memory and strength of the nervous system. *Voprosy Psikhologii* **17**, 121–124 (in Russian).
Golubeva, E. A. and Vasilenko, T. K. (1965). Effect of caffeine on the bioelectric potential indices in early stages of psychic fatigue. *In* (B. M. Teplov, ed.) "Typological features of higher nervous activity in man". Vol. 4. Prosveshcheniye, Moscow (in Russian).
Gorbacheva, V. A. (1954). An attempt to study individual and typological features of three-year-old children. *Izvestiya Academii Pedagogicheskikh Nauk RSFSR* **52**, 6–39 (in Russian).
Gorbunov, V. V. (1973). EEG investigation, different typological characteristics of higher nervous activity and professional selection. *In* "Psychophysiological bases of professional selection". Kiev (in Russian).
Gordeyeva, A. K. and Klyagin, V. S. (1977). On some manifestations of the strength of the nervous system in the bus driver's activity. *Voprosy Psikhologii* **23**, 137–142 (in Russian).
Gorozhanin, V. S. (1977). Regulation of motor activity as a problem of differential psychophysiology. *Voprosy Psikhologii* **23**, 52–63 (in Russian).
Goryńska, E. (1982). Podstawowe cechy charakterystyki czasowej zachowania i ich pomiar metodą kwestionariusza. *In* (J. Strelau, ed.) "Regulacyjne funkcje temperamentu". Ossolineum, Wroclaw–Warsaw.
Goryńska, E. and Strelau, J. (1979). Basic traits of the temporal characteristics of behavior and their measurement by an inventory technique. *Polish Psychological Bulletin* **10**, 199–207.
Gray, J. A. (1964). "Pavlov's typology". Pergamon Press, Oxford and Frankfurt.
Gray, J. A. (1967). Strength of the nervous system, introversion-extraversion, conditionability and arousal. *Behavior Research and Therapy* **5**, 151–169.

Gray, J. A. (1970). The physiological basis of introversion-extraversion. *Behavior Research and Therapy* **8**, 249–266.

Gray, J. A. (1972a). Learning theory, the conceptual nervous system and personality. *In* (V. D. Nebylitsyn and J. A. Gray, eds) "Biological bases of individual behavior". Academic Press, New York and London.

Gray, J. A. (1972b). The psychophysiological nature of introversion-extraversion: A modification of Eysenck's theory. *In* (V. D. Nebylitsyn and J. A. Gray, eds) "Biological bases of individual behavior". Academic Press, New York and London.

Gray, J. A. (1978). The 1977 Myers Lecture: The neuropsychology of anxiety. *British J. Psychology* **69**, 417–434.

Gray, J. A. (1981). A critique of Eysenck's theory of personality. *In* (H. J. Eysenck, ed.) "A model for personality". Springer Verlag, Berlin and New York.

Grodner, M. (1973). "Wpływ siły układu nerwowego i poziomu lęku na wyniki próby motorycznej w sytuacji współzawodnictwa u chłopców w wieku 12–15 lat." Unpublished M.A. thesis, University of Warsaw.

Grzegołowska-Klarkowska, H. (1980). Use of defence mechanisms as determined by reactivity and situation level of activation. *Polish Psychological Bulletin* **11**, 155–168.

Guilford, J. P. (1956). "Fundamental statistics in psychology and education". McGraw-Hill, New York.

Guilford, J. P. and Zimmerman, W. S. (1956). Fourteen dimensions of temperament. *Psychological Monographs* **70**, 1–26.

Gurevich, K. M. (1959a). The role of stimulus intensity in "alteration" of choice reaction. *In* (B. M. Teplov, ed.) "Typological features of higher nervous activity in man". Vol. 2. RSFSR Academy of Pedagogical Sciences, Moscow (in Russian).

Gurevich, K. M. (1959b). The elaboration and change of the dynamic stereotype in the assessment of mobility of nervous processes in man. *In* (B. M. Teplov, ed.) "Typological features of higher nervous activity in man". Vol. 2. RSFSR Academy of Pedagogical Sciences, Moscow (in Russian).

Gurevich, K. M. (1965). On the validity of laboratory tests of strength and balance of nervous processes. *In* (B. M. Teplov, ed.) "Typological features of higher nervous activity in man". Vol. 4. Prosveshcheniye, Moscow (in Russian).

Gurevich, K. M. (1970). "Professional fitness and basic nervous system properties". Nauka, Moscow (in Russian).

Gurevich, K. M. (ed.) (1974). "Psychophysiological problems of higher level professional experience". Vol. 1. Sovetskaya Rossiya, Moscow (in Russian).

Gurevich, K. M., Klyagin, V. S., and Serkov, M. I. (1975). The diagnosis of individual psychophysiological traits of drivers in relation to professional reliability. *In* (K. M. Gurevich and V. I. Lubovsky, eds) "Psychological diagnosis: Problems and methods". SSSR Academy of Pedagogical Sciences, Moscow (in Russian).

Gurevich, K. M. and Matveyev, V. F. (1966). On the professional fitness of operators: Theory and assessment. *In* (B. M. Teplov and K. M. Gurevich,

eds) "Problems of professional fitness of power plants operation section staff". Prosveshcheniye, Moscow (in Russian).
Gurevich, V. C. and Kolesnikov, M. S. (1955). Determination of type of nervous system in animals under freely moving conditions. *Fiziologicheskii Zhurnal SSSR* **41**, 339–345 (in Russian).
Guseva, E. P. (1975). The relation of involuntary and voluntary memorizing to some EEG characteristics in adolescents and adults, *Voprosy Psikhologii* **21**, 128–135 (in Russian).
Guseva, E. P. and Shlakhta, N. F. (1974). Some features of bioelectric brain activity indices in adolescents. *In* (V. D. Nebylitsyn, ed.) "Problems of differential psychophysiology. Electrophysiological studies on the fundamental properties of the nervous system". Vol. 8. Nauka, Moscow (in Russian).
Haber, R. N. (1958). Discrepancy from adaptation level as a source of effect. *J. Experimental Psychology* **56**, 370–375.
Halmiová, O. (1978). Einfluss der Eigenschaften des Nervensystems auf die Kategorisierungsprozesse im Gedächtnis. *Studia Psychologica* **20**, 213–216.
Halmiová, O. (1980). Effect of properties of the nervous system on performance in search task. *Studia Psychologica* **22**, 195–199 (in Russian).
Halmiová, O. and Šebová, E. (1978). Effect of properties of the nervous system and activation level on recall. *Studia Psychologica* **20**, 305–308.
Halmiová, O. and Šebová, E. (in press). Nervous system properties and coding processes. *In* (J. Strelau, F. H. Farley, and A. Gale, eds) "The biological foundations of personality and behavior". Hemisphere Publishing Corporation, Washington and London.
Halmiová, O. and Uherik, A. (1972). A note on the criteria of dynamism of the nervous processes. *In* (V. D. Nebylitsyn and J. A. Gray, eds) "Biological bases of individual behavior". Academic Press, New York and London.
Haslam, D. R. (1972). Experimental pain. *In* (V. D. Nebylitsyn and J. A. Gray, eds) "Biological bases of individual behavior". Academic Press, New York and London.
Hebb, D. O. (1955). Drives and the C.N.S. (conceptual nervous system). *Psychological Review* **62**, 243–254.
Helson, H. (1964). "Adaptation-level theory. An experimental and systematic approach to behavior". Harper and Row, New York and London.
Heymans, G. and Wiersma, E. D. (1906–1909). Beiträge zur speziellen Psychologie auf Grund einer Massenuntersuchung. *Zeitschrift für Psychologie* **42**, 81–127; **43**, 321–373; **45**, 1–42; **46**, 321–333; **49**, 414–439; **51**, 1–72.
Hjelle, L. A. and Ziegler, D. J. (1981). "Personality theories". McGraw-Hill, New York.
Hull, C. L. (1943). "Principles of behavior. An introduction to behavior theory". Appleton-Century-Crofts, New York.
Ilin, E. P. (1975). On the physiological basis of the manifestation of strength-weakness of the nervous system. *In* (B. A. Nikityuk, ed.) "Differential psychophysiology and its genetic aspects". SSSR Academy of Pedagogical Sciences, Moscow (in Russian).

Ilin, E. P. (1978). "A study of nervous system properties". Yaroslavl University Press, Yaroslavl (in Russian).
Ilina, A. I. (1961). "Sociability and temperament in school children". Permskoye Knizhnoye Izdatelstvo, Perm (in Russian).
Ilina, A. I. and Paley, I. M. (1958). The method of anamnesis in the study of types of higher nervous activity. *In* (V. S. Merlin, ed.) "Problems of psychology of personality in relation to types of higher nervous activity". Permskii Gosudarstvennyi Pedagogicheskii Institut, Perm (in Russian).
Ilina, G. N. (1959). Extinctive and differential inhibition as shown in responses "of the reverse sign". *In* (B. M. Teplov, ed.) "Typological features of higher nervous activity in man". Vol. 2. RSFSR Academy of Pedagogical Sciences, Moscow (in Russian).
Ippolitov, F. V. (1966). Materials on interanalyser differences in the strength of the nervous system in man. *Voprosy Psikhologii* **12**, 83–91 (in Russian).
Ippolitov, F. V. (1967). Interanalyser differences in the parameter of sensitivity-strength (excitation) for vision, hearing and touch. *In* (B. M. Teplov, ed.) "Typological features of higher nervous activity in man". Vol. 5. Prosveshcheniye, Moscow (in Russian).
Ippolitov, F. V. (1969). On the rate of conditioning of photochemical reflexes to visual, acoustic and tactile stimuli. *In* (V. D. Nebylitsyn, ed.) "Problems of differential psychophysiology". Vol. 6. Prosveshcheniye, Moscow (in Russian).
Ippolitov, F. V. (1972). Interanalyser differences in the sensitivity-strength parameter for vision, hearing and cutaneous modalities. *In* (V. D. Nebylitsyn and J. A. Gray, eds) "Biological bases of individual behavior". Academic Press, New York and London.
Ivanov-Smolensky, A. G. (1935). The experimental investigation of higher nervous activity in children. *Fiziologicheskii Zhurnal SSSR* **19**, 133–140 (in Russian).
Ivanov-Smolensky, A. G. (1952). "Essays on the pathophysiology of the higher nervous activity". Medgiz, Moscow (in Russian).
Ivanov-Smolensky, A. G. (1953). The study of types of higher nervous activity in animals and man. *Zhurnal vysshei nervnoi Deyatelnosti* **3**, 36–54 (in Russian).
Ivanova, M. P. (1957). Investigation of higher nervous activity in adolescents in conditions of sporting practice. *Zhurnal vysshei nervnoi Deyatelnosti* **7**, 519–523 (in Russian).
Izyumova, S. A. (1976). Properties of the nervous system in the anterior and posterior regions of the brain and man's voluntary memory. *Voprosy Psikhologii* **22**, 124–129 (in Russian).
Izyumova, S. A. (1977). Stable characteristics of asymmetry as indices of lability and their relation to information processing and information storage. *In* (M. N. Borisova *et al.*, eds) "Problems of differential psychophysiology". Vol. 9. Pedagogika, Moscow (in Russian).
Izyumova, S. A. (1980). Activatability trait, information processing, and

information storage in man. *In* (V. M. Rusalov and E. A. Golubeva, eds) "Psychophysiological investigations on intellectual self-regulation and activity". Nauka, Moscow (in Russian).

Izyumova, S. A. and Aminov, N. A. (1978). On the physiological nature of connections between the emotional stability and the properties of the nervous system in man. *Voprosy Psikhologii* **24**, 128–133 (in Russian).

Izyumova, S. A., Golubeva, E. A., Guseva, E. P., Trubnikova-Morgunova, R. S., and Pechenkov, V. V. (1977). Statistical analysis of some background and reactive indices of the electroencephalogram. *In* (M. N. Borisova *et al.*, eds) "Problems of differential psychophysiology". Vol. 9. Pedagogika, Moscow (in Russian).

Jasper, H. and Shagass, C. (1941). Conditioning the occipital alpha rhythm in man. *J. Experimental Psychology* **28**, 373–388.

Jung, C. G. (1960). "Psychologische Typen" Gesammelte Werke, Vol. 6. Rascher Verlag, Zürich and Stuttgart.

Kachura, L. P. (1965). On the type of higher nervous activity in hysterics. *In* "Clinic problems, pathophysiology, and treatment of psychological diseases". Lugansk Medical College Press, Lugansk (in Russian).

Kagan, J. (1966). Developmental studies in reflection and analysis. *In* (A. H. Kidd and J. L. Rivoire, eds) "Perceptual development in children". Inter. University Press, New York.

Kagan, J., Moss, H. A., and Siegel, I. E. (1973). Psychological significance of styles of conceptualization. *In* (J. C. Wright and J. Kagan, eds) "Basic cognitive processes in children". The University of Chicago Press, Chicago.

Kant, I. (1943). "Anthropologie in pragmatischer Hinsicht". Verlag von Philipp Reclam, Leipzig.

Kapustin, A. N. (1972). Study of aspiration level in athletes in relation to individual differences in strength of the nervous system. *In* (B. A. Vyatkin, ed.) "Temperament and sport". Vol. 1. MP RSFSR, PGPI and UOOP, Perm (in Russian).

Kapustin, A. N. (1976). The change of aspiration level under stress in sportsmen in relation to the features of the neuro-psycho-dynamics. *In* (B. A. Vyatkin, ed.) "Temperament and sport". Vol. 3. MP RSFSR, PGPI and UOOP, Perm (in Russian).

Karpova, A. K. (1974). Generality and specificity in mathematical interrelations of orthogonal indices of temperament features in different social-developmental samples. *In* (V. S. Merlin, ed.) "The problems of temperament theory". MP RSFSR and PGPI, Perm (in Russian).

Kashin, A. P. (1974). The method and technique of complex investigation of some psychophysiological features in man. *In* (N. M. Peysakhov, V. M. Shadrin, and A. P. Kashin, eds) "Problems of psychology of individual differences". Kazan University Press, Kazan (in Russian).

Kavetsky, R. E., Solodyuk, N. F., Vovk, S. I., Krasnovskaya, M. S., and Dzgoyeva, T. A. (1961). "Reactivity of the organism and type of nervous system". USSR Academy of Sciences, Kiev (in Russian).

Khalik, A. V. (1972). The influence of different sources of stress on the sportsmen's kinesthetic sensitivity in relation to strength of the nervous system. *In* (B. A. Vyatkin, ed.) "Temperament and sport". Vol. 1. MP RSFSR, PGPI and UOOP, Perm (in Russian).

Khilchenko, A. E. (1958). Methods of studying the mobility of basic nervous processes in man. *Zhurnal vysshei nervnoi Deyatelnosti* **8**, 945–948 (in Russian).

Khilchenko, A. E., Kurkchi, L. N. and Kurkchi, N. F. (1966). Developmental dynamics of mobility of man's basic nervous processes. *Voprosy Psikhologii* **12**, 123–128 (in Russian).

Khlebutina, T. A. (1962). The mobility of basic nervous processes in signal systems under different types of functional load. *Zhurnal vysshei nervnoi Deyatelnosti* **12**, 587–591 (in Russian).

Klimov, E. A. (1959). Individual occupational features of female textile multi-machine operators with respect to the mobility of nervous processes. *Voprosy Psikhologii* **5**, 66–76 (in Russian).

Klimov, E. A. (1969). "Individual style of activity determined by the typological properties of the nervous system". Kazan University Press, Kazan (in Russian).

Klonowicz, T. (1974a). Wpływ poziomu reaktywności i rodzaju instrukcji na wykonywanie prostych zadań konstrukcyjnych. *In* (J. Strelau, ed.) "Rola cech temperamentalnych w działaniu". Ossolineum, Wroclaw–Warsaw.

Klonowicz, T. (1974b). Reactivity and fitness for the occupation of operator. *Polish Psychological Bulletin* **5**, 129–136.

Klonowicz, T. (1974c). Próba zastosowania "prawa siły" do diagnozy reaktywności. *In* (J. Strelau, ed.) "Rola cech temperamentalnych w działaniu". Ossolineum, Wroclaw–Warsaw.

Klonowicz, T. (1979a). Transformation ability, temperament traits and individual experience. *Polish Psychological Bulletin* **10**, 215–223.

Klonowicz, T. (1979b). "Kwestionariusz do badania temperamentu" J. Strelaua–próba badań międzykulturowych. *Studia Psychologiczne* **18**, 83–92.

Klonowicz, T. (1982). Potrzeba stymulacji. Analiza pojęcia. *In* (J. Strelau, ed.) "Regulacyjne funkcje temperamentu". Ossolineum, Wroclaw–Warsaw.

Klonowicz, T. (in press, a). Reactivity and performance: The third side of the coin. *In* (J. Strelau, F. H. Farley, and A. Gale, eds) "The biological foundations of personality and behavior". Hemisphere Publishing Corporation, Washington and London.

Klonowicz, T. (in press, b). Temperament and performance. *In* (G. L. Mangan and T. J. H. Paisey, eds) "Contemporary approaches to temperament and personality: An East–West dialogue". Pergamon Press, Oxford.

Klyagin, V. S. (1974). Diagnostic relevance of individual stability of the total power EEG activity. *In* (K. M. Gurevich, ed.) "Psychophysiological problems of higher level professional experience". Vol. 1. Sovetskaya Rossiya, Moscow (in Russian).

# References

Klyagin, V. S. (1975). The significance of the type of nervous system for diagnosis of reliability of the management system. *In* (K. M. Gurevich and V. I. Lubovsky, eds) "Psychological diagnosis: Problems and methods". SSSR Academy of Pedagogical Sciences, Moscow (in Russian).

Klyagin, V. S., Gordeyeva, A. K., and Muldarov, V. K. (1977). Individual characteristics of the regulative activity of the central nervous system and their manifestations in indicators of car drivers' reliability. *In* (K. M. Gurevich and Yu. L. Syérda, eds) "Problems of psychological diagnosis: Theory and practice". Research Pedagogical Institute ESSR, Tallinn (in Russian).

Kłodecka-Rożalska, J. (1982). "Związek cech temperamentu chłopców w wieku 16–18 lat z poziomem wykonywania testu sprawności motorycznej w sytuacjach o różnym ładunku stymulacji". Unpublished Ph.D. thesis, University of Warsaw.

Kofta, M. (1979). "Samokontrola a emocje". Państwowe Wydawnictwo Naukowe, Warsaw.

Kokorina, E. P. (1963). Measurement of basic nervous processes in the determination of higher nervous activity using the motor method with food reinforcement. *Zhurnal vysshei nervnoi Deyatelnosti* **13**, 361–370 (in Russian).

Kokorina, E. P. (1971). The assessment of fundamental nervous processes on the basis of functional tests. *In* (V. K. Krasusky and V. K. Fedorov, eds) "Methods of assessment of properties of higher nervous activity". Nauka, Leningrad (in Russian).

Kolchenko, N. V. (1965). Mobility of fundamental nervous processes and efficiency of first and second signal systems in men differing in age. *In* (A. F. Makarchenko, ed.) "Physiology and pathology of higher nervous activity". Ldorovya, Kiev (in Russian).

Kolchina, L. P. (1976). The interrelation between behavioural-verbal indicators of social aggression and of aggression under frustration. *In* (V. S. Merlin, ed.) "Temperament". MP RSFSR and PGPI, Perm (in Russian).

Kolesnikov, M. S. (1953). Material on the description of the weak type of nervous system. *Trudy Instituta Fiziologii im. I. P. Pavlova* **2**, 120–135 (in Russian).

Kolesnikov, M. S. and Troshikhin, V. A. (1951). The small standard battery of tests for determining type of higher nervous activity in the dogs. *Zhurnal vysshei nervnoi Deyatelnosti* **1**, 739–743 (in Russian).

Komarova, T. F. (1971). Tolerance to glucose test as an assessment of the strength of the excitatory process in dogs. *In* (V. K. Krasusky and V. K. Fedorov, eds) "Methods of assessment of properties of higher nervous activity". Nauka, Leningrad (in Russian).

Konorski, J. (1958). Procesy pobudzenia i hamowania w korze mózgowej. *Acta Physiologica Polonica* **9**, 17–32.

Konorski, J. (1967). "Integrative activity of the brain". University of Chicago Press, Chicago.

Kopylov, A. G. (1956). Evaluation of the functional state of the human brain by the method of electroencephalographic curves of rhythm assimilation. *In* (N. V. Golikov and V. N. Myasishchev, eds) "Problems in the theory and practice of electroencephalography". Leningrad University Press, Leningrad (in Russian).

Kopytova, L. A. (1963). Expression of typological properties of the nervous system in the activity of machine operators when machines are idle. *Voprosy Psikhologii* **9**, 59–72 (in Russian).

Kopytova, L. A. (1964). Individual style of professional activity of operators determined by strength of the nervous system as regards excitation. *Voprosy Psikhologii* **10**, 24–33 (in Russian).

Kordyukova, M. R. (1977). The comparison of indices of mobility of the nervous system with some EEG indices. *In* (M. N. Borisova *et al.*, eds) "Problems of differential psychophysiology". Vol. 9. Pedagogika, Moscow (in Russian).

Kounin, J. S. (1943). Intellectual development and rigidity. *In* (R. G. Barker, J. S. Kounin, and H. R. Wright, eds) "Child behavior and development". McGraw-Hill, New York.

Kovač, D. and Halmiová, O. (1973). Is there a direct correlation between emotional stability and strength of nervous processes? *Studia Psychologica* **15**, 1–7.

Kozielecki, J. (1975). "Psychologiczna teoria decyzji". Państwowe Wydawnictwo Naukowe, Warsaw.

Kozlova, V. T. (1974). The manifestation of lability-inertia of the nervous processes in mental-verbal activity. *In* (K. M. Gurevich, ed.) "Psychophysiological problems of higher level professional experience". Vol. 1. Sovetskaya Rossiya, Moscow (in Russian).

Kozlova, V. T. (1975). The elaboration of diagnostic methods of mobility of nervous processes in mental-verbal activity. *In* (B. A. Nikityuk, ed.) "Differential psychophysiology and its genetic aspects". SSSR Academy of Pedagogical Sciences, Moscow (in Russian).

Kozlova, V. T. (1977). The study of manifestation of the mobility of nervous processes in cognitive-speech activity. *In* (K. M. Gurevich and Yu. L. Syérda, eds) "Problems of psychological diagnosis: Theory and practice". Research Pedagogical Institute ESSR, Tallinn (in Russian).

Kozłowski, C. (1977). Demand for stimulation and probability preferences in gambling decisions. *Polish Psychological Bulletin* **8**, 67–73.

Krasnogorsky, N. I. (1939). "Development of studies on the physiological activity of the brain in children". Biomedgir, Leningrad and Moscow (in Russian).

Krasnogorsky, N. I. (1953). Typological properties of higher nervous activity in children. *Zhurnal vysshei nervnoi Deyatelnosti* **3**, 169–183 (in Russian).

Krasnogorsky, N. I. (1954). "Studies on higher nervous activity of man and animals". Vol. 1. Medgiz, Moscow (in Russian).

Krasnogorsky, N. I. (1958). "Higher nervous activity in children". Medgiz, Leningrad (in Russian).

Krasuskaya, N. A. (1971). Assessment of strength of the excitatory process by means of caffeine administration. *In* (V. K. Krasusky and V. K. Fedorov, eds) "Methods of assessment of properties of higher nervous activity". Nauka, Leningrad (in Russian).
Krasusky, V. K. (1953). Methods of studying types of nervous system in animals. *Trudy Instituta Fiziologii im. I. P. Pavlova* **2**, 111–119 (in Russian).
Krasusky, V. K. (1959). Some evidence on the physiological characteristics of types of the nervous system. *Trudy Instituta Fiziologii im. I. P. Pavlova* **8**, 60–69 (in Russian).
Krasusky, V. K. (1963). Methods for estimating nervous system properties in dogs used in the Laboratory of Physiology and Genetics of Types of Higher Nervous Activity. *Zhurnal vysshei nervnoi Deyatelnosti* **13**, 165–176 (in Russian).
Krasusky, V. K. (1971). On some additional criteria of assessment of higher nervous activity properties. *In* (V. K. Krasusky and V. K. Fedorov, eds) "Methods of assessment of higher nervous activity properties". Nauka, Leningrad (in Russian).
Krasusky, V. K. and Fedorov, V. K. (eds) (1971). "Methods of assessment of higher nervous activity properties". Nauka, Leningrad (in Russian).
Kretschmer, E. (1944). "Körperbau und Charakter" (17/18th ed.). Springer Verlag, Berlin.
Kreutz, M. (1966). Analityczene badanie osobowości. *Nowa Szkoła* **5**, 36–39.
Krohne, H. W. and Laux, L. (eds) (1982). "Achievement, stress and anxiety". Hemisphere Publishing Corporation, Washington and London.
Król, T. Z. (1977). The relation between nervous system strength and aspiration level. *Polish Psychological Bulletin* **8**, 99–105.
Krupnov, A. I. (1970). An investigation into the relationship between EEG background indices and behavioural activity of dynamic characteristics. *Voprosy Psikhologii* **16**, 47–59 (in Russian).
Krushinsky, L. V. (1947). Inheritance of passive-defensive behaviour (cowardice) as connected with types of nervous system in the dog. *Trudy Instituta evolucionnoi Fiziologii i Patologii im. I. P. Pavlova* **1**, 39–62 (in Russian).
Kulagin, D. A. (1975). Emotionality and typological features of the nervous system in rats. *In* (B. A. Nikityuk, ed.) "Differential psychophysiology and its genetic aspects". SSSR Academy of Pedagogical Sciences, Moscow (in Russian).
Kupalov, P. S. (1952). Experimental neuroses in animals. *Zhurnal vysshei nervnoi Deyatelnosti* **2**, 457–473 (in Russian).
Kupalov, P. S. (1954). Theory of types of higher nervous activity in animals. *Zhurnal vysshei nervnoi Deyatelnosti* **4**, 3–19 (in Russian).
Lacey, J. I. (1950). Individual differences in somatic response patterns. *J. Comparative and Physiological Psychology* **43**, 338–350.
Lacey, J. I. (1956). The evaluation of autonomic responses: Toward a general solution. Reprinted from *Ann. N.Y. Acad. Sci.* **67**, 123–164.

Lang-Belonogova, N. S. and Kok, E. P. (1952). The significance of the study of anamnesis in patients for the determination of their type of higher nervous activity and for the elucidation of the functional state of the central nervous system prior to illness. *Trudy Instituta Fiziologii im. I. P. Pavlova* **1**, 493–506 (in Russian).

Lazarus, R. S. (1966). "Psychological stress and the coping process". McGraw-Hill, New York.

Leites, N. S. (1956a). Typological differences in the after-effects of the excitatory and inhibitory processes. *In* (B. M. Teplov, ed.) "Typological features of higher nervous activity in man". Vol. 1. RSFSR Academy of Pedagogical Sciences, Moscow (in Russian).

Leites, N. S. (1956b). An attempt to give a psychological description of temperaments. *In* (B. M. Teplov, ed.) "Typological features of higher nervous activity in man". Vol. 1. RSFSR Academy of Pedagogical Sciences, Moscow (in Russian).

Leites, N. S. (1963). Determination of equilibrium of the basic nervous processes by the method of delayed motor reactions. *In* (B. M. Teplov, ed.) "Typological features of higher nervous activity in man". Vol. 3. RSFSR Academy of Pedagogical Sciences, Moscow (in Russian).

Leites, N. S. (1972). Problems of interrelationship between typological features and age. *In* (V. D. Nebylitsyn and J. A. Gray, eds) "Biological bases of individual behavior". Academic Press, New York and London.

Leites, N. S., Golubeva, E. A., and Kadyrov, B. R. (1980). The dynamic aspect of mental activity and activatability of the brain. *In* (V. M. Rusalov and E. A. Golubeva, eds) "Psychophysiological investigations on intellectual self-regulation and activity". Nauka, Moscow (in Russian).

Leontev, A. N. (1978). "Activity, consciousness and personality". Prentice-Hall, Englewood Cliffs.

Leuba, C. (1965). Toward some integration of learning theory: The concept of optimal stimulation. *In* (H. Fowler, ed.) "Curiosity and exploratory behavior". Macmillan, New York.

Levey, A. B. and Martin, I. (1981). Personality and conditioning. *In* (H. J. Eysenck, ed.) "A model for personality". Springer Verlag, Berlin and New York.

Levitov, N. D. (1969). "Problems of the psychology of character". Prosveshcheniye, Moscow (in Russian).

Likhachev, L. V. (1976). Reciprocal effects of the social status, position in team and strength of the nervous system on interrelations during games of basketball players. B. A. Vyatkin (ed.) "Temperament and Sport". Vol. 3. MP RSFSR and UOOP, Perm (in Russian).

Lindsley, D. B. (1952). Psychological phenomena and the electroencephalogram. *Electroencephalography and Clinical Neurophysiology* **4**, 443–456.

Livanov, M. N. (1940). Unbalanced development of some specific EEG processes and of the Berger rhythm. *Fiziologicheskii Zhurnal SSSR* **28**, 157–171 (in Russian).

Lomov, B. F. and Ravich-Shcherbo, I. V. (eds) (1978). "The problems of genetic psychophysiology in man". Nauka, Moscow (in Russian).
Loo, R. (1978). Measurement of neo-Pavlovian properties of higher nervous activity by motor reaction-time tasks. *Pavlovian Journal of Biological Sciences* **13**, 265–269.
Loo, R. (1979). Neo-Pavlovian properties of higher nervous activity and Eysenck's personality dimensions. *International Journal of Psychology* **14**, 265–274.
Lovchikov, V. A. and Roshchina, L. V. (1971). The caffeine maximum dose as a criterion of typological distribution in dogs. *In* (V. K. Krasusky and V. K. Fedorov, eds) "Methods of assessment of properties of higher nervous activity". Nauka, Leningrad (in Russian).
Lovell, C. (1945). A study of the factor structure of thirteen personality variables. *Educational and Psychological Measurement* **5**, 335–350.
Lundberg, U. (1982). Psychophysiological aspects of performance and adjustment to stress. *In* (H. W. Krohne and L. Laux, eds) "Achievement, stress and anxiety". Hemisphere Publishing Corporation, Washington and London.
Lundberg, U. and Frankenhaeuser, M. (1978). Psychophysiological reactions to noise as modified by personal control over stimulus intensity. *Biological Psychology* **6**, 51–59.
Łukaszewski, W. (1974). "Osobowość: struktura i funkcje regulacyjne". Państwowe Wydawnictwo Naukowe, Warsaw.
Łukaszewski, W. (1975). Studia nad teorią czynności ludzkich (book review). *Psychologia Wychowawcza* **18**, 719–725.
Maciejczyk, J. (1974). Reaktywność a podejmowanie decyzji w sytuacji trudnej u pilotów. *In* (J. Strelau, ed.) "Rola cech temperamentalnych w działaniu". Ossolineum, Wroclaw–Warsaw.
Magnusson, D. and Endler, N. S. (eds) (1977). "Personality at the crossroads: Current issues in interactional psychology". Lawrence Erlbaum Associates, Hillsdale.
Maizel, N. I. (1956). The investigation of typological differences in the balance of the processes of excitation and inhibition by the photochemical conditioned reflex method. *In* (B. M. Teplov, ed.) "Typological features of higher nervous activity in man". Vol. 1. RSFSR Academy of Pedagogical Sciences, Moscow (in Russian).
Malkov, N. E. (1957). Individual differences in the formation of motor habits in high school children. "Proceedings of a conference on psychology (1–6 July, 1955)". RSFSR Academy of Pedagogical Sciences, Moscow (in Russian).
Malkov, N. E. (1966). The manifestation of individual-typological differences of nervous processes in intellectual abilities. *Voprosy Psikhologii* **12**, 38–48 (in Russian).
Malmo, R. B. (1957). Anxiety and behavioural arousal. *Psychological Review* **64**, 276–287.

Malmo, R. B. (1959). Activation: A neuropsychological dimension. *Psychological Review* **66**, 367–386.

Mangan, G. L. (1967a). Studies of the relationship between neo-Pavlovian properties of higher nervous activity and Western personality dimensions: II. The relation of mobility to perceptual flexibility. *J. Experimental Research in Personality* **2**, 107–116.

Mangan, G. L. (1967b). Studies of the relationship between neo-Pavlovian properties of higher nervous activity and Western personality dimensions: III. The relation of transformation mobility to thinking flexibility. *J. Experimental Research in Personality* **2**, 117–123.

Mangan, G. L. (1967c). Studies of the relationship between neo-Pavlovian properties of higher nervous activity and Western personality dimensions: IV. A factor analytic study of extraversion and flexibility, and the sensitivity and mobility of the nervous system. *J. Experimental Research in Personality* **2**, 124–127.

Mangan, G. L. (1978). The relationship of mobility of inhibition to rate of inhibitory growth and measures of flexibility, extraversion, and neuroticism. *J. General Psychology* **99**, 271–279.

Mangan, G. L. (1982). "The Biology of Human Conduct: East–West models of temperament and personality". Pergamon Press, Oxford.

Mangan, G. L. and Farmer, R. G. (1967). Studies of the relationship between neo-Pavlovian properties of higher nervous activity and Western personality dimensions: I. The relationship of nervous strength and sensitivity to extraversion. *J. Experimental Research in Personality* **2**, 101–106.

Mangan, G. L. and Paisey, T. J. H. (1980). New perspectives in temperament/personality research: The "behavioral" model of the Warsaw group. *Pavlovian J. Biological Sciences* **15**, 159–171.

Mann, R. D. (1959). A review of the relationships between personality and performance in small groups. *Psychological Bulletin* **56**, 241–270.

Markelov, V. V. (1976). Reciprocal effects of temperament and activity on success in competitions of accomplished athletes. *In* (B. A. Vyatkin, ed.) "Temperament and sport". Vol. 3. MP RSFSR, PGPI and UOOP, Perm (in Russian).

Marton, M. L. (1972). The theory of individual differences in neo-behaviourism and the typology of higher nervous activity. *In* (V. D. Nebylitsyn and J. A. Gray, eds) "Biological bases of individual behavior". Academic Press, New York and London.

Marton, L. and Urban, J. (1966). The relationship between typological personality traits and characteristics of the process of elaboration and extinction of conditioned links. *Voprosy Psikhologii* **12**, 92–100 (in Russian).

Maryutina, T. M. (1974). Visual evoked potentials in adults and children. *In* (V. D. Nebylitsyn, ed.) "Problems of differential psychophysiology. Electrophysiological studies on the fundamental properties of the nervous system". Vol. 8. Nauka, Moscow (in Russian).

Maryutina, T. M. (1978). On the genetic determinants of evoked potentials in man. *In* (B. F. Lomov and I. V. Ravich-Shcherbo, eds.) "The problems of genetic psychophysiology in man". Nauka, Moscow (in Russian).

Mastvilisker, E. I. (1967). The psychological determinants of the modes of reaction and kinds of activity in preschool children. *In* (V. S. Merlin, ed.) "Typological investigations in psychology of personality". UOOP and PGPI, Perm (in Russian).

Mastvilisker, E. I. (1973). The development of temperament in children. *In* (V. S. Merlin, ed.) "Outline of the theory of temperament" (2nd ed.). Permskoye Knizhnoye Izdatelstvo, Perm (in Russian).

Mastvilisker, E. I. and Dikopolskaya, G. E. (1976). Some conditions of the individual style's formation in preschool children learning. *In* (V. S. Merlin, ed.) "Temperament". MP RSFSR, and PGPI, Perm (in Russian).

Matczak, A. (1982a). Rozwojowe i temperamentalne uwarunkowania refleksyjności-impulsywności. *In* (J. Strelau, ed.) "Regulacyjne funkcje temperamentu". Ossolineum, Wroclaw–Warsaw.

Matczak, A. (1982b). "Style poznawcze. Rola indywidualnych preferencji w funkcjonowaniu". Państwowe Wydawnictwo Naukowe, Warsaw.

Matczak, A. (in press). The role of the cognitive style (abstraction–concretion) as regulator of the level of activation. *Polish Psychological Bulletin*.

Materska, M. (1972). "Treść przygotowania teoretycznego a struktura czynności praktycznych". Ossolineum, Wroclaw–Warsaw.

Materska, M. (1978). Programowanie ludzkiej działalności zadaniowej w świetle badań nad strukturą i efektywnością czynności wykonawczych. *Przegląd Psychologiczny* **21**, 425–443.

Mateyev, D. and Georgiyev, V. (1960). On the relation between fatigue and the type of higher nervous activity (ergographic data). *Fiziologicheskii Zhurnal SSSR* **46**, 141–147 (in Russian).

Matveyev, V. F. (1965). Psychological manifestation of the basic properties of the nervous system in power plant operators under conditions of simulated damage. *In* (B. M. Teplov, ed.) "Typological features of higher nervous activity in man". Vol. 4. Prosveshcheniye, Moscow (in Russian).

Matysiak, J. (1977). Reactivity in rats, measured by reaction time to nearthreshold stimuli, and "open field" behavior. *Polish Psychological Bulletin* **8**, 95–98.

Matysiak, J. (1980). "Różnice indywidualne w zachowaniu zwierząt w świetle koncepcji zapotrzebowania na stymulację". Ossolineum, Wroclaw–Warsaw.

Mayorov, F. P. (1962). Some problems in the theory of cortical inhibition. *Fiziologicheskii Zhurnal SSSR* **48**, 606–615 (in Russian).

Mayorov, F. P. and Troshikhin, V. A. (1952). The standard of nervous system type's investigation. *In* (N. A. Podkopayev) "Methods of studying conditioned reflexes". SSSR Academy of Sciences, Moscow and Leningrad (in Russian).

Melikhova, E. F. (1964). Correlation analysis of the results of different investigations of strength, balance and mobility of nervous processes in dogs. *Zhurnal vysshei nervnoi Deyatelnosti* **14**, 808–812 (in Russian).

Melnichenko, O. G. (1975). The study of individual properties of aspiration level in relation to some traits of the neurodynamics. *In* (B. A. Nikityuk, ed.) "Differential psychophysiology and its genetic aspects". SSSR Academy of Pedagogical Sciences, Moscow (in Russian).

Merlin, V. S. (1955). The role of temperament in emotional reaction to school mark. *Voprosy Psikhologii* **1**, 62–71 (in Russian).

Merlin, V. S. (1958). A method of testing the properties of the general type of higher nervous activity in man using the GSR. *Voprosy Psikhologii* **4**, 159–162 (in Russian).

Merlin, V. S. (ed.) (1964a). "Typological studies in psychology of personality and in industrial psychology". UOOP and PGPI, Perm (in Russian).

Merlin, V. S. (1964b). Typological differences in the influence of negative and positive estimation on the fluctuation of attention. *In* (V. S. Merlin, ed.) "Typological studies in psychology of personality and in industrial psychology". UOOP and PGPI, Perm (in Russian).

Merlin, V. S. (ed.) (1967a). "Typological investigations in psychology of personality". UOOP and PGPI, Perm (in Russian).

Merlin, V. S. (1967b). The interrelation between social-typological and individual factors in personality. *Voprosy Psikhologii* **13**, 34–43 (in Russian).

Merlin, V. S. (ed.) (1968). "Problems of experimental psychology of personality". Vol. 5. UOOP and PGPI, Perm (in Russian).

Merlin, V. S. (ed.) (1970a). "Problems of experimental psychology of personality". Vol. 6. UOOP and PGPI, Perm (in Russian).

Merlin, V. S. (1970b). The relationship between type and individual features of temperament. *Voprosy Psikhologii* **16**, 21–27 (in Russian).

Merlin, V. S. (ed.) (1971). "Experimental studies in personality and temperament". UOOP and PGPI, Perm (in Russian).

Merlin, V. S. (ed.) (1973). "Outline of the theory of temperament" (2nd ed.). Permskoye Knizhnoye Izdatelstvo, Perm (in Russian).

Merlin, V. S. (ed.) (1974). "The problems of temperament theory". MP RSFSR and PGPI, Perm (in Russian).

Merlin, V. S. (ed.) (1976a). "Temperament". MP RSFSR and PGPI, Perm (in Russian).

Merlin, V. S. (1976b). Problems of integral characteristics of individuality in differential psychophysiology. *In* (V. S. Merlin and B. A. Nikityuk, eds) "Problems of differential psychophysiology related to genetics". SSSR Academy of Pedagogical Sciences, Perm (in Russian).

Merlin, V. S. (ed.) (1977). "Theoretical bases, application, and methods of differential psychophysiology". MP RSFSR and PGPI, Perm (in Russian).

Merlin, V. S. and Mastvilisker, E. I. (1971). Some procedures of investigating the strength of excitatory process. *Voprosy Psikhologii* **17**, 151–155 (in Russian).

Merlin, V. S. and Nikityuk, B. A. (eds). "Problems of differential psychophysiology related to genetics". SSSR Academy of Pedagogical Sciences, Perm (in Russian).

Merlin, V. S., Pekhletsky, I. D. and Belous, V. V. (1967). On some relatively stable characteristics of temperament. *In* (V. S. Merlin, ed.) "Typological investigations in psychology of personality". UOOP and PGPI, Perm (in Russian).
Miller, G., Galanter, E. and Pribram, K. (1960). "Plans and the structure of behavior". Holt and Co., New York.
Mirkowska, A. (1976). "Poziom reaktywności a skłonność do zamierzonego oddziaływania na innych. Podatność na zmiany w nasileniu tych skłonności". Unpublished M.A. Thesis, University of Warsaw.
Morris, L. W. (1979). "Extraversion and introversion. An interactional perspective". Hemisphere Publishing Corporation, Washington and London.
Moruzzi, G. and Magoun, H. W. (1949). Brain stem reticular formation and activation of the EEG. *Electroencephalography and Clinical Neurophysiology* **1**, 455–473.
Mundy-Castle, A. C. (1953). An analysis of central responses to photic stimulation in normal adults. *Electroencephalography and Clinical Neurophysiology* **5**, 1–22.
Mundy-Castle, A. C. (1957). The electroencephalogram and mental activity. *Electroencephalography and Clinical Neurophysiology* **9**, 643–655.
Mündelein, H. (1981) "Informationsverarbeitung und Datensichtgeräten". Paper presented at the 23rd Convention of Experimental Industrial Psychologists, April 13–16, Berlin.
Nebylitsyn, V. D. (1956). The relationship between sensitivity and strength of the nervous system. *In* (B. M. Teplov, ed.) "Typological features of higher nervous activity in man". Vol. 1. RSFSR Academy of Pedagogical Sciences, Moscow (in Russian).
Nebylitsyn, V. D. (1957). Individual differences in strength-sensitivity in the visual and auditory analyzers. *Voprosy Psikhologii* **3**, 53–69 (in Russian).
Nebylitsyn, V. D. (1959a). Relationship between strength and sensitivity of the nervous system. *In* (B. M. Teplov, ed.) "Typological features of higher nervous activity in man". Vol. 2. RSFSR Academy of Pedagogical Sciences, Moscow (in Russian).
Nebylitsyn, V. D. (1959b). The typological significance of the speed of formation of a conditioned photochemical reflex. *In* (B. M. Teplov, ed.) "Typological features of higher nervous activity in man". Vol. 2. RSFSR Academy of Pedagogical Sciences, Moscow (in Russian).
Nebylitsyn, V. D. (1960a). The present state of factor analysis. *Voprosy Psikhologii* **6**, 45–60 (in Russian).
Nebylitsyn, V. D. (1960b). Reaction time and strength of nervous system. *Doklady Akademii Pedagogicheskikh Nauk RSFSR* **4**, 93–100; **5**, 71–74 (in Russian).
Nebylitsyn, V. D. (1961). Extinction with reinforcement of conditioned EEG as an index of strength of nervous system. *Doklady Akademii Pedagogicheskikh Nauk SSSR* **3**, 97–100 (in Russian).

Nebylitsyn, V. D. (1963a). The structure of the basic properties of the nervous system. *Voprosy Psikhologii* **9**, 21–34 (in Russian).

Nebylitsyn, V. D. (1963b). An electroencephalographic study of the properties of strength and balance of the nervous processes in man using factor analysis. *In* (B. M. Teplov, ed.) "Typological features of higher nervous activity in man". Vol. 3. RSFSR Academy of Pedagogical Sciences, Moscow (in Russian).

Nebylitsyn, V. D. (1964a). Cortico-reticular connections and their role in the structure of the properties of the nervous system. *Voprosy Psikhologii* **10**, 3–24 (in Russian).

Nebylitsyn, V. D. (1964b). The photic driving reaction as a function of the intensity of the pulsing light. *Zhurnal vysshei nervnoi Deyatelnosti* **14**, 569–576 (in Russian).

Nebylitsyn, V. D. (1965). Dynamism of nervous processes and individual differences in resting EEG in man. *In* (B. M. Teplov, ed.) "Typological features of higher nervous activity in man". Vol. 4. Prosveshcheniye, Moscow (in Russian).

Nebylitsyn, V. D. (1966). "Fundamental properties of the human nervous system". Prosveshcheniye, Moscow (in Russian).

Nebylitsyn, V. D. (ed.) (1969). "Problems of differential psychophysiology". Vol. 6. Prosveshcheniye, Moscow (in Russian).

Nebylitsyn, V. D. (1972a). "Fundamental properties of the human nervous system". Plenum Press, New York and London.

Nebylitsyn, V. D. (1972b). The problem of general and partial properties of the nervous system. *In* (V. D. Nebylitsyn and J. A. Gray, eds.) "Biological bases of individual behavior". Academic Press, New York and London.

Nebylitsyn, V. D. (ed.) (1972c). "Problems of differential psychophysiology". Vol. 7. Pedagogika, Moscow (in Russian).

Nebylitsyn, V. D. (ed.) (1974). "Problems of differential psychophysiology. Electrophysiological investigations of the fundamental properties of the nervous system". Vol. 8. Nauka, Moscow (in Russian).

Nebylitsyn, V. D. (1976). "Psychophysiological investigations of individual differences". Nauka, Moscow (in Russian).

Nebylitsyn, V. D., Golubeva, E. A., Ravich-Shcherbo, I. V., and Yermolayeva-Tomina, L. B. (1965). A comparative study of short methods of measuring basic properties of the nervous system in man. *In* (B. M. Teplov, ed.) "Typological features of higher nervous activity in man". Vol. 4. Prosveshcheniye, Moscow (in Russian).

Nebylitsyn, V. D. and Gray, J. A. (eds.). "Biological bases of individual behavior". Academic Press, New York and London.

Nikiforovsky, P. M. (1952). "The pharmacology of conditioned reflexes as a method for their study". SSSR Academy of Medical Sciences, Moscow (in Russian).

Norkina, L. N. (1961). Comparative data of repeated study on typological features of higher nervous activity in monkeys. *Zhurnal vysshei nervnoi Deyatelnosti* **11**, 444–449 (in Russian).

Nosarzewski, J. (1974). Styl pracy umysłowej młodzieży uwarunkowany siłą układu nerwowego. *In* (J. Strelau, ed.) "Rola cech temperamentalnych w działaniu". Ossolineum, Wroclaw–Warsaw.

Numan, R. (1978). Cortical-limbic mechanisms and response control: A theroretical review. *Physiological Psychology* **6**, 445–470.

Nuttin, J. (1965). "La structure de la personnalité". Presses Universitaires de France, Paris.

Obraztsova, G. A. (1964). Characteristics of typological features of nervous systems in rabbits using the vibration method. *In* (V. N. Chernigovsky, ed.) "Methods of study of typological features of higher nervous activity in animals". Nauka, Moscow (in Russian).

Obraztsova, G. A. (1971). Some results of investigation of the individual properties of the nervous system in the ontogenesis of animals. *In* (V. S. Krasusky and V. K. Fedorov, eds) "Methods of assessment of properties of higher nervous activity". Nauka, Leningrad (in Russian).

Obuchowski, K. (1970). "Kody orientacji i struktura procesów emocjonalnych". Państwowe Wydawnictwo Naukowe, Warsaw.

Oderyshev, B. S. (1975). Activability as a generalized property of the individual's nervous system. *In* (B. A. Nikityuk, ed.) "Differential psychophysiology and its genetic aspects". SSSR Academy of Pedagogical Sciences, Moscow (in Russian).

Oleszkiewicz, Z. (1982). Reactivity and stimulative value of chosen and rejected professions. *Polish Psychological Bulletin* **13**, 3.

Olshannikova, A. E. (1967). Indices of fatigue-producing activity and strength of the nervous system in relation to the excitatory process. *In* (B. M. Teplov, ed.) "Typological features of higher nervous activity in man". Vol. 5. Prosveshcheniye, Moscow (in Russian).

Olshannikova, A. E. (1978). Toward a psychological diagnosis of emotionality. *In* (V. V. Davydov, ed.) "Problems of general, developmental and pedagogical psychology". Pedagogika, Moscow (in Russian).

Olshannikova, A. E. and Aleksandrova, N. I. (1969). On the reliability of the motor reaction indices. *In* V. D. Nebylitsyn, ed.) "Problems of differential psychophysiology". Vol. 6. Prosveshcheniye, Moscow (in Russian).

Orlebeke, J. F. (1972). Aktivering, extraversie en sterke van het zenuwstelsel. Van Gorcum and Comp., Assen.

Paisey, T. J. H. and Mangan, G. L. (1980). The relationship of extraversion, neuroticism and sensation-seeking to questionnaire-derived measures of nervous system properties. *The Pavlovian J. Biological Science* **15**, 123–130.

Paisey, T. J. H. and Mangan, G. L. (1982). Neo-Pavlovian temperament theory and the biological bases of personality. *Personality and Individual Differences* **3** (2).

Paley, I. M. (1976). The relation between differentiation and integration in psychophysiology of individual differences. *In* (V. S. Merlin and B. A. Nikityuk, eds) "Problems of differential psychophysiology related to genetics". SSSR Academy of Pedagogical Sciences, Perm (in Russian).

Paley, I. M., Zazulina, P. L., Ivanova, E. A., Leviyeva, S. N. and Lisenkova, V. P. (1966). An attempt for complex investigation of some individual typological properties in man. *In* B. G. Ananyev and D. A. Kerimov (eds) "Man and society". Leningrad University Press, Leningrad (in Russian).
Palmer, R. D. (1970). Visual acuity and stimulus seeking behaviour. *Psychosomatic Medicine* **32**, 277–284.
Panteleyeva, T. A. (1975). The genetic factor in strength and lability of the nervous system in man. *In* (B. A. Nikityuk, ed.) "Differential psychophysiology and its genetic aspects". SSSR Academy of Pedagogical Sciences, Moscow (in Russian).
Panteleyeva, T. A. and Shlakhta, N. F. (1978). On the study of genetic determination of some indices of lability of nervous processes. *In* (B. F. Lomov and I. V. Ravich-Shcherbo, eds) "The problems of genetic psychophysiology in man". Nauka, Moscow (in Russian).
Pasynkova, A. V., Guseva, E. P., and Lipovetsky, S. S. (1980). The relation of later evoked potentials' components to indicators of activation and efficiency of learning and memorizing. *In* (V. M. Rusalov and E. A. Golubeva, eds.) "Psychophysiological investigations on intellectual self-regulation and activity". Nauka, Moscow (in Russian).
Pavlov, I. P. (1951–52). "Complete Works" (2nd ed.) SSSR Academy of Sciences, Moscow and Leningrad (in Russian).
Pawłow, I. P. (1952). "Dwadzieścia lat badań wyższej czynności nerwowej (zachowania się) zwierząt". Państwowy Zakład Wydawnictw Lekarskich, Warsaw.
Perczyńska, D. and Żuchowska-Czwartosz, E. (1976). Charakterystyka dzieci aktywnych społecznie ze względu na cechy temperamentu oraz uznawane wartości społeczne. *In* (A. Gurycka, ed.) "Aktywność i aktywizacja społeczna". Wydawnictwa Uniwersytetu Warszawskiego, Warsaw.
Pervomaysky, B. Ya. (1964). Methods of asseessment of the type of nervous system in man. *In* "Clinic problems, pathophysiology and treatment of psychological diseases". Lugansk Medical College, Lugansk (in Russian).
Petrie, A. (1967). "Individuality in pain and suffering". Chicago University Press, Chicago.
Peysakhov, N. M. (1974). The diagnosis of strength of the excitatory process by means of motor-reaction methods. *In* (N. M. Peysakhov, V. M. Shadrin and A. P. Kashin, eds) "Problems of psychology of individual differences". Kazan University Press, Kazan (in Russian).
Peysakhov, N. M. (1975). The study of contradictions as a source of progress in differential psychophysiology. *In* (B. A. Nikityuk, ed.) "Differential psychophysiology and its genetic aspects". SSSR Academy of Pedagogical Sciences, Moscow (in Russian).
Piaget, J. (1964). "Six études de psychologie". Editions Gonthier S.A., Genève.
Popescu-Neveanu, P. G. (1954). An attempt to investigate the typological features of higher nervous activity in man. "Scientific Reports of the

Leningrad University". Vol. 185. Leningrad University Press, Leningrad (in Russian).
Popielarska, M. (1972). "Poziom reaktywności a udział w sytuacjach o różnym stopniu natężenia stymulacji". Unpublished M.A. thesis, University of Warsaw.
Povorinsky, Yu. A. (1954). "The method of studying motor conditioned reflexes based on verbal reinforcement". Medgiz, Leningrad (in Russian).
Powell, G. E. (1979). "Brain and personality". Saxon House, Farnborough.
Prusakova, M. B. (1974). The problem of typological determined individual style in solving arithmetic tasks in elementary school children. *In* (V. S. Merlin, ed.) "The problems of temperament theory". MP RSFSR and PGPI, Perm (in Russian).
Pshenichny, I. P. (1960). Dynamics of blood leucocyte changes in dogs of different nervous system types. *Zhurnal vysshei nervnoi Deyatelnosti* **10**, 435–442 (in Russian).
Rabinovich, R. L. (1961). Methods for studying the mobility of basic nervous processes. *Zhurnal vysshei nervnoi Deyatelnosti* **11**, 960–965 (in Russian).
Ratanova, T. A. (1975). Subjective estimation of loudness, RT and GSR to auditory stimuli of different intensity in relation to strength of the nervous system. *In* (B. A. Nikityuk, ed.) "Differential psychophysiology and its genetic aspects". SSSR Academy of Pedagogical Sciences, Moscow (in Russian).
Ravich-Shcherbo, I. V. (1956). Study of typological differences in mobility of the nervous processes in the visual analyzer. *In* (B. M. Teplov, ed.) "Typological features of higher nervous activity in man". Vol. 1. RSFSR Academy of Pedagogical Sciences, Moscow (in Russian).
Ravich-Shcherbo, I. V. (1969). Evaluation of the strength of the nervous system by the dependence of the reaction time on the intensity of the stimulus. *In* (V. D. Nebylitsyn, ed.) "Problems of differential psychophysiology". Vol. 6. Prosveshcheniye, Moscow (in Russian).
Ravich-Shcherbo, I. V. (1976). On the problem of the essence of psychophysiological bases of individuality. *In* (V. S. Merlin and B. A. Nikityuk, eds). "Problems of differential psychophysiology related to genetics". SSSR Academy of Pedagogical Sciences, Moscow (in Russian).
Ravich-Shcherbo, I. V. (1977). Preliminary results of investigation of nervous system properties based on the twin method. *In* (A. A. Smirnov, ed.) "Psychology and psychophysiology of individual differences". Pedagogika, Moscow (in Russian).
Ravich-Shcherbo, I. V. (1978). The twins method in psychology and psychophysiology. *In* (B. F. Lomov and I. V. Ravich-Shcherbo, eds) "The problems of genetic psychophysiology in man". Nauka, Moscow (in Russian).
Ravich-Shcherbo, I. V. and Shibarovskaya, G. A. (1972). The structure of dynamism of nervous processes in children of school age. *In* (V. D. Nebylitsyn, ed.) "Problems of differential psychophysiology". Vol. 7. Pedagogika, Moscow (in Russian).

Ravich-Shcherbo, I. V., Shlakhta, N. F. and Shibarovskaya, G. A. (1969). A study of some typological indices in twins. *In* (V. D. Nebylitsyn, ed.) "Problems of differential psychophysiology". Vol. 6. Prosveshcheniye, Moscow (in Russian).

Ravich-Shcherbo, I. V. and Shvarts, L. A. (1959). Correlation between the speed of arousal and termination of nervous processes as indices of mobility of the nervous system. *Voprosy Psikhologii* **5**, 97–103 (in Russian).

Ravich-Shcherbo, I. V. and Trifonova, M. K. (1967). Age features of some electroencephalographic reactions. *In* (B. M. Teplov, ed.) "Typological features of higher nervous activity in man". Vol. 5. Prosveshcheniye, Moscow (in Russian).

Rebrov, V. P. (1965). Some data on the study of type of nervous system during the manic phase of manic-depressive psychosis complicated by infection. *In* "Clinic problems, pathophysiology and treatment of psychological diseases". Lugansk Medical College Press, Lugansk (in Russian).

Regan, D. (1972). "Evoked potentials in psychology, sensory physiology and clinical medicine". Chapman and Hall, London.

Reykowski, J. (1966). "Funkcjonowanie osobowości w warunkach stressu psychologicznego". Państwowe Wydawnictwo Naukowe, Warsaw.

Reykowski, J. (1970). Obraz własnej osoby jako mechanizm regulujący postępowanie. *Kwartalnik Pedagogiczny* **15**, 45–58.

Reykowski, J. (1974). "Eksperymentalna psychologia emocji". (2nd ed.). Książka i Wiedza, Warsaw.

Reykowski, J. (1977). Osobowość jako centralny system regulacji i integracji czynności. *In* (T. Tomaszewski, ed.) "Psychologia" (3rd ed.). Państwowe Wydawnictwo Naukowe, Warsaw.

Reykowski, J. (1979). Intrinsic motivation and intrinsic inhibition of aggressive behavior. *In* (S. Feshbach and A. Frączek, eds) "Aggression and behavior change. Biological and social processes". Praeger Publishers, New York.

Rogers, C. R. (1961). "On becoming a person: A therapist's view of psychotherapy". Houghton Mifflin, Boston.

Roget, A. (1960). Correlations between the different electroencephalographic variables. *Electroencephalography and Clinical Neurophysiology* **12**.

Rokotova, N. A. (1954). The method of nervous system type investigation in man. *Fiziologicheskii Zhurnal SSSR* **40**, 727–729 (in Russian).

Rozhdestvenskaya, V. I. (1955). An attempt to measure the strength of the excitatory process through aspects of its irradiation and concentration in the visual analyser. *Voprosy Psikhologii* **1**, 90–98 (in Russian).

Rozhdestvenskaya, V. I. (1959a). The strength of nerve cells as shown in the nature of the effect of additional stimulation on visual sensitivity. *In* (B. M. Teplov, ed.) "Typological features of higher nervous activity in man". Vol. 2. RSFSR Academy of Pedagogical Sciences, Moscow (in Russian).

Rozhdestvenskaya, V. I. (1959b) Strength of the nervous system as shown in the ability of the nerve cells to withstand persistent concentrated excitation.

*In* (B. M. Teplov, ed.) "Typological features of higher nervous activity in man". Vol. 2. RSFSR Academy of Pedagogical Sciences, Moscow (in Russian).
Rozhdestvenskaya, V. I. (1963a). Determination of inhibitory strength in man through prolonging the action of the differential stimulus. *In* (B. M. Teplov, ed.) "Typological features of higher nervous activity in man". Vol. 3. RSFSR Academy of Pedagogical Sciences, Moscow (in Russian).
Rozhdestvenskaya, V. I. (1963b). Typological features in the nervous system of man during the development of delayed photochemical reflexes. *In* (B. M. Teplov, ed.) "Typological features of higher nervous activity in man". Vol. 3. RSFSR Academy of Pedagogical Sciences, Moscow (in Russian).
Rozhdestvenskaya, V. I. (1969). Estimation criteria of induction procedure. *In* (V. D. Nebylitsyn, ed.) "Problems of differential psychophysiology". Vol. 6. Prosveshcheniye, Moscow (in Russian).
Rozhdestvenskaya, V. I. (1971). The estimation of strength of the nervous system in man based on the features of irradiation and concentration of excitation in visual analyser. *In* (V. K. Krasusky and V. K. Fedorov, eds) "Methods of assessment of properties of higher nervous activity". Nauka, Leningrad (in Russian).
Rozhdestvenskaya, V. I. (1977a). On the problem of manifestation of strength of the nervous system in different kinds of monotonous work. *In* (M. N. Borisova *et al.*, eds) "Problems of differential psychophysiology". Vol. 9. Pedagogika, Moscow (in Russian).
Rozhdestvenskaya, V. I. (1977b). The influence of strength of nervous system on work efficiency in different situations. *In* (A. A. Smirnov, ed.) "Psychology and psychophysiology of individual differences". Pedagogika, Moscow (in Russian).
Rozhdestvenskaya, V. I. (1980). "Individual differences in work efficiency". Pedagogika, Moscow (in Russian).
Rozhdestvenskaya, V. I., Golubeva, E. A., and Yermolayeva-Tomina, L. B. (1969a). On general and partial factors of the strength of the nervous system. *In* (V. D. Nebylitsyn, ed.) "Problems of differential psychophysiology". Vol. 6. Prosveshcheniye, Moscow (in Russian).
Rozhdestvenskaya, V. I., Golubeva, E. A., and Yermolayeva-Tomina, L. B. (1969b). The role of strength of the nervous system in the dynamics of mental capacity for work in different kinds of activity. *In* (V. D. Nebylitsyn, ed.). "Problems of differential psychophysiology". Vol. 6. Prosveshcheniye, Moscow (in Russian).
Rozhdestvenskaya, V. I., Golubeva, E. A., and Yermolayeva-Tomina, L. B. (1972). Alterations in functional state as affected by different kinds of activity and strength of the nervous system. *In* (V. D. Nebylitsyn and J. A. Gray, eds) "Biological bases of individual behavior". Academic Press, New York and London.
Rozhdestvenskaya, V. I., Golubeva, E. A., and Yermolayeva-Tomina, L. B., Aleksandrova, N. I., and Klyagin, V. S. (1967). On the problem of

functional state in relation to typological features of the nervous system. *In* (B. M. Teplov, ed.) "Typological features of higher nervous activity in man". Vol. 5. Prosveshcheniye, Moscow (in Russian).

Rozhdestvenskaya, V. I. and Levochkina, I. A. (1972). Functional states when performing a monotonous work and the strength of the nervous system. *In* (V. D. Nebylitsyn, ed.) "Problems of differential psychophysiology". Vol. 7. Pedagogika, Moscow (in Russian).

Rozhdestvenskaya, V. I., Nebylitsyn, V. D., Borisova, M. N. and Yermolayeva-Tomina, L. B. (1960). A comparative study of different indices of strength of the nervous system in man. *Voprosy Psikhologii* **6**, 41–56 (in Russian).

Rubinstein, S. L. (1946). "Fundamentals of psychology" (2nd ed.). Institute of Philosophy of SSSR Academy of Sciences, Moscow (in Russian).

Rusalov, V. M. (1974). Polar-amplitude asymmetry of evoked potentials. *In* (V. D. Nebylitsyn, ed.) "Problems of differential psychophysiology. Electrophysiological studies on the fundamental properties of the nervous system". Vol. 8. Nauka, Moscow (in Russian).

Rusalov, V. M. (1975). System approach in the study of general properties of the nervous system in man. *In* (B. A. Nikityuk, ed.) "Differential psychophysiology and its genetic aspects". SSSR Academy of Pedagogical Sciences, Moscow (in Russian).

Rusalov, V. M. (1977). On the nature of general and partial properties of the nervous system in man. *In* (A. A. Smirnov, ed.) "Psychology and psychophysiology of individual differences". Pedagogika, Moscow (in Russian).

Rusalov, V. M. (1979). "Biological bases of individual-psychological differences". Nauka, Moscow (in Russian).

Rusalov, V. M. and Golubeva, E. A. (eds) (1980). "Psychophysiological investigations on intellectual self-regulation and activity". Nauka, Moscow (in Russian).

Rusalov, V. M. and Kotov, L. N. (1980). On the neurophysiological content of the property of lability of the nervous system. *Voprosy Psikhologii* **26**, 150–154 (in Russian).

Ryabinina, E. P. (1977). The reliability of psychophysiological indicators in connection with a psychic state of monotony. *In* (K. M. Gurevich and Yu. L. Syérda, eds) "Problems of psychological diagnosis. Theory and practice". Research Pedagogical Institute ESSR, Tallinn (in Russian).

Sales, S. M., Guydosh, R. M., and Iacono, W. (1974). Relationship between strength of the nervous system and need for stimulation. *Journal of Personality and Social Psychology* **29**, 16–22.

Sales, S. M. and Throop, W. F. (1972). The relationship between kinesthetic aftereffects and strength of the nervous system. *Psychophysiology* **9**, 492–497.

Samarin, Yu. A. (1954). An attempt at the experimental psychological study of typological features of the nervous system in children. *Izvestiya Akademii Pedagogicheskikh Nauk RSFSR* **52**, 81–140.

Samonov, A. P. (1972). The influence of nervous system properties on activity in extreme conditions. *In* (B. A. Vyatkin, ed.) "Temperament and sport". Vol. 1. MP RSFSR, PGPI and UOOP, Perm (in Russian).

Samonov, A. P. (1974). The professional fitness of persons with strong and weak nervous system to activity performed in extreme conditions. *In* (B. A. Vyatkin, ed.) "Temperament and sport". Vol. 2. MP RSFSR, PGPI and UOOP, Perm (in Russian).

Sanocki, W. (1976). "Kwestionariusze osobowości w psychologii". Państwowe Wydawnictwo Naukowe, Warsaw.

Saprykin, P. G. and Mileryan, E. A. (1954). "An attempt to develop a method for the experimental investigation of individual features of higher nervous activity in man". Proceedings of a conference on psychology (3–8 July, 1953). RSFSR Academy of Pedagogical Sciences, Moscow (in Russian).

Schulz, P. and Schönpflug, W. (1982). Regulatory activity during states of stress. *In* (H. W. Krohne and L. Laux, eds) "Achievement, stress and anxiety". Hemisphere Publishing Corporation, Washington and London.

Semagin, V. N. (1971). Correlational analysis of the significance of some indicators of conditioned reflexes in the typological studies of nervous system. *In* (V. K. Krasusky and V. K. Fedorov, eds) "Methods of assessment of properties of higher nervous activity". Nauka, Leningrad (in Russian).

Shchukin, M. R. (1977). Coping with negative manifestations of nervous system properties in the development of the individual style of activity. *In* (V. S. Merlin, ed.) "Theoretical bases, application, and methods of differential psychophysiology". MP RSFSR and PGPI, Perm (in Russian).

Sheldon, W. H. and Stevens, S. S. (1942). "The varieties of temperament". Harper and Row, New York and London.

Shevko, G. N., Troshikhin, V. A., and Moldavskaya, S. I. (1973). Investigation of interrelations between EEG indicators and individual properties of the nervous system for professional selection's purposes. *In* (V. A. Troskikkin, ed.) "Psychophysiological bases of professional selection". Naukova Dumka, Kiev (in Russian).

Shibarovskaya, G. A. (1975). On the problem of influence of inheritance on the formation of dynamism of nervous processes. *In* (B. A. Nikityuk, ed.) "Differential psychophysiology and its genetic aspects". SSSR Academy of Pedagogical Sciences, Moscow (in Russian).

Shibarovskaya, G. A. (1978). The genotypical bases of dynamism of nervous processes. *In* (B. F. Lomov and I. V. Ravich-Shcherbo, eds) "The problems of genetic psychophysiology in man". Nauka, Moscow (in Russian).

Shlakhta, N. F. (1972). EEG in twins and some properties of nervous system. *In* (V. D. Nebylitsyn, ed.) "Problems of differential psychophysiology". Vol. 7. Pedagogika, Moscow (in Russian).

Shlakhta, N. F. (1975). The syndrome of strength of nervous system as regards excitation in adolescent twins. *In* (B. A. Nikityuk, ed.) "Differential psychophysiology and its genetic aspects", SSSR Academy of Pedagogical Sciences, Moscow (in Russian).

Shlakhta, N. F. and Panteleyeva, T. A. (1978). The investigation of genotypically determined strength of nervous system syndrome. *In* (B. F. Lomov and I. V. Ravich-Shcherbo, eds) "The problems of genetic psychophysiology in man". Nauka, Moscow (in Russian).

Shorokhova, E. V. (ed.) (1974). "The theoretical problems of personality psychology". Nauka, Moscow (in Russian).

Shtimmer, E. V. (1974). The interrelation between mental development estimated by WISC and strength of nervous system in preschool children. *In* (V. S. Merlin, ed.) "The problems of temperament theory". MP RSFSR and PGPI, Perm (in Russian).

Shvarts, L. A. (1959). Individual differences in critical frequency of flicker-fusion and duration of negative visual aftereffect. *In* (B. M. Teplov, ed.) "Typological features of higher nervous activity in man". Vol. 2. RSFSR Academy of Pedagogical Sciences, Moscow (in Russian).

Shvarts, L. A. (1960). Critical frequency of flicker fusion and properties of "clash" of nervous processes as indicators of mobility of nervous system. *Doklady Akademii Pedagogicheskikh Nauk* **1**, 69–72 (in Russian).

Shvarts, L. A. (1963). Speed of restoration of absolute visual sensitivity after fooding as an index of mobility (lability) of nervous processes, and other tests of mobility. *In* (B. M. Teplov, ed.) "Typological features of higher nervous activity in man". Vol. 3. RSFSR Academy of Pedagogical Sciences, Moscow (in Russian).

Shvarts, L. A. (1965). Speed of restoration of visual sensitivity after visual fatigue and after light exposure as indices of lability of nervous processes. *In* (B. M. Teplov, ed.) "Typological features of higher nervous activity in man". Vol. 4. Prosveshcheniye, Moscow (in Russian).

Silina, E. A. (1977). Longitudinal studies of structural relations between temperament traits: from puberty to adolescent age. *In* (V. S. Merlin, ed.) "Theoretical bases, application and methods of differential psychophysiology". MP RSFSR and PGPI, Perm (in Russian).

Simanovsky, S. M. (1964). Four variants of typological features in patients with manic-depressive psychosis. *In* "Clinical problems, pathophysiology and treatment of psychological diseases". Lugansk Medical College Press, Lugansk (in Russian).

Simonov, P. V. (1962). "Three phases in the organism's reactions to stimulus of increasing intensity". SSSR Academy of Sciences, Moscow (in Russian).

Sklarova, E. G. (1965). Typological features of higher nervous activity in neurotic patients. *In* "Clinic problems, pathophysiology, and treatment of psychological diseases". Lugansk Medical College Press, Lugansk (in Russian).

Smirnov, A. A. (1966). "Problems of psychology of memory". Prosveshcheniye, Moscow (in Russian).

Smirnov, A. A. (ed.) (1977). "Psychology and psychophysiology of individual differences". Pedagogika, Moscow (in Russian).

Smith, S. L. (1968). Extraversion and sensory threshold. *Psychophysiology* **5**, 296–297.

Smoleńska, M. Z. (1971). "Spostrzeganie podobieństwa do 'ja' a zachowania allocentryczne i egocentryczne u młodzieży wybitnie uzdolnionej". Unpublished M.A. thesis, University of Warsaw.
Soloveva, S. A. (1970). Interrelation between type of nervous system, neuropsychological tension, and strength of motivation in memory. In (V. S. Merlin, ed.) "Problems of experimental psychology of personality". Vol. 6. UOOP and PGPI, Perm (in Russian).
Soloveva, S. A. (1972). The effects of the strength of the nervous system, mental tension and the level of motivation on memorization. *Voprosy Psikhologii* **18**, 133–137 (in Russian).
Sosnowski, T. (1978). Reactivity, level of stimulation, and some features of verbal behavior in small, task-oriented groups. *Polish Psychological Bulletin* **9**, 129–137.
Sosnowski, T. and Wrześniewski, K. (in press). Polska wersja Kwestionariusza STAI Spielbergera do pomiaru lęku. *Przegląd Psychologiczny*.
Spearman, C. (1927). "The abilities of man". Macmillan, New York.
Spence, K. W. (1953). Learning and performance in eyelid conditioning as a function of intensity of the UCS. *Journal of Experimnental Psychology* **45**, 57–63.
Spence, K. W. (1956). "Behavior theory and conditioning". Yale University Press, New Haven.
Spence, K. W. (1960). "Behavior theory and learning". Prentice-Hall, Englewood Cliffs.
Spence, K. W. and Taylor, J. A. (1951). Anxiety and strength of the UCS as determiners of the amount of eyelid conditioning. *Journal of Experimental Psyhcology* **42**, 183–188.
Spielberger, C. D. (1972). Anxiety as an emotional state. In (C. D. Spielberger, ed.) "Anxiety: Current trends in theory and research". Vol. 1. Academic Press, New York and London.
Spielberger, C. D. (1976). The nature and measurement of anxiety. In (C. D. Spielberger and R. Diaz-Guerrero, eds.) "Cross-cultural anxiety". Hemisphere Publishing Corporation, Washington and London.
Spielberger, C. D., Gorsuch, R. L. and Lushene, R. E. (1970). "Manual for the State-Trait Anxiety Inventory". Consulting Psychologists Press, Palo Alto.
Stawowska, L. (1973). "Diagnoza typów osobowości". Wydawnictwo Uniwersytetu Śląskiego, Kielce.
Stawowska, L. (1977). "Rola zróżnicowania typologicznego w funkcjonowaniu jednostki". Wydawnictwo WSP, Opole.
Stern, W. (1921). "Die Differentielle Psychologie in ihren methodischen Grundlagen" (3rd ed.). J. A. Barth Verlag, Leipzig.
Strelau, J. (1958). Problem parcjalnych typów wyższej czynności nerwowej. *Psychologia Wychowawcza* **1**, 244–251.
Strelau, J. (1960). Przewaga ruchliwości analizatora wzrokowego nad słuchowym u człowieka. *Studia Psychologiczne* **3**, 181–198.

Strelau, J. (1962). O metodach badania ogólnych typów układu nerwowego człowieka dorosłego i zwierząt. *Psychologia Wychowawcza* **5**, 42–54.
Strelau, J. (1964a). The dependence of the diagnosis of the type of higher nervous activity on the kind of UCS in CR procedure. *Voprosy Psikhologii* **10**, 37–44 (in Russian).
Strelau, J. (1964b). Problemy temperamentu. *In* (L. Wołoszynowa, ed.) "Materiały do nauczania psychologii. Psychologia ogólna". Vol. 1. Państwowe Wydawnictwo Naukowe, Warsaw.
Strelau, J. (1965a). "Problemy i metody badań typów układu nerwowego człowieka". Ossolineum, Wrocław–Warsaw.
Strelau, J. (1965b). "O temperamencie i jego poznawaniu". Nasza Księgarnia, Warsaw.
Strelau, J. (1967a). Reaction time as an indicator of strength of the nervous system. *In* (V. S. Merlin, ed.) "Typological investigations in psychology of personality". UOOP and PGPI, Perm (in Russian).
Strelau, J. (1967b). Czas reakcji motorycznej jako wskaźnik siły układu nerwowego. *Przegląd Psychologiczny* **14**, 124–129.
Strelau, J. (1969). "Temperament i typ układu nerwowego". Państwowe Wydawnictwo Naukowe, Warsaw.
Strelau, J. (1970a). Nervous system type and extraversion-introversion. A comparison of Eysenck's theory with Pavlov's typology. *Polish Psychological Bulletin* **1**, 17–24.
Strelau, J. (1970b). Indywidualny styl pracy ucznia a cechy temperamentalne. *Kwartalnik Pedagogiczny* **15**, 59–77.
Strelau, J. (1972a). The general and partial nervous system types—data and theory. *In* (V. D. Nebylitsyn and J. A. Gray, eds) "Biological bases of individual behavior". Academic Press, New York and London.
Strelau, J. (1972b). A diagnosis of temperament by nonexperimental techniques. *Polish Psychological Bulletin* **3**, 97–105.
Strelau, J. (1974). Temperament as an expression of energy level and temporal features of behavior. *Polish Psychological Bulletin* **5**, 119–127.
Strelau, J. (1975a). Pavlov's typology and current investigations in this area. *Nederlands Tijdschrift voor de Psychologie* **30**, 177–200.
Strelau, J. (1975b). Różnice indywidualne. *In* (T. Tomaszewski, ed.) "Psychologia". Państwowe Wydawnictwo Naukowe, Warsaw.
Strelau, J. (1975c). Reactivity and activity style in selected occupations. *Polish Psychological Bulletin* **6**, 199–206.
Strelau, J. (1978). "Rola temperamentu w rozwoju psychicznym". Wydawnictwa Szkolne i Pedagogiczne, Warsaw.
Strelau, J. (1981). Temperament und Persönlichkeit—Beziehungen und Abhängigkeiten. *In* (T. Tomaszewski, ed.) "Zur Psychologie der Tätigkeit. Positionen und Ergebnisse polnischer Psychologen". VEB Deutscher Verlag der Wissenschaften, Berlin.
Strelau, J. (1982). Biologically determined dimensions of personality or temperament? *Personality and Individual Differences* **13**, 355–360.

Strelau, J. (in press). Temperament and personality. Pavlov and beyond. *In* (J. Strelau, F. H. Farley, and A. Gale, eds) "The biological foundations of personality and behavior". Hemisphere Publishing Corporation, Washington and London.

Strelau, J., Eliasz, A., and Klonowicz, T. (1974). Charakterystyka czasowa zachowania się—na przykładzie wybranych reakcji motorycznych i werbalnych. *In* (J. Strelau, ed.) "Rola cech temperamentalnych w działaniu". Ossolineum, Wroclaw–Warsaw.

Strelau, J., Farley, F. H., and Gale, A. (eds) (in press). "The biological foundations of personality and behavior". Hemisphere Publishing Corporation, Washington and London.

Strelau, J., Klonowicz, T., and Eliasz, A. (1972). Fizjologiczne mechanizmy cech temperamentalnych. *Przegląd Psychologiczny* **15**, 25-51.

Strelau, J. and Krajewski, A. (1974). Individual style of activity and strength of the nervous system. *In* (K. M. Gurevich, ed.) "Psychophysiological problems of higher level professional experience". Vol. 1. Sovetskaya Rossiya, Moscow (in Russian).

Strelau, J. and Maciejczyk, J. (1977). Reactivity and decision making in stress situations in pilots. *In* (C. D. Spielberger and I. G. Sarason, eds) "Stress and anxiety". Vol. 4. Hemisphere Publishing Corporation, Washington and London.

Strelau, J., Sosnowski, T. and Oniszczenko, W. (in press). The dynamics of psychophysiological changes under hypoxia and sensory deprivation in subjects with different reactivity and anxiety levels. *In* (J. Strelau, F. H. Farley, and A. Gale, eds) "The biological foundations of personality and behavior". Hemisphere Publishing Corporation, Washington and London.

Strelau, J. and Terelak, J. (1974). The alpha-index in relation to temperamental traits. *Studia Psychologica* **16**, 40–50.

Strykowska, M. (1978). Effect of reactivity on choice of strategy in solving typical operators' tasks. *Polish Psychological Bulletin* **9**, 139–145.

Strzałkowska, G. (1977). "Relacja między 'ja realnym' i 'ja idealnym' a poziomem zapotrzebowania na stymulację". Unpublished M.A. thesis, University of Warsaw.

Sukhanova, N. V. (1959). Mobility of nervous processes in motor analyser in preschool children. *Zhurnal vysshei nervnoi Deyatelnosti* **9**, 679–683 (in Russian).

Sukhareva, A. I. (1967). The use of individual properties in the process of formation of individual style of work in turner-apprentice. *In* (B. M. Teplov, ed.) "Typological features of higher nervous activity in man". Vol. 5. Prosveshcheniye, Moscow (in Russian).

Suslov, B. V. (1972). The effect of different emotion-inducing factors on the speed and accuracy of movements in fencers depending on the strength of nervous system. *In* (B. A. Vyatkin, ed.) "Temperament and sport". Vol. 1. MP RSFSR, PGPI and UOOP, Perm (in Russian).

Suvorova, V. V. (1974). The EEG indicators and the individual traits of vegetative reactivity. *In* (V. D. Nebylitsyn, ed.) "Problems of differential psychophysiology. Electrophysiological studies on the fundamental properties of the nervous system". Vol. 8. Nauka, Moscow (in Russian).

Suvorova, V. V. (1975). "Psychophysiology of stress". Pedagogika, Moscow (in Russian).

Taylor, J. A. (1953). A personality scale of manifest anxiety. *Journal of Abnormal Social Psychology* **48**, 285–290.

Teplov, B. M. (1954). An attempt to elaborate methods for investigating typological features of higher nervous activity in man. "Proceedings of a conference on psychology (3–8 July, 1953)". RSFSR Academy of Pedagogical Sciences, Moscow (in Russian).

Teplov, B. M. (1955a). The study on types of higher nervous activity and psychology. *Voprosy Psikhologii* **1**, 36–41 (in Russian).

Teplov, B. M. (1955b). The concepts of weakness and inertness of the nervous system. *Voprosy Psikhologii* **1**, 3–15 (in Russian).

Teplov, B. M. (1956). Problems in the study of general types of higher nervous activity in man and animals. *In* (B. M. Teplov, ed.) "Typological features of higher nervous activity in man". Vol. 1. RSFSR Academy of Pedagogical Sciences, Moscow (in Russian).

Teplov, B. M. (1957). The study of typological properties of the nervous system and their psychological manifestation. *Voprosy Psikhologii* **3**, 108–130 (in Russian).

Teplov, B. M. (1959). Some results of the study of strength of nervous system in man. *In* (B. M. Teplov, ed.) "Typological features of higher nervous activity in man". Vol. 2. RSFSR Academy of Pedagogical Sciences, Moscow (in Russian).

Teplov, B. M. (1960). The investigation of the properties of the nervous system as a way of studying individual psychological differences. *In* (B. G. Ananyev *et al.*, eds) "Psychological science in the USSR". Vol. 2. RSFSR Academy of Pedagogical Sciences, Moscow (in Russian).

Teplov, B. M. (1961). "Problems of individual differences". RSFSR Academy of Pedagogical Sciences. Moscow (in Russian).

Teplov, B. M. (1963a). New data for the study of nervous system properties in man. *In* (B. M. Teplov, ed.) "Typological features of higher nervous activity in man". Vol. 3. RSFSR Academy of Pedagogical Sciences, Moscow (in Russian).

Teplov, B. M. (1963b). Typological features of the nervous system and their significance for psychology. *In* (M. P. Fedoseyev, ed.) "Philosophical problems of physiology of higher nervous activity and psychology". SSSR Academy of Sciences, Moscow (in Russian).

Teplov, B. M. (1964a). Problems in the study of general types of higher nervous activity in man and animals. *In* (J. A. Gray, ed.) "Pavlov's typology". Pergamon Press, Oxford.

Teplov, B. M. (1964b). "Current status of the problem of types of higher nervous activity in man and methods of their assessment". Paper presented at the meeting of the International Congress of Anthropology and Ethnographical Sciences, Moscow (in Russian).

Teplov, B. M. (1972). The problems of types of human higher nervous activity and methods of determining them. *In* (V. D. Nebylitsyn and J. A. Gray, eds) "Biological bases of individual behavior". Academic Press, New York and London.
Teplov, B. M. (ed.) (1956–67). "Typological features of higher nervous activity in man". Vol. 1 (1956); Vol. 2 (1959); Vol. 3 (1963). RSFSR Academy of Pedagogical Sciences. Vol. 4 (1965); Vol. 5 (1967). Prosveshcheniye, Moscow (in Russian).
Teplov, B. M. and Nebylitsyn, V. D. (1963a). The study of basic properties of the nervous system and their significance in psychology of individual differences. *Voprosy Psikhologii* **9**, 38–47 (in Russian).
Teplov, B. M. and Nebylitsyn, V. D. (1963b). Experimental study of properties of the nervous system in man. *Zhurnal vysshei nervnoi Deyatelnosti* **13**, 789–797 (in Russian).
Terelak, J. (1974). Reaktywność mierzona indeksem alfa a cechy temperamentalne. *In* (J. Strelau, ed.) "Rola cech temperamentalnych w działaniu". Ossolineum, Wroclaw–Warsaw.
Terelak, J. (1982). "Człowiek w sytuacjach ekstremalnych (izolacja antarktyczna). Wydawnicto MON, Warsaw.
Terry, R. A. (1953). Autonomic balance and temperament. *J. Comparative and Physiological Psychology* **46**, 454–460.
Thomas, A. and Chess, S. (1977). "Temperament and development", Brunner/Mazel Publishers, New York.
Thomas, A., Chess, S., and Birch, H. G. (1968). "Temperament and behavior disorders in children". New York University Press, New York.
Thompson, W. R. and Schaefer, T. Jr. (1961). Early environmental stimulation. *In* (D. W. Fiske and S. R. Maddi, eds) "Functions of varied experience". The Dorsey Press, Homewood.
Thurstone, L. L. (1951). The dimensions of temperament. *Psychometrika* **16**, 11–20.
Toeplitz, Z. (1982). Krytyczna analiza Kwestionariusza Osobowości Eysencka (Eysenck Personality Questionnaire, EPQ) pod kątem próby adaptacji tego testu do warunków polskich. *In* (J. Strelau, ed.) "Regulacyjne funkcje temperamentu". Ossolineum, Wroclaw–Warsaw.
Tomaszewski, T. (1963). "Wstęp do psychologii". Państwowe Wydawnictwo Naukowe, Warsaw.
Tomaszewski, T. (1967). Aktywność człowieka. *In* (M. Maruszewski, J. Reykowski, and T. Tomaszewski) "Psychologia jako nauka o człowieku". Książka i Wiedza, Warsaw.
Tomaszewski, T. (1968). "Problemy i kierunki współczesnej psychologii". Państwowe Wydawnictwo Naukowe, Warsaw.
Tomaszewski, T. (1975). Człowiek i otoczenie. *In* (T. Tomaszewski, ed.) "Psychologia". Państwowe Wydawnictwo Naukowe, Warsaw.
Travis, L. E. and Egan, J. P. (1938). Conditioning of the electrical response of the cortex. *J. Experimental Psychology* **22**, 524–531.
Troshikhin, V. A., Kozlova, L. N., Kruchenko, Zh. A., and Sirotsky, V. V. (1971). "Shaping and development of the basic properties of the type of

higher nervous activity in ontogenesis". Naukova Dumka, Kiev (in Russian).
Troshikhin, V. A., Moldavskaya, S. I., and Kolchenko, N. V. (1978). "Functional mobility of nervous processes and professional selection". Naukova Dumka, Kiev (in Russian).
Troshikhina, Yu. G. (1971). The significance of the animals' weight in determining strength of excitation process by means of caffeine test. *In* (V. K. Krasusky and V. K. Fedorov, eds) "Methods of assessment of properties of higher nervous activity". Nauka, Leningrad (in Russian).
Trubnikova-Morgunova, R. S. (1977). Efficiency of memorizing and the strength of the nervous system. *In* (M. N. Borisova *et al.*, eds) "Problems of differential psychophysiology". Vol. 9. Pedagogika, Moscow (in Russian).
Turovskaya, Z. G. (1963). The relation between some indices of strength and mobility of the nervous system in man. *In* (B. M. Teplov, ed.) "Typological features of higher nervous activity in man". Vol. 3. RSFSR Academy of Pedagogical Sciences, Moscow (in Russian).
Turovskaya, Z. G. (1974). The relation between typological features of higher nervous activity and some characteristics of vegetative reactivity. *In* (V. D. Nebylitsyn, ed.) "Problems of differential psychophysiology. Electrophysiological studies on the fundamental properties of the nervous system". Vol. 8. Nauka, Moscow (in Russian).
Turovskaya, Z. G. (1977). Individual features of the vegetative balance and equilibrium of basic nervous processes. *In* (A. A. Smirnov, ed.) "Psychology and psychophysiology of individual differences". Pedagogika, Moscow (in Russian).
Turovskaya, Z. G., Berezhkovskaya, E. L., and Aleksandrovskaya, E. M. (1972). Individual style of work and psychophysiological characteristics of chemical operators. *Voprosy Psikhologii* **18**, 77–88 (in Russian).
Tyler, L. E. (1978). "Individuality. Human possibilities and personal choice in the psychological development of men and women". Jossey-Bass Publishers, San Francisco.
Umansky, L. I. (1958). Experimental study of typological features of children's nervous systems (using play material). *Voprosy Psikhologii* **4**, 184–190 (in Russian).
Umansky, L. I. (1960). Some problems in the study of general types of nervous system and temperaments in children. *In* (E. I. Ignatyev, ed.) "Problems of psychology of personality". Izdatelstvo MP RSFSR, Moscow (in Russian).
Umansky, L. I. (1961). The problem of partial types of higher nervous activity in man. *Voprosy Psikhologii* **7**, 154–160 (in Russian).
Uszyńska, Z. (1971). "Cechy temperamentalne a styl pracy produkcyjnej". Unpublished M.A. thesis, University of Warsaw.
Utkina, N. S. (1964). Typological differences and the effect of school marks on some features of attention. *In* (V. S. Merlin, ed.) "Typological studies in psychology of personality and in industrial psychology". UOOP and PGPI, Perm (in Russian).

Utkina, N. S. (1968). Typological differences in the manifestation of psychological tension dependent on the strength of the excitatory process. *In* (V. S. Merlin, ed.) "Problems of experimental psychology of personality". Vol. 5. UOOP and PGPI, Perm (in Russian).

Vasilenko, L. D. (1967). Psychological complex of symptoms determined by mobility of the nervous system. *In* (V. S. Merlin, ed.) "Typological investigations in psychology of personality". Vol. 4. UOOP and PGPI, Perm (in Russian).

Vasilets, T. V. (1974). Genetic bases of the mobility of nervous processes in motor reactions. *Voprosy Psikhologii* **20**, 136–140 (in Russian).

Vasilets, T. V. (1978). Mobility as a trait of nervous processes. Genetical aspect of the problem. *In* (B. F. Lomov and I. V. Ravich-Shcherbo, eds) "The problems of genetic psychophysiology in man". Nauka, Moscow (in Russian).

Vasilev, A. N. (1960). The relation between reaction times to the onset and termination of a signal as an index of strength of the nervous system. *Voprosy Psikhologii* **6**, 113–122 (in Russian).

Vatsuro, E. G. (1945). The investigation of the comparative lability of the processes of higher nervous activity as applied to the functioning of the separate analyzers. *Trudy fiziologicheskikh Laboratorii im. I. P. Pavlova* **12**, 33–57 (in Russian).

Vatsuro, E. G. and Shtodin, M. P. (1947). Mechanism underlying the behaviour of the anthropoid ape (chimpanzee). Second communication. *Trudy Instituta evolutsionnoi Fizilogii i Patologii vyssheinervnoi Deyatelnosti im. I. P. Pavlova* **1**, 211–224 (in Russian).

Voicu, C. and Olteanu, T. (1972). Study of the correlation between flexibility of attention and dynamism of nervous processes. *In* (V. D. Nebylitsyn and J. A. Gray, eds) "Biological bases of individual behavior". Academic Press, New York and London.

Vyatkin, B. A. (1964a). Typologically determined differences in efficiency of the game-method in training of sports movements. *In* (V. S. Merlin, ed.) "Typological studies in psychology of personality and in industrial psychology". UOOP and PGPI, Perm (in Russian).

Vyatkin, B. A. (1964b). Typological differences in strength of the excitation process and the influence of the situation of tension on some motor characteristics in pupils. *Voprosy Psikhologii* **10**, 39–49 (in Russian).

Vyatkin, B. A. (1967). The validity of J. Strelau's modification to investigate strength of the nervous system as regards excitation. *In* (V. S. Merlin, ed.) "Typological investigations in psychology of personality". UOOP and PGPI, Perm (in Russian).

Vyatkin, B. A. (1968). The problem of reciprocal effects of motivation, neuro-psychological tension and the features of the type of nervous system on some aspects of sports activity. "Proceedings of the 3rd meeting of the Soviet Society of Psychologists". SSSR Academy of Pedagogical Sciences, Moscow (in Russian).

Vyatkin, B. A. (ed.) (1972a). "Temperament and sport". Vol. 1. MP RSFSR, PGPI and UOOP, Perm (in Russian).
Vyatkin, B. A. (1972b). Competitive stress and individual psychological features of sportsmen. *In* (B. A. Vyatkin, ed.) "Temperament and sport". Vol. 1. MP RSFSR, PGPI and UOOP, Perm (in Russian).
Vyatkin, B. A. (ed.) (1974a). "Temperament and sport". Vol. 2. MP RSFSR, PGPI and UOOP, Perm (in Russian).
Vyatkin, B. A. (1974b). The influence of temperament on activity in sportswomen performing artistic gymnastics. *In* (B. A. Vyatkin, ed.) "Temperament and sport". Vol. 2. MP RSFSR, PGPI and UOOP, Perm (in Russian).
Vyatkin, B. A. (ed.) (1976). "Temperament and sport". Vol. 3. MP RSFSR, PGPI and UOOP, Perm (in Russian).
Vyatkin, B. A. (1978). "The role of temperament in sports activity". Fizkultura i sport, Moscow (in Russian).
Vyatkin, B. A. and Chekirov, M. M. (1976). Typological differences in the influence of competitive stress on voluntary regulation of activity in wrestlers and individualization of voluntary training. *In* (B. A. Vyatkin, ed.) "Temperament and sport". Vol. 3. MP RSFSR, PGPI and UOOP, Perm (in Russian).
Vyatkin, B. A. and Markelov, V. V. (1974). Interrelation between temperament traits and tolerance to stress of competition. *In* (B. A. Vyatkin, ed.) "Temperament and sport". Vol. 2. MP RSFSR, PGPI and UOOP, Perm (in Russian).
Vyatkina, Z. N. (1976). Nervous system properties and the teacher's individual style of activity during lecture. *In* (B. A. Vyatkin, ed.) "Temperament and sport". Vol. 3. MP RSFSR, PGPI and UOOP, Perm (in Russian).
Vygotsky, L. S. (1962). "Thought and language". Wiley, New York.
Vyrzhikovsky, S. N. and Mayorov, F. P. (1954). Material on the influence of upbringing on the habitual form of higher nervous activity in the dog. *Trudy fiziologicheskikh Laboratorii im. I. P. Pavlova* **5**, 169–191 (2nd ed.) (in Russian).
Wenger, M. A. (1942). The stability of measurement of autonomic balance. *Psychosomatic Medicine* **4**, 94–95.
Werre, P. F. (1957). The relationships between electroencephalographic and psychological data in normal adults. Universitaire Pers Leiden, Leiden.
White, K. D. and Mangan, G. L. (1972). Strength of the nervous system as a function of personality type and level of arousal. *Behaviour Research and Therapy* **10**, 139–146.
White, K. D., Mangan, G. L., Morrish, R. B. and Siddle, D. A. T. (1969). The relation of visual after-images to extraversion and neuroticism. *Journal of Experimental Research in Personality* **3**, 268–274.
Willett, R. A. (1960). Measures of learning and conditioning. *In* (H. J. Eysenck, ed.) "Experiments in personality". Vol. 2. (Psychodiagnostics and psychodynamics). Routledge and Kegan Paul, London.
Williams, R. J. (1956). "Biochemical individuality: The basis for the genetotrophic concept". Wiley, New York.

Witkin, H. (1978). "Cognitive styles in personal and cultural adaptation". Clark University Press, Worcester.
Witkin, H. A., Dyk, R. B., Faterson, H. F., Goodenough, D. R., and Karp, S. A. (1962). "Psychological differentiation". Wiley, New York.
Witoszek, A. (1967). Problemy i metody badań typów układu nerwowego człowieka (book review). *Psychologia Wychowawcza* **10**, 87–94.
Wundt, W. (1911). "Grundzüge der Physiologischen Psychologie". (6th ed.). Vol. 3. Verlag von W. Engelmann, Leipzig.
Yakovleva, V. V. (1938). Determination of mobility of the nervous processes in the dog by means of a double transformation of the conditioned stimulus. *Trudy fiziologicheskikh Laboratorii im. I. P. Pavlova* **8**, 32–42 (in Russian).
Yermolayeva-Tomina, L. B. (1960). Individual differences in the ability to concentrate attention and strength of nervous system. *Voprosy Psikhologii* **6**, 84–95 (in Russian).
Yermolayeva-Tomina, L. B. (1963). The use of GSR indices in determination of typological properties of nervous system in man. *In* (B. M. Teplov, ed.) "Typological features of higher nervous activity in man". Vol. 3. RSFSR Academy of Pedagogical Sciences, Moscow (in Russian).
Yermolayeva,Tomina, L. B. (1969). The estimation of the indices of typological properties of the nervous system by skin galvanic procedure. *In* (V. D. Nebylitsyn, ed.) "Problems of differential psychophysiology". Vol. 6. Prosveshcheniye, Moscow (in Russian).
Yermolayeva-Tomina, L. B. (1971). The estimation of equilibrium of the nervous system based on GSR indicator. *In* (V. K. Krasusky and V. K. Fedorov, eds.) "Methods of assessment of properties of higher nervous activity". Nauka, Leningrad (in Russian).
Yusim, E. D. (1975). Psychophysiological investigations of individual differences in motor memory. *Voprosy Psikhologii* **21**, 130–136 (in Russian).
Zarzycka, M. (1980). "Rola cech temperamentu i osobowości w powodowaniu wypadków przez maszynistów PKP". Unpublished Ph.D. thesis, University of Warsaw.
Zhorov, P. A. and Sitkovskaya, O. D. (1974). The role of cortex-sub-cortex relations in voluntary regulation of alpha rhythm. *In* (V. D. Nebylitsyn, ed.) "Problems of differential psychophysiology. Electrophysiological studies on the fundamental properties of the nervous system". Vol. 8. Nauka, Moscow (in Russian).
Zhorov, P. A. and Yermolayeva-Tomina, L. B. (1972). Concerning the relation between extraversion and the strength of the nervous system. *In* (V. B. Nebylitsyn and J. A. Gray, eds) "Biological bases of individual behavior". Academic Press, New York and London.
Zuckerman, M. (1979). "Sensation seeking: Beyond the optimal level of arousal". Lawrence Erlbaum Assoc. Publishers, Hillsdale.
Zuckerman, M. (1980). Sensation seeking and its biological correlates. *Psychological Bulletin* **88**, 187–214.
Zyryanova, N. G. (1970). On the relationship between indices of two motor procedures when determining the strength of the nervous system. *Voprosy Psikhologii* **16**, 158–161 (in Russian).

# Chapter Notes

## CHAPTER 1

1. Speaking about "unconditioned inhibition" I have in mind, in accordance with Pavlov, all alterations of inherited inhibition; namely, protective (transmarginal) inhibition, sleep, and negative induction (external inhibition). In turn, using the notion "conditioned inhibition" all kinds of learned, acquired inhibitions should be considered, i.e. extinction, delay, differentiation, and conditioned inhibition in its narrow sense (as used by Pavlov).
2. This understanding of Pavlov's types of NS based on his first, and later rejected, classification may be found in recent publications thus being a source of misunderstanding (e.g. Zuckerman, 1979, p. 38).
3. The quotations from Pavlov's works are, for technical reasons, taken from the Polish translation.
4. Genotype refers to the genetic programme inherited by a given individual, whereas innate traits are the result of the interaction between genotype and the prenatal environment. The term phenotype was used by Pavlov to characterize the actual nervous activity which is the resultant of the TNS properties (genotype) and the whole system of temporal connections formed during the individual's life. The phenotype has been identified with what psychologists call "character" (Pavlov, 1952, p. 594).
5. The speed of conditioning used by Pavlov as one of the criteria for diagnosing the strength of excitation (see p. 15) was mentioned in the first place as the accepted standard. It is, therefore, difficult to accept Nebylitsyn's position when he states that ". . . Pavlov, in all his reported studies, did not mention speed of CR formation as an index of nervous system strength" (1972a, p. 15). Also Mangan (1982) acknowledges the fact that Pavlov used the speed of conditioning as index of strength of excitation.
6. The essence of this method is that instead of using UCSs which serve as reinforcement to a given reaction (in this case the motor reaction) verbal commands like: "press" are used. If the child, after several instructions, presses the bulb before the command "press" is given, this reaction is verbally reinforced by "good". If the child hesitates as to how to react, a signal to deliver the reaction is given, e.g. "well?". If the child makes a mistake he is informed by the word: "wrong", and so on. The CR is assumed to be evoked if the child presses the bulb to a given auditory or visual signal without being given the command "press". This method has been strongly criticized, among other things, by Soviet psychologists who objected to the verbal stimuli used by Ivanov–Smolensky as UCSs. It has been show that the speed of reaction formation adequate to the experimenters expectations should not be considered as an indicator of the ability to form conditioned reflexes but as the ability to follow the instruction.

7. This book was published in Russian in 1966.
8. The term lability was introduced into the physiology of higher nervous activity in 1901 by Vvedensky, who treated it as the speed of elementary reactions of the nervous system realized during functional activity. Also Ukhtomsky used the notion lability, stating that it might be measured by the number of separate excitatory periods arising in the nerve tissue in a given unit of time (see Troshikhin et al., 1978).
9. This index of mobility is used in our research as one of the main criteria of the mobility of behaviour (see p. 194).
10. The EEG method was used earlier in Teplov's laboratory (see Nebylitsyn, 1961) in the extinction with reinforcement method for diagnosing the strength of nervous system (see p. 77), where the phenomenon of alpha-blocking to visual stimuli was used as the unconditioned response in the CR procedure (see also Travis and Egan, 1938; Jasper and Shagass, 1941).
11. Golubeva, sharing Pavlov's position, assumes as unconditioned all those processes which take place without learning, and as conditioned those which are acquired during ontogenesis, thereby, using these terms quite broadly.
12. The question arises, whether arousability and activability are not synonyms because both of them relate to individual differences in activation. However, according to Gray (1964), it seems that arousability has a definite content which differs from the Russian psychophysiologists' understanding of activatability.
13. This is a new understanding of the relation between strength and dynamism, which, of course, makes the picture of the interrelations between the separate properties more complicated than hitherto.
14. Golubeva differentiates between the terms "balance" and "equilibrium", which is a novel approach.
15. The description and criteria of all these methods used in the twin studies may be found in Chapter 2.
16. Discussing the relation between general and partial NS properties I have suggested that one of the possible ways to solve this problem is to treat the general NS properties from the functional point of view and the partial ones as structurally determined (Strelau, 1969, 1972a).
17. When hypothesizing about the relationship between mobility of NS and memory, Teplov had in mind mobility in the broad meaning of the term. After differentiation between mobility in the narrow sense (measured by the "alteration" method) and lability of nervous processes understood as the individual's typical speed of initiation and termination of the nervous processes (see p. 31) Teplov's hypotheses should be restricted to lability.
18. For example, the Czechoslovakian psychologist Halmiová conducted several studies devoted to the relation of memory and TNS, however, all of them may be included into the framework of research typical for the Teplov-Nebylitsyn school (cf. Halmiová, 1978; Halmiová and Šebová, 1978, in press). Note that, among Russian psychologists (see Golubeva, 1980a) is a tendency to link verbal and non-verbal memory with Pavlov's typology, based on the distinction between the so-called first and second signal systems; the predominance of the first ("artists") being typical for non-verbal memory and the second ("thinkers") for verbal memory. Since this typology is not related to temperament it is not discussed here.
19. These are the volumes I have in my collection; however, there may be some with which I am not familiar. The same relates to other books published by Merlin's group.

20. This position is not quite clear. Style of action understood as the typical way in which any activity is performed is closely related to the question "how" a given activity proceeds and this essential question distinguishes the area of temperament from the area of ability, for which the questions "what" and "how well" are the most representative (e.g. Thomas et al., 1968; Buss and Plomin, 1975; Burks and Rubenstein, 1979).
21. They are measured by using combined methods some of which are described in the literature, though they are mostly used for other purposes (e.g. TAT, Jung's association experiment or Cattell's unstructuralized drawings). Most of these methods have been developed in Merlin's laboratory. The method used to measure temperament traits makes it hard to compare these traits with analogical ones, at least by name, known from the psychological literature. For this reason I have refrained from describing the diagnostic methods used by Merlin and his students.
22. It is not explained in this paper nor in any others why these particular NS properties have been taken into account.
23. Within the Moscow group Rusalov's (1979) research may serve as an example of a systems theory approach.
24. One of Merlin's closest students, Vyatkin (1978) has proposed a very different list of temperamental traits. He mentions: sensitivity, reactivity, activity, relation between reactivity and activity, speed of reaction, rigidity, and extraversion–introversion. Taking these temperamental traits as a starting-point we may expect different types as well as different species-specific structures of temperament.

## CHAPTER 2

1. The photochemical reflex has to be understood as the change of visual sensitivity caused by light stimuli. A given number of connections of the UCS (light) with an indifferent stimulus (e.g. sound) leads to the evocation of a CR. Visual sensitivity changes under the isolated action of the CS (sound), formerly presented together with the light. This phenomenon has been used by Dolin (1936) in studies of CR in humans.
2. Peysakhov (1974) proposes only two stimuli. In the auditory experiment sounds of 40 dB (weak) and 120 dB (strong) were used.

## CHAPTER 4

1. Gray's (1967) paper published in *Behavior Research and Therapy* was not available to me for a long time and its translation, which appeared in *Voprosy Psikhologii* in the second half of 1968 was not published until my book (Strelau, 1969), in which I gave a detailed discussion of the interrelations of E/I and NS properties, had already appeared in print.
2. Mangan and Farmer (1967) were not isolated in their treatment of the relation between E/I and NS properties. Marton and Urban (1966) also concluded that introverts correspond with the strong type of NS, because of their predominance of excitation over inhibition; the converse being the case in extraverts. But at the same time, considering the balance of NS properties (excitation and inhibition) as an independent dimension, they came to conclusions different from Mangan's. In Marton and Urban's opinion extraversion–introversion corresponds with balance

of NS but not with strength, which is regarded by the authors as a dimension related to neuroticism.
3. In a study comparing Eysenck's concept of E/I with Pavlovian typology I acknowledged the fact (Strelau, 1969, 1970a) that one of the main differences between both these concepts consists of the understanding of balance (equilibrium) of nervous processes. In Pavlov's theory equilibrium is the outcome of the positions held by an individual on two dimensions (strength of excitation and strength of inhibition). This means that an individual may be considered balanced when possessing both weak excitation and inhibition processes as well as strong excitation and inhibition. In Eysenck's theory, equilibrium of nervous processes should be regarded as one dimension, where the ideal balance between excitation and inhibition should be considered as a point situated in the middle of this dimension.
4. All experiments, where the extinction of the orienting response is the measure of NS properties, must be treated very cautiously, since this phenomenon has served as the index of several NS properties, e.g. strength, mobility, dynamism, and balance of the nervous system (see Nebylitsyn, 1972a).
5. In this context it must be regarded as strange that Morris (1979), in his book *Extraversion and Introversion*, devoted a chapter to the discussion of this dimension in relation to other personality dimensions with no mention of Pavlovian typology at all. Not one researcher in this area from socialist countries is included in the author's index to his book.
6. This paradigm must be treated with great caution because of the limitation which follows from the specificity of the CR procedure, as demonstrated by Eysenck and Levey (1972). Such variables as strength of UCS and CS, and time-interval, as well as kind of reinforcement (continuous vs. partial), play an important role in determining the speed and ease of conditioning; therefore, any conclusion about the speed of conditioning in relation to personality dimensions must be seen to be limited (Gray, 1981).
7. It should be noted that strength of inhibition is limited to conditioned inhibition only and, as measured by the STI, is primarily manifested in restraining from reactions, in their delay, and in the ability to interrupt actions when needed (see p. 126).
8. As stated by such as Spielberger *et al.* (1970), the correlation of the IPAT Anxiety scale with other measures of this dimension is quite high. Correlating the results of the IPAT Anxiety scale with Taylor's MAS and Spielberger's STAI A-Trait scale the authors obtained the following correlation coefficients: (a) males—IPAT-MAS = 0.73; IPAT-STAI = 0.76; (b) females—IPAT-MAS = 0.85; IPAT-STAI = 0.75.
9. For a detailed description of the modification of Eysenck's theory of E/I and neuroticism, especially as regards their physiological interpretation, as well as for the interdependency between these dimensions and the primary dimensions distinguished by Gray—anxiety and impulsivity the reader should refer to Gray's publications (Gray, 1970, 1972b, 1978, 1981). Despite the differences in the interpretation of Eysenck's basic dimensions of personality and their physiological correlates, when using the notions of extraversion and neuroticism, Gray probably has in mind the same phenomena as Eysenck, since Gray does not criticize Eysenck's inventories for measuring the dimensions in question.
10. It is not clear from this study how the diagnosis of emotional stability was performed.
11. The denominations of traits in the separate factors have been given in accordance with the names used by the respective authors themselves.

## CHAPTER 5

1. In 1966 I obtained a six-month scholarship at Teplov's laboratory. It allowed me not only to conduct a study on partial NS properties (Strelau, 1969) but also to get acquainted with the methods used in that laboratory; and, most important, to establish close friendship with the late Nebylitsyn and his associates.
2. Speed of conditioning was used as the index of strength by Pavlov (see chapter 1) and was included into the Standard of TNS investigation accepted by the Academy of Medical Sciences. The same index was used for mobility diagnosis by Ivanov–Smolensky. Finally, Nebylitsyn used it as the main index of dynamism.
3. In this study, which included 190 male adults, aged 20–40 years, in each group, 24 traits were assessed using Eysenck's MPI, Taylor's MAS, Guilford-Zimmerman's GZTS, Thurstone's TTS, and Strelau's STI. The results of each group were submitted to factor analysis by the method of principal components and Kaiser's Varimax.
4. Our understanding of temperament differs in this respect from Eliasz's (1981), who considers temperament to be the dynamics of behaviour which includes state-reactivity. The physiological mechanism of temperament thus understood is, of course, much broader and includes all functional changes of the organism taking part in the process of regulation of stimulation.
5. Hebb used to use the term "arousal" to refer to central processes of the conceptual nervous system. Some psychophysiologists (see e.g. Fiske and Maddi, 1961) distinguish between central excitation caused mainly by the cortex-reticular formation loop, which they call activation, and peripheral excitation, determined by the autonomic nervous system and endocrine system, denoted arousal. For this reason, when referring to Hebb's centrally determined "optimal level of arousal" we will use the phrase "optimal level of activation".
6. The diagnosis of reactivity was accomplished by a special method adapted to rat investigation by Matysiak (1977). It consists of measuring RT to light stimuli of near-threshold intensity in avoidance conditioning. The reactivity index is composed of the mean RT to CSs (5 lx light) in ten trials. The shorter the RT the higher the reactivity in rats.
7. The factor analysis was based on Hotelling's principal components' method and Kaiser's Varimax. In the discussion the factors extracted after rotation are taken into account.

## CHAPTER 6

1. The Soviet psychologists, taking as point of departure the division of actions into executive and orienting ones proposed by Galperin, have considered the dependency between type of NS and style of action from the point of view of the equilibrium between executive and orienting reactions (see p. 64).
2. A special study aimed at investigating the structure of activity within the framework of Tomaszewski's theory has been conducted by Materska (1972).
3. Here again we assume that the homogeneous actions are performed in an intensive manner for a long time and with rather high motivation. Such examples as: solving mathematical problems, driving a car over a long distance, or continuous working at the turning lathe may be mentioned.

4. A more systematic presentation of some of our studies as regards the relation between reactivity and style of action as compared with the research conducted in this area by Soviet psychologists may be found elsewhere (Strelau, 1975c, 1978; Klonowicz, in press, b).
5. The effort (or so-called operational costs) was computed using the ratio of the sum of all operations performed to the quality of work, the latter measured by weighted points.
6. The following reasoning underlies this assumption. As stated in Chapter 5, reactivity directly determines the need for stimulation. Eliasz (1974) has argued that neuroticism should be considerd as a factor modifying the need for stimulation. This stems from the fact that in neurotic individuals, due to the generalization of anxiety, more stimuli and psychic states may gain high physiological intensity than compared with emotionally stable individuals.
7. The coefficient of skewness for which the formula is: $SK = 1 - 2p/\sqrt{p(1-p)}$ was taken from Kozielecki (1975).
8. The methods used by Vyatkin as well as by the whole Merlin group for diagnosing the temperament traits under discussion are not generally accepted and they have a rather local character (see note 24 to Chapter 1).
9. According to our assumption, in standard testing conditions (total relaxation with eyes closed) the stimulation will be too weak to evoke the appropriate bioelectric changes in low-reactive persons and this would be reflected in a high alpha index. High-reactive persons, identified by a low alpha index, are those who, because of their higher sensitivity, react to the experimental situation even though there is no specific stimulus. However, as shown in one of our studies (Strelau and Terelak, 1974), the alpha index does not correlate with reactivity as measured by STI, thus throwing some doubt on the justification for using the alpha index as a measure of reactivity.
10. There is no easy way of determining the level of stimulation in these two experimental settings, but there can be no doubt that Mackworth's vigilance test, one of the tasks administered in conditions of monotony, is less stimulating than the solving of arithmetic problems, in which the subject has to engage with some determination.
11. In this study trait anxiety was also under control, however, for our purposes the results for this dimension, discussed elsewhere (Strelau *et al.*, in press), are omitted here.

## CHAPTER 7

1. This argument is somewhat simplified because there are many other mechanisms which may cause reduction in discrepancy between the real and ideal self, the defence mechanism being the best example (Reykowski, 1970; Łukaszewski, 1974; Grzegołowska-Klarkowska, 1980).
2. The two scales were used as equivalent forms to retest the Machiavellian tendency after training aimed specifically at changing this tendency. Half of the group took Mach IV and the other half Mach V before the training sessions. According to Christie and Geis (1970) both methods may be used interchangeably. Nevertheless, for caution's sake the results have been changed to standard scores to make them comparable.

3. This disproportion in the number of strong and weak types of NS results from the rather strange criterion used by Król for diagnosing the strong type, where even those individuals whose performance decreased were included.
4. Because of the small number of functional answers these have been excluded from the statistical analysis.

# Appendix 1

# Strelau Temperament Inventory (STI)

Initials .............................. Age............... Sex...............

Education ........................... Occupation ...........................

Date of testing ...................... Remarks ..............................

The questions in this inventory refer to various traits of temperament. The replies given to these questions will not be evaluated in terms of right or wrong because each type of temperament has its advantages.

The data derived from the replies will be used for scientific purposes, hence the importance attached to the truthfulness of the replies.

Please answer the questions one by one without looking back to earlier replies.

Questions may be answered with one of three alternative replies: "yes", "no", or "?" (don't know)[1]. The "don't know" reply should be given whenever there is hesitation in choosing between "yes" or "no". Circle your reply in the following manner:

Can you easily forget a wrong done to you?   (Yes)   ?   No

Are you capable of controlling a strong emotion? Yes   (?)   No

| Scores | Nervous System Properties | | | |
|---|---|---|---|---|
| | Strength of Excitation | Strength of Inhibition | Equilibrium of NP | Mobility of NP |
| Raw score | | | | |
| Standard score | | | | |

---

[1] For the sake of space, the three alternative responses, "yes", "?", "no", will be omitted here. In the actual questionnaire sheet they should follow each question, making a column in the right margin of the sheet.

1. Do you make friends easily?
2. Are you capable of restraining yourself from doing something until you are given the signal to do it?
3. Does a brief rest remove your work fatigue?
4. Can you work in adverse circumstances?
5. In a discussion, can you resist the temptation to resort to non-substantial, emotional arguments?
6. Is it easy for you to resume work after a long break (caused by a holiday or the summer vacations)?
7. Can you forget your fatigue when immersed in work?
8. Having asked someone to perform a job, can you wait patiently until it's finished?
9. Do you easily fall asleep, irrespective of the hour of day, once in bed?
10. Can you easily keep a confidence?
11. Is it easy for you to resume a task you interrupted some weeks or months ago?
12. Do you show patience in supplying explanations?
13. Do you like occupations which involve mental exertion?
14. Do you feel bored or sleepy when performing monotonous work?
15. Do you easily fall asleep after a strong emotion?
16. Can you refrain from showing your superiority when necessary?
17. Do you have difficulties in controlling irritation or anger?
18. Do you behave in your customary manner in the presence of strangers?
19. In the face of hardships, do you still feel in control of the situation?
20. Are you capable of adapting your conduct to the behaviour of others in a group when necessary?
21. Do you readily assume responsible jobs?
22. Is your mood usually influenced by your surroundings?
23. Do you easily survive a defeat?
24. Do you talk as freely as usual in the presence of a person whom you want to impress?
25. Do unexpected changes in your day's schedule irritate you?
26. Do you have a ready answer to every argument?
27. Do you keep calm when waiting for some important announcement which could change the course of your life?
28. Are you quick in settling down when on holiday?
29. Are you quick in reacting to unexpected stimuli?
30. Can you easily adjust your gait or eating habits to someone who talks or eats much slower than you?
31. Do you fall asleep quickly when in bed?
32. Do you readily take the floor at meetings or other gatherings?
33. Are you easily upset?
34. Do you have difficulties in disengaging yourself from a job when engrossed in it?
35. Can you refrain from talking when this disturbs someone?
36. Are you hot-tempered?

37. When working with a partner, can you easily fall in step with him?
38. Do you always think twice before deciding on a course of action?
39. When reading a book etc., do you find it easy to follow the author's line of argument from start to finish?
40. Are you quick to join in a conversation with fellow travellers?
41. Can you refrain from arguing with someone who is wrong, when such argument is bound to be ineffective?
42. Do you like work requiring manual dexterity?
43. Do you change your mind when confronted with new arguments?
44. Do you easily get accustomed to a new job routine?
45. Can you work at night after a full day's work?
46. Do you read novels quickly?
47. Do you often give up plans because of some difficulty?
48. Can you keep calm when the situation requires it?
49. Do you wake quickly and without difficulty?
50. Can you restrain the impulse to react without forethought?
51. Does noise disturb you at your work?
52. Can you resist the temptation to tell people the truth, when restraint is desirable?
53. Can you control yourself when waiting for an exam, an unpleasant confrontation etc.?
54. Do you quickly get accustomed to a new environment?
55. Do you like frequent changes and diversions?
56. Does a night's sleep remove the fatigue caused by a hard days' work?
57. Do you shun those occupations which involve different operations in quick succession?
58. Do you solve your problems by yourself, as a rule?
59. Do you put forward your own arguments before the other party has stopped presenting his?
60. Would you jump into the water to rescue a drowning person, provided you could swim?
61. Can you work (or study) hard?
62. Can you refrain from making comments when these are out of place?
63. Do you prefer to have your permanent seat at work, at the table, in the lecture hall, etc.?
64. Do you easily switch from one occupation to another?
65. When facing a crucial decision, do you weigh carefully all the "pros" and "cons"?
66. Are you quick in overcoming obstacles?
67. Do you have difficulty in restraining your curiosity when an opportunity arises to take a look at someone's things or notes?
68. Do you get bored when performing stereotyped operations?
69. Is it easy for you to heed the rules of conduct in public places?
70. Can you refrain from superfluous gesticulation etc. while talking, addressing a gathering, or passing an oral test?
71. Do you like to stay in a place full of hustle and bustle?

72. Do you like strenuous occupations?
73. Are you able to concentrate on your work for any length of time?
74. Do you like those occupations which call for quick movements?
75. Do you preserve your calm in difficult situations?
76. Do you rise immediately upon wakening when necessary?
77. Having done a job, can you wait patiently for the others to finish theirs, if necessary?
78. Having witnessed an unpleasant or distressing sight, can you carry on with your customary efficiency?
79. Are you quick in looking through the day's newspapers?
80. Does it ever happen that your speech is so fast that it becomes incomprehensible?
81. Can you work as usual when you have had little sleep at night?
82. Are you capable of working uninterruptedly for a long time?
83. Does a headache or toothache seriously interfere with your work?
84. When there is a need to finish a job, do you proceed with it despite the fact that your colleagues are enjoying themselves or waiting for you?
85. Are you quick in responding to unexpected questions?
86. Do you speak rapidly?
87. Are you able to work while waiting for guests?
88. Do you easily change your opinion in the face of cogent arguments?
89. Are you patient?
90. Are you able to adapt to someone else's tempo of work if it is slower?
91. Can you plan your work in such a way as to perform more than one assignment at a time, when this is possible?
92. Does good-humoured company help you to recover from depression?
93. Can you perform several operations at a time without much exertion?
94. Do you preserve your composure having witnessed a road accident?
95. Do you like a job that calls for performing diverse operations?
96. Do you keep calm when seeing the suffering of a person dear to you?
97. Are you self-reliant in a critical situation?
98. Do you feel at ease in numerous or unknown company?
99. Can you interrupt a conversation at once when time has run out?
100. Do you easily adapt to the way other people work?
101. Do you like to change your occupation frequently?
102. In an accident, do you feel an urge to show initiative?
103. Can you restrain a smile when it is out of place?
104. Starting your work, do you get in high gear right at the beginning?
105. Would you question a generally accepted view if you were sure you were right?
106. Can you suppress momentary moods of dejection?
107. Do you find it difficult to fall asleep after a full day of strenuous and fatiguing brainwork?
108. Are you able to wait quietly in a long queue?
109. Can you abstain from lodging complaints when these are obviously useless?

## Appendix 1

110. Are you able to argue calmly in a heated debate?
111. Do you react at once to a sudden change in the situation?
112. Can you behave quietly when asked to do so?
113. Do you easily submit to painful medical or surgical treatment?
114. Can you work with great intensity?
115. Do you readily change your place of entertainment or rest?
116. Do you have difficulties in adapting to a new daily schedule?
117. Do you eagerly offer your help in an accident?
118. Do you refrain from excessive shouting or gesticulation at a sports event?
119. Do you like work that involves talking to many people?
120. Can you control your mimicry (pulling faces, smiling ironically etc.)?
121. Do you like occupations which require you to perform vigorous movements?
122. Do you consider yourself a person of courage?
123. Does your voice fail you in a critical situation?
124. Are you able to overcome despondency after failure?
125. Are you able to sit or stand quietly for a long time, when asked to do so?
126. Are you able to control your mirth if this could hurt someone?
127. Do you easily switch from sadness to good humour?
128. Are you easily thrown out of gear?
129. Is it easy for you to heed the rules of conduct accepted in your milieu?
130. Do you like to make public addresses?
131. Are you quick in starting your work, without tedious preparation?
132. Do you feel an urge to rescue people in danger even if this were to endanger your own life?
133. Are your movements vigorous?
134. Do you like assignments involving responsibility?

# Appendix 2
# Nursery School Child's Reactivity Rating Scale (RRS$_1$)

Administration date .................................................................

Child's full name ...................................................................

Nursery school number ............................................................

Nursery School teacher's full name ............................................

*Instruction:* Please assess on a 5-point scale the intensity of each of the enumerated behavioural traits, as manifested in the assessed child. Specific observed manners and forms of behaviour should be considered in the assessment. The cipher 1 denotes the lowest degree of intensity of a given trait (definite lack). For instance, when the trait of vigour or springiness of movement is assessed the cipher 1 will be marked when the child's observed movements are definitely lacking in vigour and springiness. The cipher 5 denotes the maximum intensity of a given trait (definitely manifests the given behavioural trait—the movements are springy and very vigorous). The cipher 3 is an intermediary assessment and denotes moderate intensity of the given trait. Encircle the selected cipher.

1. Is capable of concentrated attention

    1————————2————————3————————4————————5

| | | |
|---|---|---|
| Cannot concentrate on current activity (drawing, cut-outs, etc.); engages in conversation with others, looks at their work. | While working is very involved in current activity, but also interrupts work easily (engages in something else) but in a moment resumes the task. | Completely engrossed by current activity. Does not interrupt the task even for a moment. When invited to play with others refuses to participate. |

## Appendix 2

2. Is resistant to setbacks

1————————2————————3————————4————————5

| Under the influence of failure (criticism etc.) discontinues current activity (drawing, cut-outs, etc.), has to be encouraged to complete it. | Under the influence of failure may just as often become discouraged in his/her work, as he/she is willing to pass on to the next tasks assigned him/her. | Failure does not discourage him/her in his work. Willingly passes to next tasks, which are carried out more carefully. |

3. Shows initiative in organizing joint play with others.

1————————2————————3————————4————————5

| During group work or play subordinates him/herself to others (precisely carries out directions given by others, shows no opposition). | During group activity he/she may just as well subordinate him/herself to others, as try to lead the play him/herself. | Readily undertakes organisation of joint play, likes to lead others (imposes a play theme, assigns roles). |

4. Does not abandon current activity on encountering obstacles

1————————2————————3————————4————————5

| Even a small obstacle (difficulty etc.) makes him/her abandon the task. If he/she has to complete it, resorts to other's help. | Confronted with an obstacle he/she may just as well become discouraged toward the task, or make an effort to deal with it on his/her own. | Obstacles do not discourage him/her in carrying out a task. Tries to deal with encountered difficulties alone. |

5. In the presence of an unknown adult behaves as usual.

1————————2————————3————————4————————5

| Is timid in the presence of an unknown adult (reddens, averts gaze, answers with monosyllables). | In the presence of an unknown adult is initially timid, reddens, averts gaze. After a while begins to talk, willingly answers questions. | The presence of an unknown adult does not intimidate him/her. Treats conversation with an unknown adult as something natural. |

6. Shows no tension before an important task

1————————2————————3————————4————————5

| During a competition is tense, works nervously, is anxious about the final result (e.g. asks the teacher whether he/she is doing well). | During a competition may be tense (and then work nervously), but just as often may behave in that manner during the execution of non-competitive tasks. | During a competition behaves in the same manner as during the execution of other tasks. No manifestation of tension is observed. |

7. Willingly carries out tasks demanding considerable exertion

1————————2————————3————————4————————5

| Avoids long or tiresome activities (painstaking puzzles etc.), prefers easy, uninvolving tasks (playing with blocks, cars. etc.). | Engages just as willingly in easy uninvolving tasks as in more difficult and complicated ones (puzzles, games). | Likes very involving activities, which demand effort and resistance to possible difficulties which might appear during their execution (e.g. complicated puzzles or other kinds of games). |

8. In the presence of unknown persons behaves as usual

1————————2————————3————————4————————5

| Is timid in the presence of unknown adults, avoids public appearances (e.g. in front of a group of parents during school ceremonies). | In the presence of unknown persons may just as often be timid, as behave normally. | The presence of unknown persons does not intimidate him/her. Shows off willingly in front of others (recites, sings). |

9. Seeks the company of other children

1————————2————————3————————4————————5

| Prefers to play alone; prefers to sit at the table than join others playing. | Just as often plays alone, as with others. | Prefers to associate with others in joint play. Prefers to play with others than alone. |

# Appendix 3
# Pupil's Reactivity Rating Scale (RRS$_2$)

Administration date ..............................................................

Pupil's full name ................................................................

Elementary school number ......................... Class..................

Teacher's full name ..............................................................

Subject taught ....................................................................

*Instruction:* Please assess on a 5-point scale the intensity of each of the enumerated behavioural traits, as manifested in the assessed child. Specific observed manners and forms of behaviour should be considered in the assessment. The cipher 1 denotes the lowest degree of intensity of a given trait (definite lack). For instance, when the trait of vigour or springiness of behaviour is assessed the cipher 1 will be marked when the child's observed movements are definitely lacking in vigour and springiness. The cipher 5 denotes the maximum intensity of a given trait (definitely manifests the given behavioural trait—movements are springy and very vigorous). The cipher 3 is an intermediate assessment and denotes moderate intensity of the given trait. Encircle the selected cipher.

1. Is capable of concentrated atention

1—————2—————3—————4—————5

| Cannot concentrate on current activity. Noise in the hall, others' conversations or other interfering factors distract him/her from task performance. | While working is very engrossed by the task; however, can easily interrupt work (e.g. joins others' conversation) and after a moment resumes the task. | Is capable of concentrating on a task. Conversation, noise and other interferences do not interrupt his/her work. |

2. Is resistant to setbacks

1—————2—————3—————4—————5

| Under the influence of failure (reproof, bad mark) cries, does not prepare for school (does not do homework), does not offer to answer questions in class. | Under the influence of failure he/she may just as well become discouraged toward his/her work, or willingly pass on to the next tasks assigned him/her. | Failures mobilize him/her to study even more (offers to answer more questions, prepares homework more carefully). Does not become discouraged toward his/her work. |

3. Shows initiative in organizing play or work with others

1—————2—————3—————4—————5

| Avoids situations in which he/she would have to take initiative. Prefers to subordinate to others both in group work and play (executes others' directions, prefers to put their ideas into practice). | During group work just as often subordinates to others as tries to lead the group. | Likes to organize and lead play and work with others (distributes tasks, roles, determines work method, rules of the game etc.). |

4. Does not abandon performance of current activity on encountering an obstacle

1————————2————————3————————4————————5

| | | |
|---|---|---|
| Even a small obstacle (e.g. problem encountered during task execution) make him/her discouraged toward his/her work. Does not attempt to overcome the obstacle (e.g. find the error), immediately abandons the task. | Upon encountering an obstacle may either become discouraged or attempt to deal with the task on his own. | Upon encountering an obstacle (e.g. during answering, doing an exercise) does not abandon a task. Tries on his own to find the error or, another way of doing the exercise. |

5. In the presence of the teacher and less-known persons behaves as usual

1————————2————————3————————4————————5

| | | |
|---|---|---|
| Is timid in the presence of the teacher and less known persons (averts gaze, reddens when asked a question, answers with monosyllables). | In contact with the teacher and less known persons is initially timid (reddens). After a while begins to talk and answer questions. | The presence of the teacher and less known persons does not intimidate him/her. Treats talking with them as something natural. |

6. Shows no tension before an important task

1————————2————————3————————4————————5

| | | |
|---|---|---|
| Before a test, class exercise or individual answer is very tense (sits rigidly, nervously manipulates pen or other object). Shows nervousness during answering (reddens, hands tremble). | Before a test, class exercise or important individual answer, may either be tense or manifest no tension. | During a test, class exercise or individual answer behaves as usual. Shows no signs of tension. |

7. Willingly carries out tasks demanding considerable exertion

1————————2————————3————————4————————5

| | | |
|---|---|---|
| Does not undertake to execute long, fatiguing tasks, prefers simple ones as preparing charts, tables, etc. | Executes just as often easy, uninvolving tasks as reaches for more difficult and complicated ones. | Likes to execute involving tasks, demanding effort and problem-solving (preparing ingenious decorations, a wall-newspaper for a given occasion, etc.) |

8. In the presence of a group of unknown persons behaves as usual

1————————2————————3————————4————————5

| | | |
|---|---|---|
| Is timid in the presence of a group of unknown persons (reddens, answers with monosyllables). Never offers to answer questions during a visit of inspection. | The presence of unknown persons initially makes him timid (reddens, answers with monosyllables). After a while begins to behave as if among well-known persons. | The presence of unknown persons during a lesson (inspection) does not intimidate him. He/she offers to answer as during a normal lesson. Treats talking with these persons as something normal. |

9. Seeks the company of other persons

1————————2————————3————————4————————5

| | | |
|---|---|---|
| During breaks prefers to remain in class. Does not join others in play or talk. Prefers to be alone or with a close friend. | Can be seen just as often alone (or with one friend) as in a larger group. | Spends breaks in the hallways. Participates in games, usually of movement, with others, or talks in a large group. |

10. Willingly assumes independent and responsible functions

1————————2————————3————————4————————5

| | | |
|---|---|---|
| Never offers to fulfil functions for which he alone would be responsible (e.g. work in class self-government). Refuses them when proposed by class. | Just as often presents him/herself for responsible functions as avoids them. | Willingly accepts responsible tasks. Presents him/herself for independent class or school functions. |

# Appendix 4
# Pupil's Reactivity Rating Scale (RRS$_3$)

Administration date ............................................................

Pupil's full name ...............................................................

High school (type and number) ....................... Class...............

Teacher's full name ............................................................

Subject taught ..................................................................

*Instruction:* Please assess on a 5-point scale the intensity of each of the enumerated behavioural traits, as manifested in the observed pupil. Specific observed manners and forms of behaviour should be considered in the assessment. The cipher 1 denotes the lowest degree of intensity of the given trait (definite lack). For instance, when the trait of springiness and vigour of movement is assessed, the cipher 1 will be marked when the pupil's observed movements are definitely lacking in vigour and springiness. The cipher 5 denotes the maximum intensity of the given trait (definitely manifests the given behavioural trait—his movements are springy and very vigorous). The cipher 3 is an intermediary assessment and denotes moderate intensity of the given trait. Encircle the selected cipher.

1. Is capable of concentrated attention

   1————————2————————3————————4————————5

| | | |
|---|---|---|
| Cannot concentrate on current activity, others' conversations or other irrelevant stimuli distract him/her from task performance. | When performing a task is very concentrated, but can break off easily to engage in something else (e.g. talking with others). | Can focus on current activity (problem-solving, reading). Irrelevant stimuli (talk, noise etc.) do not distract him/her from task performance. |

2. Is resistant to setbacks

1————————2————————3————————4————————5

Transitory failures (criticism, reproof, bad notes) discourage him/her from studying. Begins to show up unprepared at school. Does not do homework.

Under the influence of failure, he/she may both become discouraged from studying or become more mobilized for study.

Failures mobilize him/her to studying well. Prepares thoroughly for lessons. When questioned is capable of answering not only on the current lesson, but also about preceding ones. During the lesson, more often offers to answer. Does not show signs of tension.

3. Shows initiative in organizing play or work with others

1————————2————————3————————4————————5

Avoids situations in which he/she would have to take initiative. During group work (or play) prefers to subordinate him/herself to others (carries out orders, does not present own ideas, does not discuss proposed problem-solving methods).

As often avoids situations in which he/she would have to take initiative as undertakes to organize and lead different forms of team work.

Likes to organize and direct team work (e.g. preparation of the artistic part of a school ceremony). Willingly undertakes to organize different kinds of enterprises in class and school.

4. Does not abandon performance of current activity on encountering an obstacle

1————————2————————3————————4————————5

Even a small obstacle (e.g. difficulty in solving a problem at the blackboard) makes him/her abandon a task.

Upon encountering an obstacle may either abandon a task or attempt to deal with it.

Encountered obstacles do not discourage him/her from further tasks. Attempts to overcome them (e.g. find and correct errors).

# Appendix 4

5. In the presence of the teacher and less-known persons behaves as usual

1————————2————————3————————4————————5

| Is timid in the presence of the teacher and less known persons (averts gaze, reddens when asked questions, answers with monosyllables). | In contact with the teacher and less known persons is initially timid (reddens). After a while begins to talk. Answers questions willingly. | The presence of the teacher and less-known persons does not intimidate him/her. Treats talking with them as something normal. |

6. Shows no tension before an important task

1————————2————————3————————4————————5

| During answering or writing a test is tense (reddens, hands tremble). | During answering or writing a test may be tense, but just as often may behave as usual. | During answering or writing a test is calm, behaves as usual. |

7. Willingly carries out tasks demanding considerable exertion

1————————2————————3————————4————————5

| Avoids long, tiring activities, prefers to undertake easy tasks (execution of small teaching aids, graphs, etc.). | Just as often avoids long, tiring activities as undertakes tasks which demand big effort and resistance to difficulties that may arise during their execution. | Willingly undertakes tasks which demand big effort and resistance to possible difficulties which may arise during their execution. May, for instance, undertake to prepare an extracurricular paper or produce ingenious decorations. |

8. In the presence of a group of unknown persons behaves as usual

1————————2————————3————————4————————5

| Is timid in the presence of a group of unknown persons (reddens, answers with monosyllables). Never presents him/herself to answer during an inspection. | The presence of unknown persons initially intimidates him (reddens, answers with monosyllables). After a while begins to behave as if in a group of well-known persons. | The presence of unknown persons during a lesson (inspection) does not intimidate him/her. Presents him/herself to answer as in a normal lesson. Treats talking with these persons as something normal. |

9. Seeks the company of other persons

1————————2————————3————————4————————5

| During breaks prefers to be alone. Usually reads or glances through a book or paper. If he/she talks, then only with one friend (a close one). | During breaks just as often talks only with a close friend as joins group discussion. | During breaks talks with friends. Likes to join others' discussions. |

10. Willingly assumes independent and responsible functions

1————————2————————3————————4————————5

| Never assumes responsibility for execution of a group task. Even when picked out by the class refuses fulfilling a function which would demand work on his/her own. | Just as often refuses responsible tasks and independent functions as assumes responsibility for execution of a group task. | Willingly executes responsible tasks. Fulfills independent class and school functions. Never refuses if this type of task is suggested by the class. |

11. In case of conflict strongly defends own opinion

1————————2————————3————————4————————5

| Does not like to take the risk of misunderstandings, always aims to compromise (during discussions, role divisions etc.). | Just as often is capable of a reasonable compromise as to hold own opinion. | Is able to maintain his/her views regardless of conflicts with others which might arise. |

# Appendix 5
# Temporal Traits Inventory (TTI)

Initials ................................... Age............ Sex...............

Education ........................... Occupation ...........................

Date of testing ....................... Remarks ..............................

The aim of this questionnaire is to determine certain temperament-related traits. It consists of a number of questions pertaining to different life situations which anyone may encounter. After each question, there is a choice of three answers: "yes" "question mark" and "no".[1] Read each question carefully and then decide which of the answers is true for you and encircle it. Give only one answer to each question. Mark "question mark" only in cases when you simply can't decide between "yes" or "no". If you want to change an earlier answer, cross out the circle previously made and mark the correct answer. Remember, there are no "good" or "bad" answers. The important thing is that they be sincere and well-considered. Answer the questions in order. There is no time limit.

1. Do you always wake up at the same time?
2. Are your physiological functions regular?
3. Do you stop worrying quickly after a reprimand at work (a bad mark in class)?
4. Do you get tired quickly in a situation where you have to switch attention from one thing to another alternately?
5. Was it difficult for you in school to get into a new lesson on a different subject after the break (for instance, English after Maths or vice versa)?

---

[1] See footnote to Appendix 1.

6. Were you always one of the first in school athletic contests (physical education classes, sports, games)?
7. Do you often involuntarily count different objects?
8. Do you usually make up your mind slowly, after careful thought?
9. When you hear an unpleasant remark about yourself, do you think of it over and over again?
10. Do you always wash in a hurry, even though you have plenty of time?
11. When you get an important instruction, do you always have to wait a little before you start carrying it out?
12. Do you tolerate easily changes in your daily schedule?
13. When you can dispose of your own time, do you work and relax regularly (at fixed hours)?
14. Are you often asked by others to speak more slowly?
15. Are you in general indifferent as to the time you have dinner?
16. When you are working on something (studying), is it easy for you to break off from your work?
17. Do you easily tolerate sudden changes in your normal sleeping hours (e.g. on a long trip)?
18. If someone causes you unpleasantness, do you think about it for a long time?
19. Can you work normally after a sleepless night?
20. If something unnerves you in the morning, does your irritation quickly pass?
21. Does it often happen that you hum the same tune over and over again?
22. Does it often happen that you think so deeply about something that you don't reply immediately to a question put to you?
23. If you quarrel in the evening with someone, do you wake up thinking about it?
24. Can you manage to pay attention to more than one topic of conversation at a time?
25. At meetings, lectures or lessons, do you often make the same doodles, or write the same signs (letters, ciphers)?
26. Is it hard for you to concentrate once again on a book when someone has distracted you from it?
27. Do you jump out of the way immediately on hearing a car honking behind you?
28. When you are at summer camp or on an organized vacation, does it take you a while to get used to the new daily schedule?
29. On your way home from work (school, university), do you keep on thinking about what happened there?
30. When you began working (going to school or to college), did you quickly get used to your new requirements and duties?
31. If you had your way, would you work (study) at various hours of the day, and not the same ones?
32. Do you usually get hungry at the same time every day?
33. Do you get over your anger quickly after a quarrel?

34. When you are working (studying) and you hear a sudden noise outside, do you immediately interrupt your work?
35. Are you sometimes at a loss for words?
36. Are there regular hours when you work (study) best?
37. Is it difficult for you to concentrate on work (study) before an important meeting with someone?
38. Were you quick at getting used to new teachers at school?
39. When you have been learning something by heart (text, vocabulary), do you involuntarily keep repeating it throughout the day?
40. Do you react immediately to hearing your name being mentioned in a large group of people?
41. Do you need a lot of time in the morning to get washed, dressed and have breakfast, in order to get to work (school) on time?
42. Do you need considerable time to get packed before a trip?
43. Do you mind sudden changes in your meal hours?
44. Do you always try to be one of the first to get onto a bus?
45. Just before an exam can you deal with other unconnected matters?
46. After a long interval during which you did not practice a well-known activity, do you get back into shape slowly?
47. If somebody says something hurtful to you, do you always have an immediate comeback ready?
48. If somebody calls you, do you usually take a moment before responding?
49. After a long period of absence from work (school), is it difficult for you to get into things again?
50. If somebody interrupts your work (studying), does it take you a while to fix your attention again?
51. Does your mind often return to a conversation you had during the day?
52. After the topic of conversation has been changed, do you often still keep thinking about the one before?
53. Do you quickly scan through the newspapers?
54. Do you usually fall asleep at the same time?
55. Are you usually a fast eater?
56. Do you usually quickly drop your resentment toward somebody who has acted insultingly towards you?
57. Do you often regret that you didn't act more quickly (e.g. that you didn't answer back)?
58. Do you attach importance to regular mealtimes?
59. Do you cross the street more quickly than other people?
60. When you hear an ambulance signal on the street, do you immediately turn to look in that direction?
61. In talking with others, do you involuntarily repeat certain movements (for instance, drumming your fingers, swinging your leg, twisting your hair, breaking matches, rolling a pen, etc.)?
62. Do you fall asleep just as easily when you go to bed at different times?
63. Is it hard for you to get used to a new place (on vacation, after moving, etc.)?

64. Does it often happen for you to have thoughts recurring over and over again?
65. When you hear someone at the door, do you usually delay a moment before opening?
66. Can you calmly eat lunch after a heated exchange with your boss (teacher)?
67. Can you work intellectually after protracted physical effort?
68. Do you usually leave home at the last minute before going to an important meeting?
69. Do you quickly get back into work after vacation?
70. When you are unnerved, do you repeat certain actions (walking back and forth, eating, etc.)?
71. Do you quickly shift subjects of conversation?
72. Do you usually have a lot of ideas for spending free time?
73. When you are eating with others, are you usually one of the last to finish?
74. After an important conversation with your boss (teacher), do you usually stop bothering about it right away?
75. Does your mind often return to decisions you have already made?
76. Does tidying up and putting away your things generally take a lot of time?
77. In school did you react to the bell immediately?
78. Do you tend to go downstairs slowly?
79. Do you walk more quickly than other people of the same age?
80. When the green light comes on, are you one of the last to step down from the pavement?
81. Do you easily (quickly) go from joy to sadness and from sadness to joy?
82. Do you usually reply at once to questions?
83. Do you sometimes involuntarily count your own steps?
84. Do you think you would not have any difficulty in doing shiftwork (working days and nights, alternately)?
85. Do you sometimes count the steps you are walking on?
86. When you are doing housework, do you easily forget unpleasant situations you had that day at work (school)?
87. When you are in a bad humour, can cheerful company quickly change your mood?
88. If you didn't get something done that day as you had planned to do, do you keep thinking about it?
89. When you are faced with a problem, do you focus on one way of handling it?
90. Do you take your time over coffee (tea) when you are in a café or restaurant?
91. Were you a fast runner at school, compared with your classmates?
92. Are you one of the first to rise from your place in the cinema, when the picture is over?
93. In a conversation, do you often repeat something several times, or return to the same thought (topic)?
94. Do you consider yourself fast on the uptake?

## Appendix 5

95. When somebody enters the room suddenly where you are at work with other people, do you immediately turn around in his direction?
96. Do you usually get dressed quickly, even when you are in no hurry?
97. Do you quickly forget about an accident you saw in the street?
98. Do you open your mail without delay?
99. After an exam (test, class exercise), do you keep living it over for some time afterwards?
100. In school did you finish timed classwork more slowly than your classmates?
101. While you're talking, do you often stumble or repeat words or phrases?
102. When you have a problem to solve, do you usually have several ideas at a time on how to solve it?
103. Do you speak more slowly than others?
104. If there is a problem to solve, do you keep returning to it?
105. Do you often wake up in the night?
106. Do you often catch yourself repeating in your mind some words or sentences?
107. After a setback at work (school), do you keep thinking about it?
108. Do you catch yourself doing things over and over (combing hair, arranging your clothes)?

MAKE SURE YOU HAVE ANSWERED ALL THE QUESTIONS!

# Author Index

Adrian, E. D., 101, 286
Akimova, M. K., 67, 107, 220, 225, 286
Aleksandrova, N. I., 75, 85, 88–89, 94, 109, 286, 313, 317
Aleksandrovskaya, E. M., 66, 326
Alekseyeva, M. S., 25, 286
Allport, G. W., 173, 286
Aminov, N. A., 161, 301
Ananyev, B. G., 324
Anastasi, A., 199, 286
Anokhin, P. K., 6, 51–52, 179, 286–287
Apter, I. M., 24, 287
Argyle, M., 233, 287
Asch, S. E., 265
Asratyan, E. A., 15, 24, 97, 287
Atkinson, J., 236, 274, 277, 287

Bakulev, A. N., 115, 287
Bales, R. F., 231–233, 287
Barker, R. G., 304
Barkhudaryan, S. S., 33, 287
Barnes, G. E., 29, 141, 287
Basan, L. I., 115, 287
Baymetov, A. K., 62, 65, 287
Bazylevich, T. F., 75, 88, 96, 177, 287
Becker-Carus, C., 110, 288
Belenkaya, L. Ya., 22, 293
Belous, V. V., 28, 34, 62, 67–69, 157, 288, 310
Berezhkovskaya, E. L., 66, 326
Berlyne, D. E., 179, 186, 278–279, 288

Białowąs, D., 265–268, 288
Birch, H. G., 172, 175, 177, 184, 191, 195, 208, 258, 260, 325, 332
Birman, B. N., 24, 115, 288
Biryukova, Z., 22, 116, 288
Bitterman, M. E., 33, 105, 288
Blaydon, J., 136, 295
Bloom, B. S., 42, 288
Boiko, E. I., 90–91, 205, 288
Borisova, M. N., 26, 31, 33, 37–38, 74, 78–80, 84–85, 87, 97–99, 105, 107, 286, 288, 296 300–301, 304, 317–318, 326
Brebner, J. M. T., 56, 150, 152, 192, 289
Bruner, J. S., 186, 240, 279, 290
Brzezicki, E., 172, 290
Buchsbaum, M. S., 76, 142, 177, 290
Bundych, T. B., 98–100, 290
Burdina, V. N., 17, 290
Burks, J., 172, 208, 290, 332
Busalov, A. A., 115, 287
Buss, A. H., 171–172, 175, 184, 194, 208, 290, 332
Butler, J. M., 269, 290

Cameron, B., 237, 290
Carlier, M., 32, 131–132, 136, 147, 152–154, 159, 162–163, 197, 290
Carriol, J., 110, 295
Castaneda, A., 176, 291
Cattell, R. B., 48, 140, 159, 161, 194, 291, 332

# Author Index

Cazzullo, C. L., 150, 291
Chebykin, D. A., 17, 22, 33, 290–291
Chekirov, M. M., 135, 328
Chernigovsky, V. N., 19, 294, 313
Chess, S., 171–172, 175, 177, 184, 191, 195, 208, 224, 258, 260, 325, 332
Choynowski, M., 151, 291
Christie, R., 272, 291, 335
Chudnovsky, V. E., 116, 171, 291
Chuprikova, N. I., 32, 75, 177, 291
Ciosek, M., 153, 163, 230, 291
Cole, M., 287
Coles, M., 136, 295
Colquhoun, W. P., 196, 291
Conrad, K., 173, 256, 291
Cooper, C., 56, 152, 192, 289, 290
Cymes, I., 211, 216–217, 224, 291
Cytawa, J., 23–24, 115, 292
Czyżkowska, A. M., 211, 218–219, 292

Danch, I., 67, 80, 292
Danielak, M., 226–227, 292
Danilova, N. N., 92, 292
Davidenkov, S. N., 24, 134, 292
Davydov, V. V., 286, 297, 313
Davydova, A. N., 115, 292
Delafresnaye, J. F., 295
Depue, R. A., 290
Diamond, S., 174, 292
Diaz-Guerrero, R., 321
Dikopolskaya, G. E., 64, 66, 222–223, 225, 309
Dolin, A. O., 292, 332
Dorfman, L. Ya., 135, 292
Duffy, E., 41, 170, 174, 176–177, 179, 257, 292
Dyk, R. B., 277, 328
Dymond, R. F., 290
Dzgoyeva, T. A., 17, 177, 301

Edwards, J., 290
Edwards, W., 237, 292

Egan, J. P., 325, 331
Eliasz, A., 27, 105, 114, 130, 168, 170–172, 176, 179, 181–182, 185–187, 191, 206, 230–231, 234–237, 274–275, 292–293, 322–323, 334–335
Elkin, D. G., 22, 293
Endler, N. S., 260, 263, 307
Erlenmeyer-Kimling, L., 48, 293
Ewald, G., 174, 193, 293
Eysenck, H. J., 3, 13, 22, 29, 35–36, 58, 76, 136, 138–139, 143–152, 154, 159–160, 162, 164–166, 173, 176, 179, 192, 194, 244, 264, 293, 298, 328, 333–334
Eysenck, S. B. G., 152, 293

Fahrenberg, J., 115, 293
Farley, F. H., 290, 294–295, 299, 302, 322–323
Farmer, R. G., 76, 147–148, 161, 308, 332
Faterson, H. F., 277, 328
Feather, N. T., 274, 277, 287
Fedorov, V. K., 13, 15–16, 19, 25, 33, 134, 293–294, 303–305, 307, 313, 317, 319, 326, 329
Fedoseyev, M. P., 324
Feshbach, S., 294, 316
Festinger, L., 264, 294
Fiske, D. W., 58, 135, 179, 185, 187–188, 197, 211, 294, 325, 334
Fowler, H., 306
Frankenhaeuser, M., 179, 247, 294, 307
Franks, C. M., 115, 136, 294
Frączek, A., 283, 294, 316
Freeman, G. L., 174, 188, 294
Friedensberg, E., 198–201, 211, 216–217, 222–225, 294
Friedman, I., 269, 295
Friedman, M., 247, 295
Frigon, J. Y., 146, 151–152, 161, 295
Furukawa, T., 179, 295

Gagné, R. M., 22, 33, 295
Galanter, E., 209, 310
Gale, A., 110, 136, 290–291, 294–295, 299, 302, 322–323
Galen, 11, 24, 255
Galperin, P. Y., 64, 334
Gantman, Yu. N., 275–277, 295
Gardner, R. W., 277–278, 280, 295
Gastaut, G., 110, 295
Gastaut, H., 108, 110, 295
Geis, F., 272, 291, 335
Georgiyev, V., 23–24, 309
Gerasimov, V. P., 67, 295
Gerstmann, S., 115–116, 295
Gilliland, K., 146, 152, 295
Glass, D. C., 247, 295
Goldwurm, G. F., 150, 291
Golikov, N. V., 34, 101, 104, 295, 303
Golubeva, E. A., 26, 34–35, 37, 39–41, 48, 53–54, 59–61, 74–75, 78–81, 85–88, 90, 93–104, 109, 168, 286, 289, 296–297, 300–301, 304, 306, 312, 314, 317–318, 326
Goodenough, D. R., 277, 328
Gorbacheva, V. A., 115, 297
Gorbachevsky, I. I., 38
Gorbunov, V. V., 107, 297
Gordeyeva, A. K., 67, 72, 215, 297, 303
Gorozhanin, V. S., 55, 297
Gorsuch, R. L., 157, 321, 333
Goryńska, E., 129, 195, 197–198, 201, 297
Gray, J. A., 4, 13–14, 28–29, 35, 40, 76, 79, 82–83, 118, 136, 139–141, 143–146, 148–150, 152, 156, 159–160, 170, 174, 179–180, 184, 187, 192, 289, 291, 293, 296–300, 306, 308, 312, 317, 322, 324, 327, 329, 332–333
Greenfield, P. M., 290
Grodner, M., 205, 242–243, 247, 298
Grzegołowska-Klarkowska, H., 263, 298, 335

Guilford, J. P., 129, 165, 173, 184, 199, 244, 298, 334
Gurevich, K. M., 26, 31, 33, 37, 42, 53, 67, 72, 74–75, 97–99, 105, 109, 214, 220, 247, 286, 289, 292, 295, 298, 302–304, 318, 323
Gurevich, V. C., 22, 299
Gurycka, A., 314
Guseva, E. P., 39, 59, 75, 81, 93, 95–96, 99, 101–104, 108–109, 296, 299, 301, 314
Guydosh, R. M., 76, 140, 257, 318

Haber, R. N., 186, 299
Haier, R., 142, 177, 290
Haigh, E. V., 269, 290
Halmiová, O., 13, 109, 150, 161, 299, 304, 331
Haslam, D. R., 30, 150, 176, 299
Hebb, D. O., 170, 179, 185–186, 188–189, 299, 334
Helson, H., 179, 181, 186–188, 299
Heymans, G., 174, 184, 194, 299
Hippocrates, 11, 18, 24, 255
Hjelle, L. A., 275, 299
Hull, C. L., 138, 145, 156, 299

Iacono, W., 76, 140, 257, 318
Ignatyev, E. I., 326
Ilin, E. P., 21, 35, 40, 51, 178, 187, 299
Ilina, A. I., 115–116, 233–234, 300
Ilina, G. N., 75, 300
Ippolitov, F. V., 29, 34, 50, 78, 80, 86–87, 300
Ivanov-Smolensky, A. G., 14, 19, 22, 24–25, 31, 36, 49, 51, 139, 155, 300, 330, 334
Ivanova, E. A., 23, 49, 86, 92, 313
Ivanova, M. P., 300
Izyumova, S. A., 39, 59, 61, 75, 96, 99, 101–102, 104, 108–109, 161, 296, 300–301

Jakubowicz, J., 23–24, 292
Jarvik, L. F., 48, 293

Jasper, H., 301, 331
Johnson, J., 142, 177, 290
Jung, C. G., 138, 301, 332

Kachura, L. P., 24, 301
Kadyrov, B. R., 39, 109, 306
Kagan, J., 277, 279–280, 301
Kant, I., 167, 174, 193, 301
Kapustin, A. N., 78, 92, 276–277, 301
Karp, S. A., 277, 328
Karpova, A. K., 146, 152, 161, 301
Kashin, A. P., 98–100, 105, 290, 301, 314
Kavetsky, R. E., 17, 177, 301
Kerimov, D. A., 313
Khalik, A. V., 135, 301
Khilchenko, A. E., 32, 106–108, 194, 196, 206, 302
Khlebutina, T. A., 107, 302
Khozak, L. E., 25
Kidd, A. H., 301
Klimov, E. A., 62–65, 116, 302
Kline, P., 295
Klonowicz, T., 89, 105, 114, 128, 168, 170, 173, 179, 192–193, 206, 211, 218–220, 224, 246–252, 254, 268, 302, 322–323, 335
Klyagin, V. S., 42, 67, 72, 74–75, 85, 94, 109, 215, 230, 297–298, 302–303, 317
Kłodecka-Rożalska, J., 165, 242–247, 303
Kofta, M., 159, 303
Kok, E. P., 115, 305
Kokorina, E. P., 19, 22, 303
Kolchenko, N. V., 31–32, 72, 105–107, 134, 147, 197, 230, 303, 325, 331
Kolchina, L. P., 78, 80, 92, 303
Kolesnikov, M. S., 14–15, 22, 155, 299, 303
Kolodnaya, A. Ya., 31, 33, 97–99, 289
Komarova, T. F., 18, 303
Konorski, J., 6, 33, 177, 179, 303

Kopylov, A. G., 101, 303
Kopytova, L. A., 64, 72, 78, 81, 90–92, 135, 304
Kordyukova, M. R., 107, 135, 304
Korotkin, I. I., 25
Kotov, L. N., 100, 318
Kounin, J. S., 194, 304
Kovač, D., 161, 304
Kozielecki, J., 304, 335
Kozlova, L. N., 16–17, 171, 325
Kozlova, V. T., 31–32, 100, 107, 134, 304
Kozłowski, C., 237–240, 304
Krajewski, A., 211, 214, 224, 323
Krasnogorsky, N. I., 14, 19–24, 139, 304
Krasnovskaya, M. S., 17, 177, 301
Krasuskaya, N. A., 15, 304
Krasusky, V. K., 13–19, 22, 134, 155, 290, 303–305, 307, 313, 317, 319, 326, 329
Kretschmer, E., 173–174, 179–180, 194–195, 256, 305
Kreutz, M., 173, 305
Krohne, H. W., 58, 305, 307, 319
Król, T. Z., 274–277, 305, 336
Kruchenko, Zh. A., 16–17, 171, 325
Krupnov, A. I., 104, 305
Krushinsky, L. V., 155, 305
Kulagin, D. A., 161, 305
Kupalov, P. S., 13, 16, 36–37, 305
Kurkchi, L. N., 107, 302
Kurkchi, N. F., 107, 302

Lacey, J. I., 115, 305
Lang-Belonogova, N. S., 115, 305
Laux, L., 58, 305, 307, 319
Lazarus, R. S., 241, 306
Leites, N. S., 26, 36–37, 39, 64, 109, 116, 156, 171, 173, 286, 289, 296, 300–301, 304, 306, 317, 326
Leontev, A. N., 170, 173, 257, 306
Leuba, C., 185, 306
Levey, A. B., 13, 22, 29, 35, 76, 139, 143, 152, 306, 333
Levitov, N. D., 173, 306

Leviyeva, S. N., 49, 86, 92, 313
Levochkina, I. A., 53, 93, 317
Likhachev, L. V., 233, 306
Lindsley, D. B., 110, 306
Lipovetsky, S. S., 75, 109, 314
Lisenkova, V. P., 49, 86, 92, 313
Livanov, M. N., 92, 306
Lomov, B. F., 26, 289, 306, 308, 314–315, 319, 327
Loo, R., 13, 76, 147–150, 306–307
Lovchikov, V. A., 15, 307
Lovell, C., 173, 307
Lubovsky, V. I., 286, 298, 302
Lundberg, U., 247, 307
Lushene, R. E., 157, 321, 333
Lynn, R., 295
Łukaszewski, W., 187, 269, 307, 335

Maciejczyk, J., 246–247, 307, 323
Maddi, S. R., 58, 135, 179, 186–188, 197, 211, 294, 325, 334
Magnusson, D., 260, 263, 307
Magoun, H. W., 110, 311
Maizel, N. I., 22, 307
Makarchenko, A. F., 303
Malkov, N. E., 106, 173, 307
Malmo, R. B., 174, 307
Maltzman, I., 287
Mangan, G. L., 13, 34, 76, 118, 131, 136, 143–144, 146–148, 150, 152, 154, 159, 161–163, 166, 171, 189, 192, 293, 302, 307–308, 313, 328, 330, 332
Mann, R. D., 233, 308
Markelov, V. V., 71, 308, 328
Martin, I., 76, 139, 306
Marton, M. L., 13, 150, 156, 161, 308, 332
Maruszewski, M., 325
Maryutina, T. M., 75, 308
Mastvilisker, E. I., 63–66, 68, 78, 81, 91–92, 222–223, 225, 308–310
Matczak, A., 170, 173, 277–282, 309
Materska, M., 209, 219, 309, 334
Mateyev, D., 23–24, 309
Matthews, B. H., 101, 286

Matveyev, V. F., 53, 72, 116, 298, 309
Matysiak, J., 170, 180, 189, 309, 334
Mayorov, F. P., 6, 14, 16, 22, 155, 309, 328
Melikhova, E. F., 31, 309
Melnichenko, O. G., 276, 309
Merlin, V. S., 14, 51, 53, 62–64, 67–71, 78, 81, 91–92, 112, 136, 139, 156, 167, 171, 173, 208, 222, 225, 241, 257, 261, 287–288, 300–301, 303, 308–310, 313, 315, 319–320, 322, 326–327, 331–332, 335
Mileryan, E. A., 27, 106, 319
Miller, G., 209, 310
Mirkowska, A., 272–273, 311
Moldavskaya, S. I., 31–32, 72, 105–107, 134, 147, 197, 230, 319, 325, 331
Morris, L. W., 311, 333
Morrish, R. B., 161, 328
Moruzzi, G., 110, 311
Moss, H. A., 277, 279–280, 301
Muldarov, V. K., 67, 215, 303
Mundy-Castle, A. C., 101, 110, 311
Mündelein, H., 215, 311
Myasishchev, V. N., 295, 303
Myers, J., 237, 290
Myrsten, A. L., 179, 294

Naquet, R., 110, 295
Nebylitsyn, V. D., 3, 14, 21–22, 24–31, 33–35, 37–40, 49–53, 58, 62, 67, 72–74, 76, 78–80, 84–90, 92–101, 103–104, 108–109, 111–112, 114–115, 126–127, 131, 134, 136, 139, 148–149, 156, 161, 167–169, 176–178, 180, 183–184, 187, 192, 196, 205–206, 257, 286–287, 289, 291, 293, 296–300, 306, 308, 311–313, 315, 317–319, 322–327, 329–331, 333–334
Nikiforovsky, P. M., 1–2, 8, 312

## Author Index

Nikityuk, B. A., 63, 296, 299, 304–305, 309–310, 313–315, 318–319
Nordheden, B., 179, 294
Norkina, L. N., 19, 312
Nosarzewski, J., 211, 220–221, 312
Numan, R., 96, 179, 312
Nuttin, J., 234, 312

Obraztsova, G. A., 16, 19, 313
Obuchowski, K., 279, 313
Oderyshev, B. S., 40–41, 313
Oleszkiewicz, Z., 142, 228–229, 313
Olshannikova, A. E., 26, 88–89, 286, 289, 296, 300–301, 304, 313, 317, 326
Olteanu, T., 13, 327
Olver, R. R., 290
Oniszczenko, W., 249, 253–254, 323, 335
Orlebeke, J. F., 13, 140, 161–162, 313
Orlikowska, H., 116, 295
Oszmiańczuk, J., 153, 163, 230, 291

Paisey, T. J. H., 13, 76, 131, 143–144, 146–147, 152, 154, 159, 162–163, 166, 189, 192, 293, 302, 308, 313
Paley, I. M., 38–40, 49, 86, 92, 115, 184, 300, 313
Palkina, T. P., 67, 69, 288
Palmer, R. D., 179, 313
Panteleyeva, T. A., 44, 46–48, 78, 96, 99, 102, 313–314, 319
Pasynkova, A. V., 75, 109, 314
Pavlov, I. P., 1–15, 18–30, 32–33, 36, 39–42, 56, 58, 62, 67, 69, 73, 76–77, 79, 84, 104–106, 115, 117–118, 125–127, 131, 134, 136–137, 139, 142, 145–146, 151, 154–156, 167–169, 171, 176, 192, 194, 257, 314, 330, 334
Pechenkov, V. V., 39, 59, 75, 96, 101–102, 104, 109, 296, 301

Pekhletsky, I. D., 67, 310
Perczyńska, D., 233–234, 314
Pervomaysky, B. Ya., 24, 115, 314
Petrella, F., 150, 291
Petrie, A., 141–142, 176, 192, 257, 290, 314
Pcysakhov, N. M., 27, 88, 90–92, 290, 301, 314, 332
Piaget, J., 278, 314
Plomin, R., 171–172, 175, 184, 194, 208, 290, 332
Podkopayev, N. A., 309
Popescu-Neveanu, P. G., 13, 36, 314
Popielarska, M., 227–228, 314
Post, B., 179, 294
Povorinsky, Yu. A., 23, 314
Powell, G. E., 26, 35, 76, 118, 150, 192, 314
Pribram, K., 50, 209, 310
Prusakova, M. B., 65–66, 222, 224, 315
Pshenichny, I. P., 18, 315

Rabinovich, R. I., 107, 315
Ratanova, T. A., 176, 315
Ravich-Shcherbo, I. V., 26, 31, 33, 37, 42, 44–47, 74, 76, 78–80, 86–89, 93–99, 102–103, 107–109, 286, 289, 296, 300–301, 304, 306, 308, 312, 314–317, 319, 326–327
Rebrov, V. P., 24, 316
Regan, D., 75, 316
Reykowski, J., 241, 257, 259, 264, 269, 271, 283, 316, 325, 335
Rivoire, J. L., 301
Rogers, C. R., 270, 290, 316
Roget, A., 108, 110, 295, 316
Rokotova, N. A., 36, 105, 316
Rosenman, R. H., 247, 295
Roshchina, L. V., 15, 307
Rozhdestvenskaya, V. I., 26, 29, 34–35, 53–59, 61, 74–85, 87, 94–97, 100, 109, 144, 211, 248, 286, 289, 296–297, 300–301, 304, 316–318, 326

Rubenstein, M., 172, 208, 290, 332
Rubinstein, S. L., 170, 209, 257, 318
Rusalov, V. M., 25–26, 28, 51–52, 74–75, 90, 99–100, 168, 180, 286, 289, 296, 300–301, 304, 306, 314, 317–318, 326, 332
Ryabinina, E. P., 80, 90, 318

Sales, S. M., 76, 140–141, 257, 318
Samarin, Yu. A., 115–116, 318
Samonov, A. P., 72, 135, 318
Sanocki, W., 120, 319
Saprykin, P. G., 27, 106, 319
Sarason, I. G., 323
Schaefer, T. Jr., 30, 325
Schoen, R. A., 277–278, 280, 295
Schönpflug, W., 241, 319
Schulz, P., 241, 319
Schwarth, G. E., 290
Semagin, V. N., 22, 176, 319
Serkov, M. I., 67, 75, 215, 298
Shadrin, V. M., 290, 301, 314
Shagass, C., 301, 331
Shapiro, D., 290
Shchukin, M. R., 64–65, 72, 225, 319
Sheerer, C., 295
Sheldon, W. H., 173, 256, 319
Shevko, G. N., 107, 319
Shibarovskaya, G. A., 37, 44, 46–48, 76, 108–109, 315, 319
Shlakhta, N. F., 44–48, 78, 81, 95–96, 102, 104, 109, 299, 314–315, 319
Shorokhova, E. V., 257, 319
Shtimmer, E. V., 63, 65–66, 222, 319
Shtodin, M. P., 19, 327
Shvarts, L. A., 31, 33, 37, 97–101, 103, 289, 297, 315, 320
Siddle, D. A. T., 161, 328
Siegel, I. E., 277, 279–280, 301
Silina, E. A., 67–68, 320
Silverman, J., 177, 290

Simanovsky, S. M., 24, 320
Simonov, P. V., 58, 320
Singer, J. E., 247, 295
Sinkevich, Z. L., 25
Sirotsky, V. V., 16–17, 171, 325
Sitkovskaya, O. D., 109, 329
Skinner, B. F., 191
Sklarova, E. G., 24, 320
Smirnov, A. A., 26, 59, 61, 289, 291, 296, 315, 317–318, 320, 326
Smith, S. L., 320
Smoleńska, M. Z., 265, 320
Solodyuk, N. F., 17, 177, 301
Soloveva, S. A., 60, 81, 320–321
Sosnowski, T., 158, 170, 231–233, 249, 253–254, 321, 323, 335
Spearman, C., 49, 194, 321
Spence, K. W., 138, 156, 264, 321
Spielberger, C. D., 157, 267, 321, 323, 333
Stawowska, L., 128–129, 230, 321
Stern, W., 25, 321
Stevens, S. S., 173, 256, 319
Strelau, J., 7, 13, 16, 22, 25, 27–28, 30, 32, 34–35, 42, 50–51, 76, 79–80, 87, 90, 105, 111–112, 114, 117–119, 134, 136, 138, 143, 146–147, 153–154, 156, 158–159, 162–165, 167–168, 171, 173–176, 179–180, 185, 191–193, 195, 197, 201, 205–206, 210–212, 214, 224, 242, 244–246, 249, 253–254, 264, 274, 290, 294–295, 297, 299, 302, 309, 312, 321–323, 325, 331–335
Strykowska, M., 240, 323
Strzałkowska, G., 269–271, 283, 323
Sukhanova, N. V., 23, 323
Sukhareva, A. I., 225, 323
Suslov, B. V., 71, 78, 81, 323
Suvorova, V. V., 53, 168, 179, 323
Syerda, Yu. L., 295, 303–304, 318
Šebová, E., 299, 331

Taylor, J. A., 138, 157, 160, 165, 244, 321, 323, 333–334

# Author Index

Teplov, B. M., 7, 14–16, 21–22, 24–32, 34, 36–39, 41–43, 49, 51–53, 58, 60, 62, 67, 73–74, 78–79, 82, 84, 86, 97, 99–102, 104, 111, 114, 126–127, 131, 136, 139, 155–156, 167–169, 171, 176, 178, 183, 187, 192–193, 196, 207, 257, 288–289, 296–298, 300, 306–307, 309, 311–313, 315–317, 320, 323–326, 329, 331, 334
Terelak, J., 130–134, 153, 158, 163, 165, 175, 230, 245, 325, 335
Terry, R. A., 179, 325
Theofrastus, 255
Thomas, A., 171–172, 175, 177, 184, 191, 195, 208, 224, 258, 260, 325, 332
Thompson, W. R., 30, 325
Throop, W. F., 76, 141, 318
Thurstone, L. L., 165, 173, 184, 244, 325, 334
Toeplitz, Z., 152, 325
Tomaszewski, T., 170, 190, 209, 241, 257, 260, 316, 322, 325, 334
Travis, L. E., 325, 331
Trifonova, M. K., 109, 316
Troshikhin, V. A., 14–17, 19, 22, 31–32, 72, 105–108, 134, 147, 171, 206, 230, 303, 309, 319, 325, 331
Troshikhina, Yu. G., 15, 326
Trubnikova-Morgunova, R. S., 39, 60–61, 96, 101–102, 104, 109, 296–297, 301, 326
Turovskaya, Z. G., 29, 49, 66, 78–79, 84–87, 96–99, 134, 168, 326
Tyler, L. E., 42, 326

Uherik, A., 109, 150, 299
Ukhtomsky, A. A., 331
Umansky, L. I., 23, 51, 116, 326
Urban, J., 13, 150, 156, 161, 308, 332
Urbańska, J., 116, 295
Uszyńska, Z., 212–213, 224, 326

Utkina, N. S., 70–71, 78, 92, 261, 326

Vasilenko, L. D., 147, 327
Vasilenko, T. K., 97, 297
Vasilets, T. V., 32, 45–46, 107, 327
Vasilev, A. N., 91, 327
Vatsuro, E. G., 19, 327
Voicu, C., 13, 327
Vovk, S. I., 17, 177, 301
Vvedensky, N. E., 98, 101, 105, 196, 331
Vyatkin, B. A., 62, 67, 71–72, 78, 81, 92, 135, 222, 225, 243, 246–247, 292, 301, 306, 308, 318, 323, 327–328, 332
Vyatkina, Z. N., 128, 328
Vygotsky, L. S., 170, 328
Vyrzhikovsky, S. N., 16, 155, 328

Welford, A. T., 289
Wenger, M. A., 179, 328
Werre, P. F., 108, 328
White, K. D., 150, 161, 328
Wiersma, E. D., 174, 184, 194, 299
Willett, R. A., 136, 328
Williams, R. J., 179, 328
Witkin, H., 193, 277, 328
Witoszek, A., 117, 329
Wołoszynowa, L., 321
Wright, H. R., 301
Wright, J. C., 304
Wrześniewski, K., 158, 321
Wundt, W., 167, 173–174, 193, 256–257, 329

Yakovleva, V. V., 15, 329
Yermolayeva-Tomina, L. B., 7, 22, 31, 33–35, 53–54, 74–76, 78–80, 84–88, 93–99, 103, 109, 148, 289, 312, 317–318, 329
Yusim, E. D., 61, 329

Zarzycka, M., 132–134, 153, 158, 163, 230, 239, 329

Zazulina, P. L., 49, 86, 92, 313
Zhorov, P. A., 109, 148, 329
Ziegler, D. J., 257, 299
Zimienko, V. D., 22, 293
Zimmerman, W. S., 165, 173, 184, 244, 298, 334

Zuckerman, M., 35, 58, 142–143, 152, 159, 177, 179, 188, 192, 197, 211, 257, 293, 329–330
Zyryanova, N. G., 88, 329
Żuchowska-Czwartosz, E., 233–234, 314

# Subject Index

Abstraction index (AI), 280–282
Activatability, *see also* Equilibrium of NP, 38–41
  alpha index, 39, 108–110
  alpha rhythm amplitude, 39, 108–109
  alpha rhythm frequency, 39, 108–109
  and dynamism of NP, 39
  EEG, 39, 108–110
  energetic mobilization of NS, 38, 41
  and equilibrium of NP, 39–40, 109
  genetic determination, 45–48
  level of activation, 40
  and memory, 61
  sensitivity, 38–39
  and strength of NS, 40
  total energy of alpha rhythm, 39
  total energy of beta rhythm, 39
  total energy of theta rhythm, 39
Activation, level of, 4, 34, 110, 170, 334
  and efficiency, 56–57
  individual differences in, 170, 174, 177, 180
  normal, 186
  optimal, 185–186, 334
  optimal stimulation, 185
  and reactivity, 181–182, 231, 234, 241
  and strength of NS, 4, 29, 56–57, 139, 160
Activity, 184–190, 244, 332
  definition of, 184–185, 207
  as direct source of stimulation, 187–188, 262
  as indirect source of stimulation, 188–189, 262
  optimal level of activation, 185–187, 189, 191, 207, 262
  as regulator of stimulation need, 185, 187–191, 207, 225, 231
  "response hungry" vs. "stimulus hungry", 192
Adaptation, level of
  theory of, 181, 186
Anxiety, 67–69, 138, 160, 176, 244, 264
  behavioural inhibition system (BIS), 160
  and equilibrium of NP, 158–159, 164–165
  and extraversion-introversion, 160
  group pressure, 265–268
  measured by IPAT scale, 333
  measured by MAS, 138, 157–158, 333
  measured by STAI, 157–158, 250, 265, 333
  and mobility of NP, 158–159, 164–165
  and nervous system properties, 139, 154–159
  passive-defensive reflex, 155, 157
  self-control, 159
  stimulative value of situation, 250, 252
  and strength of NS, 71, 154–158, 160, 164–166

## Subject Index

Arousability, 40, 170, 174, 184
  and activatability, 40, 331
  cortertia, 140
  and strength of NS, 29, 40, 144
Arousal, *see* Activation, level of
Augmenting/reducing dimension, 142, 177
  and strength of NS, 29, 141–142

Balance of nervous processes, *see* Equilibrium of nervous processes

Cognitive style
  abstraction-concreteness, 277–282
  developmental characteristic, 279–282
  field dependency vs. field-independency, 277
  as personality dimension, 277
  reflection-impulsivity, 277
  stimulative value of, 278–279, 282
  and strength of NS, 193
Concentratability, 37–38, 140
  discrimination threshold, 37–38
  latency period, 37
  as nervous system trait, 37
Conditionability, 22, 138, 149

Desensitization, 181–182
Durability, 193–194
  and lability of NP, 194
  and perseveration, 194
  and persistence of reaction, 195
  and reccurence of reaction, 195
Dynamism of nervous processes (NP), 24, 33–35, 108, 140, 149, 169
  alpha index, 108–109
  alpha rhythm amplitude, 108–109
  alpha rhythm frequency, 108–109
  conditionability, 35, 149
  EEG methods, 34
  and lability, 35
  speed of conditioning, 31, 33–35, 76, 108
  speed of OR extinction, 76, 108, 150, 162
  total energy of alpha rhythm, 109
Dynamism of nervous system, *see* Dynamism of nervous processes

EEG
  hyper-vs. hypo-excitable individuals, 108
  and nervous system traits, 34–35, 75, 78–79
EEG balance, *see* Activatability
Emotional excitability, 67–69
Emotional reactivity
  and neuroticism, 161
  and strengh of NS, 161
Emotional stability, 67, 69, 71, 244, 333
  and activatability, 161–162
  and lability of NP, 161–162
  and strength of NS, 161
Emotionality, 67, 69, 165, 175, 185
Energetic level of behaviour, 174–176, 191
  activatability, 184
  activity-passivity, 174
  biotonus, 174
  in Buss and Plomin's typology, 175
  energy life, 174
  intensity of emotion, 174
  physiological mechanism of, 179–181
  Psychästesie, 174
  Psychomotolität, 174.
  strength of NS, 174
  in Thomas and Chess' typology, 175
  vigorousness, 175
Equilibrium of nervous processes (NP), 1–3, 8–9, 16, 36–37, 41, 76, 140, 165, 175, 244, 331
  and activatability, 39, 41
  alpha index, 37
  between conditioned excitation and inhibition, 39
  in dynamism of excitation and inhibition, 34, 36–37, 41, 76

Equilibrium processes—cont.
  in lability of excitation and inhibition, 36
  in mobility of excitation and inhibition, 16, 36
  Pavlov's methods of diagnosing, 8–9
  as principle of organization of NS properties, 36–37
  in strength of excitation and inhibition, 8, 16, 36, 76
  between unconditioned excitation and inhibition, 39
Extraversion–introversion, 67–69, 138, 149, 264, 332
  and activity, 192, 244
  and dynamism of NP, 67, 149–150
  and equilibrium of NP, 153–154, 164, 332–333.
  measured by EPI, 147, 152–153
  measured by EPQ, 147–148, 150, 152
  measured by MPI, 148, 151–152, 161, 244
  and mobility of NP, 143, 147–148, 152, 164–166
  and nervous system properties, 35–36, 139, 143–154, 333
  and strength of NS, 29, 55–56, 67, 139, 143–148, 151–154, 160, 164–165, 332

Functional mobility, 32, 105–106, 197

General type of nervous system, see Type of nervous system

Impulsivity, 67, 69, 160, 244
  behavioural activation system (BAS), 160
  and extraversion–introversion, 152, 160
  and strength of NS, 152
Individual differences, 255–258
  in conditioning, 1
  in personality, 255–257
  in temperament, 255–257
Individuality
  biochemical, 179
  neuroendocrine, 179
Induction, law of, 82
Inhibition
  conditioned, 6, 145, 149, 154, 330, 333
  external, 6, 330
  internal, 6
  preventive, 58
  protective, 3, 146, 330
  reactive, 144–146, 149
  temporal, 145–146
  transmarginal, 58, 142, 146, 161, 211, 330
  unconditioned, 6, 145, 149, 330
Intensive dimension of behaviour, 41, 170, 257
  and activatability, 41
  and level of activation, 174

Lability of nervous processes (NP), 31, 98, 101–102, 140, 196–197, 330
  adequate optical chronaxie, 97–99, 101
  click-fusion frequency, 100
  critical frequency of flashing phosphene, 100
  critical frequency of flicker fusion, 98–101
  delayed conditioned reflex, 31
  genetic determination, 45–46
  and memory, 59, 331
  photic driving reaction, 101–103
  photic driving reaction in beta band, 98–103
  speed of visual sensitivity restoration, 98–101
  total energy of beta rhythm, 102–104
  trace conditioned reflex, 31
Lability of the nervous system, see Lability of nervous processes

# Subject Index

Liveliness of behaviour, 196–197
  and lability of NP, 196
  and mobility of behaviour, 196
  speed of reaction, 196
  tempo of reaction, 196

Machiavellianism
  cool syndrome, 272
  measured by Mach scale, 272
  soft-touch syndrome, 272
Masculinity, 165, 175, 244
Mobility of behaviour, 135, 193–197
  and activity, 233–234
  and functional mobility, 196
  measured by speed of reaction change, 193–194, 206
  measured by STI, 198
  measured by TTI, 195, 201
  and mobility of nervous processes, 135, 193, 198
  perseveration of behaviour, 196
  and reactivity, 197, 234
  rigidity, 194
  speed of reaction, 196
  tempo of reaction, 196
Mobility of nervous processes (NP), 1–2, 9, 15–16, 30–33, 41, 140, 197
  and activity, 233, 244
  adequate optical chronaxie, 97
  after-effect of stimuli, 32
  alteration of the signal value of stimuli, 10, 15, 31–33, 73, 104–105
  developmental changes, 16–17
  and equilibrium of NP, 132–133
  genetic determination of, 15, 32, 43, 45
  and inertia, 9, 58
  and lability of NP, 9, 31, 41
  and memory, 331
  and paranoia, 147
  Pavlov's methods for diagnosing, 9–10
  physiological mechanism of, 9, 32
  speed of conditioning, 23–24, 30–31, 33
  speed of reaction change, 32, 73, 105–108
  and strength of NS, 31, 131–135, 147
  trace conditioned reflex, 9, 31
  visual after-image, 31
Mobility of the nervous system, *see* Mobility of nervous processes
Modulation of stimulus intensity and sensitivity, 192

Nervous system properties, *see also* Type of the nervous system, 1, 14–16, 140, 151, 167–169
  and abilities, 33, 49, 105, 107–108, 169
  and Cattell's personality traits, 140
  and conditioning, 1, 22, 24, 34, 333–334
  developmental changes, 16–17, 19, 42
  and efficiency of action, 62, 70–72
  as explanatory concepts, 117–118, 168
  genetic determination of, 42–49
  measured by interview, 115–117
  measured by observation chart, 116, 118
  measured by observation method, 115–117
  and memory, 58–62, 331
  methodological principles, 27–28, 67, 73, 151
  and motivation, 169
  polarity-amplitude assymetry of EP, 75
  stability of, 11–12, 17, 21, 25
  and temperament, 33, 118, 168–169
Neuroticism, 159–161, 244, 264, 269
  and anxiety, 159–160
  discrepancy between real and ideal self, 269–270
  and dynamism of NP, 150, 162
  and equilibrium of NP, 162–165
  hyperactivity, 164

Neuroticism—cont.
  measured by EPI, 146, 161–162
  measured by EPQ, 150, 162
  measured by MPI, 161–162
  and mobility of NP, 162–164
  and nervous system properties, 159–164
  and strength of NS, 144, 146–147, 159–166

Optimal discrepancy, 186

Partial traits of the nervous system, 25, 29–30, 49–52, 73, 111–115, 136, 151, 180
  horizontal, 51
  kind of effector, 50–51, 112–114
  kind of UCS, 25, 34–35, 49–50, 112
  level of the organism's functioning, 51
  perceptual brain system, 50
  regulatory brain system, 50
  specificity of sensory modality, 19, 49–51, 73, 84, 86, 90, 97–98, 111
  vertical, 51
Perseverance of behaviour, 195–197
  durability, 196
  lability of NP, 196
  mobility of behaviour, 195–196
  persistence of reaction, 195–196
  recurrence of reaction, 195–196
Persistence of reaction, 195
  measured by TTI, 195, 201
Personality, 255–258
  as generator of stimulation, 263, 271–272
  influence on temperament, 262–263
  as product of social environment, 257–258, 284–285
Psychoticism, 138, 152

Reactivity, 171–172, 176–184, 257, 264, 332
  and abstraction-concreteness, 278–282
  and activatability, 184
  and activity, 188–192, 225–226, 234
  and aggressive behaviour, 283
  and anxiety, 267–268
  and augmenting/reducing dimension, 193
  and capacity, 178, 183
  and cautious vs. risky behaviour, 237–240, 262
  and cognitive style, 193, 277–282
  and defence mechanisms, 263
  definition of, 177–178
  and discrepancy between real and ideal self, 269–272, 283
  and efficiency of performance, 214–216, 220–222, 224, 240–247
  and functional structure of activity, 209–224
  and group pressure, 264–268
  and hetorogeneous vs. homogeneous actions, 210–211, 220–221
  and intensity of reaction, 176–181
  and level of aspiration, 235–236, 274–277
  and Machiavellianism, 272–274
  measured by RRS, 198
  measured by slope of RT curve, 205–206
  measured by STI, 171, 183, 198, 264
  and neuroticism, 269–271
  physiological mechanism of, 178–182
  as a primary temperament trait, 190–191
  psychophysiological cost, 247–254
  and sensitivity, 178, 183
  as a state, 181–182
  stimulation-avoiding activity, 189
  stimulation need, 186–189, 211, 261–262
  stimulation processing coefficient

(SPC), 180–181, 188
stimulation-seeking activity, 189
and stimulative value of activity,
  226–231, 233
and stimulative value of
  stimulation, 171–172, 230–233,
  239, 241–261
and strategy of action, 234–240
and strength of NS, 183–184,
  193, 198, 206
stress resistance, 232, 241–248
and style of action, 209–225, 335
and style of self-regulation,
  234–237, 274
and temporal structure of activity,
  210, 214, 220–221
as a trait, 181–182
Reactivity rating scale (RRS),
  198–201, 342–352
  for nursery school children,
    198-199, 342–344
  for primary school pupils,
    198–199, 345–348
  reliability, 199–201
  for secondary-school pupils,
    198–199, 349–352
Recurrence of reaction, 195
  measured by TTI, 195–201
Regularity of reaction, 195–196
  measured by TTI, 195, 201
Rhythmicity of reaction, 193–196
  and mental tempo, 195
  regularity of reaction, 195
  tempo of reaction, 194
Rigidity, 67–69, 195, 332

Sensation seeking, 177, 257
  and activity, 192
  and type of NS, 142–143
Sensitivity, 38, 183, 332
  activity, 192
  arousability, 192
  capacity, 178, 183, 187, 206
  and extraversion-introversion,
    145, 192

and stimulus modulation
  intensity, 192
Sensitization, 181–182
Sociability, 165, 175
Speed of reaction, 193–196, 332
  and lability of NP, 193
  measured by TTI, 195, 201
Stimulation, regulation of, 181–190
  active, 182
  passive, 182
  standard of, 185–186
  system, 186
Strelau Temperament Inventory
  (STI), 118–120, 198, 337–341
  diagnosis of equilibrium of NP
    by, 119, 127
  distribution of scores, 127–129
  factor analysis, 131–132, 147
  general description, 120–127
  mobility of NP scale, 124–126, 198
  reliability, 119, 129–131
  sex differences, 128–129
  strength of excitation scale,
    121–122, 125, 135–136, 183, 198
  strength of inhibition scale,
    122–126
  validity, 119–120, 126, 131–136
Strength of excitation, 3–4, 16,
  28–30, 177
  caffeine trial, 4–5, 14–15, 30,
    82–83
  change of excitability under food
    deprivation, 4–5, 14
  change of sensitivity under
    caffeine, 74
  change of sensitivity under
    distractors, 74, 76
  change of simple RT, 73, 81,
    90–92
  critical frequency of flashing
    phosphene, 74
  driving reaction in alpha and beta
    bands, 93
  driving reaction to stimuli of low
    frequency, 81, 85, 87, 92–97
  evoked potentials, 75

Strength of excitation—cont.
  extinction with reinforcement, 28, 73, 77–81, 84–85, 87, 90, 92, 94–95, 331
  induction method, 28, 79–80, 82–85, 87, 94–95.
  intensity of nervous processes, 4
  intensity of stimuli, 4–5, 14, 156
  measured by Kraepelin test, 113, 274–275
  Pavlov's methods for diagnosing, 4–6
  physiological basis, 3
  protective (transmarginal) inhibition, 3, 76–78, 90
  sensitivity, 22, 29, 86, 178, 192
  sensitivity, threshold, 76, 80, 84–86, 94–95, 145
  slope of RT curve, 73, 80, 85–90, 92, 94–95
  and speed of conditioning, 5, 14, 22, 31, 33–34, 156, 330
  as a state, 4, 147–148
  and strength of inhibition, 6, 132–134
  threshold of concentration, 76, 79, 82–84
  threshold of irradiation, 76, 79, 82–84
  as a trait, 3–4, 148
  variance of EEG amplitude, 74
  working capacity (endurance), 3, 5, 29, 33, 77–78, 86, 118, 178, 214–215, 230, 244
Strength of inhibition, 6–8, 16, 75–76, 159
  bromine, 7
  differentiation, 7–8, 15
  Pavlov's methods for diagnosing, 7–8
  as a trait, 7
Strength, law of, 86, 92, 156, 176–177
Strength of nervous processes, *see* Strength of the nervous system
Strength of the nervous system (NS), *see also* Strength of excitation, 1–4, 28–30, 41, 168, 183, 257
  and dynamism of NP, 41, 331
  efficiency of performance, 53, 55–56, 60–61, 65, 70–72, 261
  emotional tension, 60, 71
  and equilibrium of NP, 132–133
  fatigue, 54–55, 58, 144–145
  genetic determination of, 43–44
  and level of aspiration, 274–277
  and memory, 60
  and monotony, 54–55, 58, 145
  and motivation, 54–55, 60, 71
  and sensation seeking, 142–143
  and stimulation seeking, 56, 140–141
  stimulative value of situation, 52–58, 60–61, 64–65, 70–72
  and stimulus intensity modulation, 141–142
  and strength of excitation, 3
  and stress, 53, 70–72
Style of action, 63–66, 207–211, 331
  developmental characteristic, 222–225
  and intellectual abilities, 66, 208, 223–225
  and mobility of NP, 64
  and nervous system properties, 63–67, 208, 334
  as regulator of stimulation need, 208–211, 225
  and strength of NS, 64–66, 222
  and structure of activity, 64, 209, 222
  and temperamental traits, 63, 208
Style of work, *see* Style of action

Temperament, 11, 20–21, 62–63, 67–72, 140–143, 165, 171–174, 255–258, 283–285
  and abilities, 208, 332
  and adjustment, 63, 68–69
  as biologically determined, 173–174, 257, 284

changes caused by environment, 171–172, 284
constitutional concepts of, 173, 256
definition of, 171, 334
developmental changes, 69, 171
and efficiency of action, 246–247
factors of, 67–68, 147, 165, 245–246
as formal traits of behaviour, 172–173, 257
in interaction with surroundings, 259–262
methods for diagnosing, 69, 173
national, 172
and personality, 173, 255–285
physiological mechanism of, 118, 167–168, 180, 197
regulative theory of, 167–206
as relatively stable features, 171–172
structure of, 67–69, 165, 175, 245–246
systems approach to, 68–69, 332
typology of, 255–256
Tempo of reaction, 193–196
and activity, 194
and lability of NP, 194
measured by TTI, 195, 201
mental tempo, 194
Temporal characteristics of behaviour, 167, 174, 197, 259
physiological mechanism of, 197
Temporal Traits Inventory (TTI), 201–205, 353–357
distribution of scores, 202
factor analysis, 204–205
reliability, 202–203
sex differences, 202–204
validity, 204–205
Thoughtfulness, 165, 175
Type A, 68, 247
Type B, 68

Type of higher nervous activity, *see* Type of nervous system
Type of nervous system (TNS), 1–3, 5–6, 10–13, 139–140
and adjustment, 12–13, 17–18, 24
characteristics of, 12–13, 20–21
classification of, 2, 10–11, 18, 330
excitable, 23
general and partial, 25, 49–52, 74, 331
as genotype, 11, 42, 169, 330
inhibitory, 2, 6, 23
mobile, 23
and phenotype, 330
with predominance of excitation over inhibition, 2
with predominance of inhibition over excitation, 2, 6
slow, 23
standard for diagnosing in dogs, 14–15
strong, balanced, mobile, 11–12
strong, balanced, slow, 11–12
strong, excitable, unbalanced, 20
strong, optimal excitation, balanced and quick, 20
strong, excitation, balanced and slow, 20
strong, unbalanced, 9–12
and temperament, 2, 6, 11, 18, 20, 49, 62, 67
weak, 6, 10, 12–13, 21, 169
choleric, 11–12
melancholic, 2, 6, 11–13
model of invariance, 68–69
phlegmatic, 11–12
sanguine, 11–12
taxonomy, 68
Typology
Ivanov-Smolensky's, 23–25
Krasnogorsky's, 19–23

Vigorousness, 165, 167, 244

## LIBRARY OF DAVIDSON COLLEGE

Books on regular loan may be checked out for **two weeks**. Books must be presented at the Circulation Desk in order to be renewed.

A fine is charged after date due.

Special books are subject to special regulations at the discretion of the library staff.

APR 2 2 1993